Louisiana at 40

The Collection Today

40

Louisiana Museum of Modern Art

Special issue published on the occasion of the exhibition
Louisiana at 40 – The Collection Today
18 June – 30 August, 1998

Note:
The numbers of the captions refer to the List of Works on pages 128-144

Translation
Ernst Dupont, Paula Hostrup-Jessen,
James Manley, Annette Mester

Layout
Hovedkvarteret ApS, Copenhagen

Printing and Lithography
Grafodan Offset

Distribution
Louisiana
DK-3050 Humlebæk, Denmark
Tel: +45 4919 0719
Fax: +45 4919 3505
e-mail: museumshop@louisiana.dk
Louisiana Revy, Vol. 38 No. 3, June 1998

Opening hours
Daily 10 am – 5 pm
Wednesdays 10 am – 10 pm

ISBN 87-90029-30-5

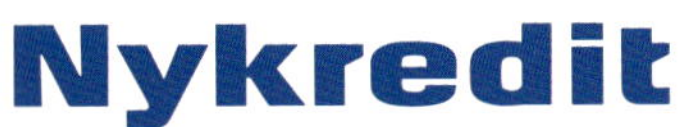

Main sponsor of Louisiana's exhibitions 1998

Contents

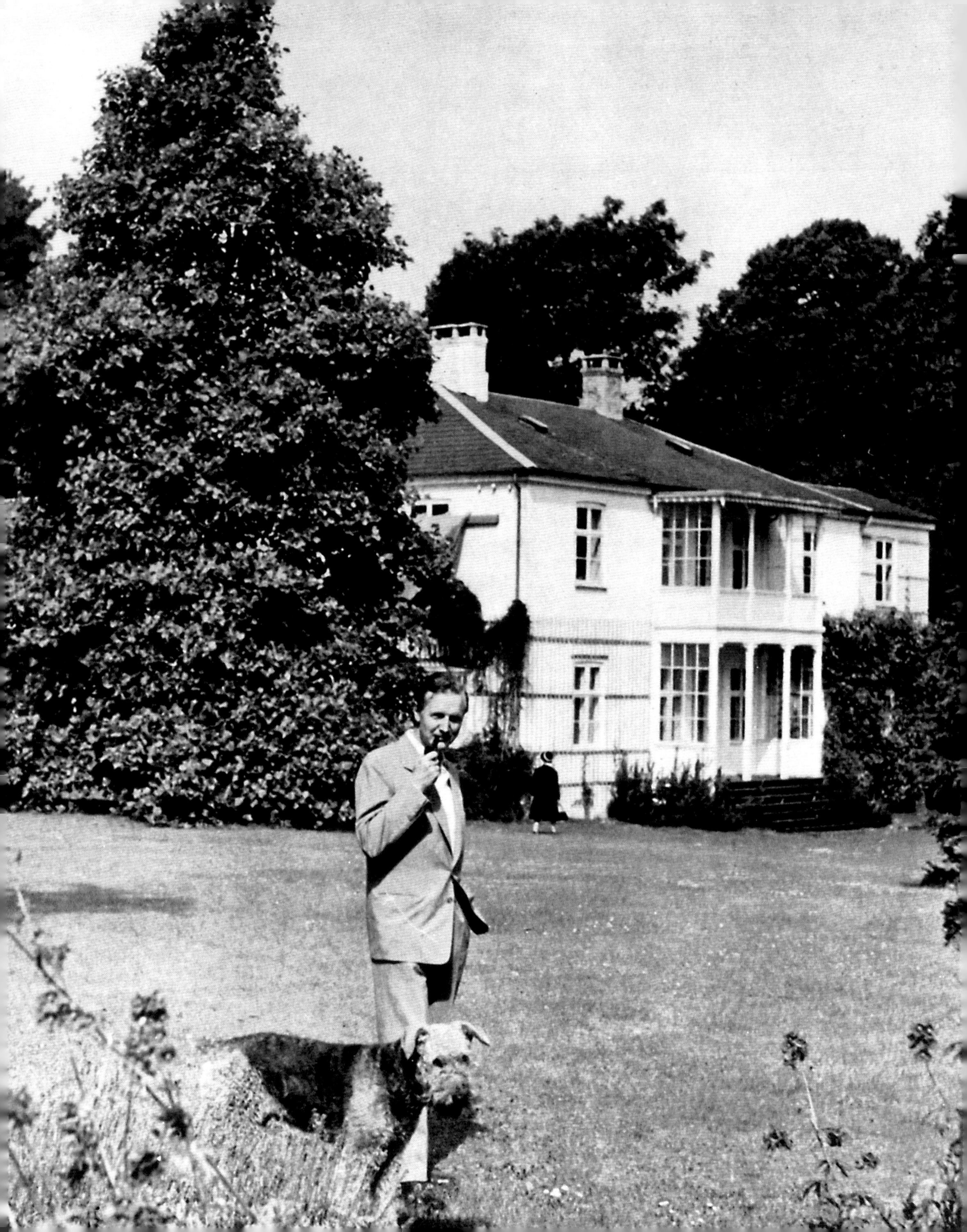

Introduction

Knud W. Jensen

At Louisiana landscape, architecture, and art are intimately connected.

The old trees in the park, the lake in the wood fed by the Humlebæk stream, the beechwood on the slopes that stretch towards the sea, the terrace which faces south and offers an unobstructed view of the Sound – the quintessence of Danish nature – a cultural landscape created by the care and concern of previous generations.

The place was ideal for a museum, but the site made demands; in a sense it became our superior, dictating the arrangement of both buildings and sculptures.

A museum of modern art must have generous exhibition facilities and large quantities of extra space; a considerable part of the total building complex was therefore placed underground or dug into the slopes. The buildings above the ground line three sides of the site, showing respect for the park and leaving the vista open towards the Sound.

Architects Jørgen Bo, Vilhelm Wohlert and (later) Claus Wohlert tackled the challenges of the site by acknowledging and appreciating its special character. Extensions were added over the years on the basis of the experience acquired. The present-day result is a museum complex whose ground plan makes it different from all other museums. The Augustinus Foundation, the Velux Foundation of 1981 and a number of other foundations have financed about half the complex.

Just as the building extensions were made possible by cultural foundations, the growth of the art collection was the result of donations from the New Carlsberg Foundation, gifts from collectors and artists, and the museum's own purchases financed by the Louisiana Foundation. It was actually like one great partnership. As demonstrated also in other countries, this is the only feasible way to establish a museum of modern art. Almost half of the collection consists of donations from Danish and foreign foundations, artists and collectors.

The development of both buildings and the collection has been parallel and mutually beneficial. Specific exhibition rooms seemed to be ideal for specific parts of the collection.

The original Danish collection grew into an international collection which focuses on significant groups of art works, created in Europe or in the US in the latter half of the 20th century.

It was never the museum's ambition to cover all essential movements in post-war-art, but to concentrate on certain focal points, for instance the 24 sculptures of the Giacometti collection. From the very beginning we have taken a keen interest in sculpture, for which the park offers marvellous opportunities.

Many different categories of people visit and use the museum. Along with such traditional forms as painting and sculpture, the museum has shown films, presented architecture and design, music, theatre and literature. At Louisiana visual art will always be the main priority, but there is an appreciation of the importance of supplementary activities that may enrich and enliven the milieu. Over the years there have been performances of music, film and theatre, there have been panel discussions, happenings and seminars. The wider the scope for experience, the more Louisiana lives up to its ideal: to be 'a meeting place of the arts', and an institution deeply involved in the world of today.

On the occasion of Louisiana's 40th anniversary on August 14, 1998, the collection will be on display throughout the entire museum, with a retrospective emphasis on the original starting point: Danish art. The exhibition will offer an opportunity to see – or see again – works that have not been on show for many years.

The collection has grown so much during the past forty years that it is impossible to show it in its entirety, so a selection has been made. We hope the exhibition will please the large number of people who have often expressed a wish to see 'once again' the works exhibited in the early years.

English translation by Ernst Dupont

Knud W. Jensen with his dog Trofast after the acquisition of Louisiana, 1955

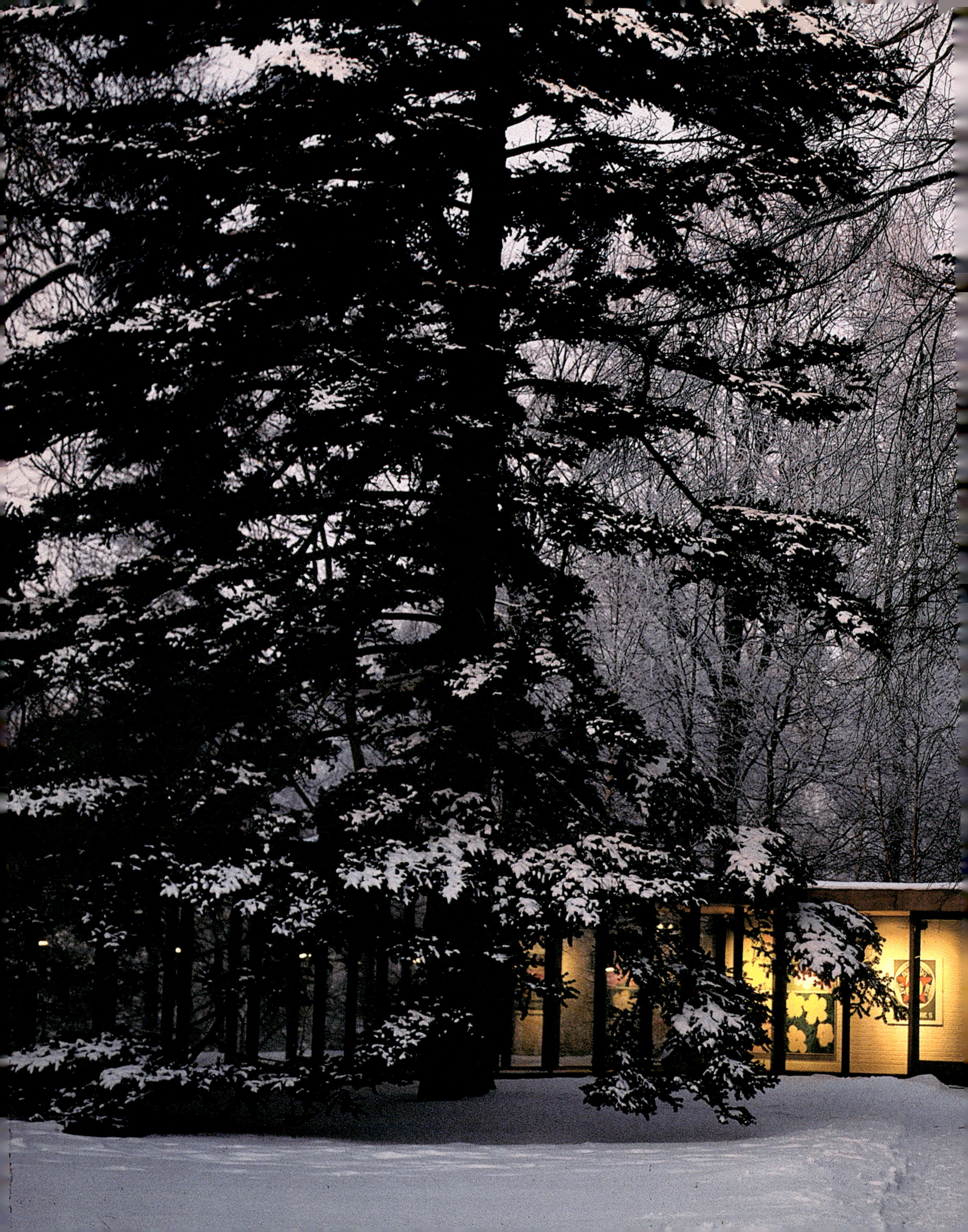

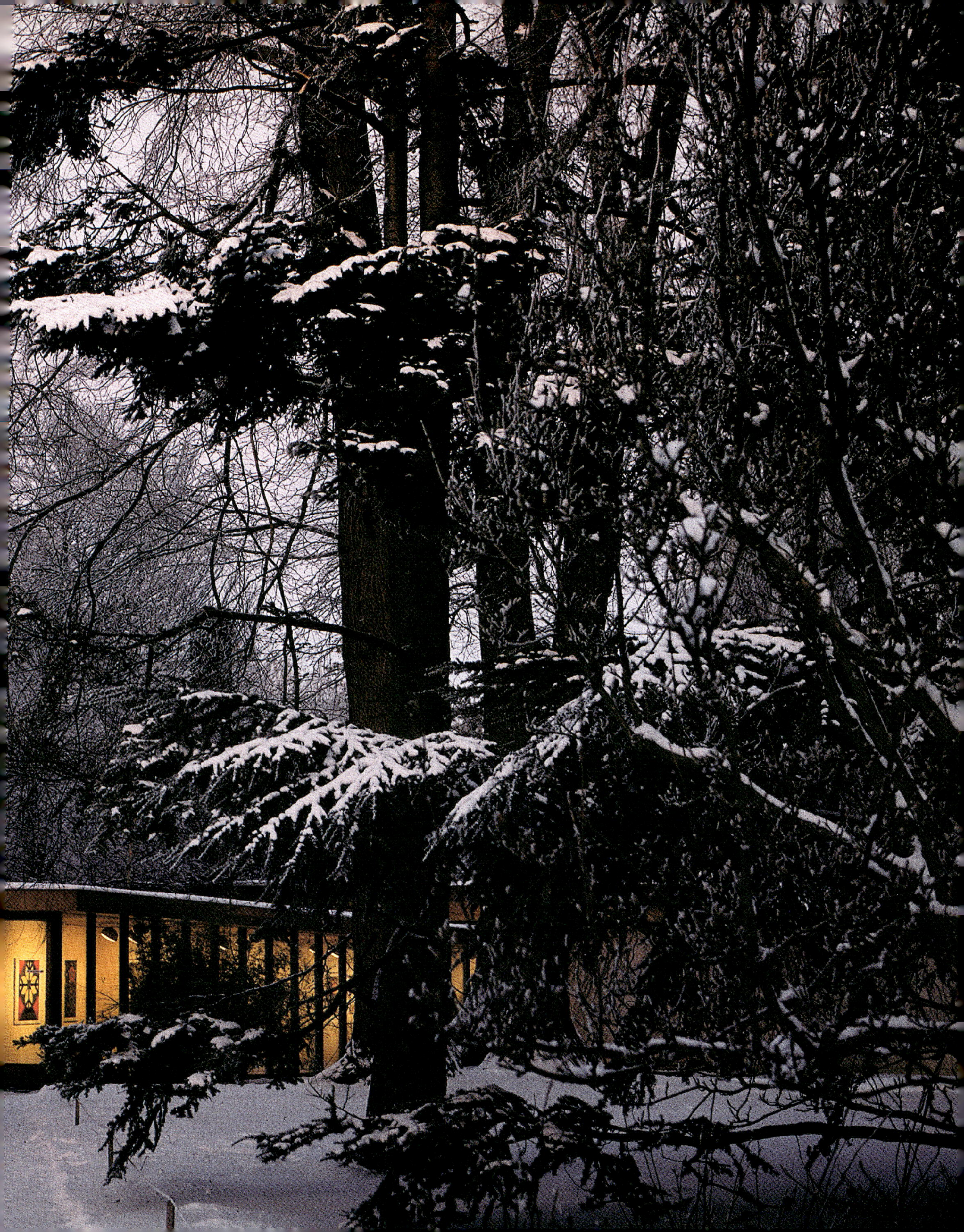

The Spirit of the Place

Steen Estvad Petersen

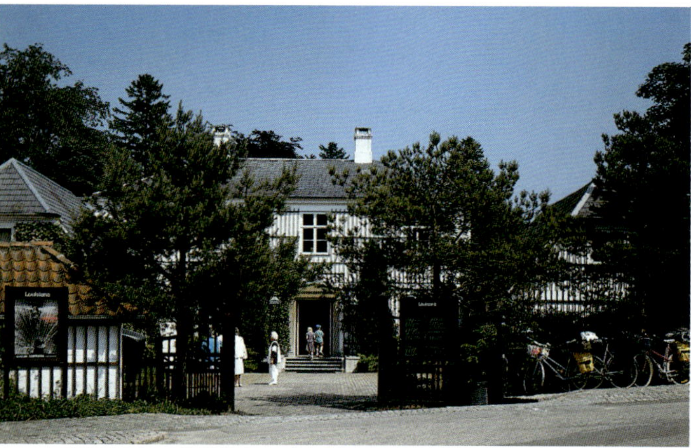

The main entrance to Louisiana is through the old stable yard in front of Alexander Brun's country house, built in 1855

One might ask what it is that determines the "genius loci" – the spirit of a place. A particular work of art, or architecture, or a certain landscape alone will not do it. Only when unity is achieved – when art, architecture and landscape come together to heighten our experience of a place – do we get that almost indefinable feeling: this is special.

Knud W. Jensen: Stedets Ånd ("The Spirit of the Place"), *Copenhagen, 1994*

There is no better way to describe the special quality of Louisiana.

Three arts – visual art, architecture and landscape design – together make up the extraordinary unity that for 40 years now has contributed to the museum's international reputation.

This interplay of the arts is what makes Louisiana unique.

At a time when prestigious museums are emerging at an almost inflationary rate all over the world, Louisiana holds a special position. Despite its 40 years, the place is still young. The outdatedness that characterises many other museums with fewer years behind them is not a problem Louisiana shares.

This is because Louisiana's spirit is rooted in a centuries-old architectural tradition that is the very antithesis of the monumental or proclamatory. The architecture at Louisiana is characterised by a highly conscious placement of buildings in relation to the topography of the landscape, a careful choice of building materials and respect for the park's old, richly crowned trees.

Actually, it is all quite simple. The special quality of Louisiana could also be explained by the fact that here, at all times and at every turn, we are presented with the exquisite – and spared the didacticism and pedagogic bombardment of the senses that invariably result in museum fatigue.

From Alexander Brun's old main building, visitors are gently guided through an architectural design so varied and responsive to the surrounding landscape that fatigue never sets in. Spacious rooms with high ceilings from which the light pours down follow intimate, dark rooms. Stairs lead deep below ground level and then up into the light. You are drawn along on a course of spatial and sensual experience that first leads to a wall, then makes a turn to one side, then opens onto an old tree, a view over a lake or a forest of ferns. The acoustics change from soft to hard, the heated air of the galleries gives way to the coolness of long glass corridors where you are protected from the weather by a screen but still outside, in nature.

The architectural design subtly incorporates reposes in which you can digest your impressions and become recharged.

It is a type of architecture that comes close to being an 'understatement', but is typical of a particularly Scandinavian sensibility and traditional respect for the spirit of a place.

In other words, Louisiana represents an architectural tradition which, despite its complexity, is highly attentive to the spirit of the place and the functions of a museum and employs materials that age with beauty. The undulating landscape, the old trees and the location right on the Sound have been given priority at all stages of the building of the museum.

This unconditional deference to the place actually enhances the architecture and the art framed by it. The continuous interplay between a wide range of sense impressions makes for a richness of experience and gives the

At Louisiana nature plays an important role. The visitor is at the same time inside as well as outside in the old park where the sculptures are placed as eye-catchers in the green vegetation

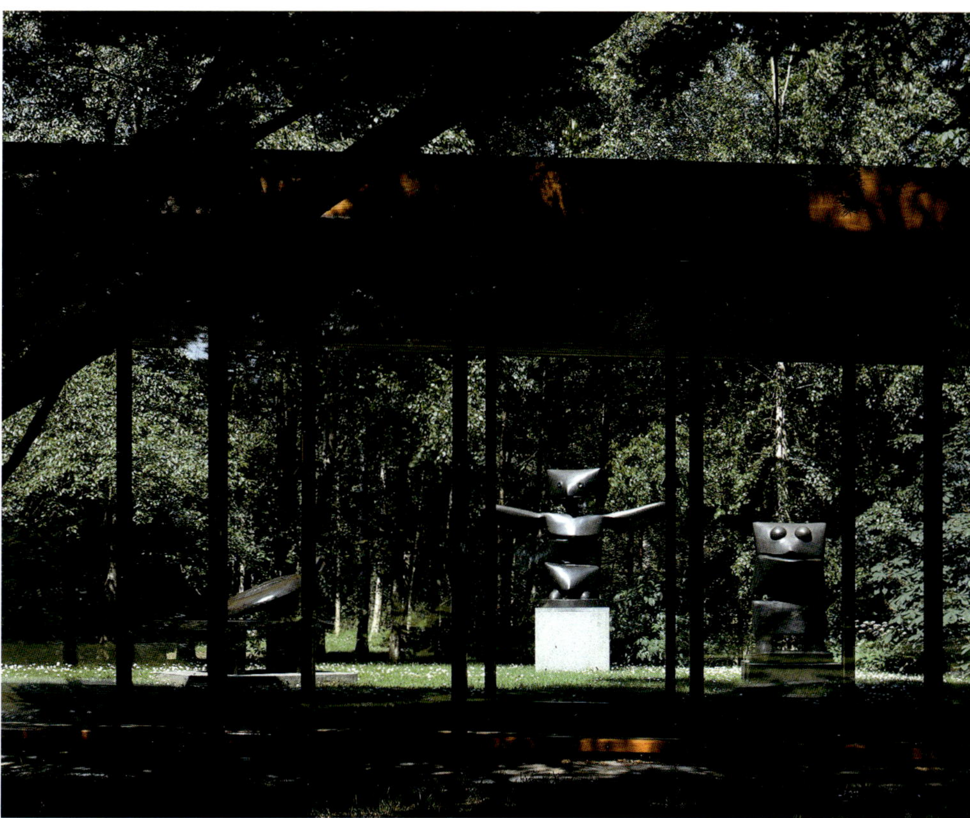

place the special character that its architects and builder intended.

It is therefore surprising that Louisiana, as an internationally well-known art museum, has had relatively few imitators in the rest of the world. The main reason is that few other art museums have had the advantages of Louisiana's extravagant building site.

Most art museums are located in densely populated cities where building sites are small and expensive. To be able to place pavilions within a spacious, pastoral landscape – as in Humlebæk – is extremely rare. Many of the elements were already there when Knud W. Jensen purchased the old country house in 1954. It had light, air, vistas and space.

But the uniqueness of Louisiana also has to do with differences in architectural traditions. The down-to-earth, simple and relaxed approach is typical of Scandinavian architectural traditions at their best, whereas the more international kind of architecture is often conceived on a large, impressive scale and tends to pay less attention to the purpose of the buildings and their immediate surroundings.

There are, admittedly, a few museums that resemble Louisiana, such as the Rijksmuseum Kröller-Müller in Holland and the Insel Hombroich in Germany, but in each case either the landscape is so unlike that of Louisiana or the basic concept is so divergent that they seem very different.

So, in a multitude of international museums, Louisiana stands apart – not just because of its location but because of the level of continuity maintained throughout its various building phases. All along, the builder Knud W. Jensen, the architects Bo and Wohlert, and the landscape designers Holscher and Nørgaard have worked side by side, engaged in a mutual dialogue that has been going on for 40 years. One result of this has been the coherence of ideas governing every stage in the development of the museum.

The economic conditions for the museum have varied, and the original criteria have changed – a natural result of the fact that the last four decades have been among the most dynamic and pluralistic in Danish history. But since the start of the museum in 1958, these shifts, rather than resulting in violent changes of style, have taken the form of a gradual adaptation to new currents and needs.

The museum's development was brought full circle with the underground Graphics Wing, opened in 1991, connecting the North Wing of the museum - built between 1958 and 1976 – with the South Wing, built in 1982. The ring was closed. Apart from the current expansion of the museum shop to mark Louisiana's 40th anniversary, the park has now reached its density limit.

The expansive urge that charac-

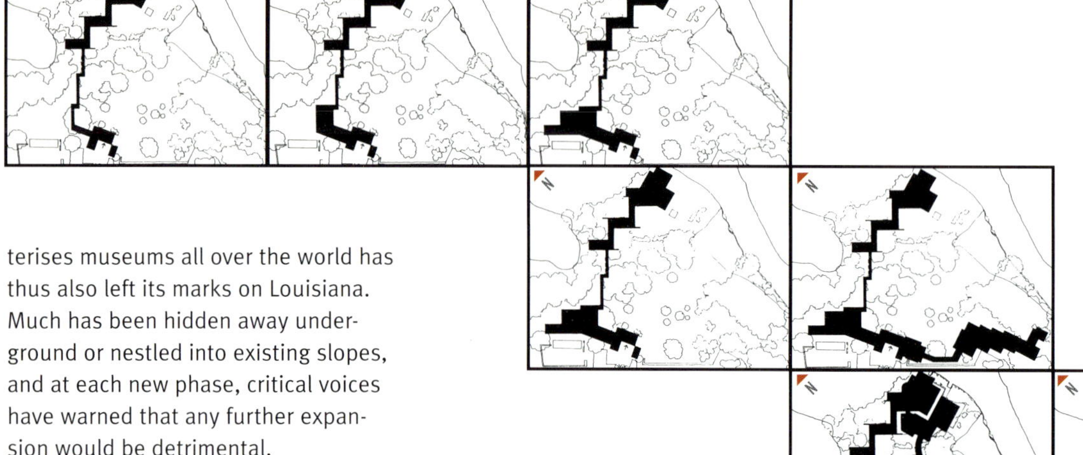

Plan of Louisiana's seven major expansions

terises museums all over the world has thus also left its marks on Louisiana. Much has been hidden away underground or nestled into existing slopes, and at each new phase, critical voices have warned that any further expansion would be detrimental.

With the latest expansion, it seems as if the saturation point has finally been reached. It will be hard to crowd the landscape further without endangering the unique character of the museum.

No one could have predicted that all of this would happen so fast – in less than half a century – when the first sod was turned in 1958.

Knud W. Jensen, who in 1954 purchased the late classicist country house – built in 1855 – originally wanted to build an exhibition pavilion at the far end of the slope facing the Sound as a supplement to the original main building. But he and the architects Jørgen Bo and Vilhelm Wohlert decided to connect the buildings, so that the original house would become the entrance to the new buildings, with the enclosed 'path' through the park as the dominant theme of the design.

The architectural inspiration for the new buildings came from both sides of the Pacific. It came from Vilhelm Wohlert's studies at Berkeley University and his encounter with the wood houses of the Bay Area, and from the simple, wooden modules of Japanese architecture. Both of these traditions were adapted to Danish conditions with Jørgen Bo's extraordinary sensitivity to the qualities of a landscape.

Along with the tradition founded by Kaare Klint at the Academy in Copenhagen, all these foreign elements were fused with the tradition of functionalism which is deeply rooted in Scandinavia. Without abandoning the Modernistic credo of form being dictated by function, this tradition was adapted to the spirit of the place and the architectural traditions of the region.

In the period from 1963 to 1973, the building that houses the changing exhibitions was built, and the Concert Hall next to the Museum Café was built in 1976.

The South Wing was added in 1982, and the two 'arms' were connected by the underground Graphics Wing in 1991. Three years later the Children's Wing was built – dug in under and budding off the original North Wing – and finally this year the building will be completed with a foyer and a museum shop.

Each of these seven different phases in the museum's 40 years of existence has cost blood, sweat and tears. The formal language of the architecture – the long, horizontal, whitewashed walls, the laminated wooden ceilings, the dark-red tile floors and the large glass areas opening onto the natural surroundings – expresses the branched-out character of the museum complex and represents a level of quality that establishes it as one of the absolute high points of modern Danish building and landscape architecture.

How to achieve a delicate balance between the exhibited works of art and the museum architecture is a contentious issue among artists, curators and architects all over the world. There have been numerous conferences on the subject, and magazines abound with discussions of the relationship between art and architecture. Should the art museum primarily be a neutral frame around the art, or should it be a culture centre, or a mega-sculpture to which the art is subordinated?

Opinions vary as much as the museum buildings themselves, and often strike an almost religious note. The numerous and highly prestigious museum buildings can be roughly divided into three categories: the shrine, the sculpture, and the bare 'storage room'.

To the first category, for instance, belongs the shrine inside the Ny Carlsberg Glyptotek, designed by Henning Larsen and built in 1996, as well as the

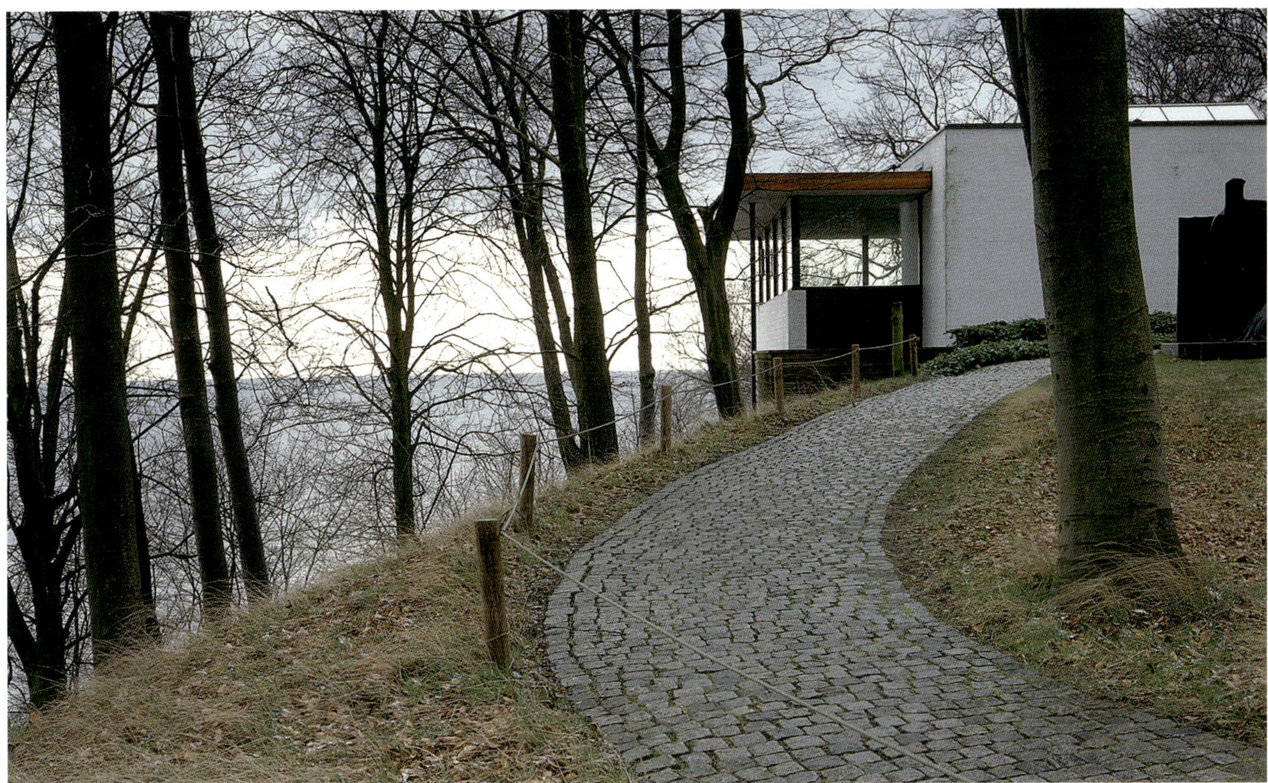

The South Wing from 1982 ends in a lookout pavilion reminiscent of the kiosk at Top Kapı Sarayı in Istanbul overlooking the Golden Horn

Architecture Museum in Frankfurt am Main, both of which represent 'in-fill' architecture, or 'houses within houses', made for small, special collections.

The second category is represented by such expressive sculptural buildings as Arken in Ishøj, near Copenhagen, designed by Søren Robert Lund and built in 1995, and the Guggenheim Museum, Bilbao, designed by Frank O. Gehry and built in 1997. The architecture of these museums engages in a dialogue with the art to the extent that many artists accuse it of being both dictatorial and choking.

To the third category belongs, for instance, Brandts Klædefabrik in Odense, Denmark, designed by Kristian Isager and built in 1981. Here former factory halls provide a frame around the exhibitions. This category also includes the Pompidou Centre, Paris – designed by Renzo Piano and Richard Rogers and built in 1980 – which on the outside resembles a high-tech oil platform, but on the inside has the appearance of a series of storage rooms placed one on top of the other.

Louisiana, however, will not fit within this rough division, since the museum is located at a point where all three categories intersect. Here we have the shrine, as well as the sculpture and the storage room. We get a natural – you could almost say musical – alternation between all three types of places within a multiplicity of spatial constellations where one never takes precedence over another. There is a razor's-edge balance, at times brought close to the hazardous, but this delicate interplay of architecture, art and landscape results in a rare harmony that gives the now wide-spreading museum complex its very special character. An interplay that functions at its very best when the place is populated.

Louisiana, in other words, is one of the 'great' places. Without really being so. Its atmosphere reminds me of Japanese or Islamic gardens – miniature worlds of beauty, peace, and timelessness. The mind rests. The senses imperceptibly open up to impressions.

English translation by Annette Mester

When we experience a great man-made work, we are at first filled with a quiet joy,
a spiritual well-being that makes us open and receptive.
As these experiences accumulate, they take us into a happy state of mind.
Anyone who has walked for hours inside a cathedral, a temple, a garden with fountains,
or a beautiful city has experienced this.
The great places move and delight us.

Knud W. Jensen: Stedets Ånd ("The Spirit of the Place"), *Copenhagen, 1994*

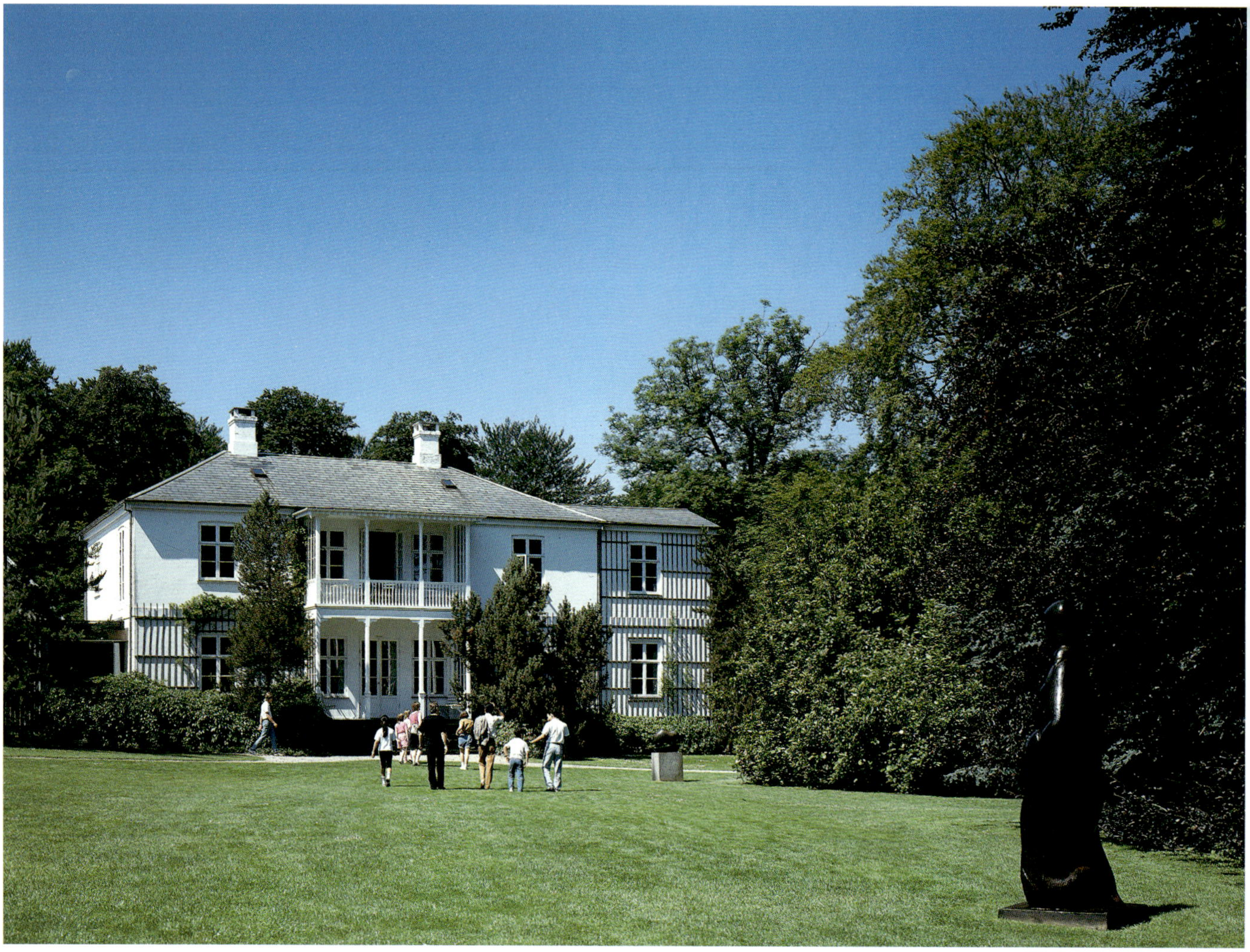

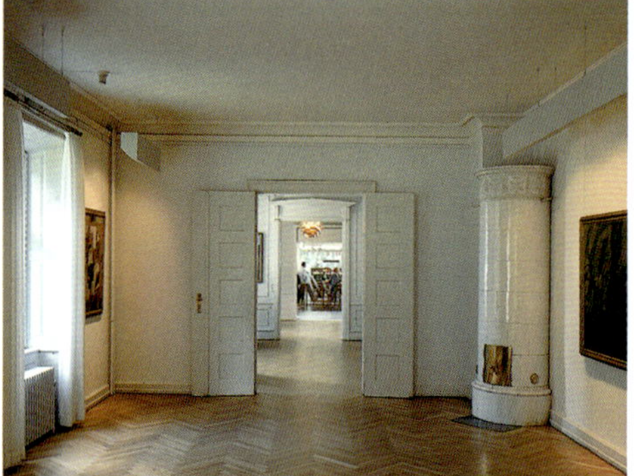

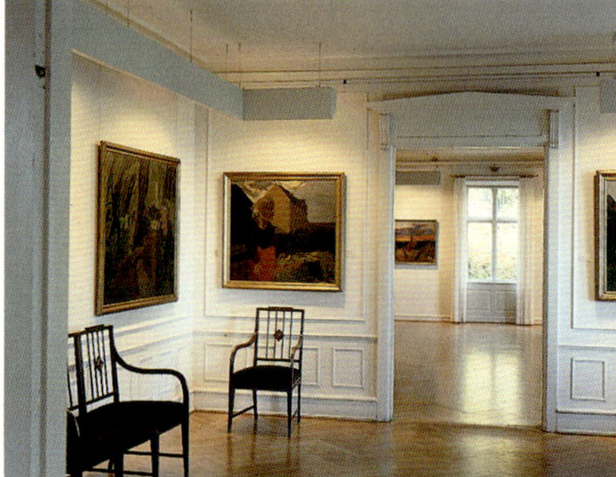

When Louisiana opened as a museum 40 years ago, it was in an old patrician house. Today, each and every guest will start the visit through the old house with the double doors that lead into the friendly private atmosphere which is the hallmark of the 100-year-old house. This sense of intimacy, the first thing meeting the visitor, has intentionally been maintained and extended to the other parts of the museum

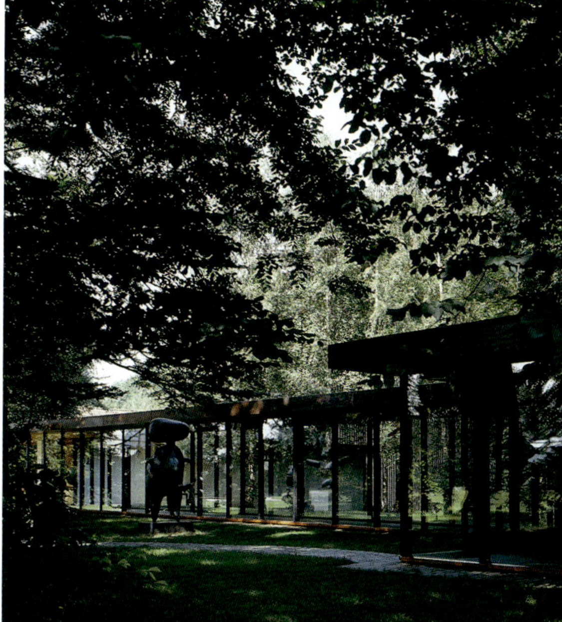

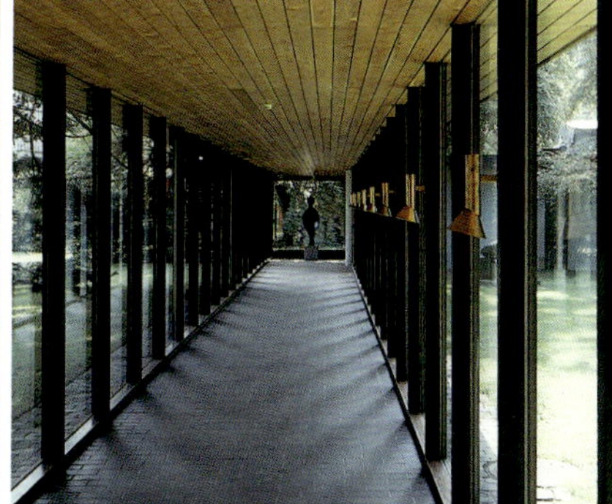

Long glass corridors connect the old house with the exhibition areas in the West, North, and South Wing. Louisiana's guests thus walk 'indoors in nature' from one wing to the other

The large nine-trunked beech dominates the view from the glass corridor at the West Wing

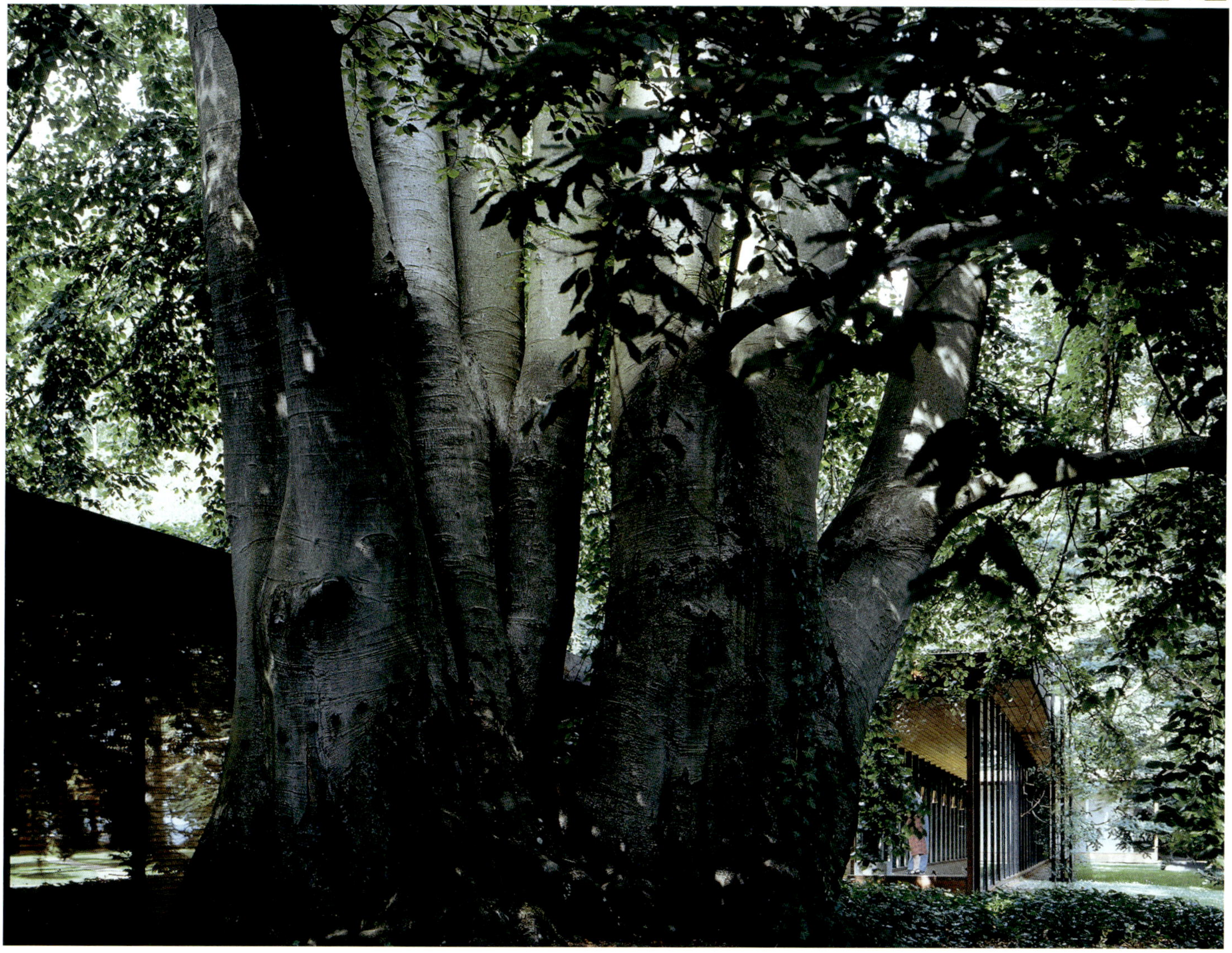

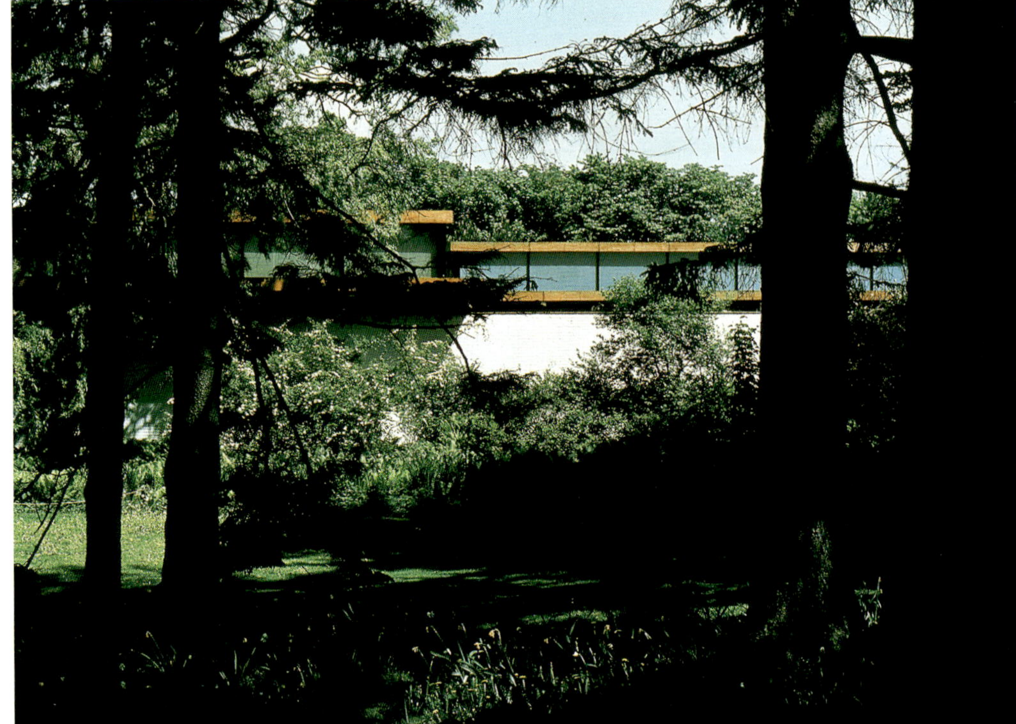

The full-grown trees of the park have – partly – determined the architecture. Rather than cutting trees, to make room for the buildings, these have in many cases been placed among the trees. The respect for the loveliest trees of the park, combined with the wish to use the most breathtaking views, has resulted in the unique and unconventional Louisiana ground plan

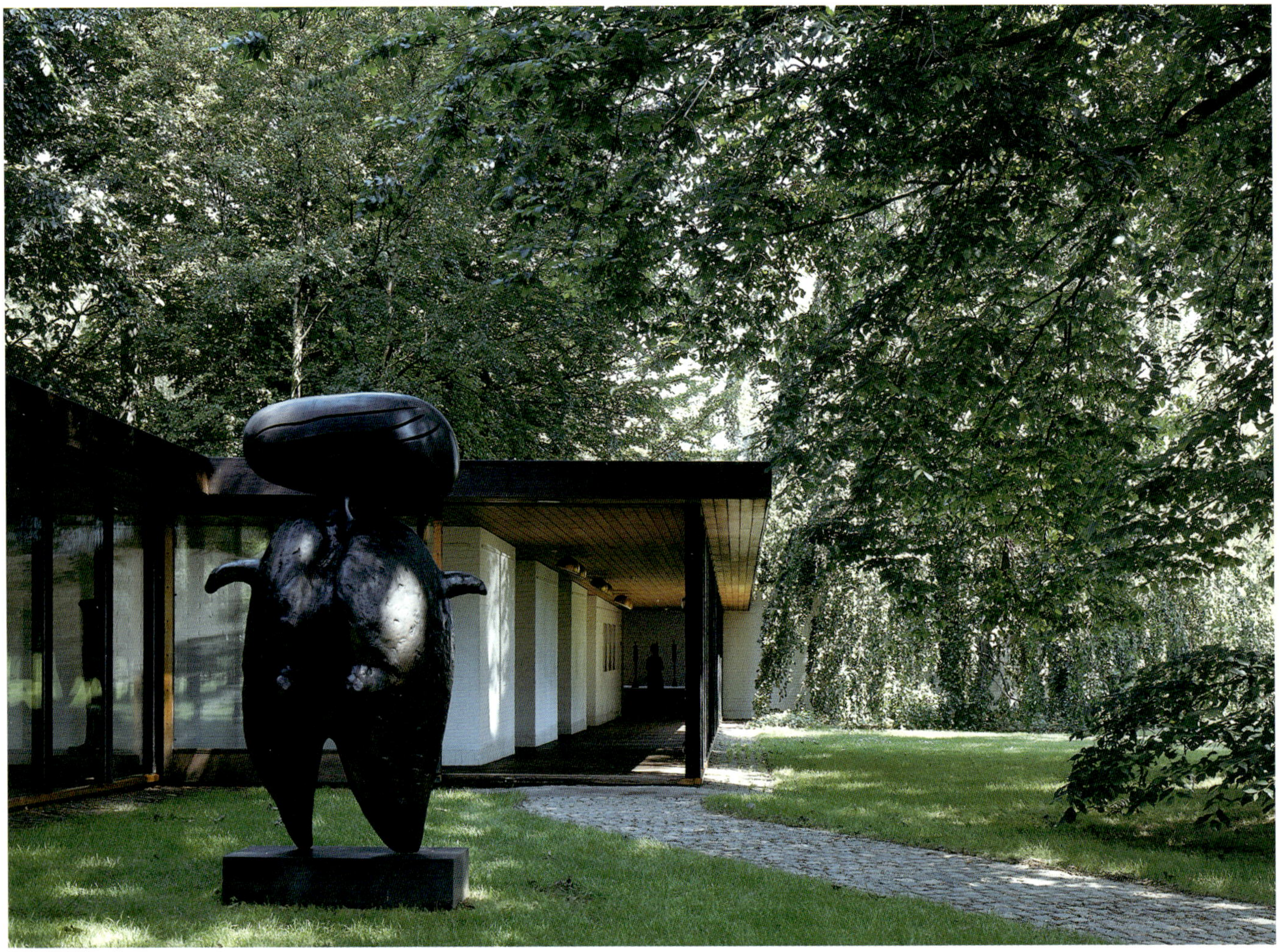

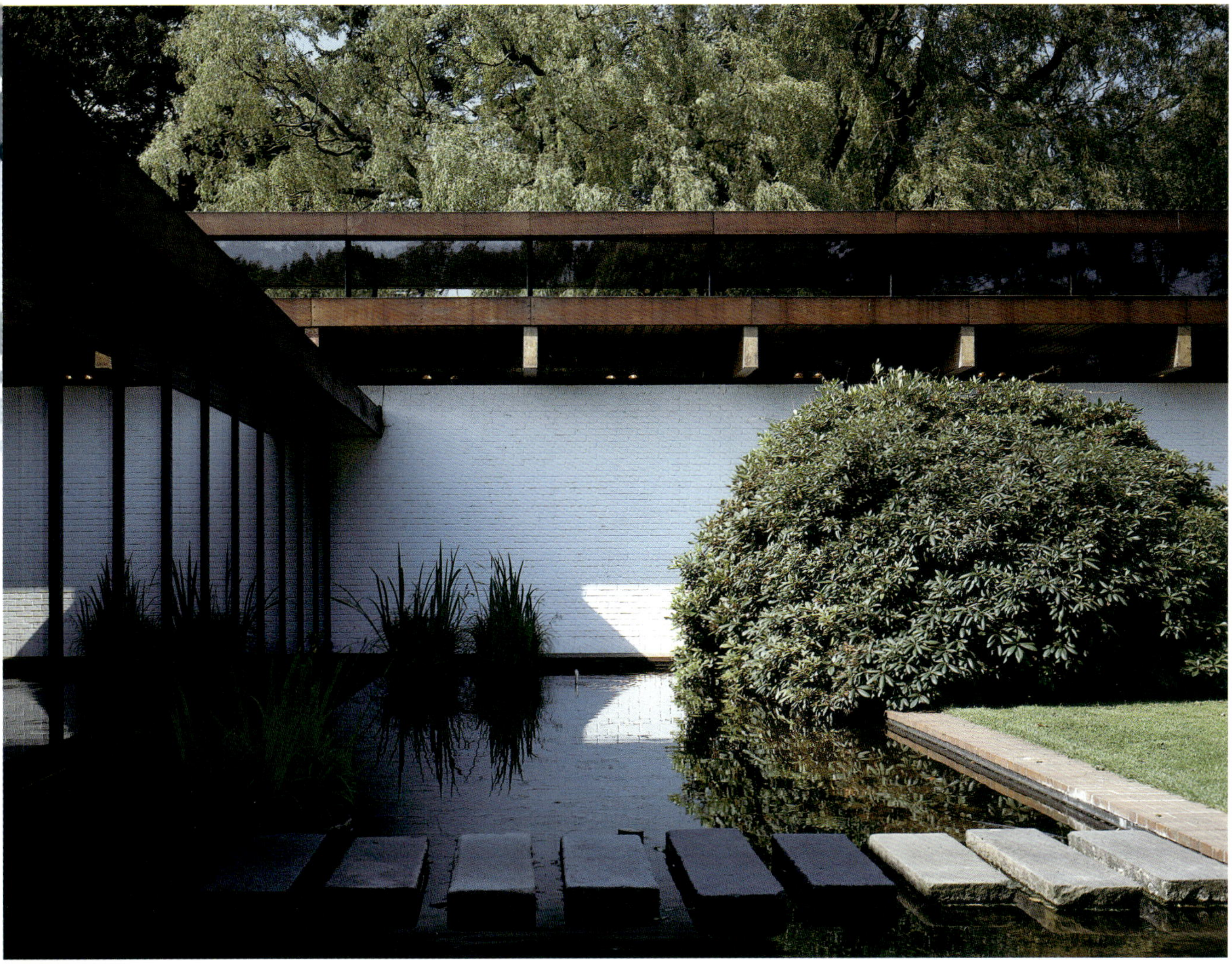

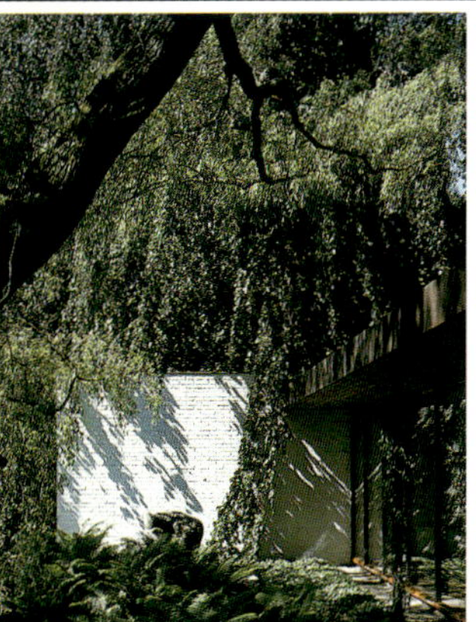

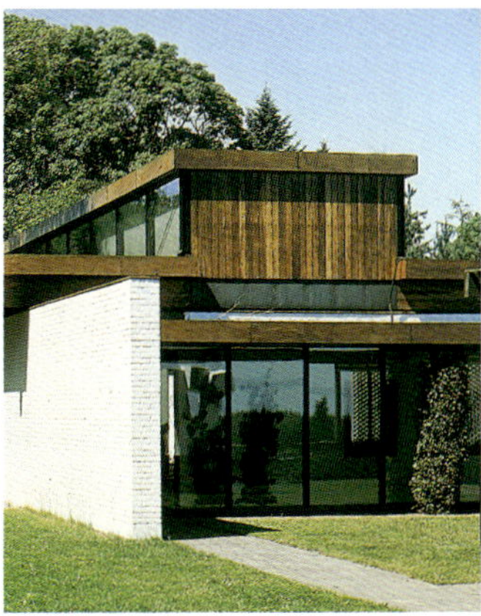

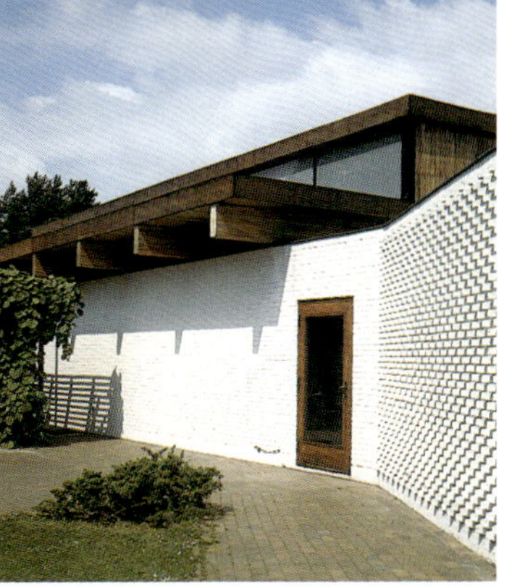

The buildings dating from Louisiana's first building stage of 1956-58 stand out through their visible structures and sterling materials. Whitewashed brick surfaces form a contrast to the dark wooden structures. Large window sections open towards the surrounding nature, contributing to architectural lightness reminiscent of traditional Japanese architecture

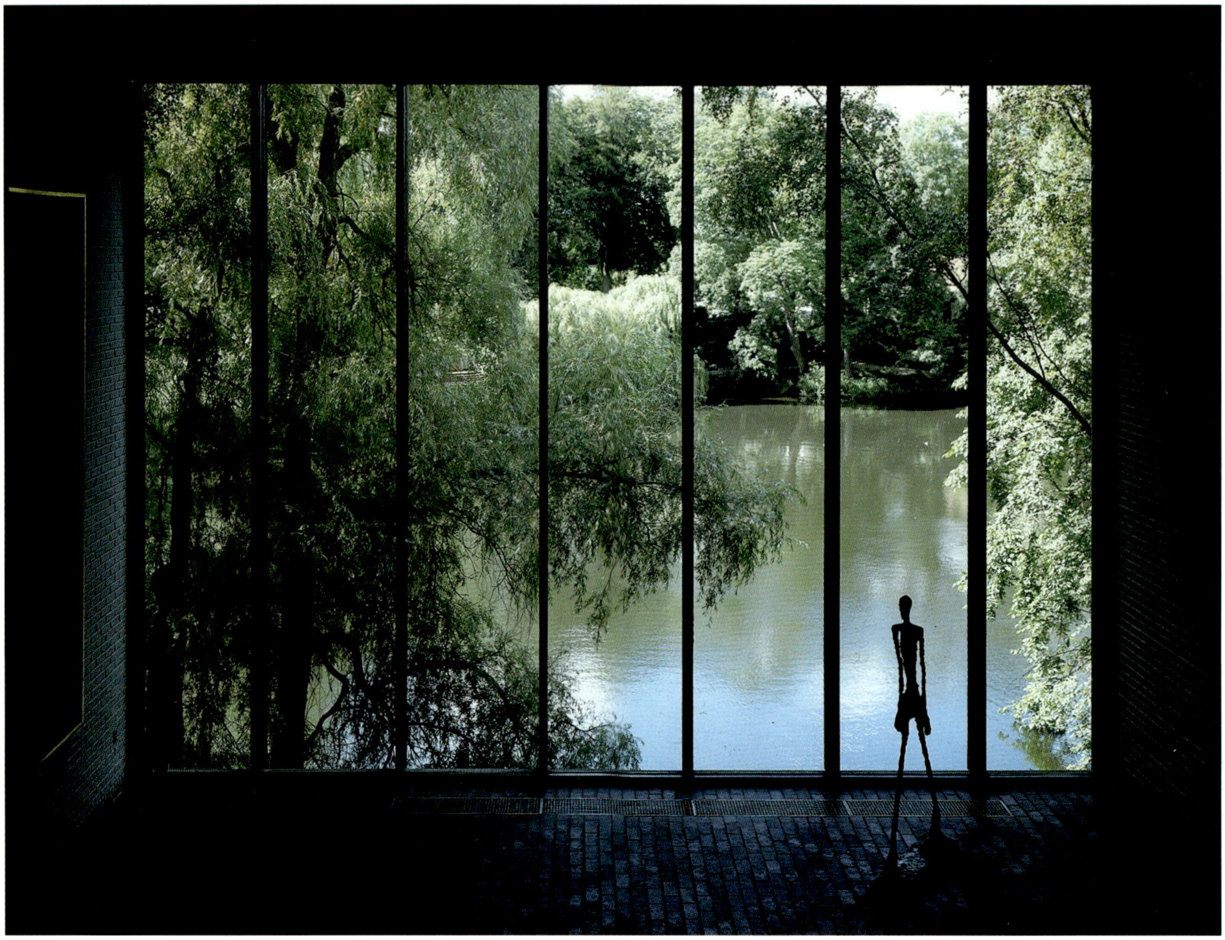

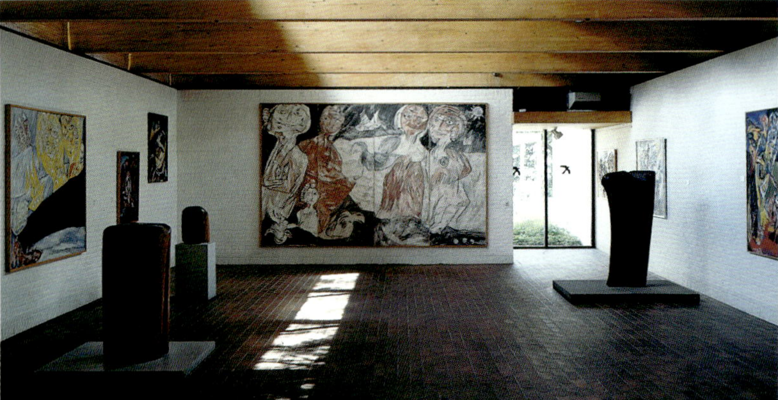

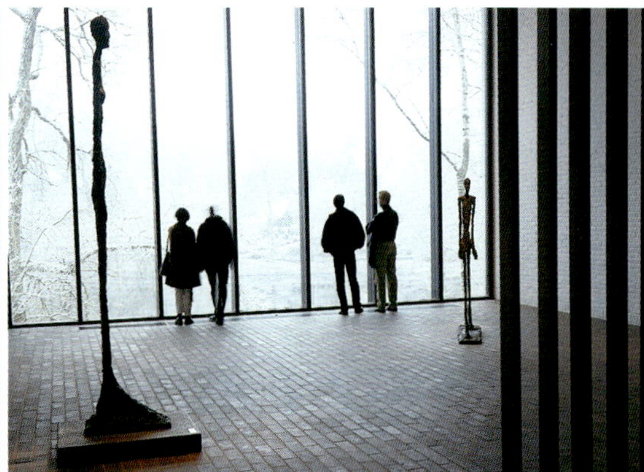

The interplay of nature, architecture, and art, one of the basic parts of Louisiana's architecture philosophy, is expressed most beautifully in the Giacometti room. From here, there is a view of the Lake Garden and Humlebæk Lake

In the part of the museum built in 1958, mainly art of the 50s is shown, above all by the Cobra group artists. Here, the bottom left picture shows paintings by Carl-Henning Pedersen and sculptures by Erik Thommesen

The architecture in this part of the museum carries the typical mark of the 60's: Red clinker floors, whitewashed brickwork, and untreated pine ceilings

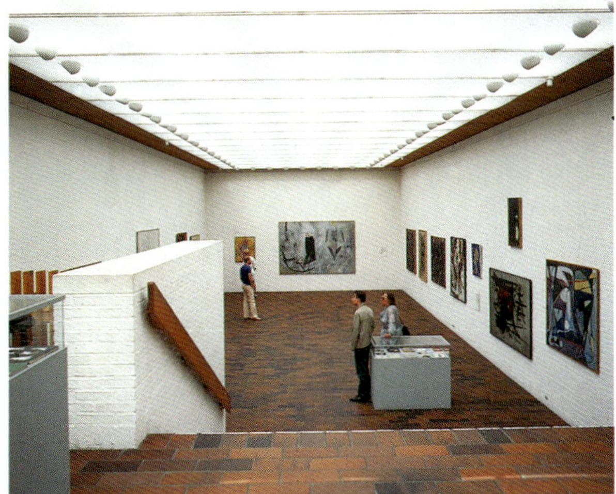

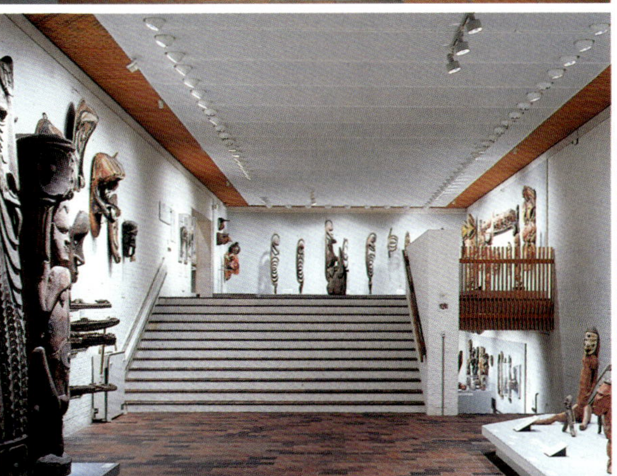

The West Wing stood ready in 1973. At the time, the museum had long been needing an exhibition area which would meet the requirements of the large, temporary exhibitions. It was paramount to the procedures of the museum not to have to dismantle large parts of the permanent collection to make room for the temporary exhibitions. The building style has consciously been kept neutral to allow for the highly varied exhibitions. Also, creating optimal light conditions has been given a high priority: Adjustable roof light, depending on the season and on the time of the day. The exhibition area is 1,000 sq. metres, distributed on three levels, interconnected by stairs and handicap lifts

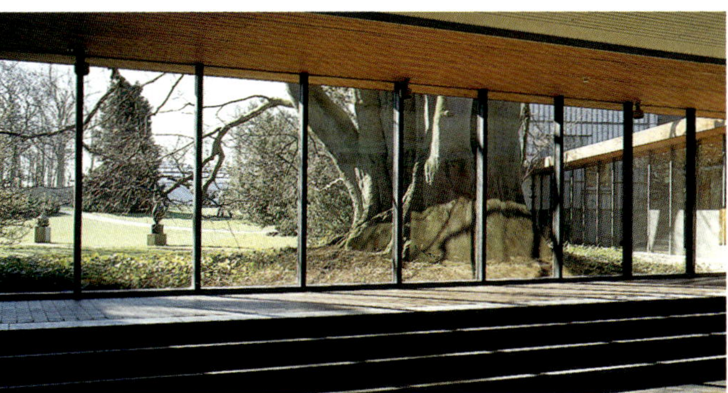

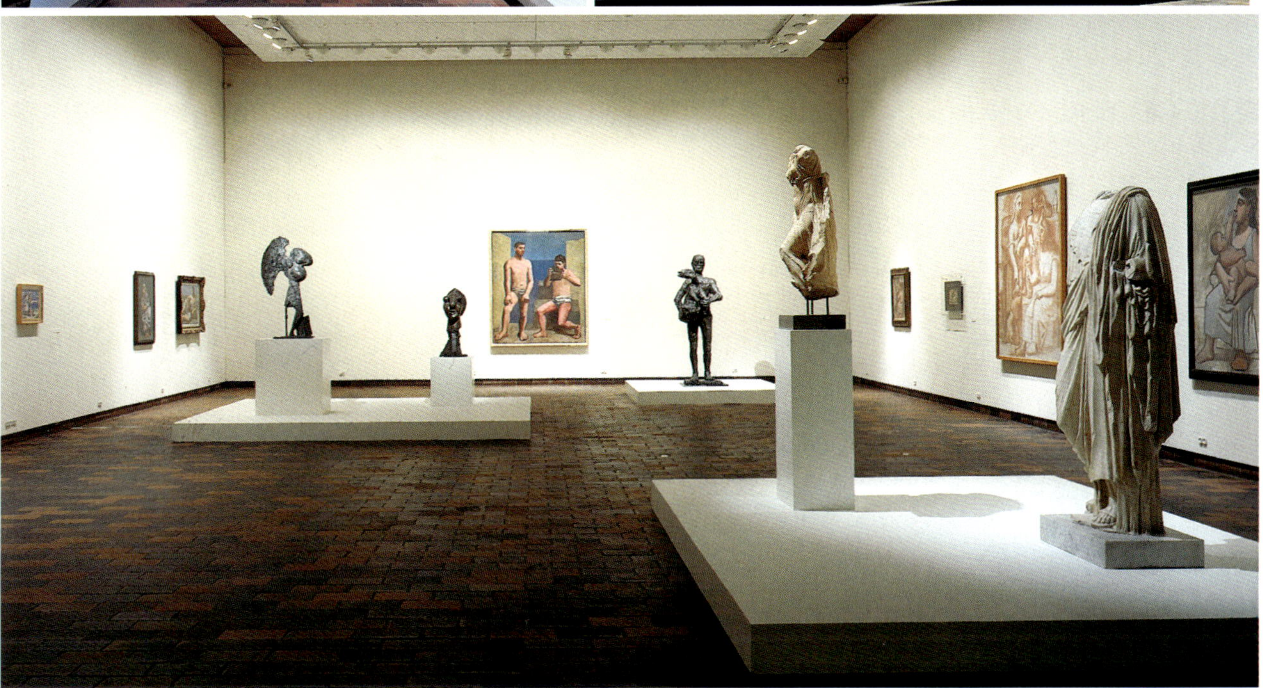

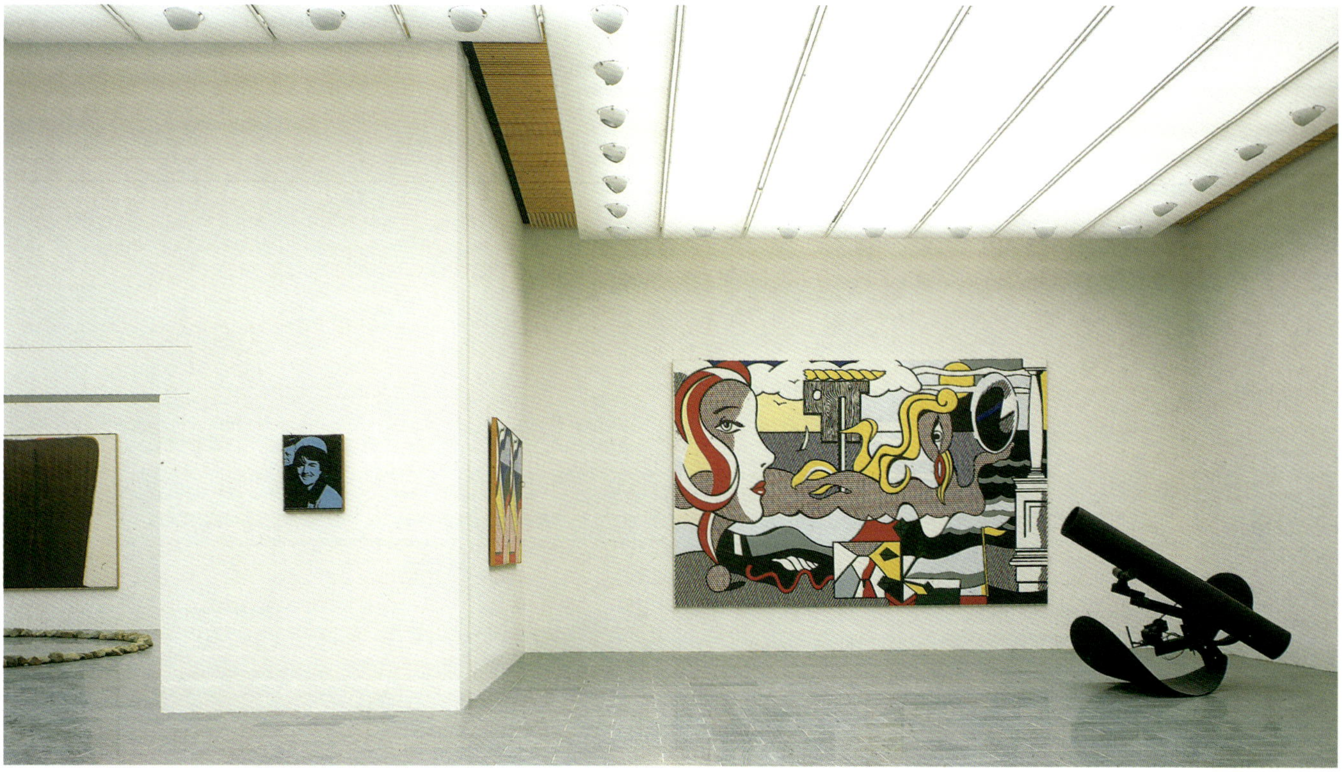

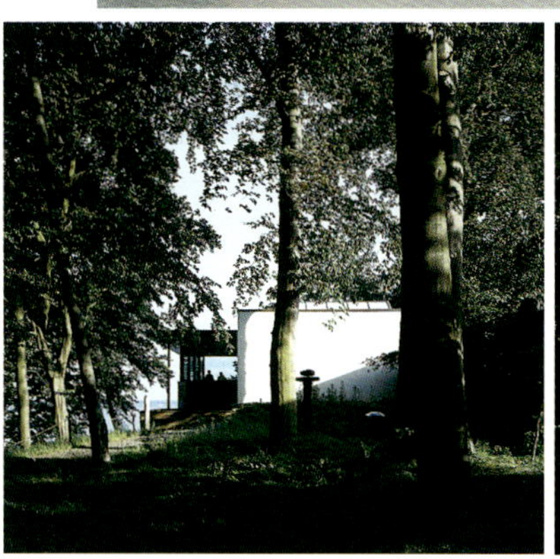

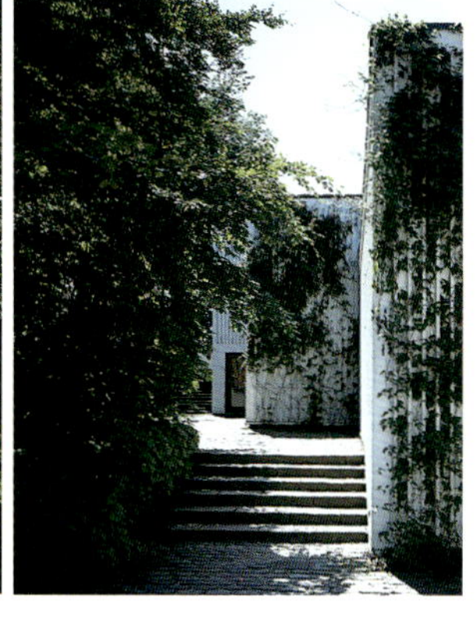

The South Wing opened in 1982 to make room for the growing collection of the museum. The lack of space was also due to the development of the new art. Not only did the formats become larger but new ways of expression, such as installations, were added, too. So it is characteristic of the architecture of this wing that importance has been attached to having high-ceilinged rooms with large proper wall and floor surfaces. Viewed from the outside, you do not gain an impression of the dimensions of the rooms as the buildings have been integrated in the steeply rising ground. Along the east side of the South Wing, small court areas have been created, offering good conditions for the sculptures

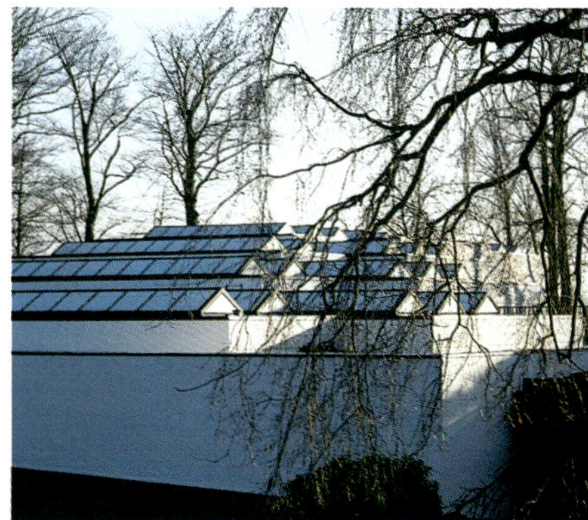

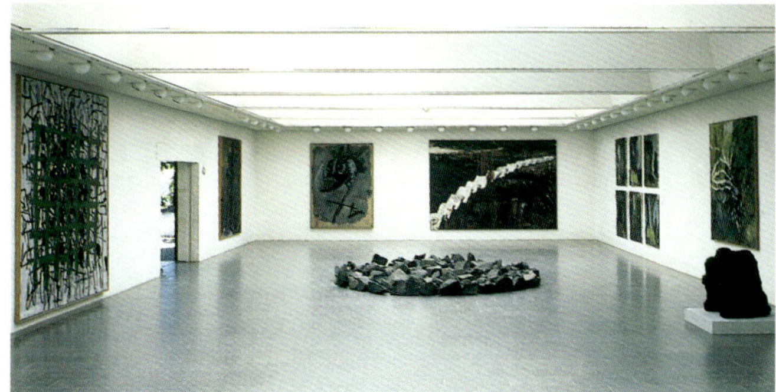

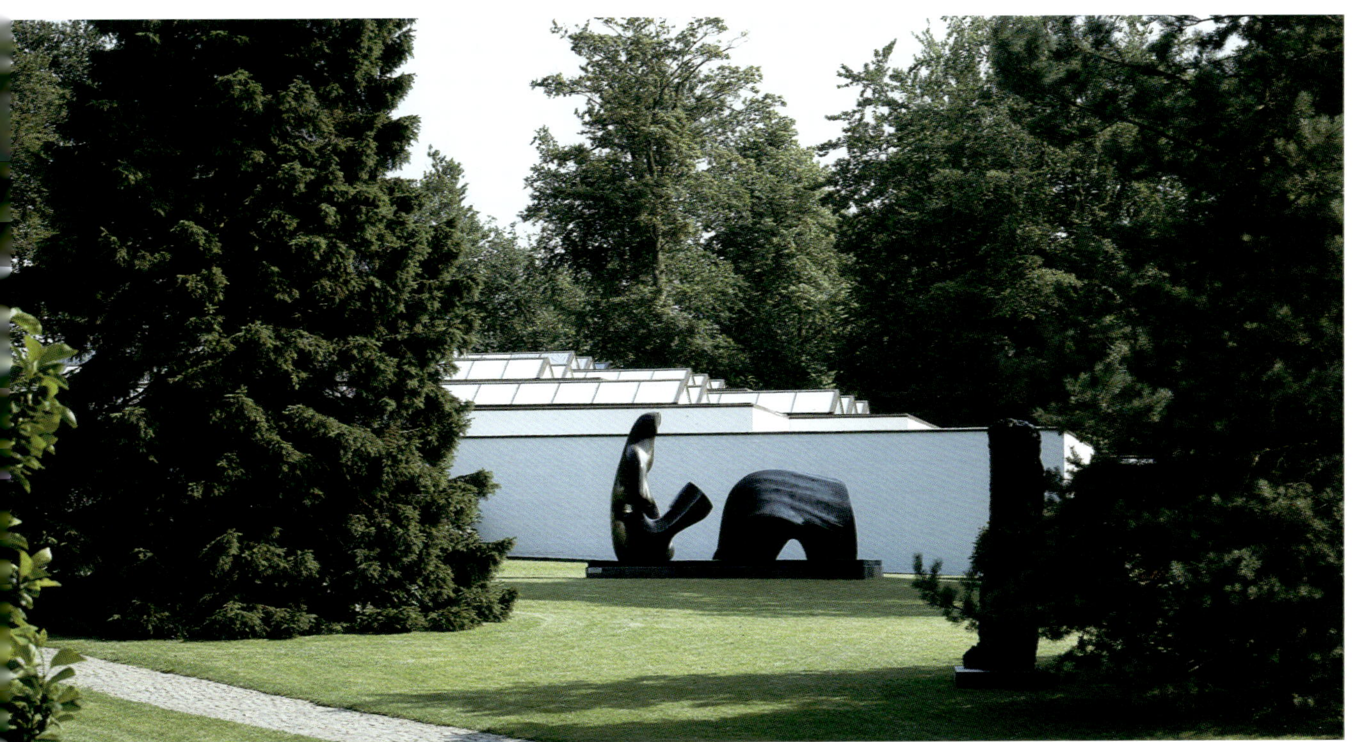

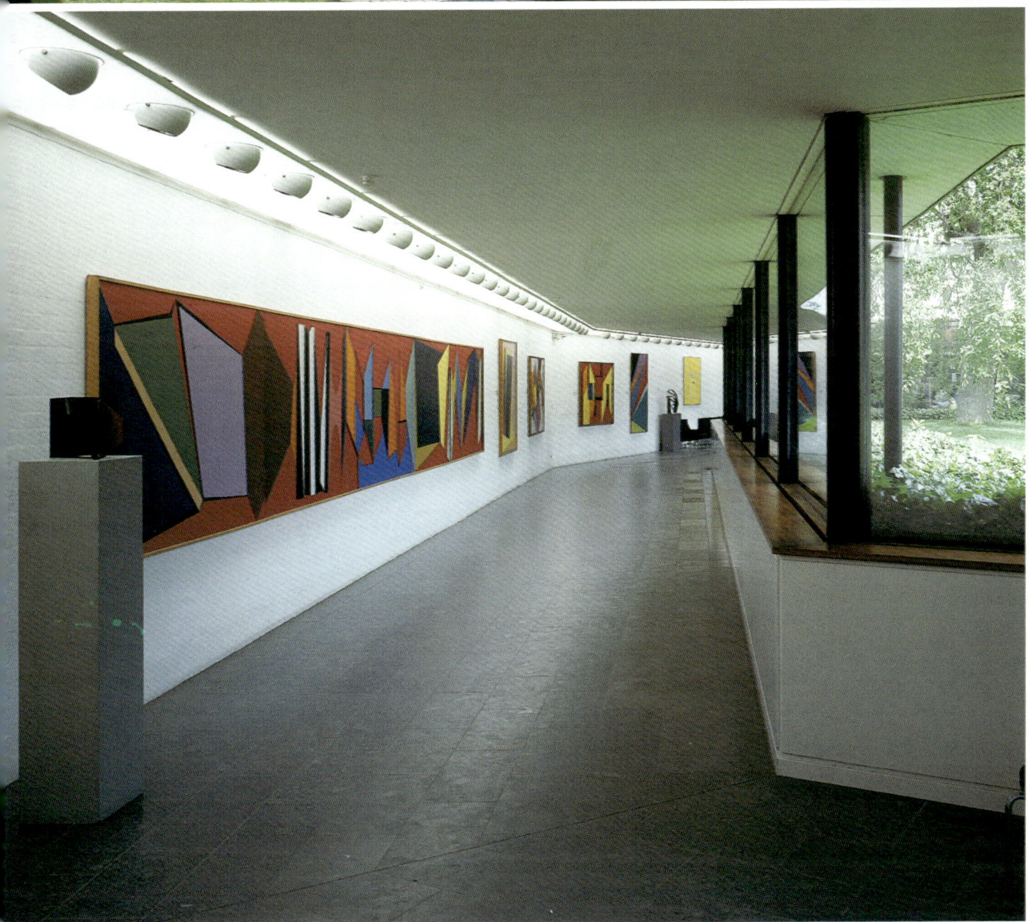

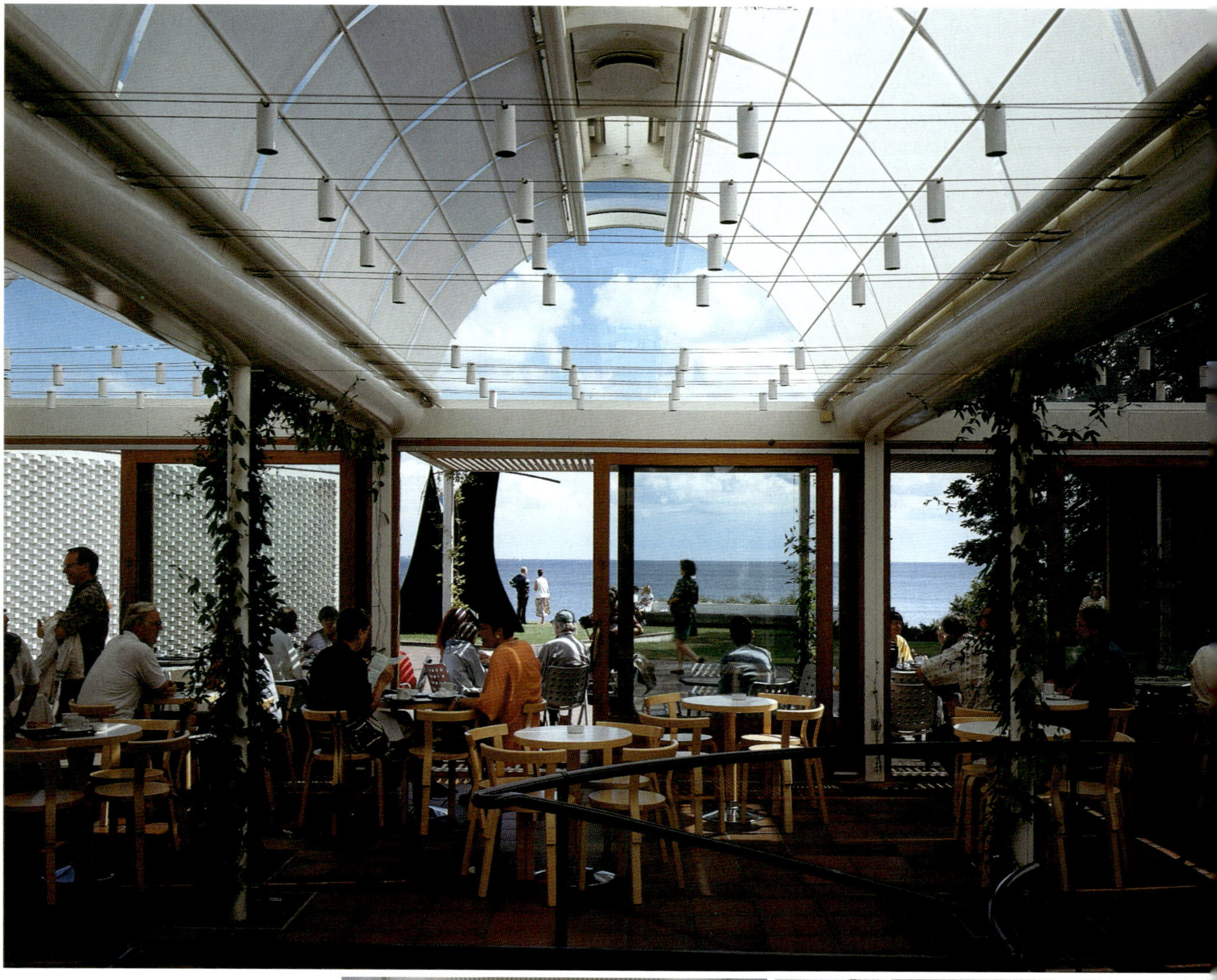

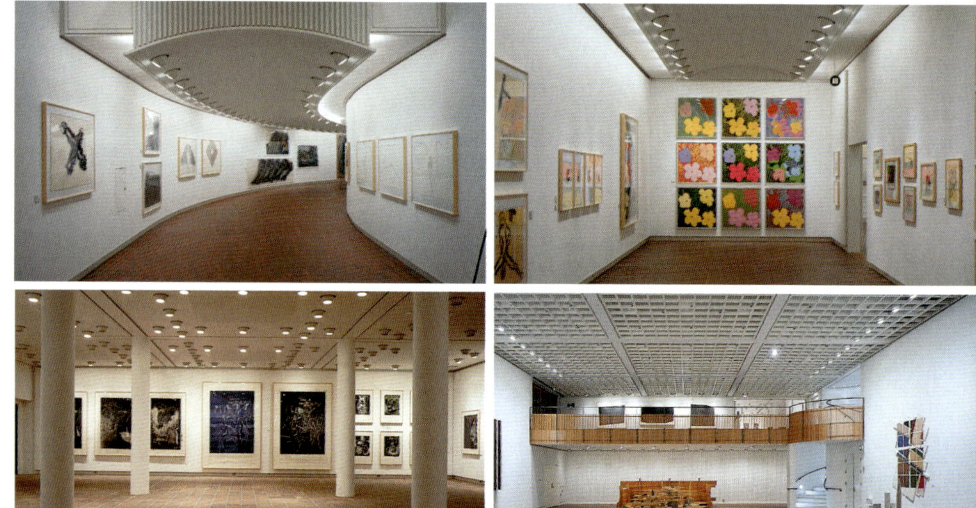

The most recent major increase of the exhibition area was made in 1991. With the new extension, the Graphics Wing, which is mainly below ground level, several wishes have been fulfilled all in one. First, the museum now has an exhibition area with artificial lighting, ideal for art on paper, such as drawings and prints and photographs. Next, the North Wing has been connected with the South Wing. You may thus walk round the entire museum without having to go back or cut across the park area. Last but not least, through the underground placing of this extension, the museum has managed to keep the beautiful view of the park and of the Sound. The Graphics Wing connects south and north, to the other architecture of the museum through two glass pavilions, the northern one making a rest area with benches and lush plants. The other pavilion works both as a rest area, and as a natural extension of the museum café

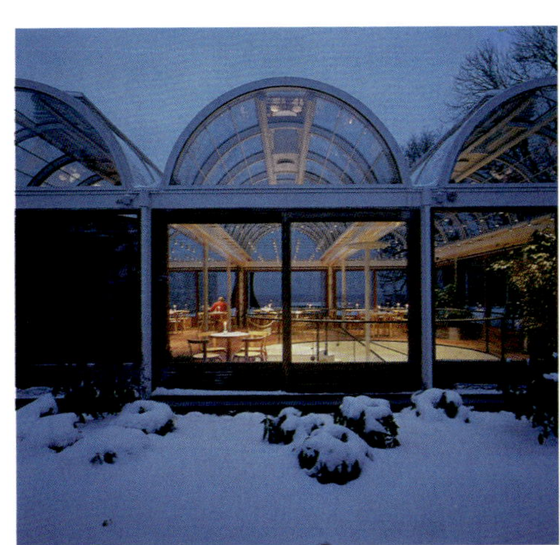

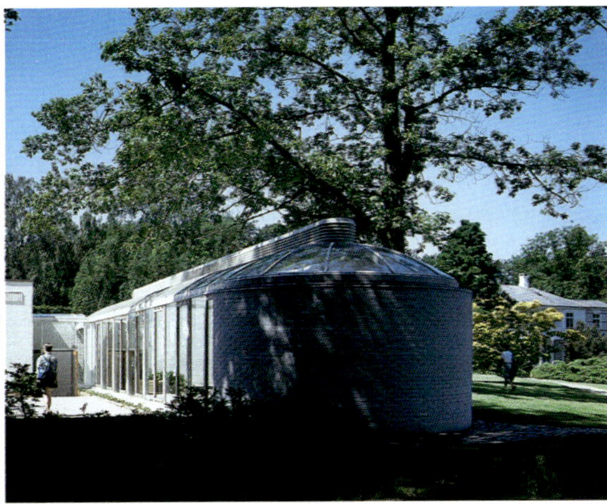

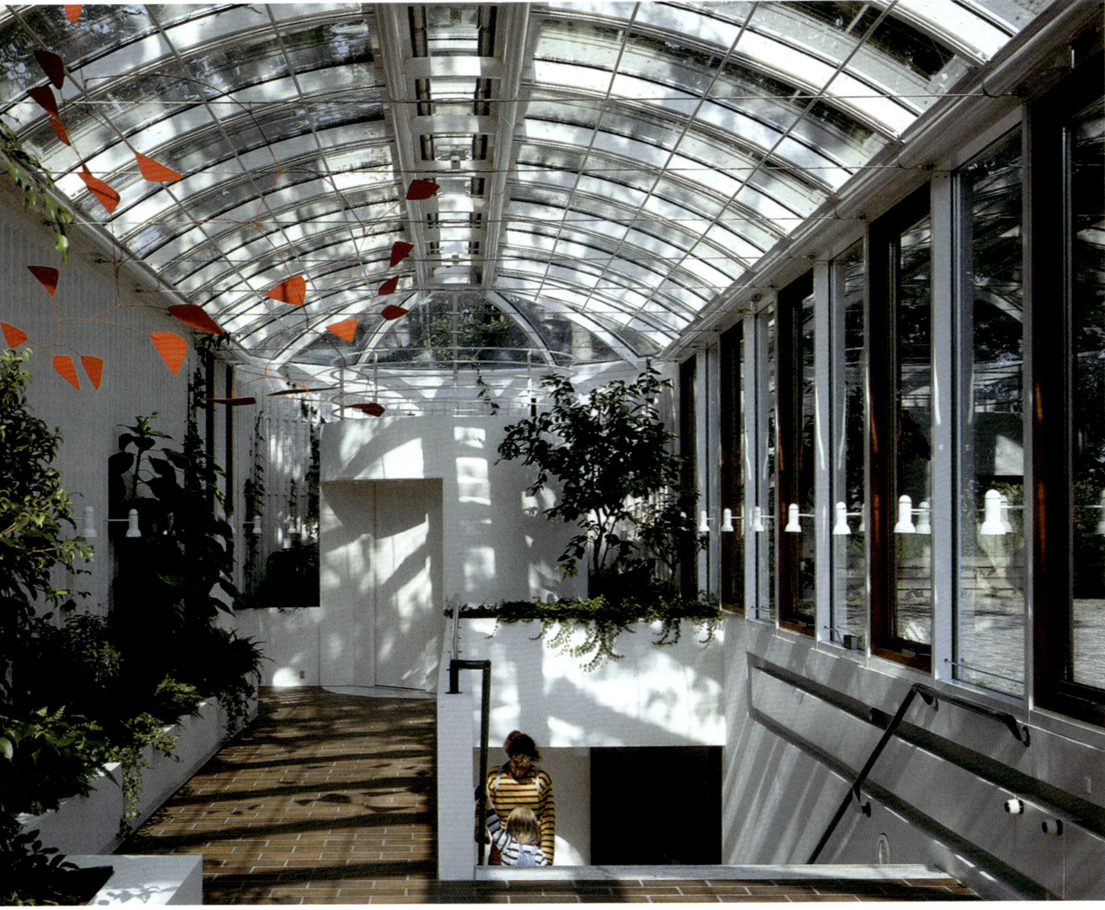

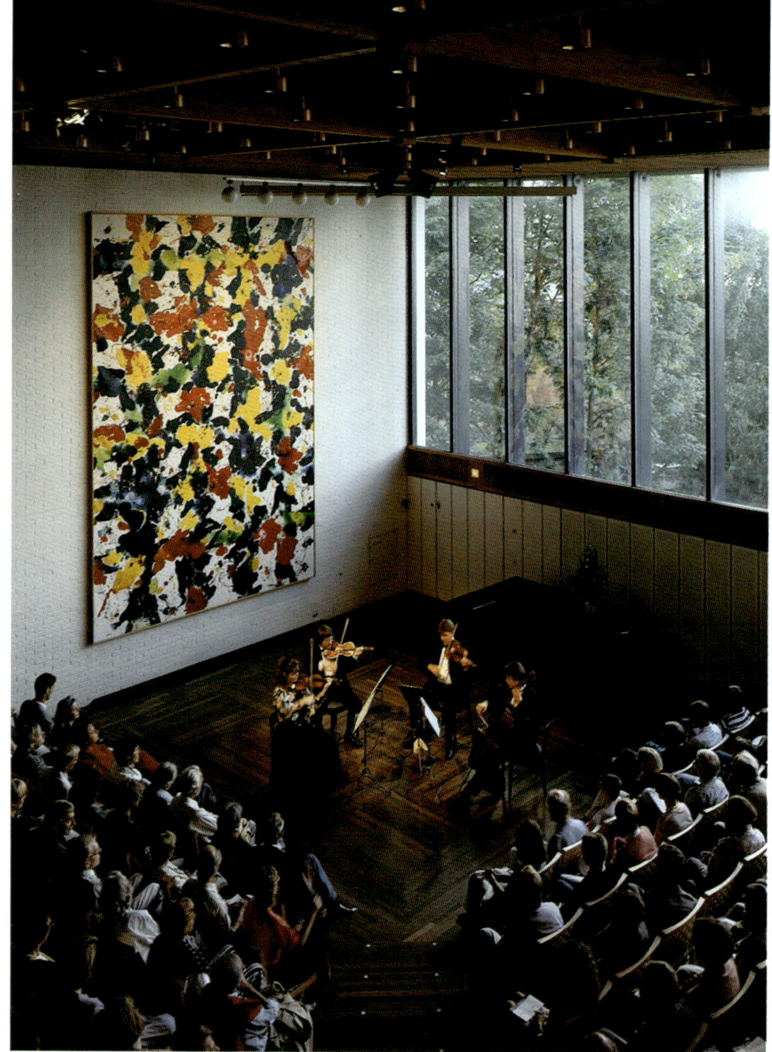

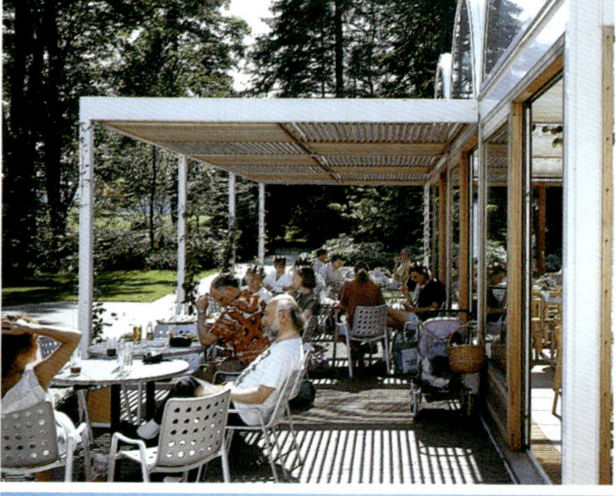

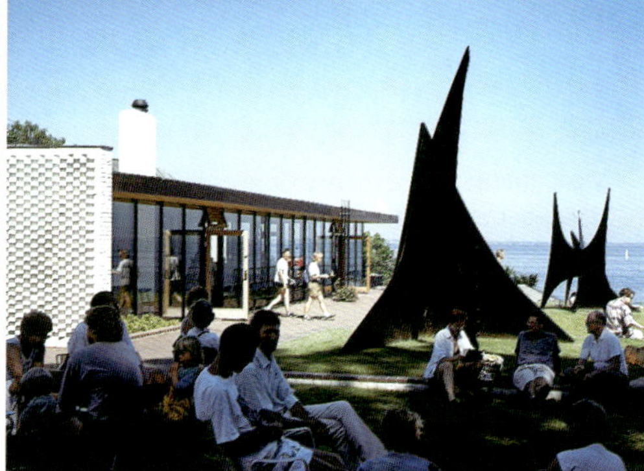

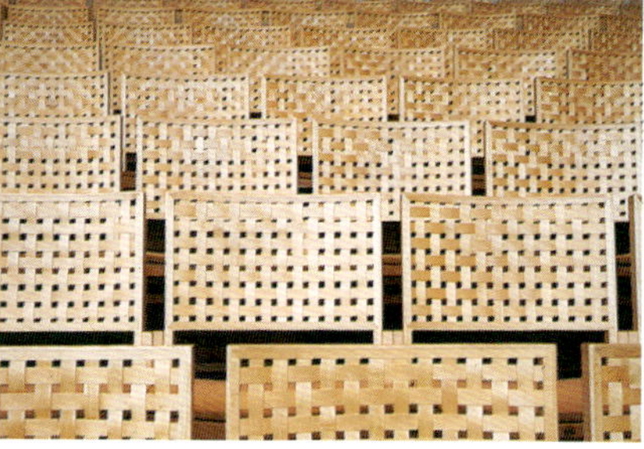

Ever since being built in 1976, the Concert Hall has provided the framework for Louisiana's weekly concerts. Panel discussions, author meetings, poetry readings, and discourses on a broad spectrum of culture also take place here. The chairs were designed by Poul Kjærholm, and the walls decorated by Sam Francis whose large paintings were made specifically for this room

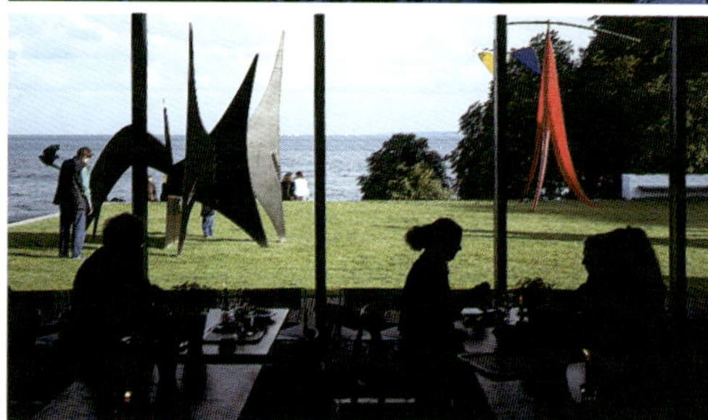

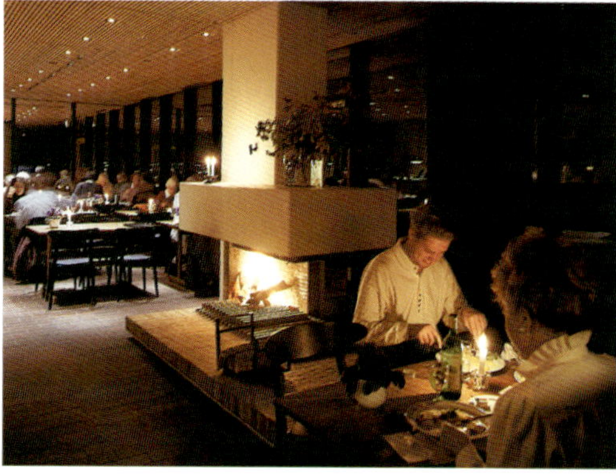

Since the first ideas and plans on the location of the various Louisiana building sections were forged, it has been definite that the cafeteria was to be placed with the best possible view. Many details have changed over the years. The area has been extended in stages, the name has been changed from the cafeteria to the museum café. The view, however, remains the most beautiful conceivable; in the course of time, it has also been accompanied by Calder's distinctive sculptures

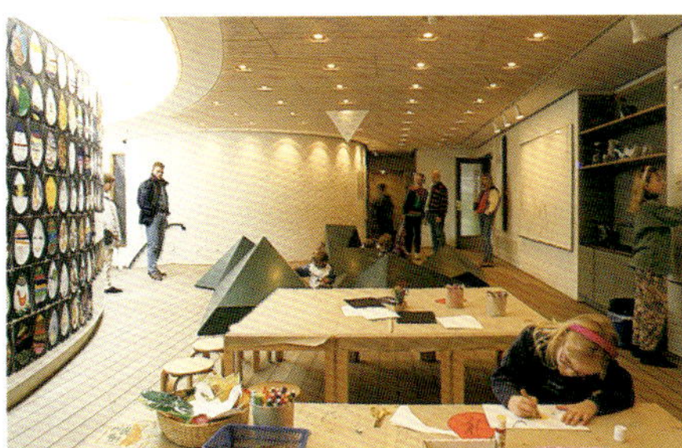

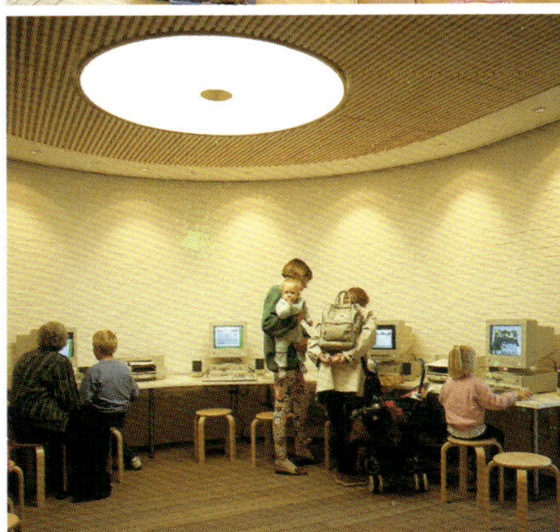

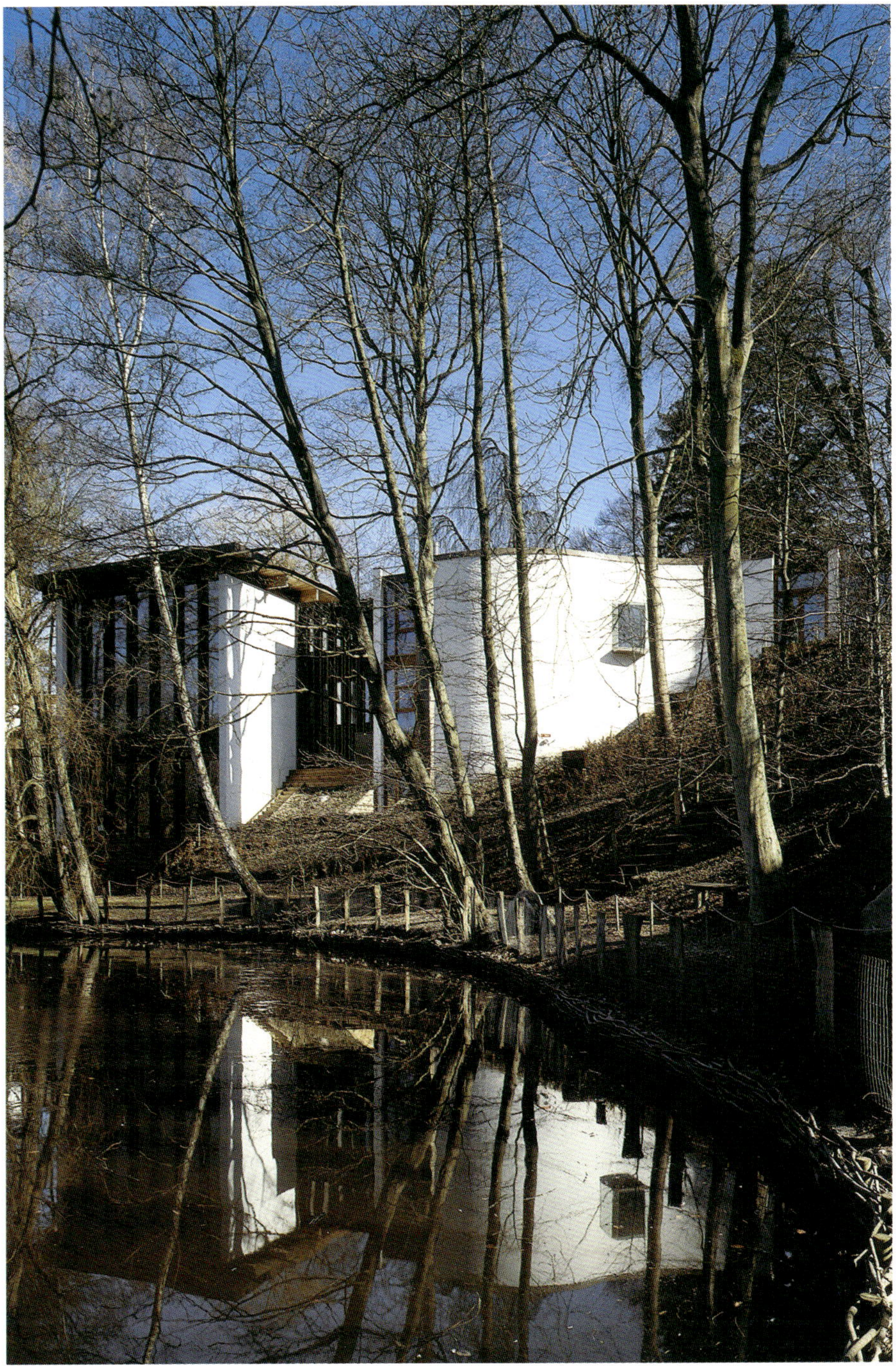

From the earliest years of Louisiana, visitors' children have benefited from the opportunity to draw or have stories read to them in the so-called children's room. In the course of time, the room became dated, both for size and convenience, fostering the idea of creating a place where the children could learn about art, and express themselves in art as well

In the autumn of 1994, the new Children's Wing was inaugurated. The area is distributed on three floors. The first floor contains a reading room and a drawing room for infants. The intermediate floor offers a children's cinema and a computer room. The bottom floor contains a workshop room and an eating area. From here, there is a view of and entrance to the Lake Garden, in summertime an imaginative playground with slides, caves, and huts. In the trees, ingenuous bird's nests have been built, so big that the children can lie down in them

A Romantic Garden

Gertrud Købke Sutton

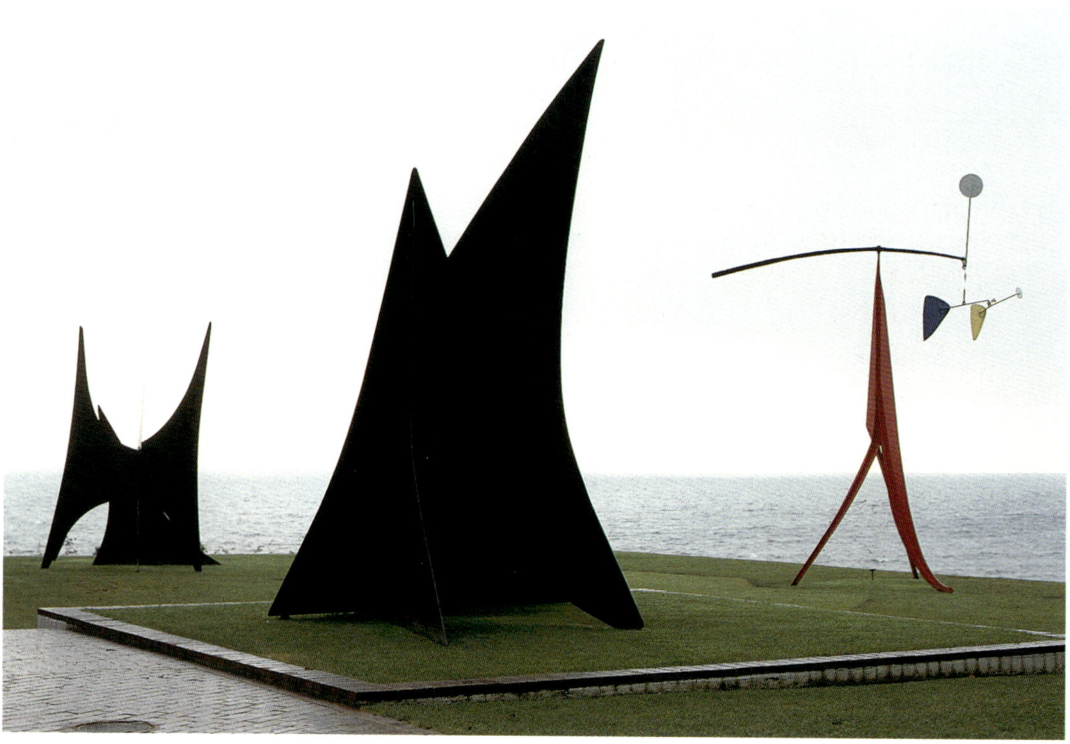

Alexander Calder's three sculptures in front of the museum café

The Louisiana Museum Park is a Romantic garden with sculptures.

"They add a new element, something man-made, to nature, which without them would become almost too overpowering," wrote Knud W. Jensen in 1972. And he continued: "The good sculptures always hold their own in the contest. The only danger that threatens outdoor sculpture exhibitions is overcrowding. The individual work needs to be seen without too much competition from other works of art – or in a tightly controlled landscape garden setting."

Back in 1954, the young Knud W. Jensen, with his dog Trofast, climbed over the gate to the unoccupied Louisiana and went exploring in the park around the abandoned country house. At that time it was just a century since the original builder of Louisiana, Alexander Brun, had acquired the deed to the land. He was a man with good ideas and an interest in trees – both fruit trees and the more exotic kinds. The fruit trees bore porcelain plates with their names, for he had grafted new pear varieties; and there were beehives, a pheasant warren and a greenhouse. At the water level of the Sound, protected from the sea air by a wall, lay an old rose garden, and on the outermost part of the beech-covered sea slope stood a tea pavilion. Humlebæk Lake, which had been dredged and turned into a privateer harbour during the Napoleonic war, was surrounded by a marshy wilderness. There, the royal buccaneer ships could lie in wait, well hidden behind a strong thrown-up bastion with sheer sides.

The Louisiana Park has its background in Danish culture and a tradition that goes back to the 1700s, and its appeal to the emotions is still felt strongly today. The way the Louisiana Park looks is the way we feel, deep down, that the Danish countryside is – beautiful, well-tended, grassy-green and sky-blue.

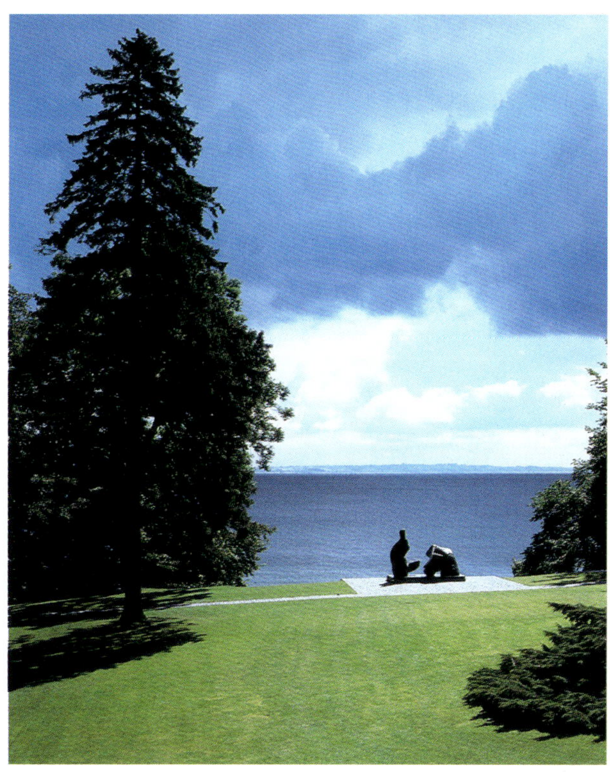

View of the Sound with Henry Moore's *Reclining Figure No. 5* from 1963-64

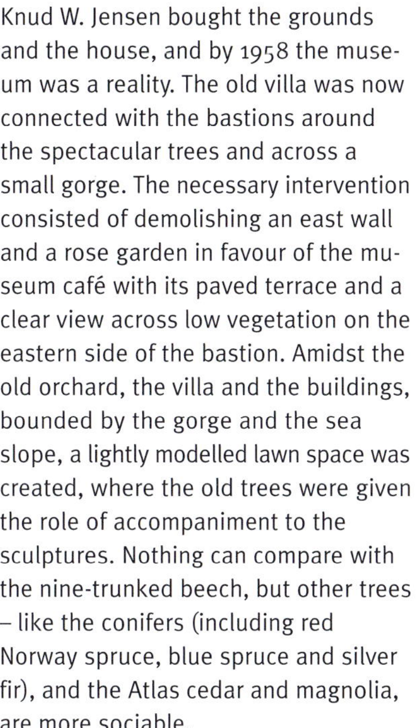

Knud W. Jensen bought the grounds and the house, and by 1958 the museum was a reality. The old villa was now connected with the bastions around the spectacular trees and across a small gorge. The necessary intervention consisted of demolishing an east wall and a rose garden in favour of the museum café with its paved terrace and a clear view across low vegetation on the eastern side of the bastion. Amidst the old orchard, the villa and the buildings, bounded by the gorge and the sea slope, a lightly modelled lawn space was created, where the old trees were given the role of accompaniment to the sculptures. Nothing can compare with the nine-trunked beech, but other trees – like the conifers (including red Norway spruce, blue spruce and silver fir), and the Atlas cedar and magnolia, are more sociable.

In his book *Labyrinten* ("The Labyrinth"), 1792-93, Jens Baggesen described how important it is to be able to sit amidst nature: what escapes your attention when you are in motion is at last captured when you sit still. From that instant you are "a nobler, a more human, being". There are perhaps not so many benches in the Louisiana Park – because benches interfere with space and sculpture – but there are lawns and steps and the marvellous museum café, from which, at rest, one can turn one's attention to art and nature.

Everything in the Danish landscape, and in a park like Louisiana's, can be formed. Even the softness of the soil is organic and manipulable. Humanity – living or in the form of a work of art – absorbs and echoes this softness; we are made of the same stuff, just as we reflect the growing forms of the trees.

Henry Moore's *Reclining Figure No. 5* from 1963-64, which has almost become synonymous with Louisiana, helps to demarcate the space; it draws in the sea and the sky, captures the formless in its malleable humanoid lump, and unites with the flatness of the lawn and the depth of the space. It is the key figure of the whole complex – yet without having been created for the setting.

The white, textured walls of the architecture, on the other hand, are important as a starting-point for and link with other intentions and expressive forms than the anthropomorphic. The non-figurative sculptures have a different kind of dialogue with their surroundings.

The plateau in front of the museum café, where the ground disappears and sea and sky open up, is the perfect foil for upward-soaring sculptures; and what could be more relevant than iron mobiles and stabiles by Alexander Calder? It is liberatingly beautiful.

Louisiana has two large open areas: the lawn in front of the house and the old tennis court by the beach. The upper plateau is framed on three sides by buildings. The northern one, the Bo and Wohlert museum building, was once half hidden below the old, distinguished trees whose trunks were reflected in the glass walls. But after the ravages of Dutch elm disease much that was once whole has been destroyed, and coming years will see changes in the composition of the Park. In the half-light among the trees the sculptures stood like organic growths or open frameworks which captured and framed nature. What was once an ivy-covered sanctuary is now exposed, and Henry Moore's large *Three Piece Reclining Figure: Draped* (1974-75) tries provisionally to fill out the emptiness of a space where two tree stumps testify to

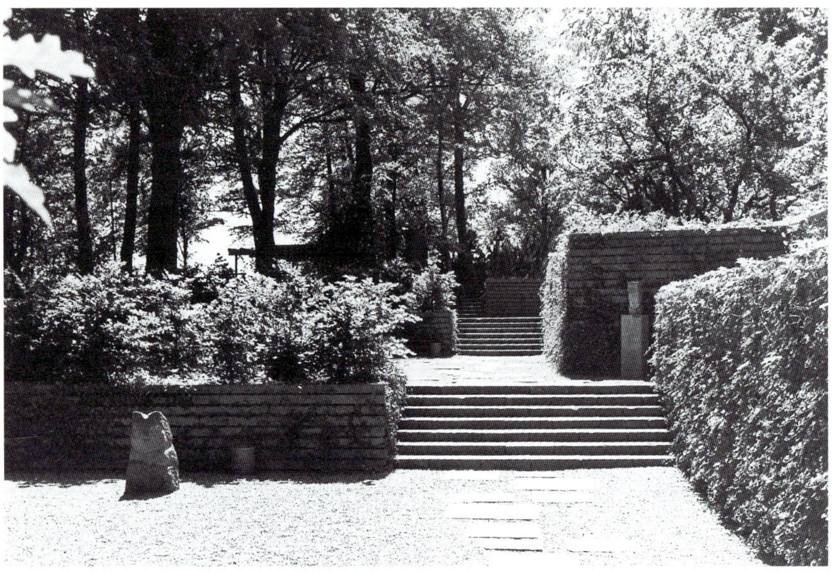
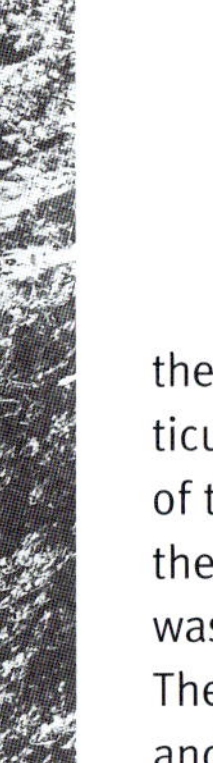

The three levels of terraces created by Edith and Ole Nørgaard in 1963-64. This complex was removed to make way for the South Wing in 1982

the format of the dead elms. In this particular part of the Park, the experience of the interplay of changing seasons, the angle of the sun, rain or moonlight, was and still is essential to the sculpture. The space is not static, but fluctuating, and over the years Knud W. Jensen remained extraordinarily faithful to his ideas and demonstrated his tirelessness in analysing and revising the interplay of art and nature.

A far more difficult matter is the low-lying area below, with its organically meandering retaining wall towards the beach. The area is large and the sides are high, and what sculpture can compete with a location that must relate both to the surrounding slopes and to an observer who must either be above or below? This is the most difficult space in the Park from a sculptural point of view, and the present solution is not optimal. Perhaps the place should represent the pause, the non-activated space – or perhaps it should be presented as a site-specific commission to an artist. A maze could be created here!

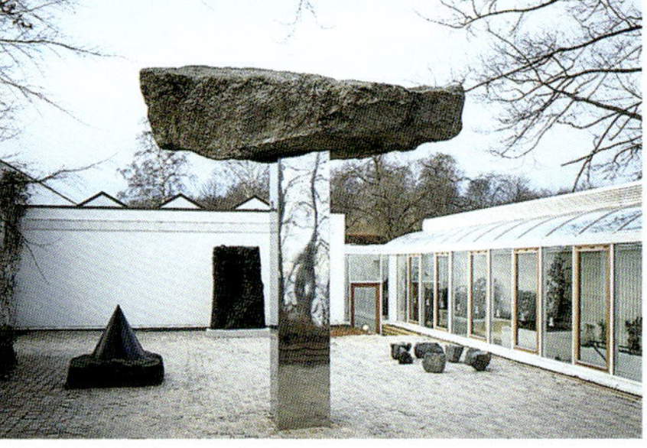

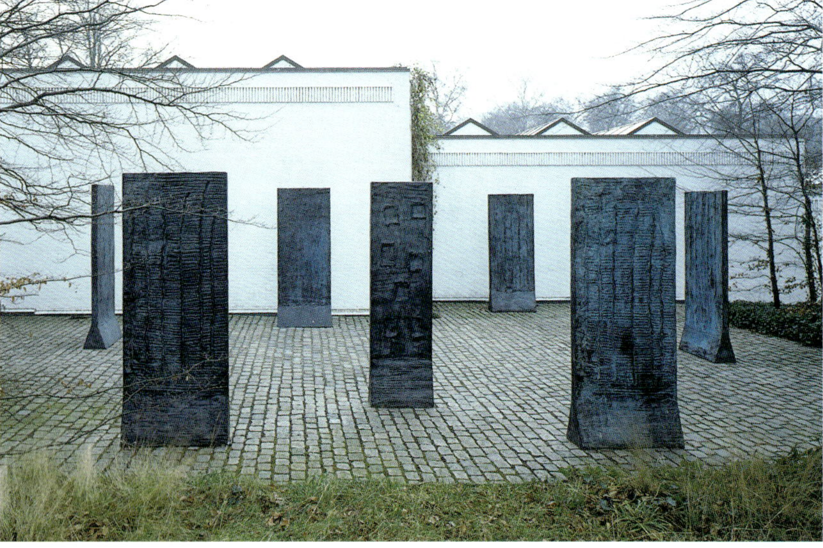

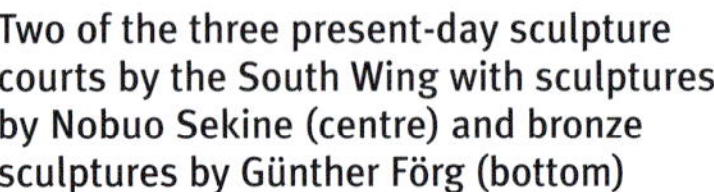

Two of the three present-day sculpture courts by the South Wing with sculptures by Nobuo Sekine (centre) and bronze sculptures by Günther Förg (bottom)

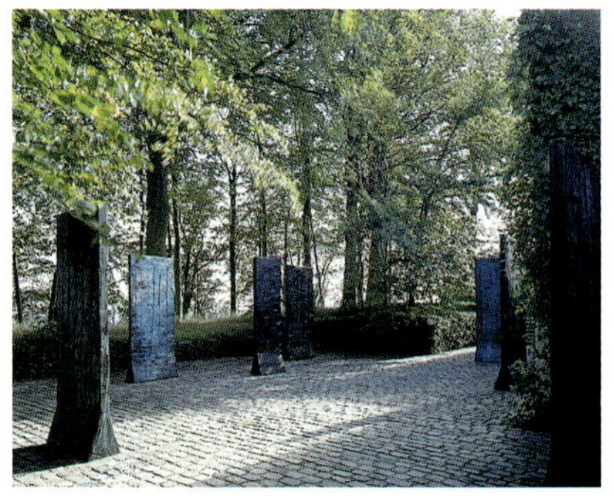

210
Günther Förg:
Seven Bronze Steles, 1988.

Sculpture in the open air was the watchword of the sixties, and the function of the Louisiana Park as a setting for sculpture became the centre of Knud W. Jensen's attention in connection with his interest in Middelheim near Antwerp, an equally old park which in the 1960s was the great inspiration as an outdoor museum of modern art. A selection of works from Middelheim was presented at Louisiana in 1964.

The museum had prepared itself well for this task. The landscape gardener Ole Nørgaard was asked to create the sculptural space between the old orchard and the sea slope, and the work was done in 1963-64. The three-metre rise in the terrain was split into three terraces, a thematic parallel to the three pavilions of the museum. The terraces were bounded by ivy-clad boarding, high enough to form a backdrop for the art, but not so high that they covered the gnarled crowns of the fruit trees, and very low in relation to the Sound and the beech wood. The open, but clearly demarcated outside spaces stood the test with the Middelheim exhibition. But, as Nørgaard put it: "A thorough viewing of a large sculptural collection can be a great strain; pauses and relief are necessary. The most important element in the solution to this problem is a large viewing floor built out over the steep coastal slope, from which there is a view of the Sound and no chance to see any sculpture." *(Knud W. Jensen:* Mit Louisiana-liv ("My Louisiana Life"), *Copenhagen, 1993.)*

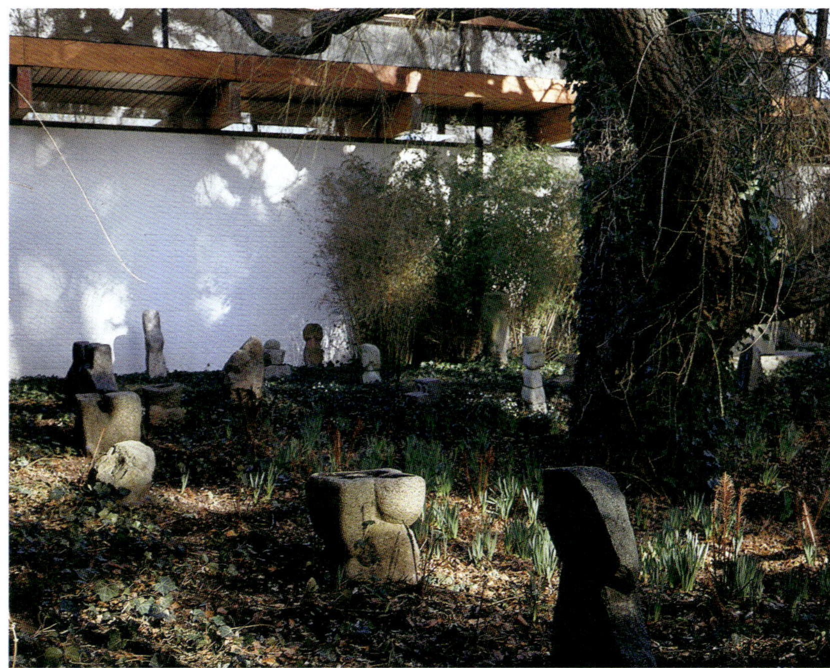

Henry Heerup's sculptures have now been set up outside the glass corridor leading from the old house to the museum café

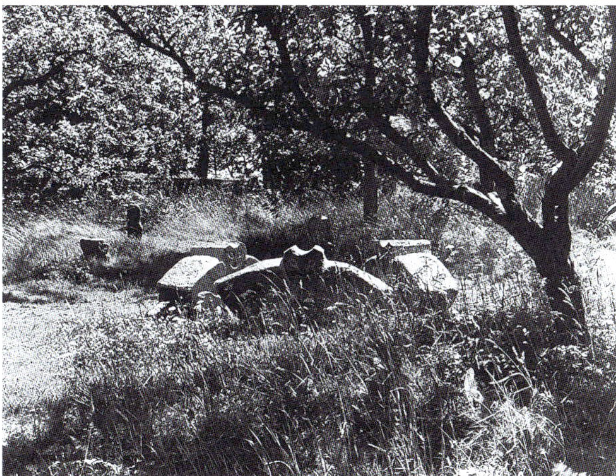

The old orchard with granite sculptures by Henry Heerup

Knud W. Jensen noted that the sculpture gardens "confirmed our view that one can place many sculptures together in a precise landscape garden setting, while there are limits to how many one can set up on lawns between trees in a park landscape like Louisiana's without the sculptures interfering with one another or 'swimming' in the rich vegetation." It was not the intention that the sculpture gardens should be permanent in nature, but that changing sculptures and configurations should be tried out in a constant quest for the best conditions and the most moving experiences.

In their own way, Nørgaard's terraces anticipated the extension of the museum with the South Wing in 1982, an annexe which meant the definitive removal of the old orchard. The terraces now function as pavement and forecourt to the buildings. And the conservatory of the Graphics Wing has cut off any interplay with the large lawn. All in all, this means that the sculptures of the Park today lead a more enclosed, museum-like life. The space created by Günther Förg's large bronzes is however in itself so architectural that the sculptures determine their own boundaries. Others must be viewed with the slope as background, while Nobuo Sekine's *Phases of Nothingness* (1972-78) live their own wondrous, introverted looking-glass life.

When the apple orchards were eliminated – only one tree is left – so too was the place where Henry Heerup's small granite sculptures throve so well. They stood as if they were offshoots from the roots of the trees, half hidden in the tall grass. Today they are planted in a semicircle below a splendid golden weeping willow – another relic of the old gardens. They present themselves to the visitor passing through the glass corridor behind. In summer they hide among the fern leaves, and in winter they emerge from their cocoon and stand naked; they wax and wane in inverse proportion with the seasons, but this very rhythm, these shifting degrees of visibility, are quite in keeping with the 'nature' of the figures.

Like most of the sculptures in the Park, Heerup's stones are movable. This means that there are always new ways of testing interrelationships, whether with plants, architecture or other works of art – an antithesis to the concept of 'site-specific' or works created by the artist at and for the site.

The golden willow stands by a depression in the ground which is the beginning of the small gorge between the bastion and the Park, and which debouches on to the flat terrain by the Sound. This was where Richard Serra chose his site in 1986, and used his large walls as a sudden termination of the soft fall of the landscape. From each side, one a little higher up the slope than the other, his immense steel plates, *The Gate in the Gorge* (1986) project in the cleft almost like geological phenomena. They shape the passage and block or restrict the view, depending on where you are in the gorge. Their format is brutal, but their colour and weathering natural. Serra has given the place sculptural meaning and a new function in the Park.

Enzo Cucchi, too, chose his own spot. Towards the south, where the trees extend down to the beach, was where he wanted to place his work from 1984, *Scultura Africa* ("Africa Sculpture"). Flat as a pancake, grey as a frozen puddle, it lies on the ground and looks like the African continent. Its presence gives weight and meaning to an anonymous strip of land between beach and slope. It is truly cut out for its location.

Above this, George Trakas has conceived a site-specific work, *Self Passage* (1986-88), consisting of small 'sheep paths' along the slope. One leads down to three platforms in a fan shape, projecting a couple of metres beyond the sandy beach and thus crossing the boundary of the museum, and when you sit on the edge you have left art behind and are alone with sand and water – the same idea as inspired Ole Nørgaard. The other path leads up to an iron foundation of convex forms along the South Wing. Trakas' intervention has a certain ambivalence towards nature. He accommodates his composition to the landscape, but projects lines and forms with the aid of cement and cast iron. The work does not yield to the order of nature, but demands intervention and maintenance, just like Jean Dubuffet's large lump of ferrocement, *Manoir d'essor* ("Dynamic Manor") (1969-82) – behind the museum café – which for aesthetic as well as practical reasons must really be regarded as 'site-specific'. The sculpture is based on a model from 1969 which, at the request of Louisiana, was enlarged with this precise placing behind the Japanese water garden in mind. A wall of plants and the architectural framework support the lump. It has a space, and it dominates it. Elsewhere, the banks between the museum and the Humlebæk lake rather form a passage or ramp; nevertheless the effect of Max Ernst's three fabulous animals, *Le Grand Assistant* ("The Great Assistant"), *La Grenouille* ("Frog") and *La Tortue* ("Tortoise") from 1967-74, is formidable but is primarily due to the convincing 'presence' of the works of art, almost regardless of location, provided their territorial boundaries are respected.

In the book *Den romantiske have* ("The Romantic Garden"), which is about sensibility and landscape gardening in the eighteenth and at the beginning of the nineteenth century, the author Christian Elling writes that one of the requirements of the Romantic garden was that certain parts of the garden – often open lawns and gentle lake shores – had to be bright as day and sun-drenched. Others were to suggest night moods. The intensity of the emotions was to be conveyed by the plants growing there. Conifers make the heart "ache with the pains of life" and the soul "is filled with awesome ideality." Weeping willows and oaks speak their understandable language, and the melancholy mood was enhanced by the planting of memorial groves and by making old graves part of the complex.

The gardens of Louisiana have all the ingredients that were required to move the Romantic mind – more indeed than most of the gardens of the period: an open, bright south side and a gloomy and menacing north side with a woodland lake, deep and black as a crater, whose steep sides are pockmarked with graves, as well as a Böcklin-like bastion, a true Toteninsel. What an artist could make of that!

Yet "Nicht diese Töne! Sondern freudenvollere..." The whole Lake Garden is dedicated to the children. This happened in 1978 when Louisiana invited its guests to the exhibition "Children are a People". True, the lake had been visually involved in the new museum in 1958 with the Giacometti Room built into the slope and the large window with the lake as backdrop; but otherwise the area lay unused. The children dispelled the Romantic elegy and Charon's ferry became a little ferry they could pilot themselves – but that too is an action with roots in Romanticism, when crossing a channel was to be an experience, almost an exploit. So the affair would often be made more difficult than necessary, among other

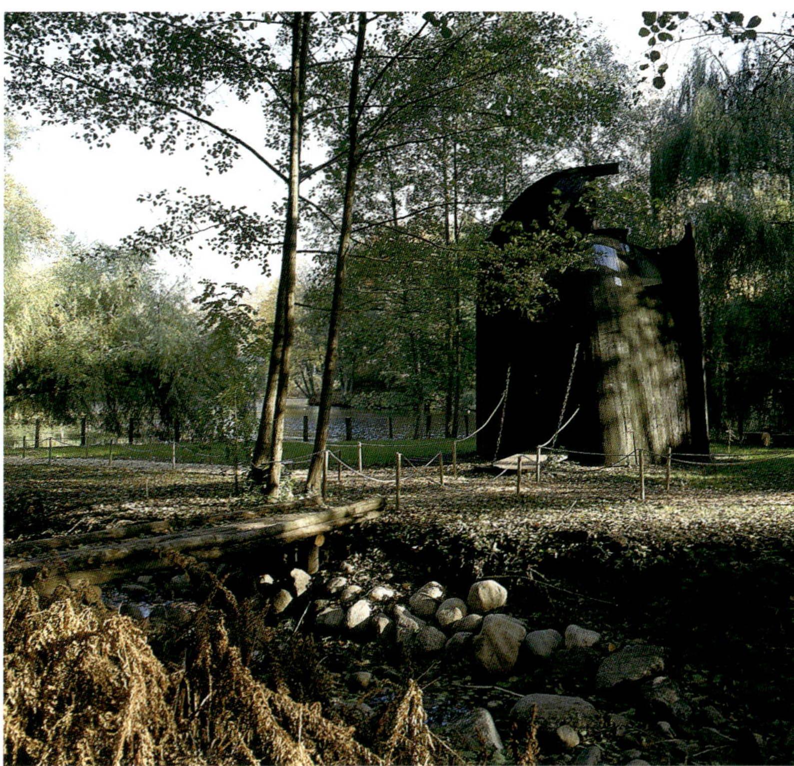

Anders Thygesen's "Opera House" in the Lake Garden

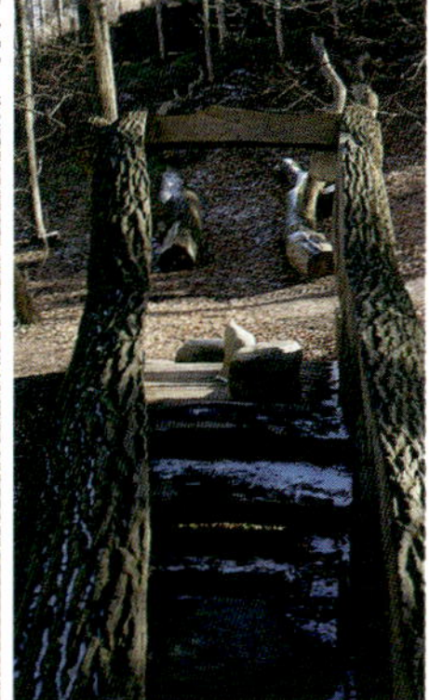

Alfio Bonanno designed the bridge over the stream in the Lake Garden and the nests into which the children can climb

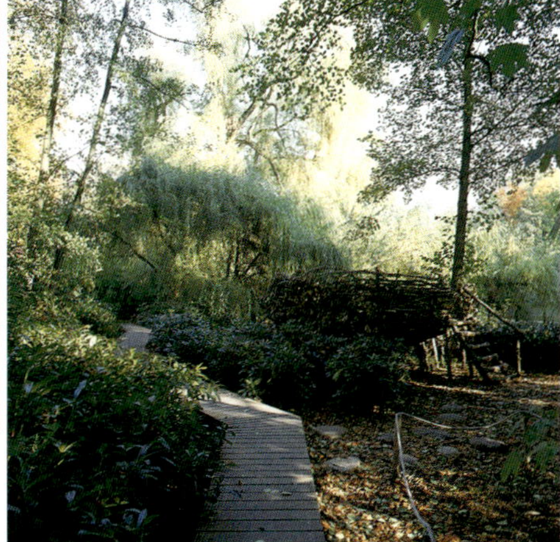

ways by using small ferries. In the Frederiksberg Gardens, for example, a light Chinese boat managed transport over the Andebakke Island with the aid of a rope.

And Louisiana's small rope-drawn ferry, created by the American artist Victor IV (Bulgar Finn), which the children themselves could sail, has now gone; as a substitute there is now a bridge over the Humlebæk stream. It is dramatic in form, but not in practice. It consists of a large oak split lengthwise, whose two halves are wedged apart by the bridge planks. The artist is Alfio Bonanno. He does not try to create form around him, but to establish an interplay where the sculpture contributes lines and a process moving from the stream up over the slope, becoming part of the natural surroundings.

Jean Dubuffet and Enzo Cucchi were given the disposal of sites which were optimal for concrete works, just as Anders Thygesen's boat-shaped *Operahus* ("Opera House") (1978), after being moved, has created a 'site' through its placing on a small tongue of land by the lake. Dani Karavan's *Square* (1982) was designed for the south-east terrace facing Tycho Brahe's Uranienborg, while Susanne Ussing's children's house (1978) of glass and seaweed was embedded in the lake slope. But only in the cases of Trakas, Serra and Bonanno is the whole concept based on the landscape, and the dialogue with nature is crucial to the form of the works – indeed to their very existence.

The Louisiana Park meets all the requirements of the Romantic garden with its charming house, historic bastion, exotic trees and bushes, a lake with a past and a sea slope where the beeches are mirrored in the water, as well as contemporary art as the aesthetic element. Here, in unique fashion, the Danish and the international, history, architecture, art and nature meet in a subtle play of contrasts. The young Knud W. Jensen's wildest dreams have become reality.

English translation by James Manley

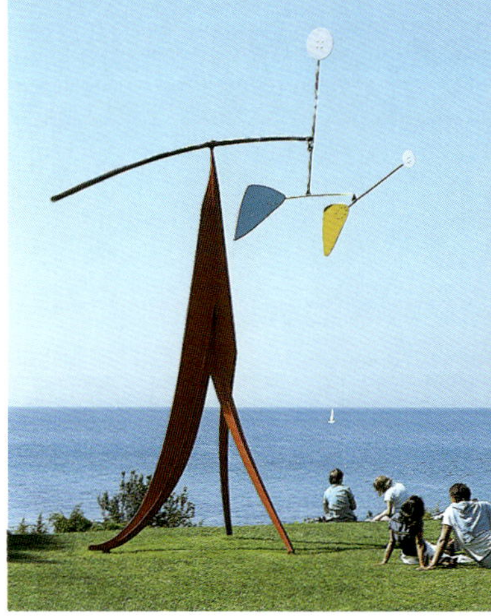

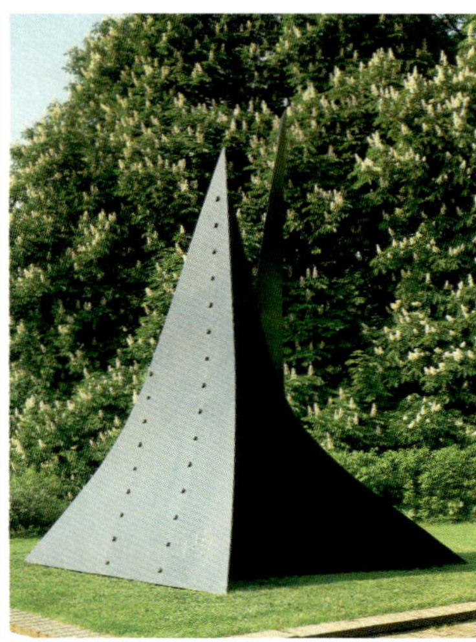

96
Alexander Calder:
Slender Ribs, 1963

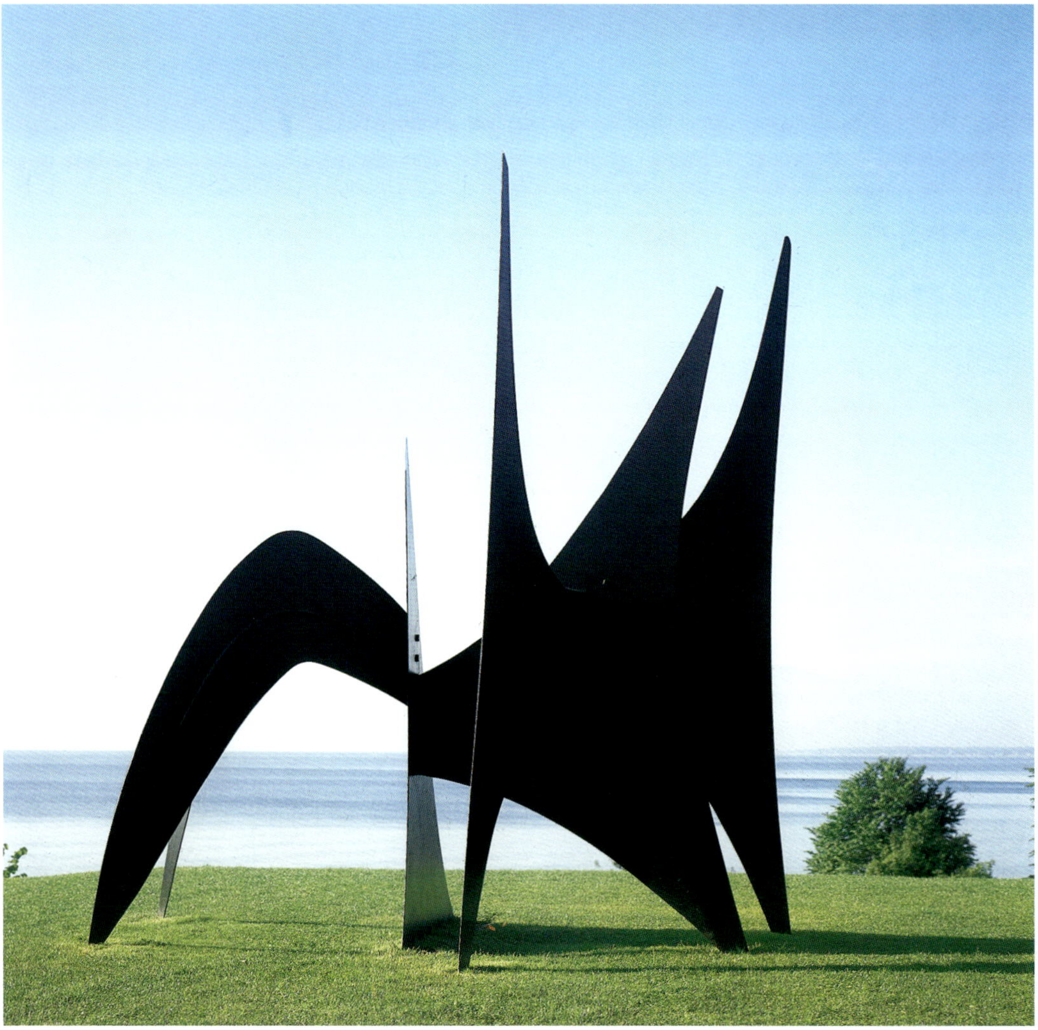

97, 98
Alexander Calder:
Little Janey-Waney, 1964/76 (left)
Almost Snow Plough, 1964/76 (right)

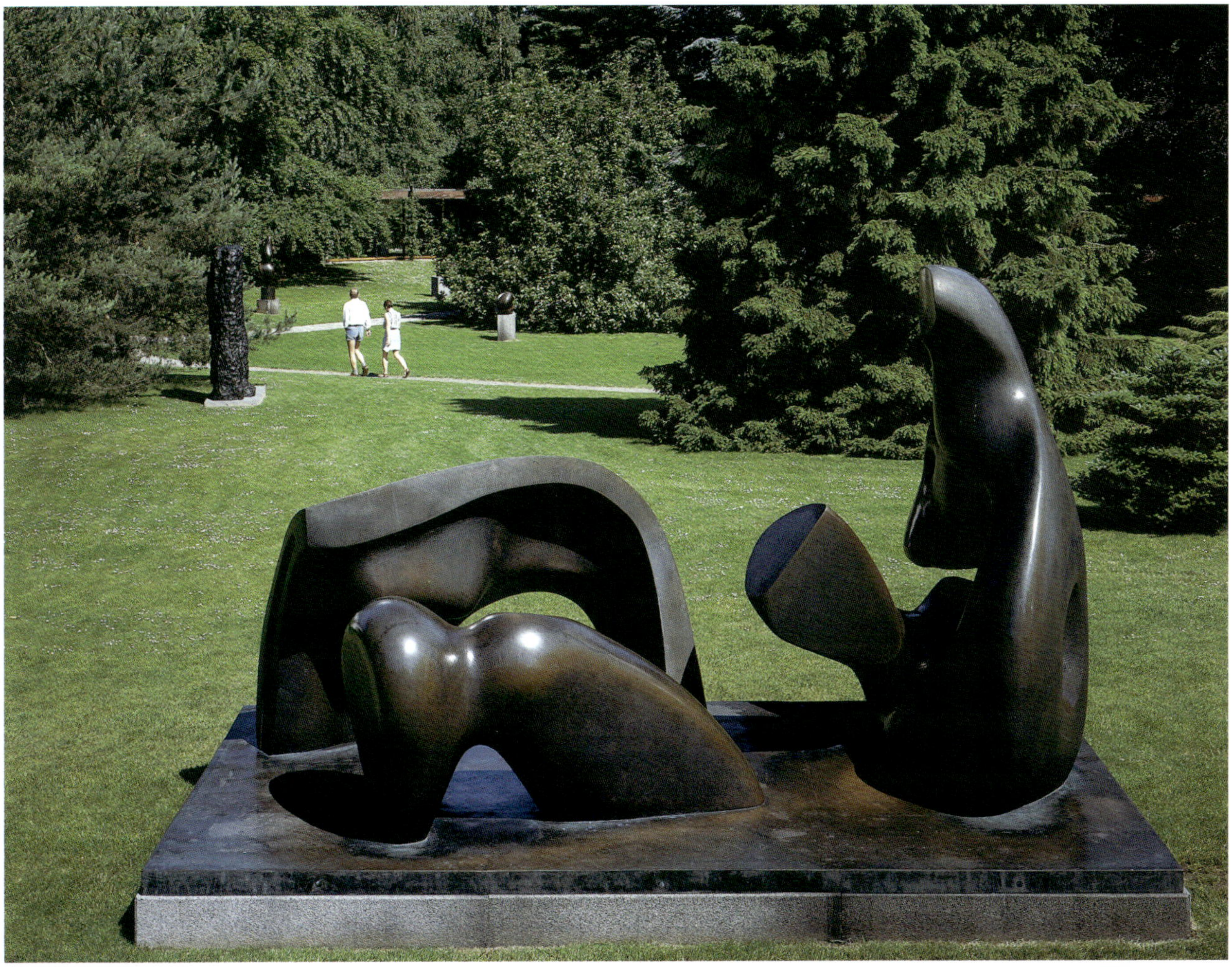

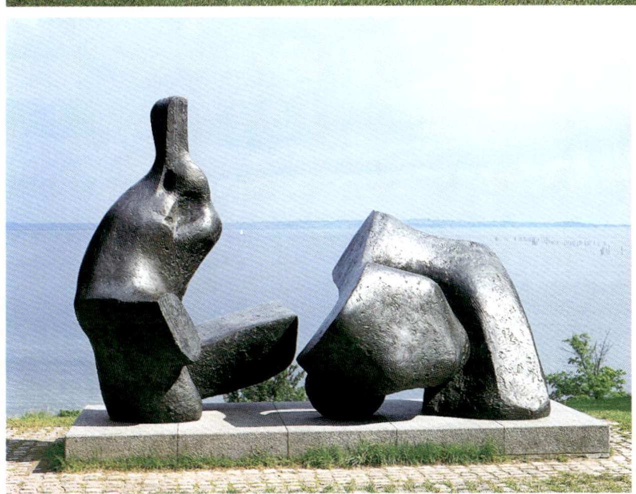

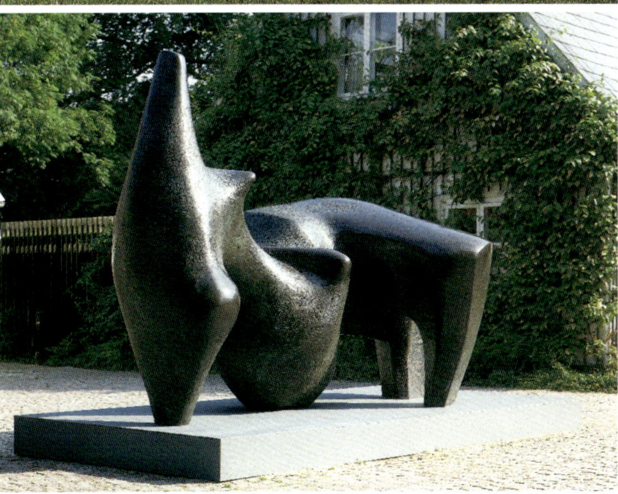

595, 593, 594
Henry Moore:
Three Piece Reclining Figure: Draped, 1974-75 (top)
Reclining Figure No. 5 (Seagram), 1963-64 (bottom left)
Reclining Figure, 1969-70 (bottom right)

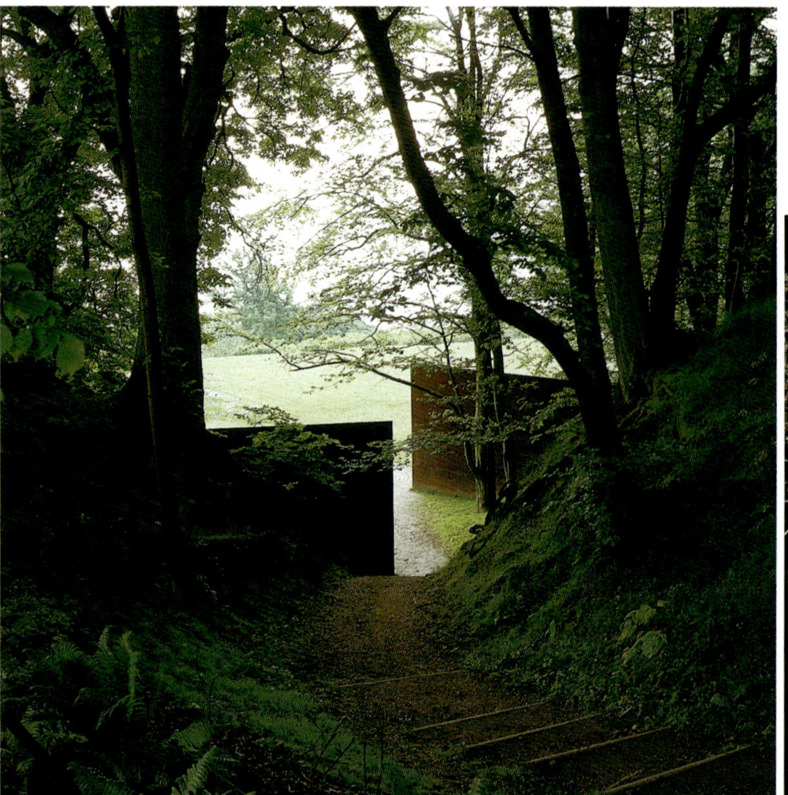

821
Richard Serra:
The Gate in the Gorge, 1986

The gorge seen from below

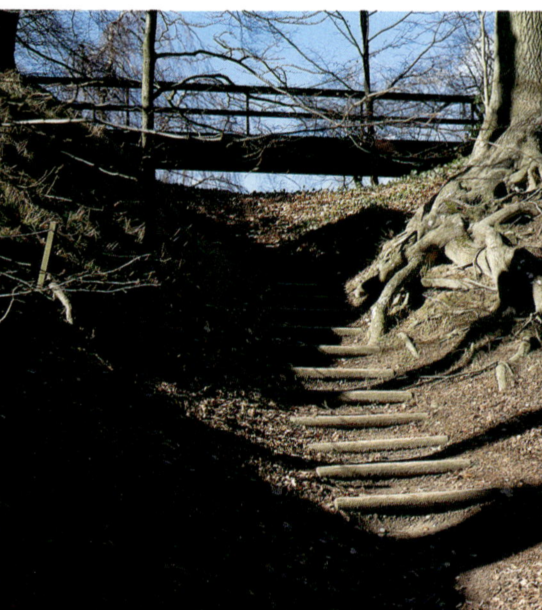

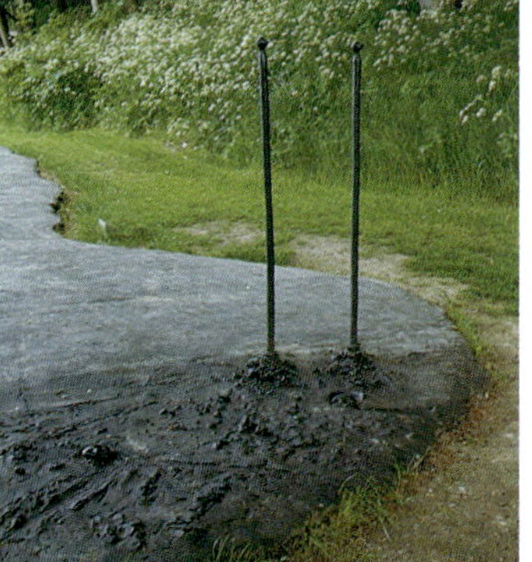

Detail of the "Africa Sculpture"

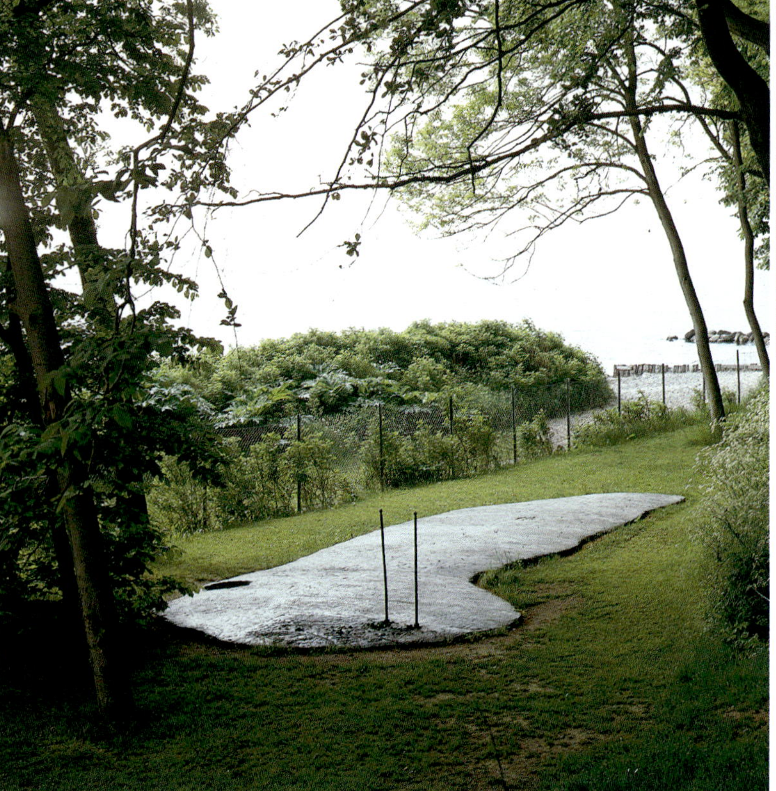

119
Enzo Cucchi:
Africa Sculpture, 1985

155
Jean Dubuffet:
Dynamic Manor, 1969/82

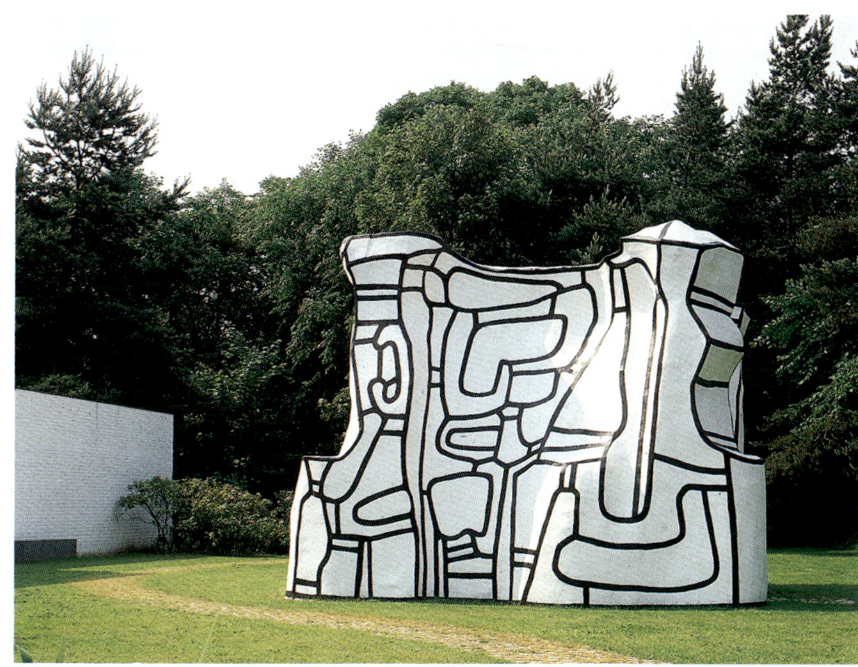

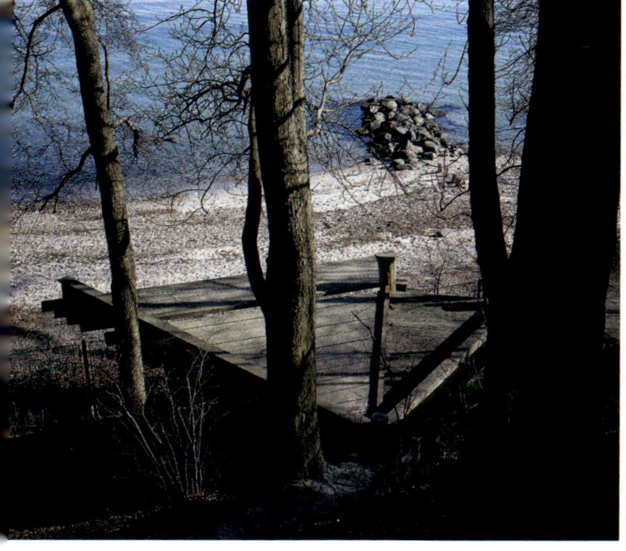

892
George Trakas: Self Passage, 1986-88

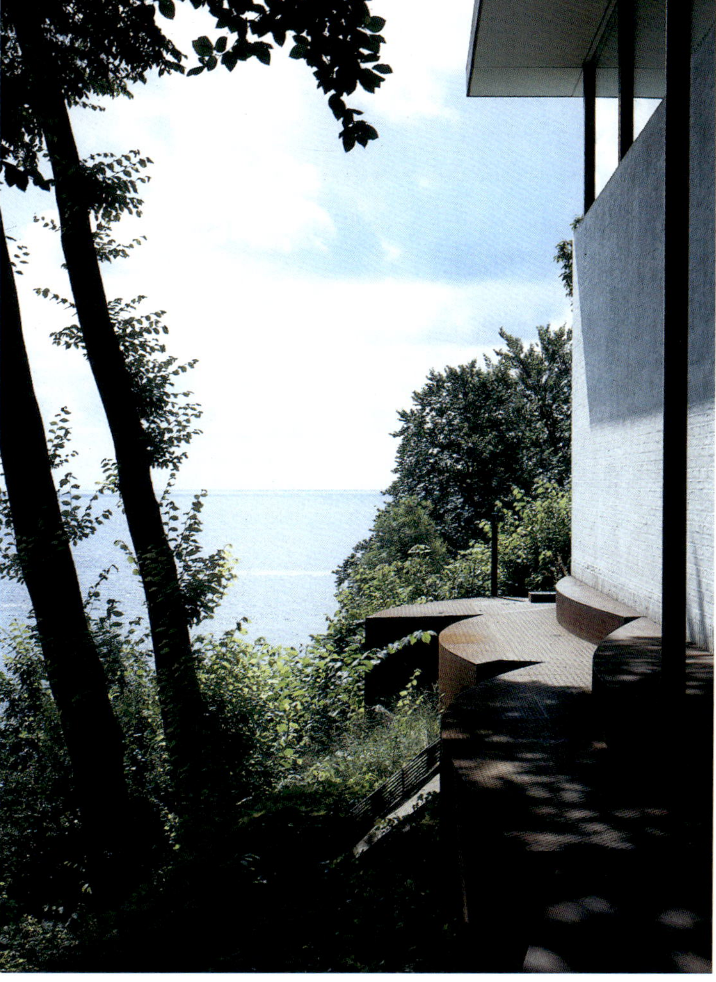

892
George Trakas:
Self Passage, 1986-88

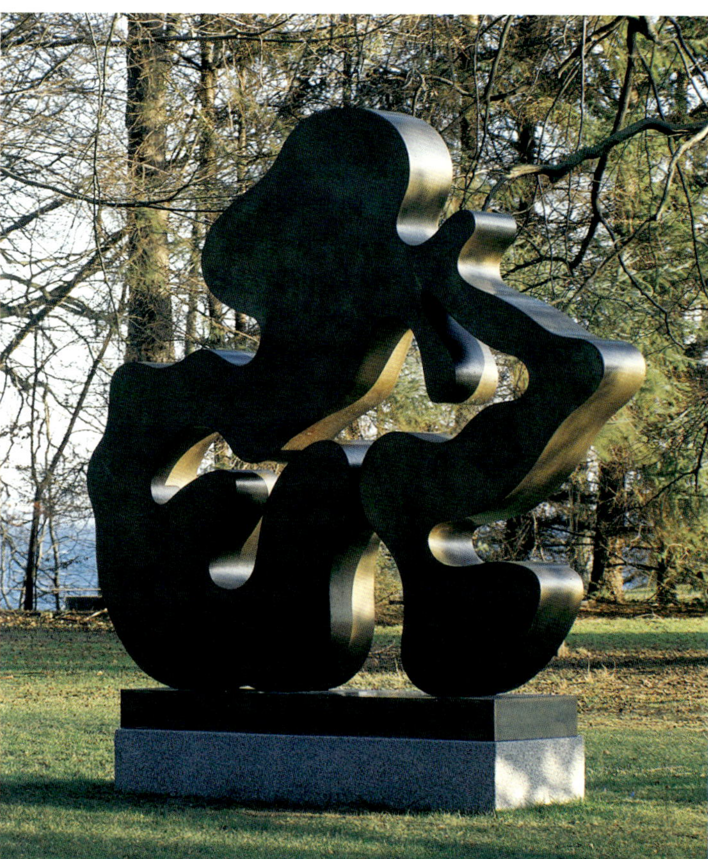

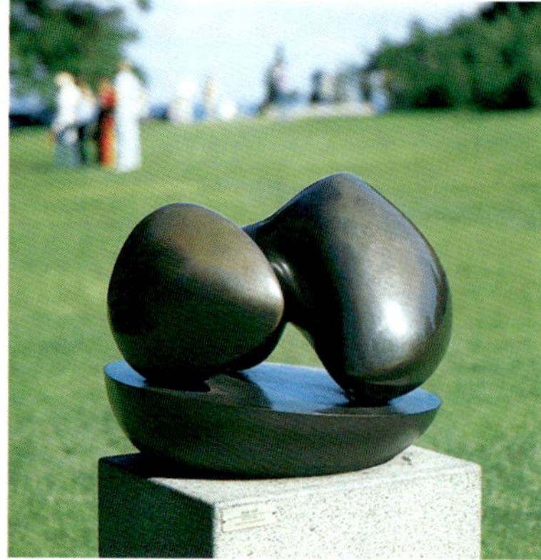

46
Jean Arp:
Human Concretion on an Oval Bowl, 1948

49, 45
Jean Arp:
Threshold Sculpture: Reflection, 1960/82

Stacked Bowls, 1947

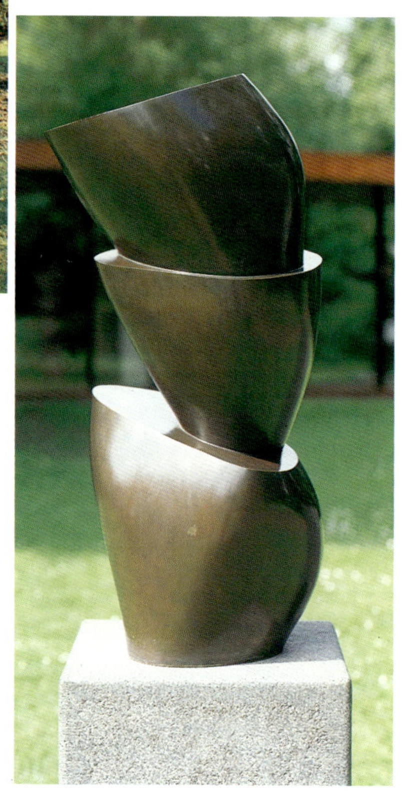

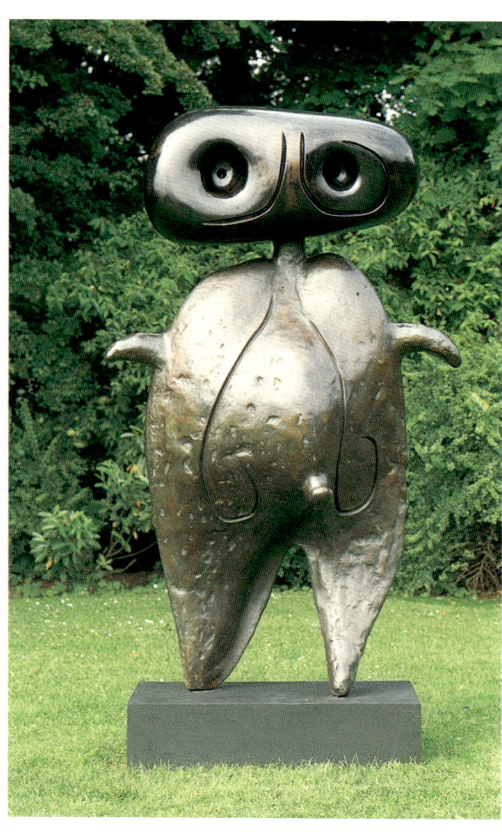

589
Joan Miró:
Figure, 1970

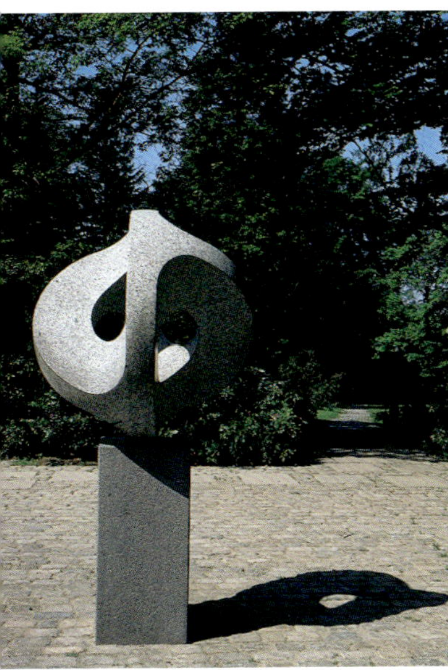

67
Max Bill:
Construction, 1937

823
Joel Shapiro: Untitled, 1985-86

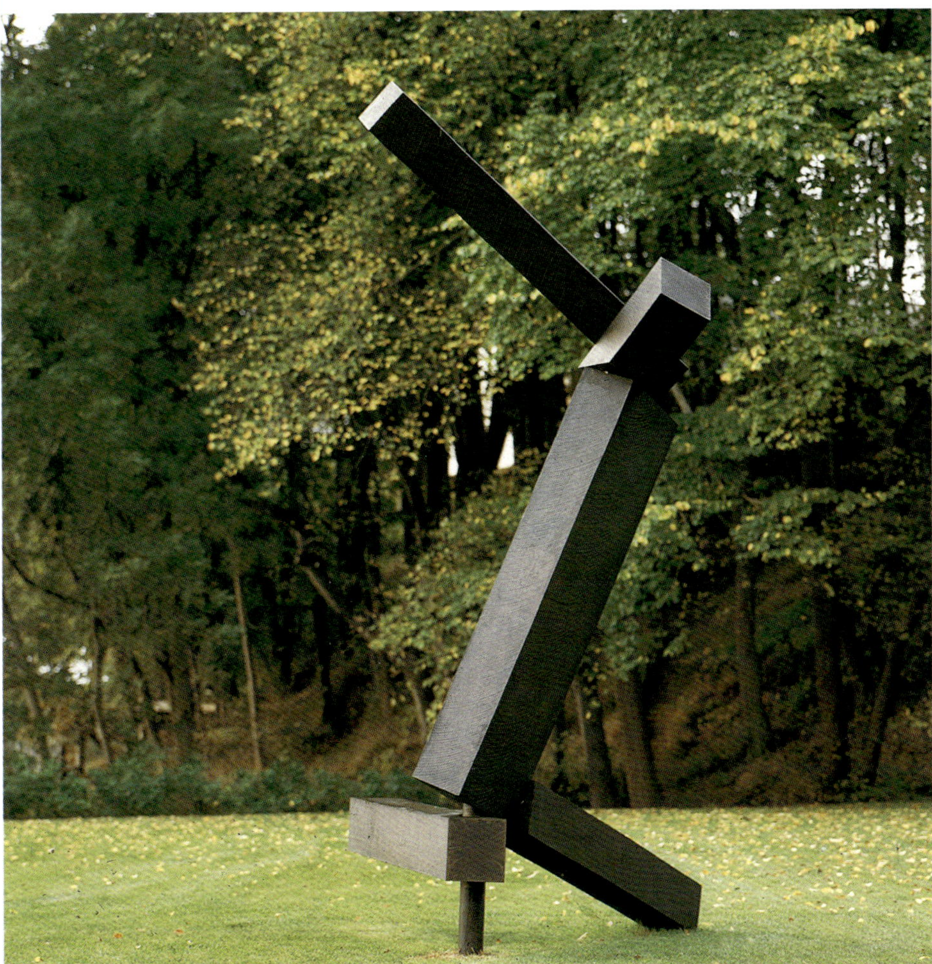

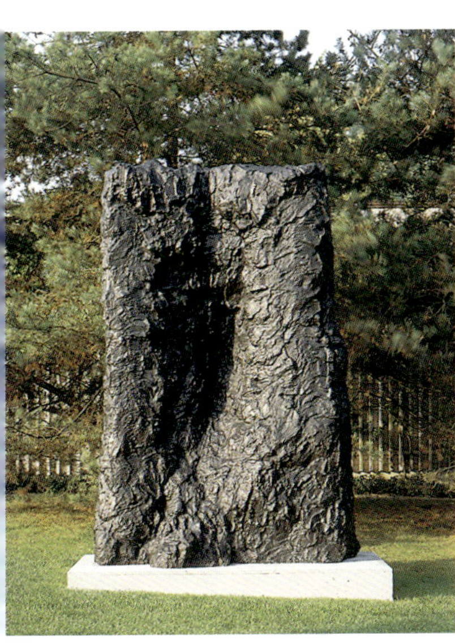

460
Per Kirkeby:
Gate II, 1987

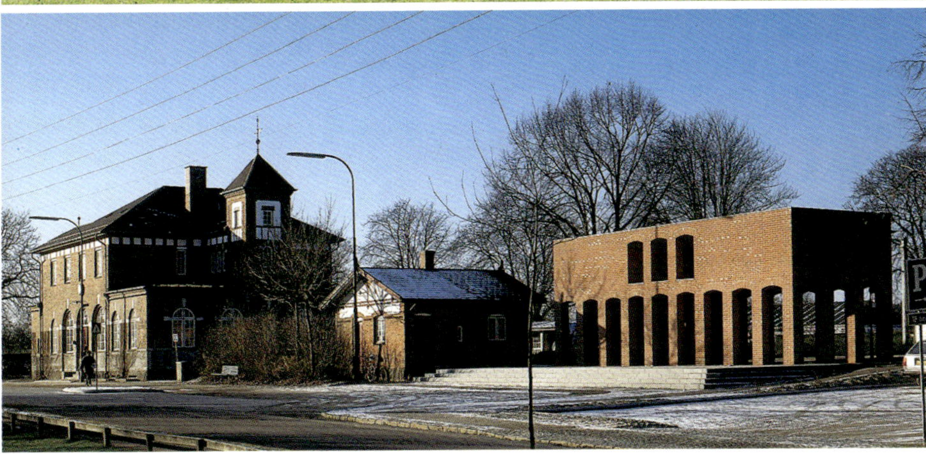

461
Per Kirkeby: Untitled. Brick sculpture at Humlebæk Railway Station, 1994

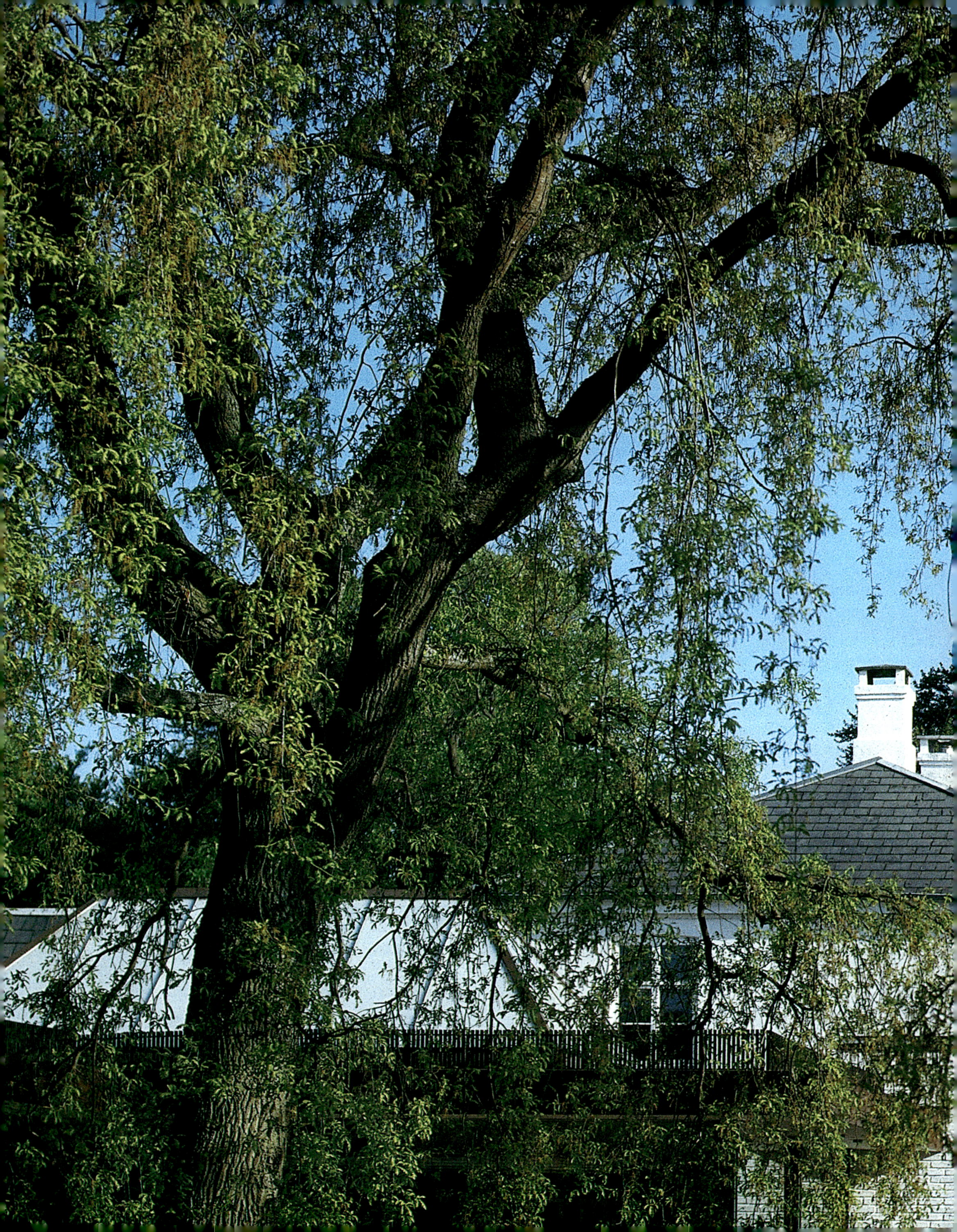

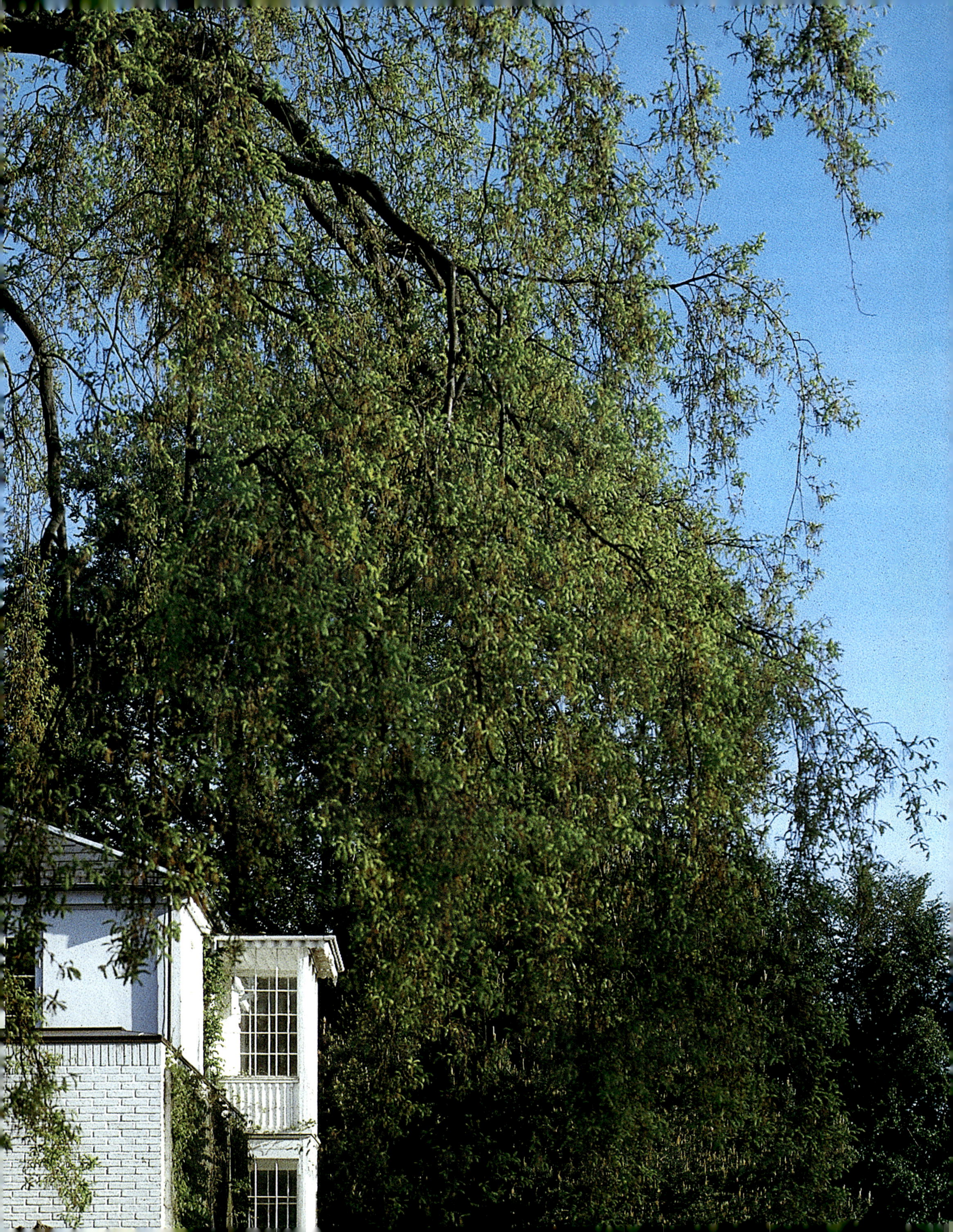

The Classics

Looking Back – Exhibitions and Events – presents a selection of the exhibitions and activities that have taken place at Louisiana since the opening of the museum in 1958.

The exhibitions have been grouped thematically and, as an introduction to each category, there is a list of the exhibitions shown over the last 40 years, complemented by a selection of installation shots from some of them.

At the bottom of each page is a chronologically arranged series of photographs, showing selected events from all 40 years.

The exhibitions fall into the following categories:
The Classics
Other Cultures
Thematic Exhibitions
The Postwar Generation
Contemporary Art
Architecture & Design
Photography

The division of the exhibitions into categories has been made from the point of view that a. o. the category "The Postwar Generation" comprises the group of artists who presented new aspects of art when first exhibiting at Louisiana while today they are recognized artists with a significant place in the history of modern art. Also, the category "Contemporary Art" reflects the position of the artists at the time their works were shown at the museum.

1959	Niels Larsen Stevns
1960	Malevich
1962	August Strindberg
1963	Vincent van Gogh
1963	Max Ernst
1964	Edvard Munch: Graphic Works from the Munch Museum, Oslo
1964	Munch – Picasso – Klee from Rolf Stenersen's Collection
1965	Alberto Giacometti
1967	Bonnard
1967	The Nolde Museum Visits Louisiana
1968	Toulouse-Lautrec
1968	Picasso
1969	Vincent van Gogh: Drawings
1969	Georges Braque & Henri Laurens
1970	Marc Chagall
1970	George Grosz
1970	Naum Gabo
1971	Klee – Kandinsky
1972	Man Ray
1973	Salvador Dali
1975	Miró
1975	Edvard Munch
1976	Giacometti
1981	Picasso from the Picasso Museum, Paris
1982	Gauguin in Tahiti
1983	Marc Chagall
1983	René Magritte
1985	Henri Matisse
1985	Russian Avant-garde 1910-1930 from Museum Ludwig, Cologne and other Museums
1986	Emil Nolde – The Nolde Museum Visits Louisiana
1988	Edvard Munch – Painter and Photographer
1988	The Late Works of Picasso 1953-73
1989	Salvador Dali
1990	La Dation Chagall
1992	Edward Hopper: Selected Works from the Whitney Museum of American Art and other American Collections
1992	Pierre Bonnard
1993	Claude Monet Works from 1880 to 1926
1994	Toulouse-Lautrec and Paris
1996	Picasso and the Mediterranean
1997	Alberto Savinio

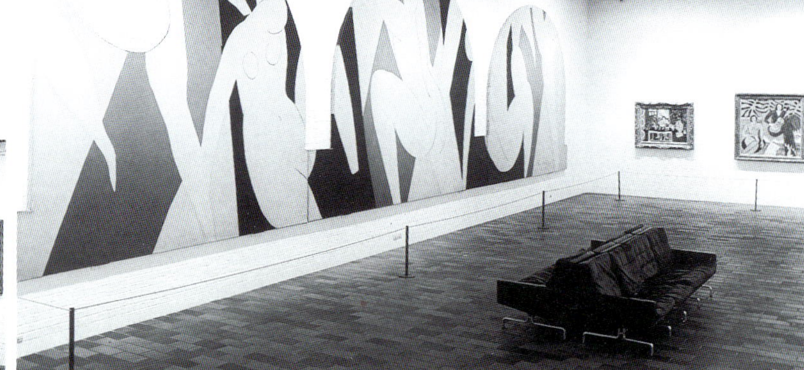

Henri Matisse, 1985

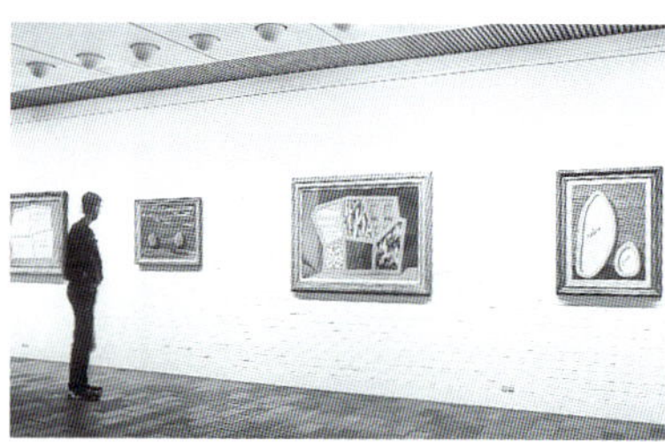

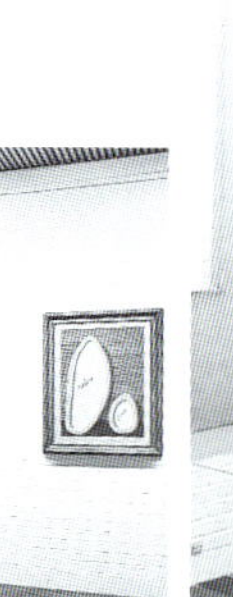

René Magritte, 1983

1958 The Opening of Louisiana

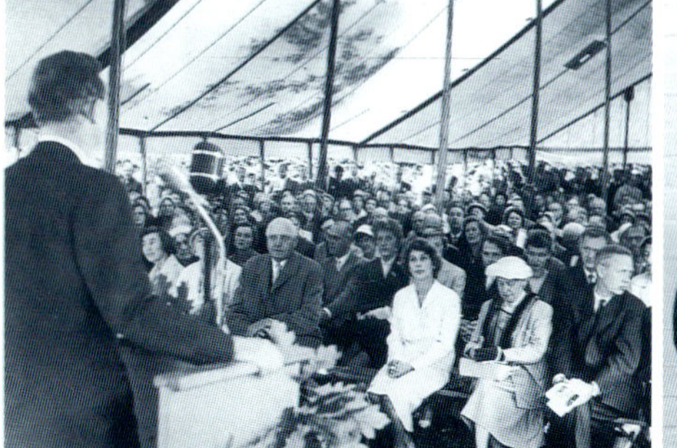

Jørgen Bo

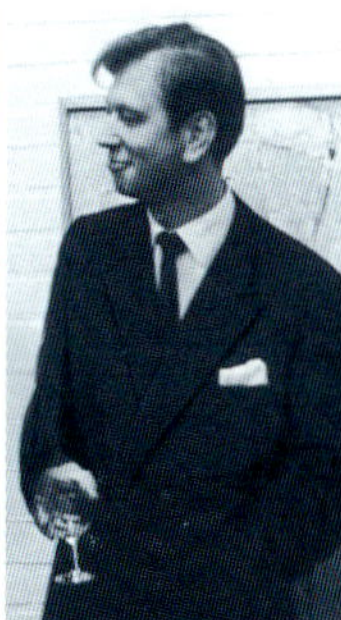

Bidda and Vilhelm Wohlert

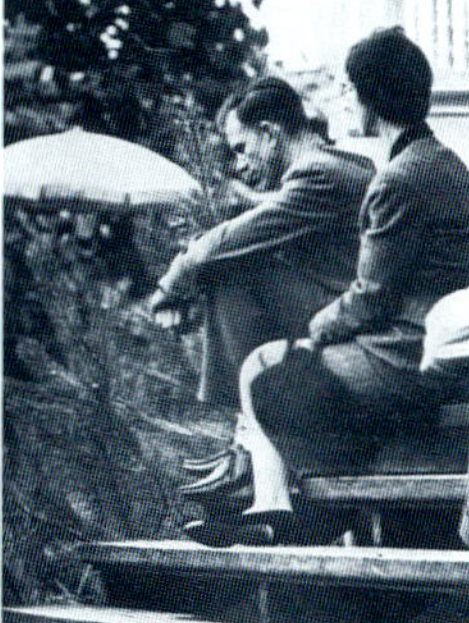

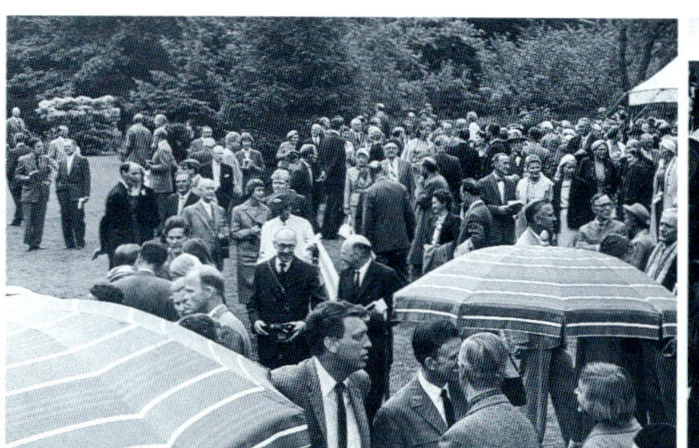

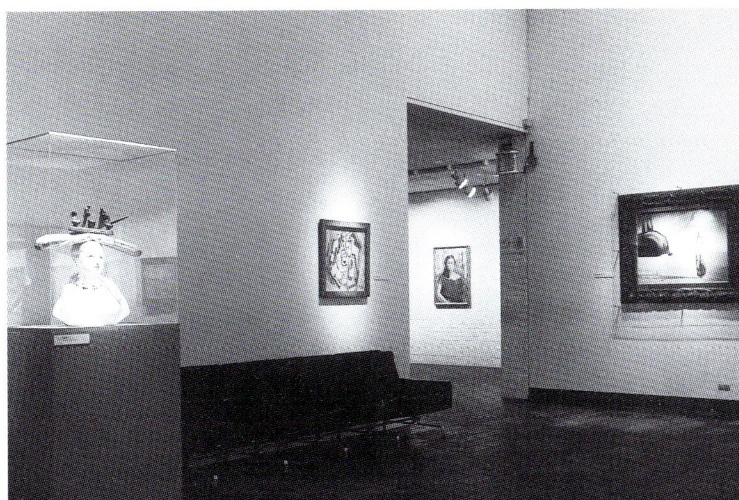
Salvador Dali, 1989

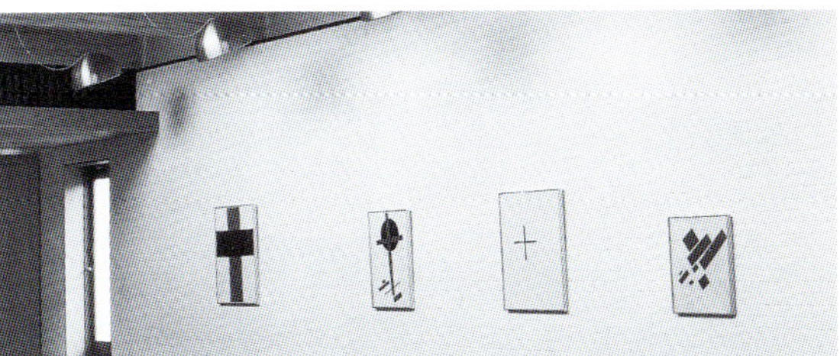
Malevich, 1960

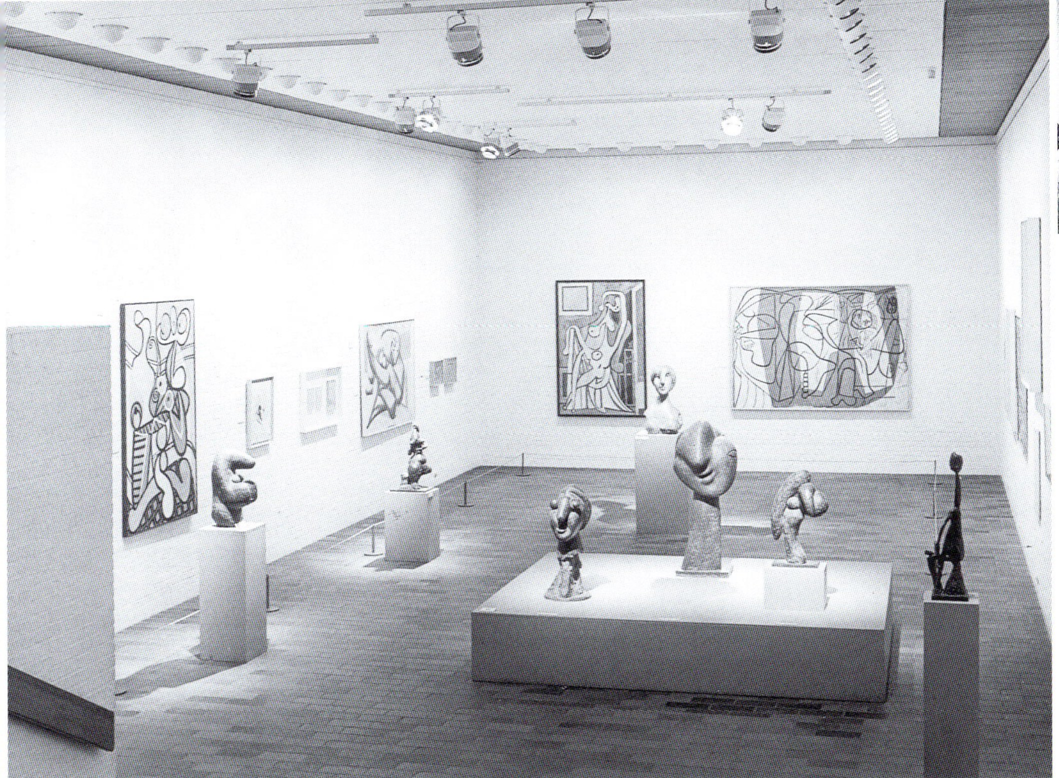
Picasso from the Picasso Museum, Paris, 1981

La Dation Chagall, 1990

The architects of Louisiana Jørgen Bo and Vilhelm Wohlert receive the Wood Award

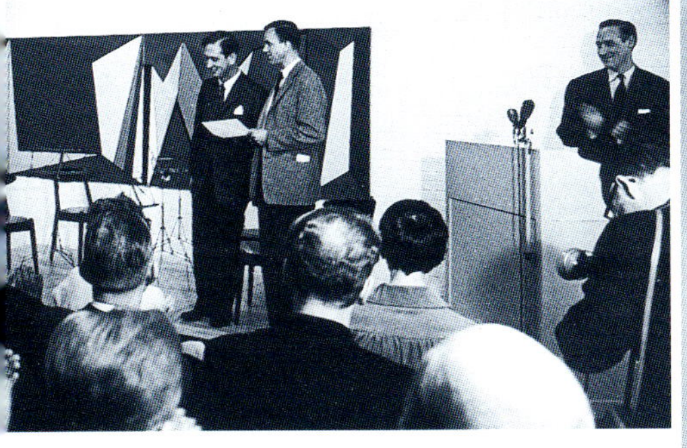

1959 The Danish Music and Ballet Festival

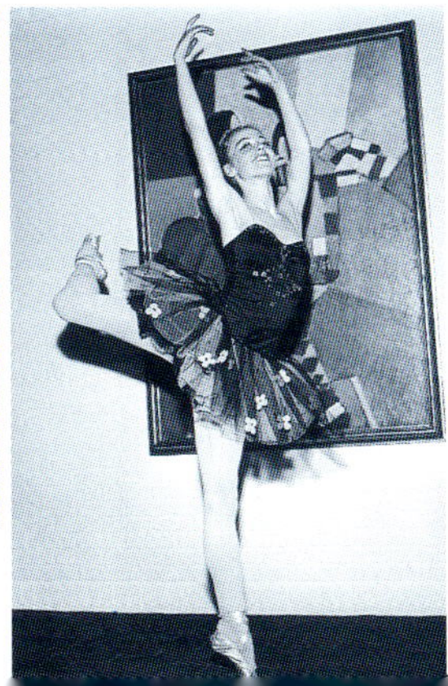

Concert on the balcony of the old villa

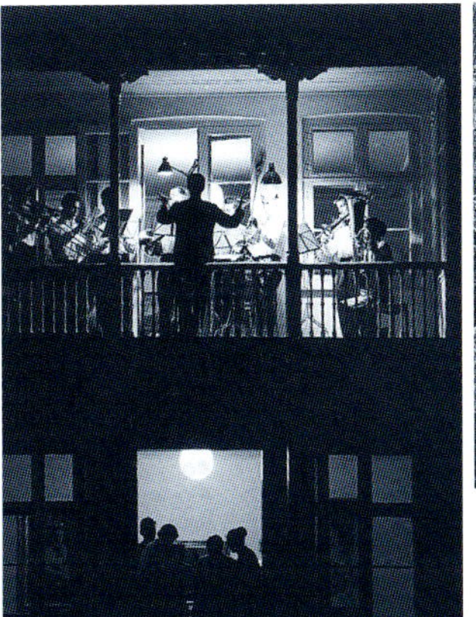

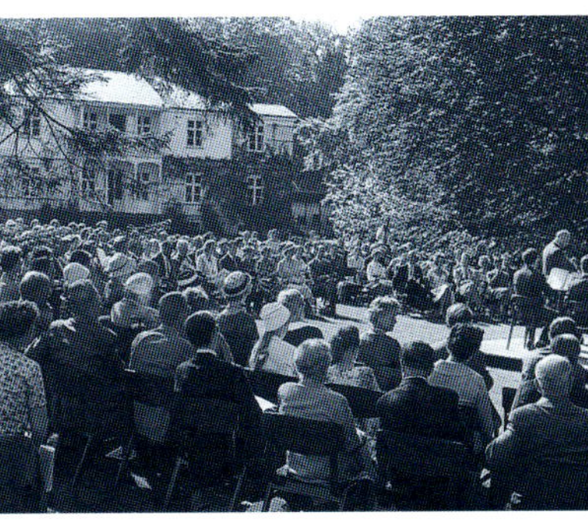

Russian Avant-garde 1910-1930 from Museum Ludwig, Cologne and other Museums, 1985

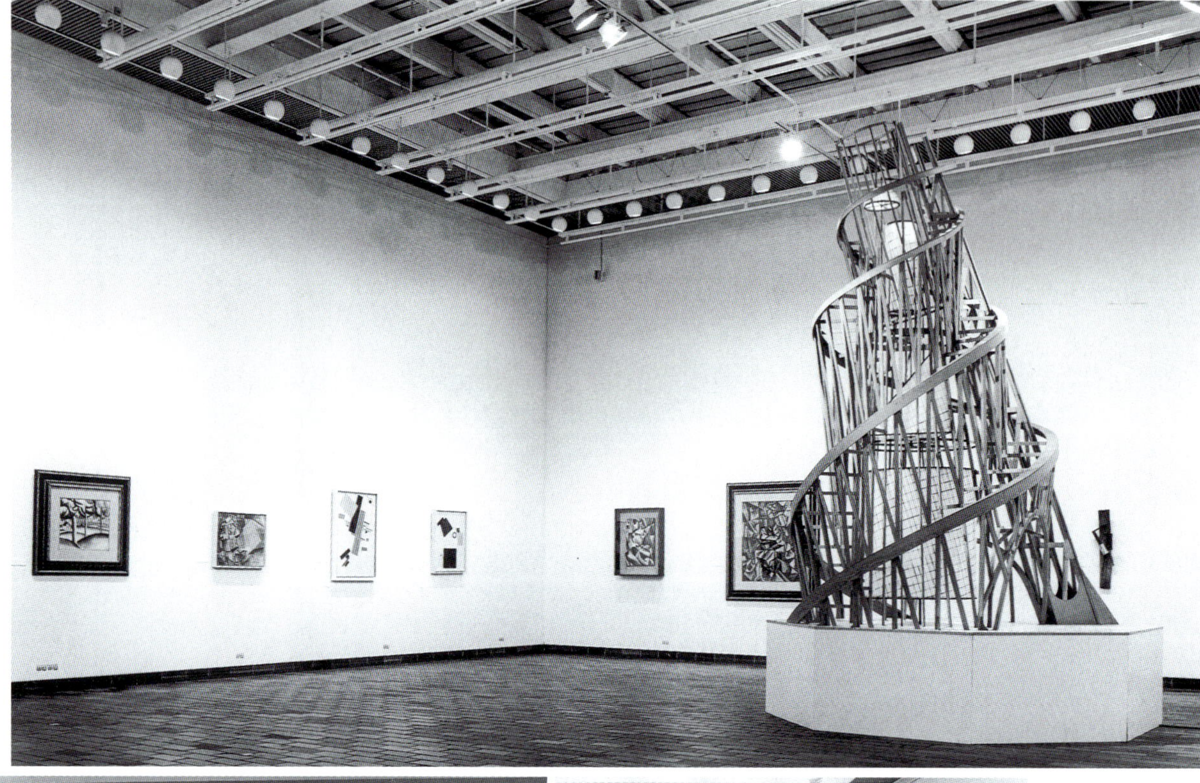

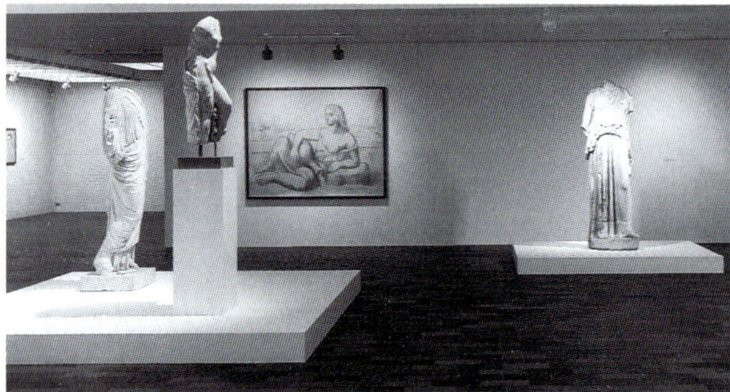

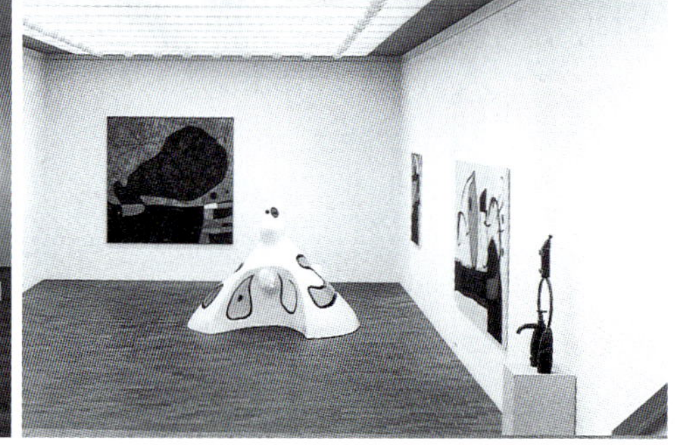

Picasso and the Mediterranean, 1996

Miró, 1975

1960 Pontus Hultén and Knud W. Jensen

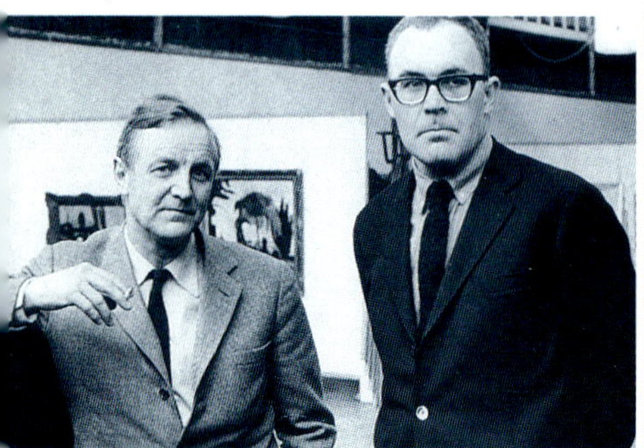

1961 Jean Tinguely. "Sketch for the End of the World"

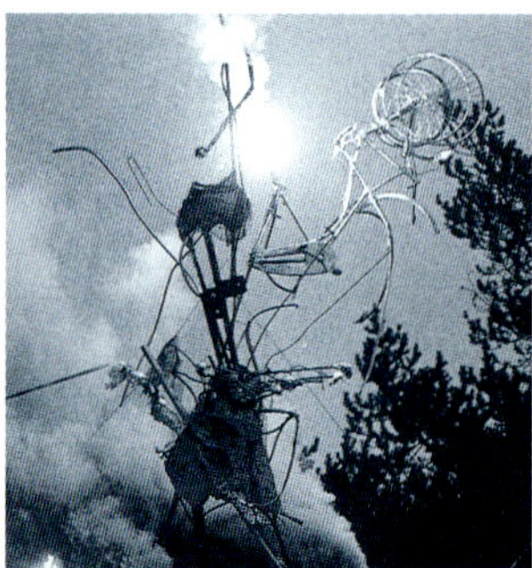

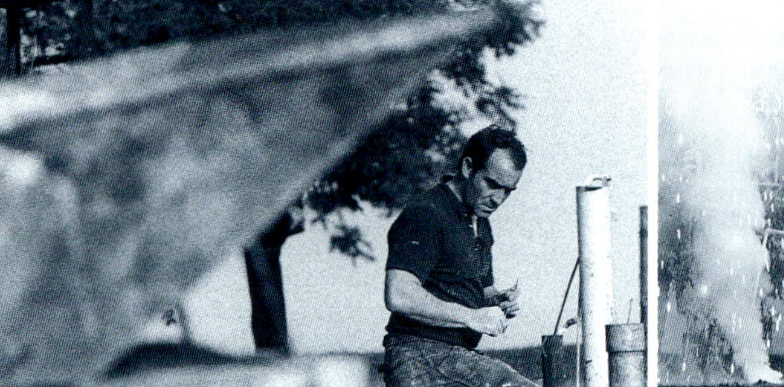

Toulouse-Lautrec and Paris, 1994

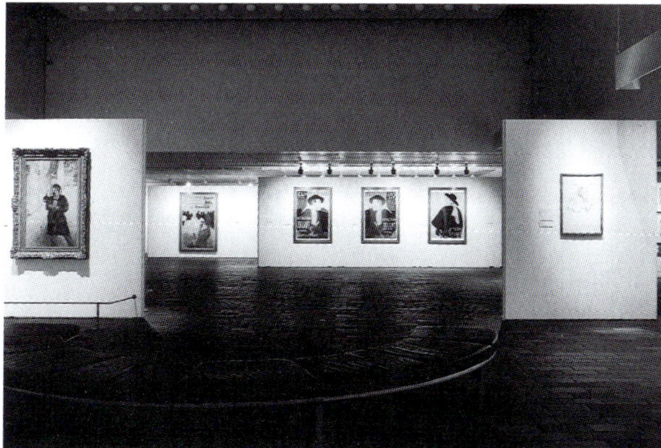

Claude Monet. Works from 1880 to 1926, 1993

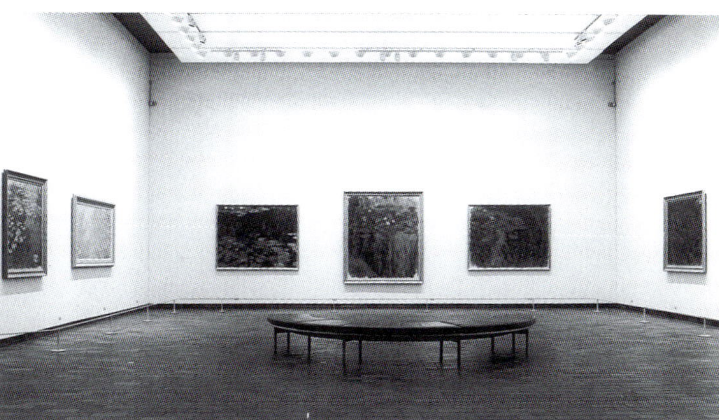

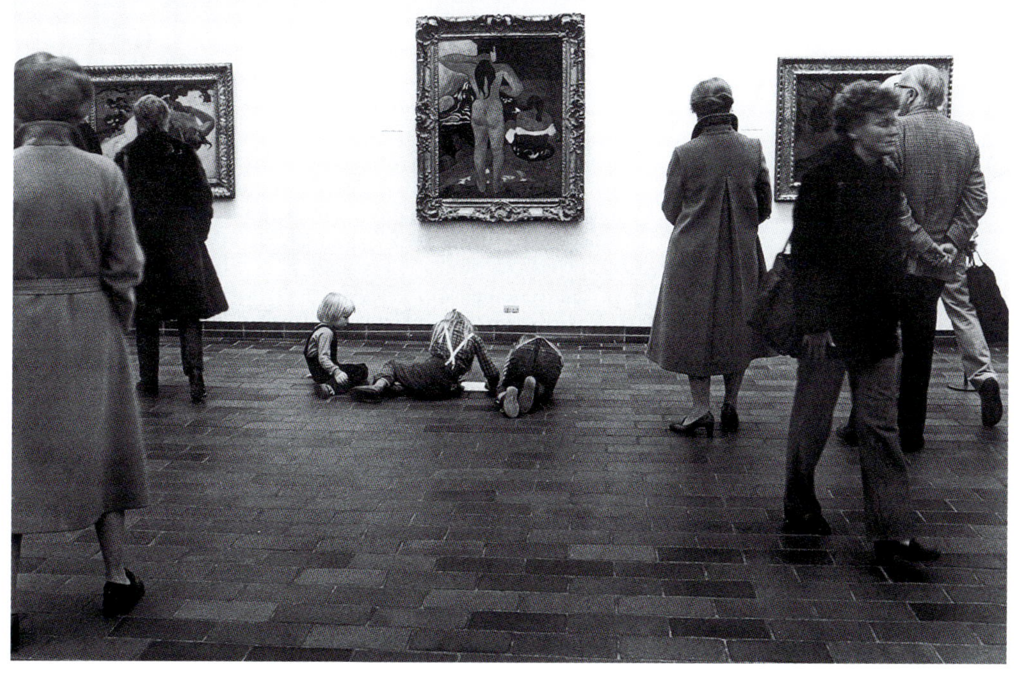

Gauguin in Tahiti, 1982

The exhibition "Movement in Art"

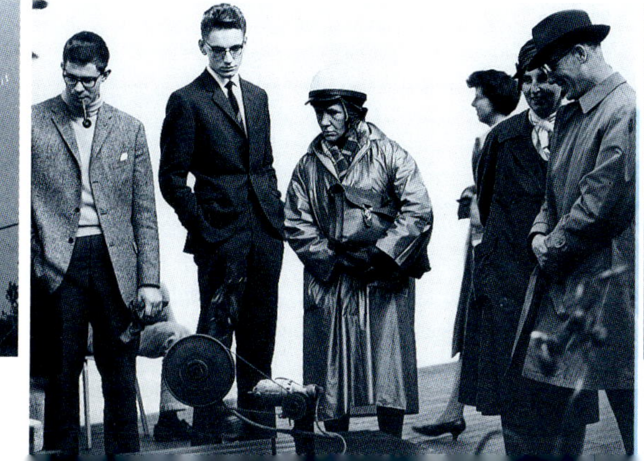

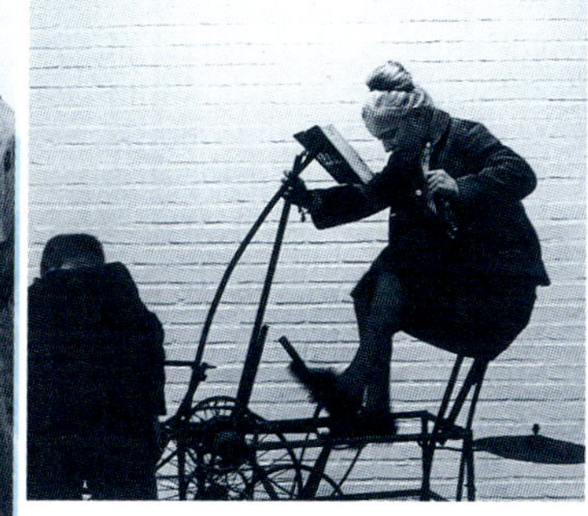

1964 Henry Moore's first visit to Louisiana

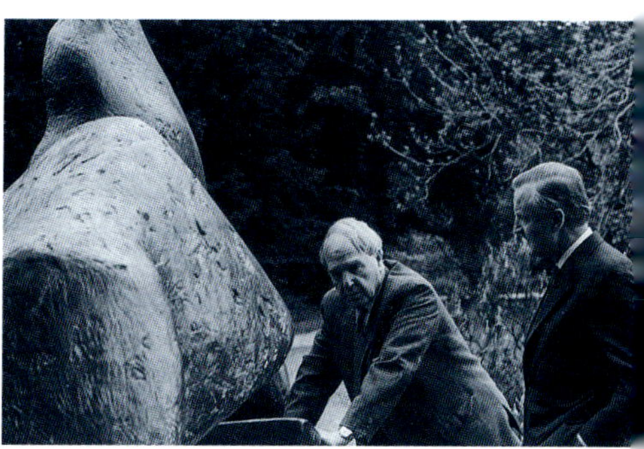

Other Cultures

1962	5000 Years of Egyptian Art
1962	Gold from Peru
1963	Mexican Masterpieces
1963	Sengai
1965	Hidden Treasures – Art from Oceania and Africa
1969	Art from Greenland
1974	Tantra
1974	Japan at Louisiana
1975	The Navajo Blanket
1976	Akhenaton and Nefertiti
1977	Balinese Art
1977	Chinese Peasant Paintings
1977	Pompeji A.D. 79
1978	Babylon – Art from Mesopotamia
1980	Treasures of China
1981	Folk Art from Morocco
1981	The Gold of El Dorado
1984	Treasures of Ireland
1987	Art from the World of Islam 8th-18th Century
1987	The Art of Mexico – Before the Spaniards
1989	African Art
1989	Treasures from Turkey
1991	Oceania – Art from Melanesia
1994	Aratjara – Aboriginal Art
1997	Men and Gods. New Discoveries from Ancient China

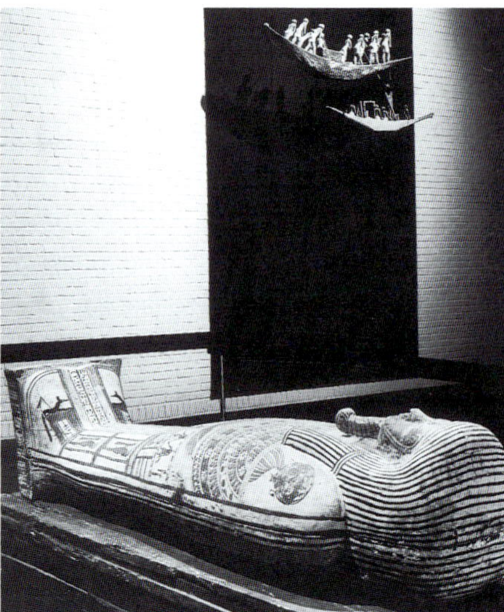
5000 Years of Egyptian Art, 1962

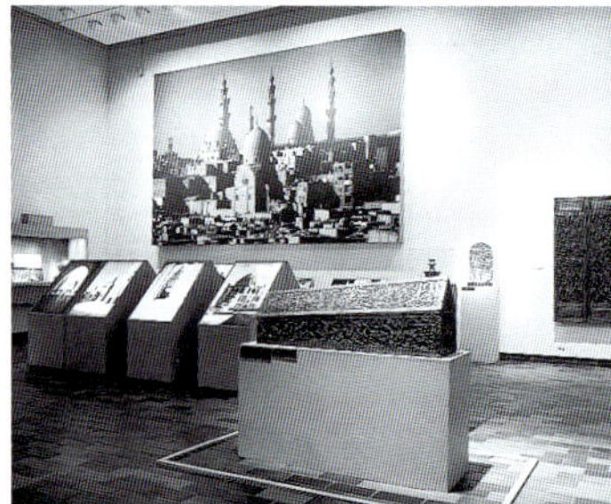
Art from the World of Islam
8th-18th Century, 1987

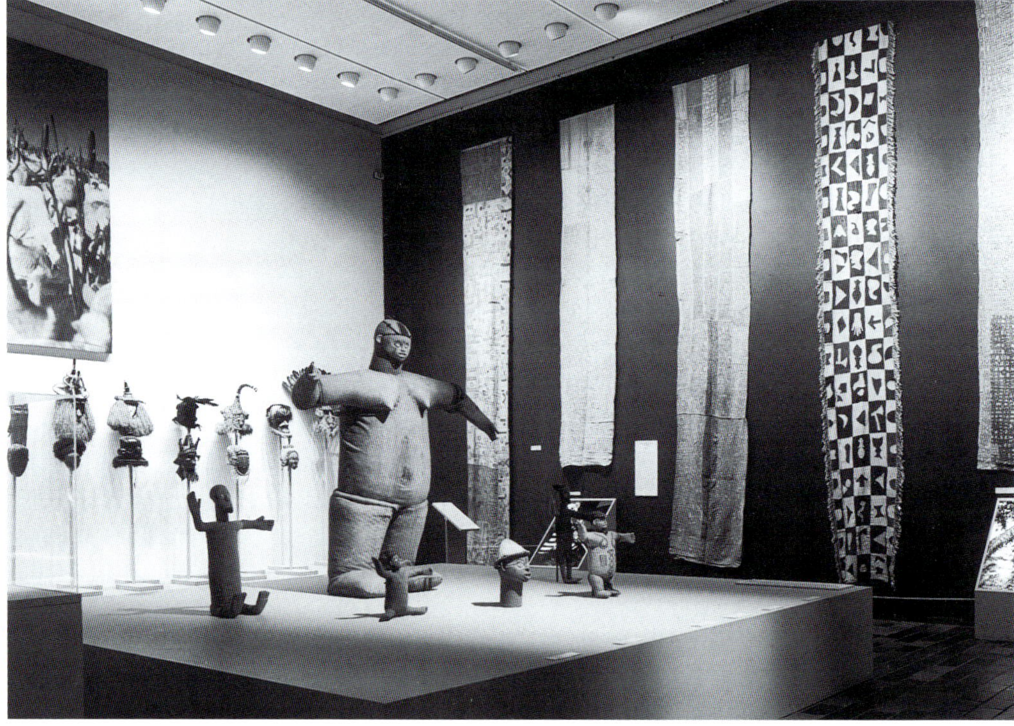
African Art, 1989

1965 Alberto Giacometti

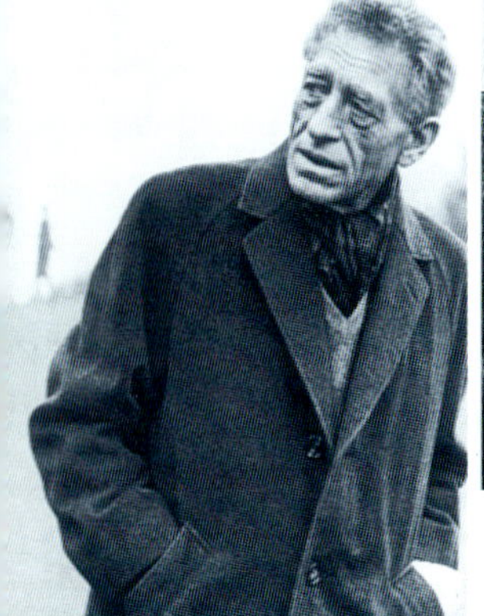

1967 Henry Heerup's birthday

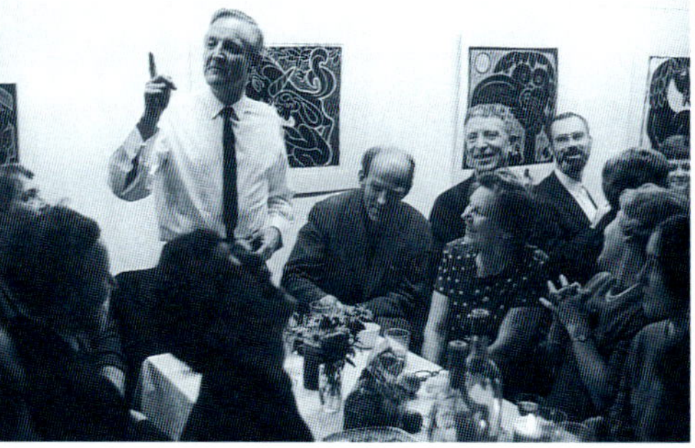

1968 From Louisiana's 10th anniversary

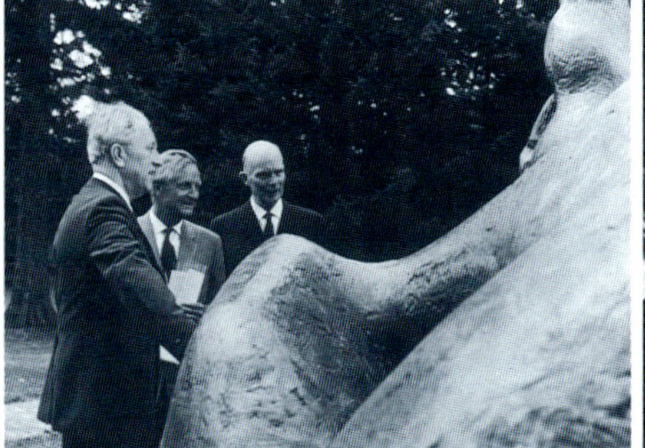

1969 Henry Kahnweiler

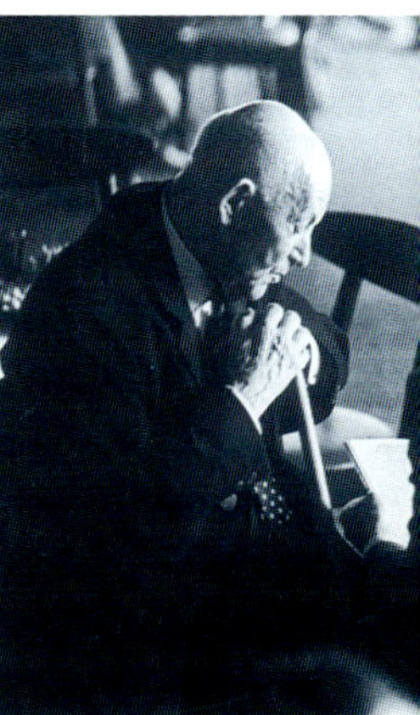

Oceania – Art from Melanesia, 1991

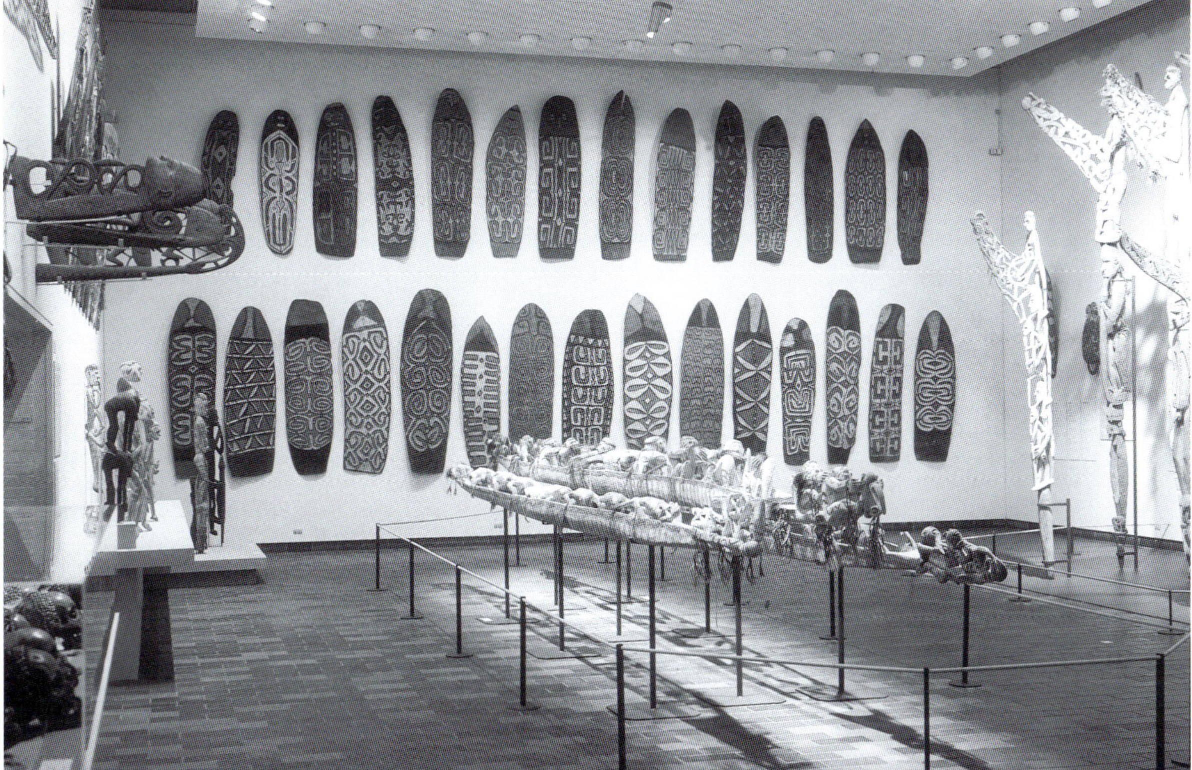

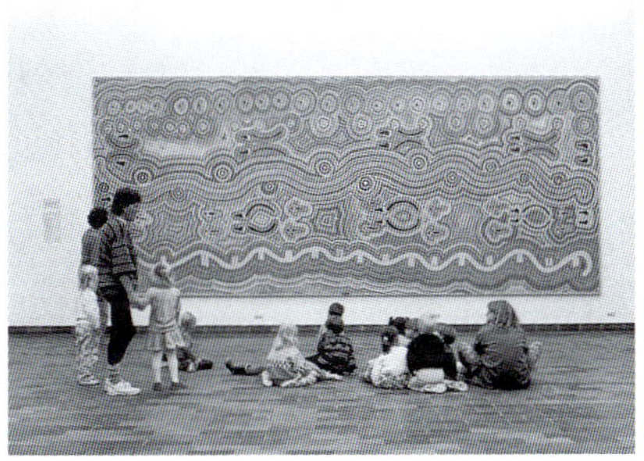

Aratjara – Aboriginal Art, 1994

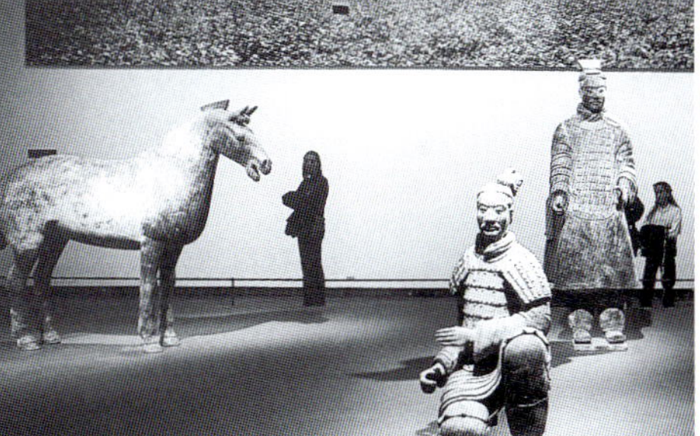

Treasures of China, 1980

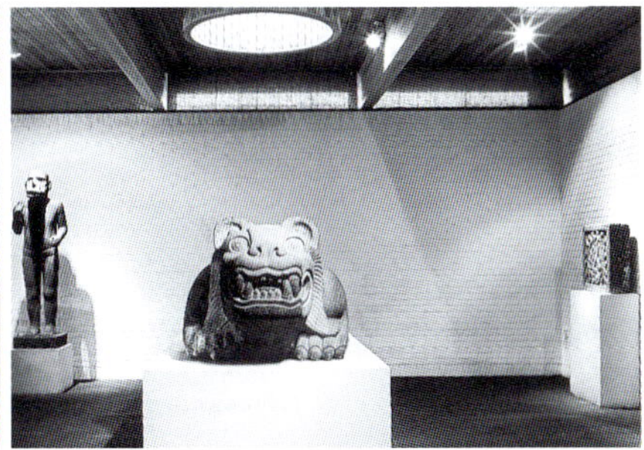

Mexican Masterpieces, 1963

970 Henry Heerup and Knud W. Jensen

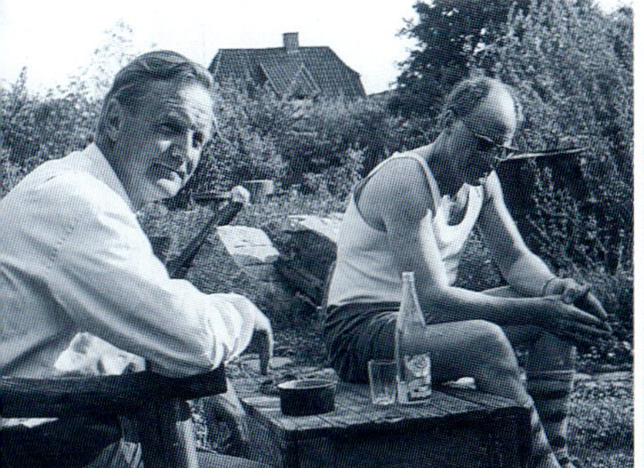

Naum Gabo and Knud W. Jensen

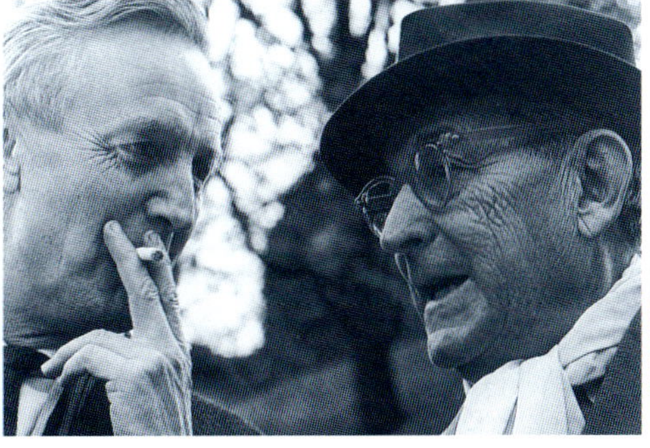

Bjørn Nørgaard: The horse slaughter

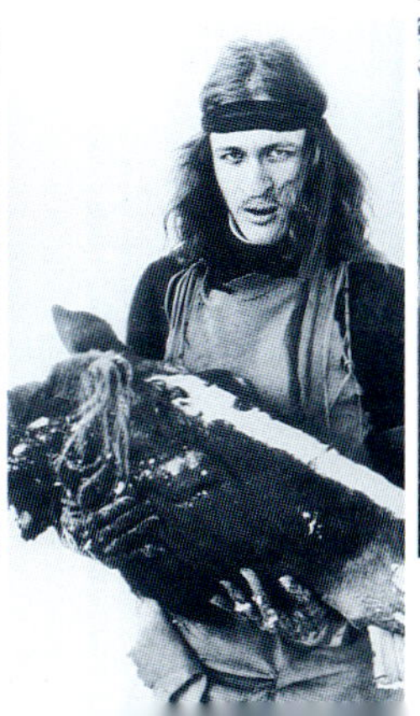

1976 Henry Moore

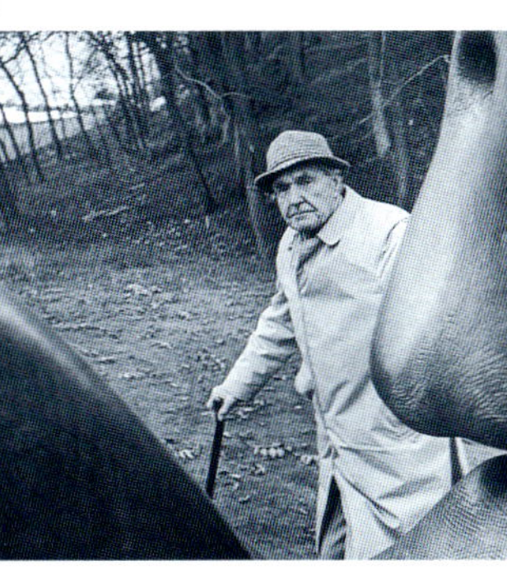

Thematic Exhibitions

1959 Art from Czechoslovakia
1960 Vitality in Art
1960 Moderna Museet Visits Louisiana
1961 The Henie-Onstad Collection
1961 Italian Culture of Today
1961 Movement in Art
1961 Stedelijk Museum Visits Louisiana
1962 Icelandic Art
1963 100 Years of Norwegian Art
1964 Since Bonnard – French Drawings and Watercolours
1964 Collection Bo Boustedt
1964 Art from Abroad in Denmark
1964 Middelheim Visits Louisiana
1965 Art in Concrete
1965 The Graindorge Collection
1965 The Hulton Collection
1966 Göteborgs Konstmuseum Visits Louisiana
1967 The Peggy Guggenheim Collection from Venice
1967 "Six Surrealists" Dali, Delvaux, Max Ernst, Magritte, Miró, Tanguy
1969 Finland at Louisiana
1969 Italian Art 1910-35
1971 Word and Image
1971 American Art 1950-70
1972 Naive Art
1975 Moderna Museet Visits Louisiana
1977 Artists for Amnesty
1978 Constructivism from the McCrory Collection
1978 Children Are a People
1979 Surrealism from MOMA, New York
1979 Outsiders
1980 Stedelijk Visits Louisiana
1982 Aftermath: France 1945-54 – New Images of Man
1984 Expressionism from the Buchheim Collection
1985 Time – The Fourth Dimension
1985 Homo Decorans – Man who Decorates
1986 Colour Since Matisse
1986 Portrait of a Collector: Stephane Janssen
1986 The Global Dialogue – Primitive and Modern Art
1986 Constructivism in the Louisiana Collection after the Gift from the Riklis -McCrory Collection
1987 The London School: Six Figurative Painters
1988 Comics and Art
1989 International Images for the Rights of Man and Citizen – a Poster Exhibition
1991 Vienna 1900 – Art & Design
1992 Spain at Louisiana
Photography and Design 1970-92
1993 At the Edge of Chaos – New Images of the World
1994 From Van Gogh to Gerhard Richter
Major Works from Museum Folkwang, Essen
1995 Japan Today
1997 Sunshine & Noir
Art in L.A. 1960-97
1997 The New Carlsberg Foundation's Gifts to Louisiana

Other thematic exhibitions are listed under "Contemporary Art" p. 56

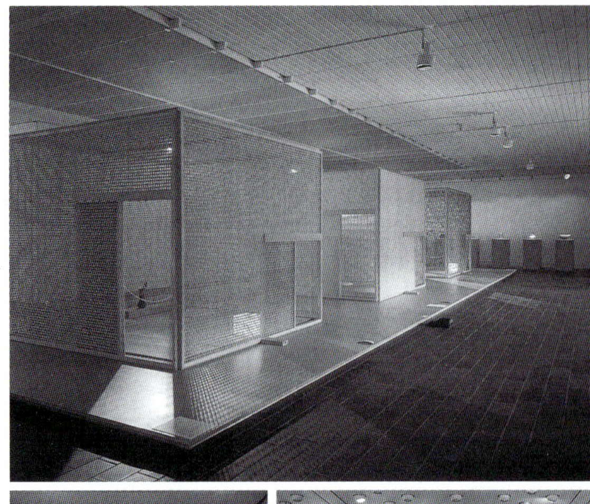

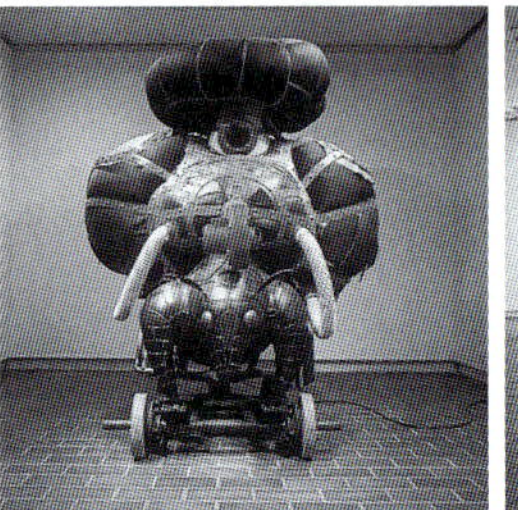

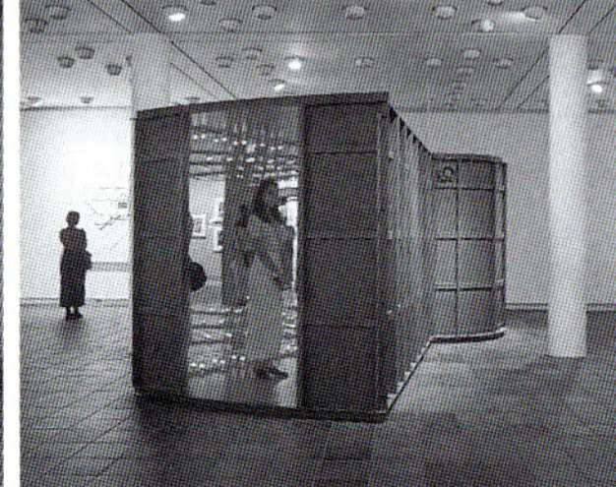

Japan Today, 1995

Vienna 1900 – Art & Design, 1991

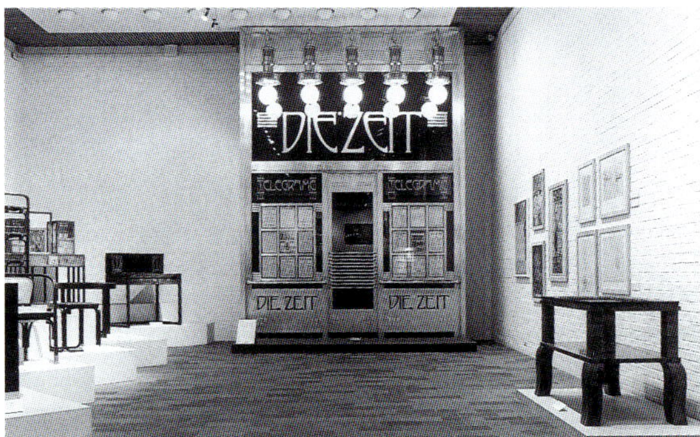

1976 Soho Downtown Manhattan. Performance

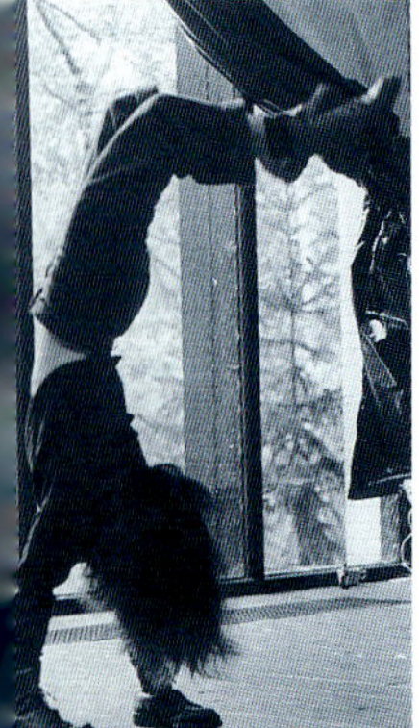

1977 Billedstofteater

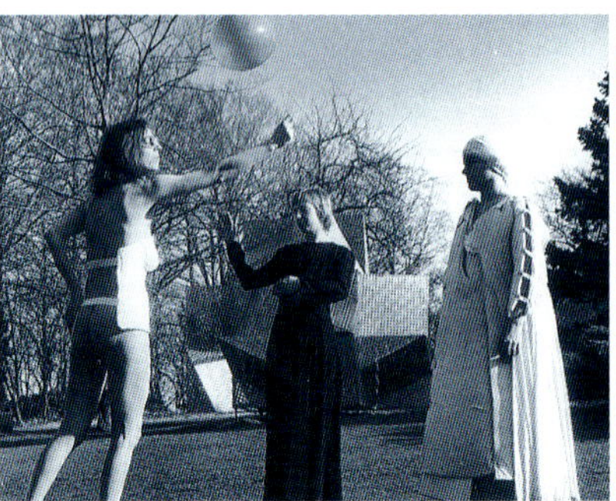

Herman D. Koppel

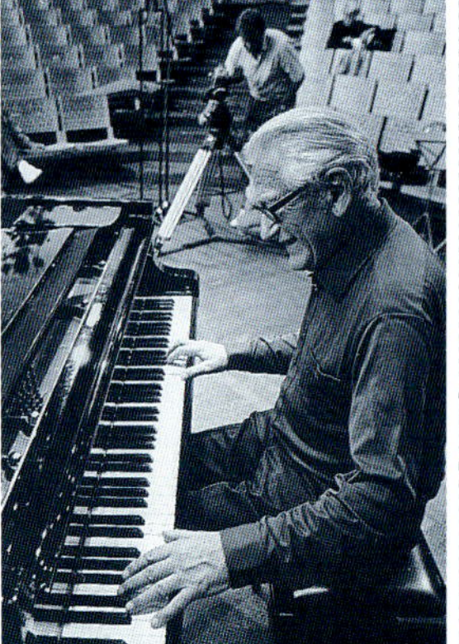

The event "Friend and Foe". Ebbe Kløvedal Reich

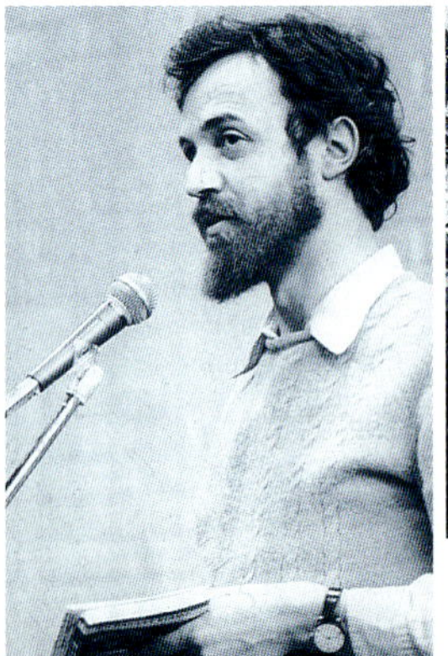

Poul Dissing and Benny Andersen

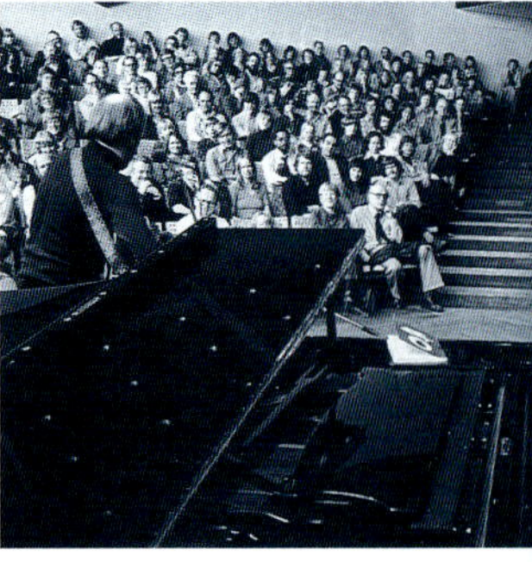

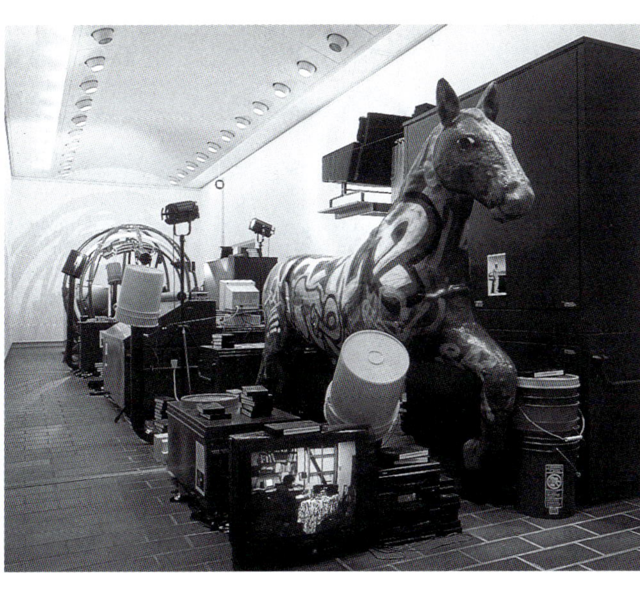

Sunshine & Noir. Art in L.A. 1960-97, 1997

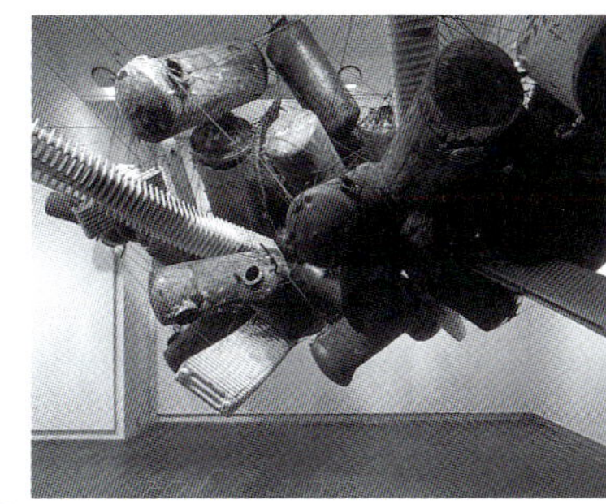

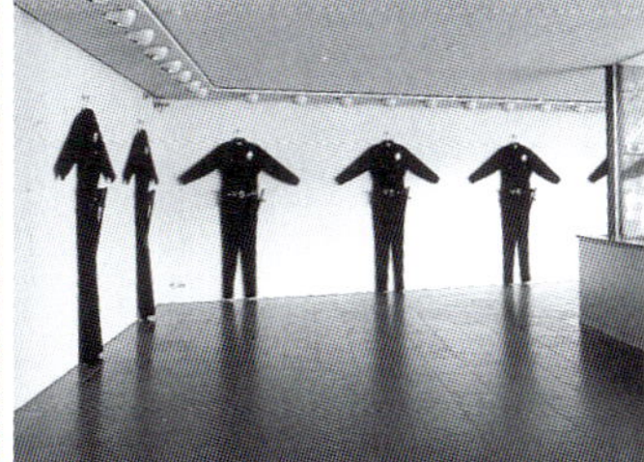

Vienna 1900 – Art & Design, 1991

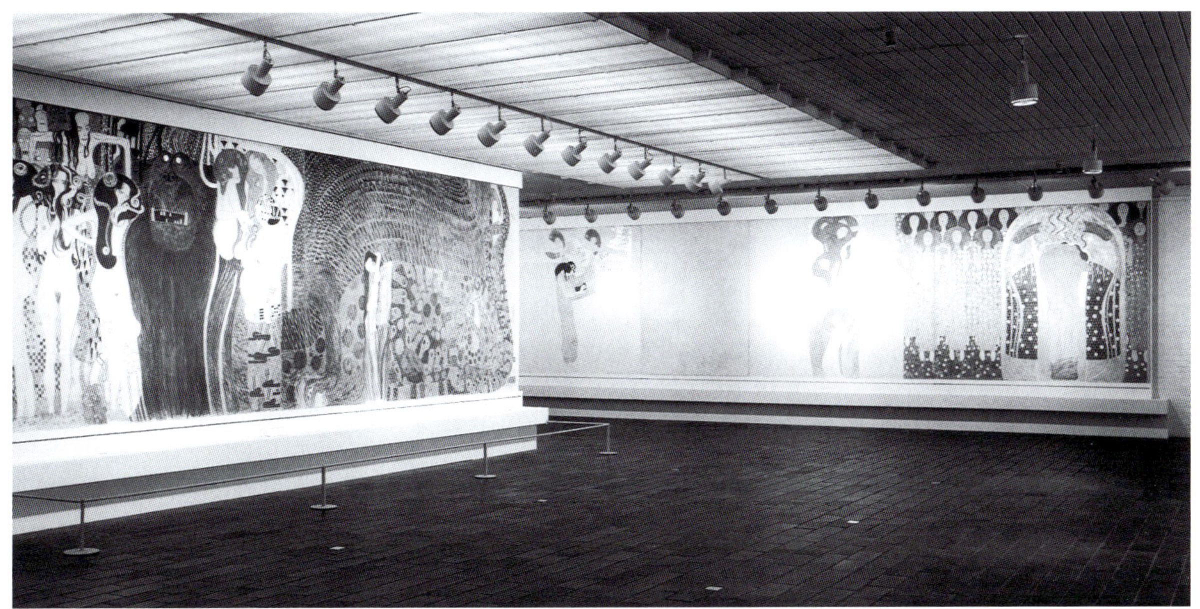

Poul Kjærholm

Pip Simmons Theatre Group

Michala Petri

1978 Vita Andersen

"The Revolt from the Centre". K. Helweg Petersen, Niels I. Meyer and Villy Sørensen

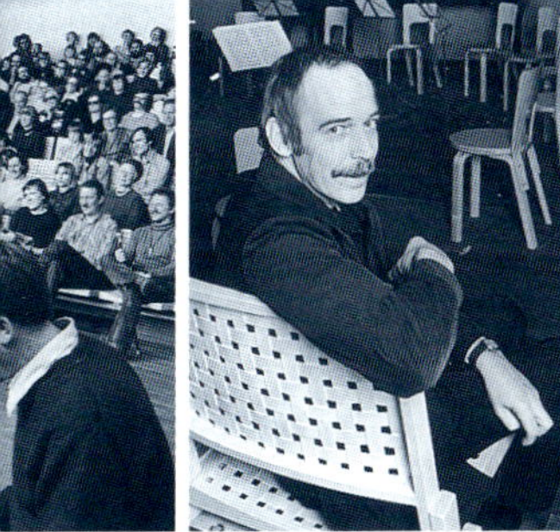

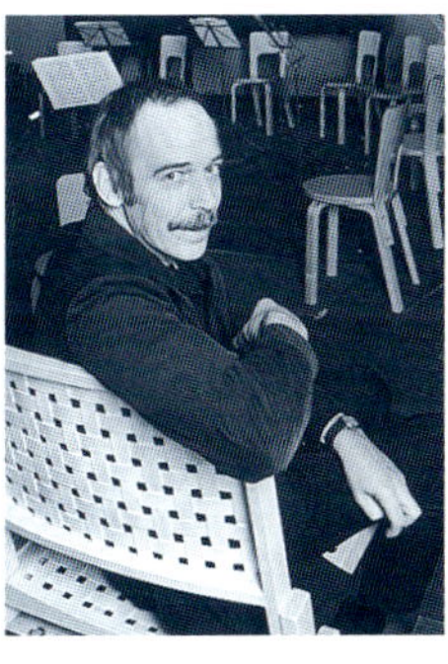

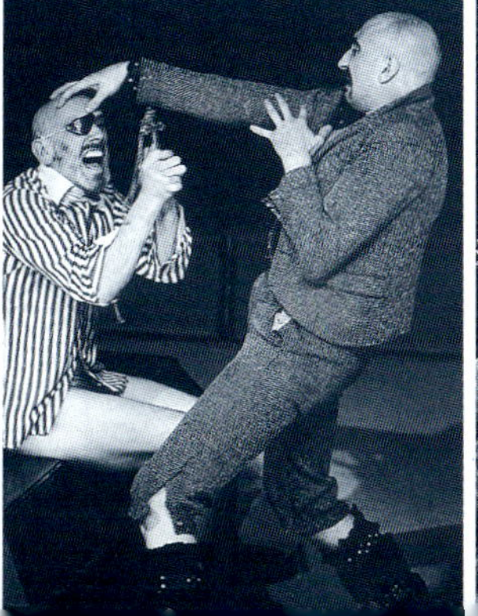

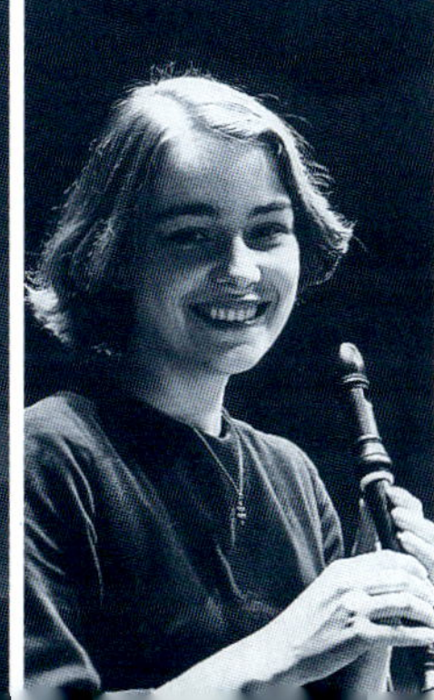

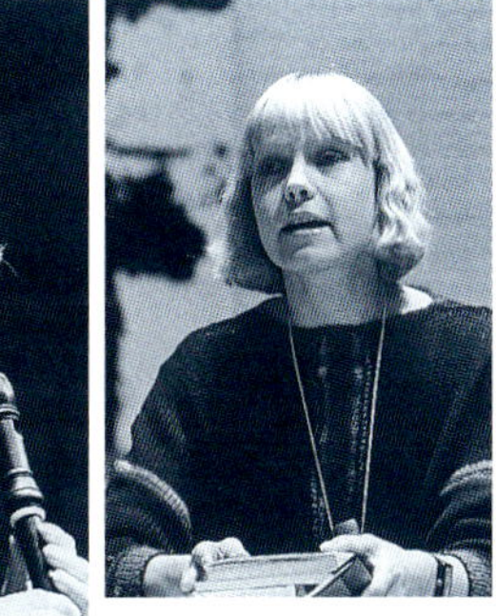

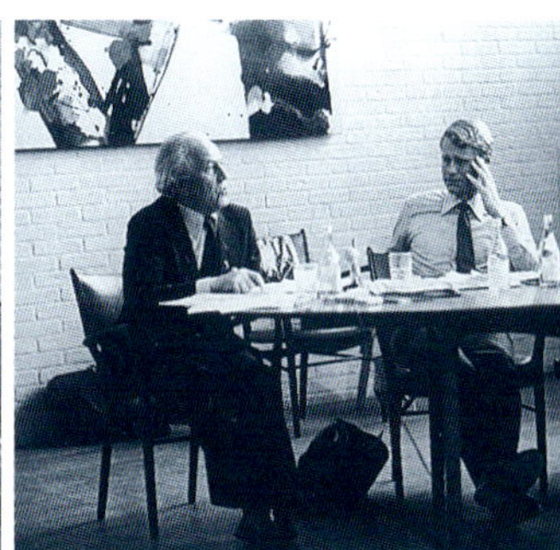

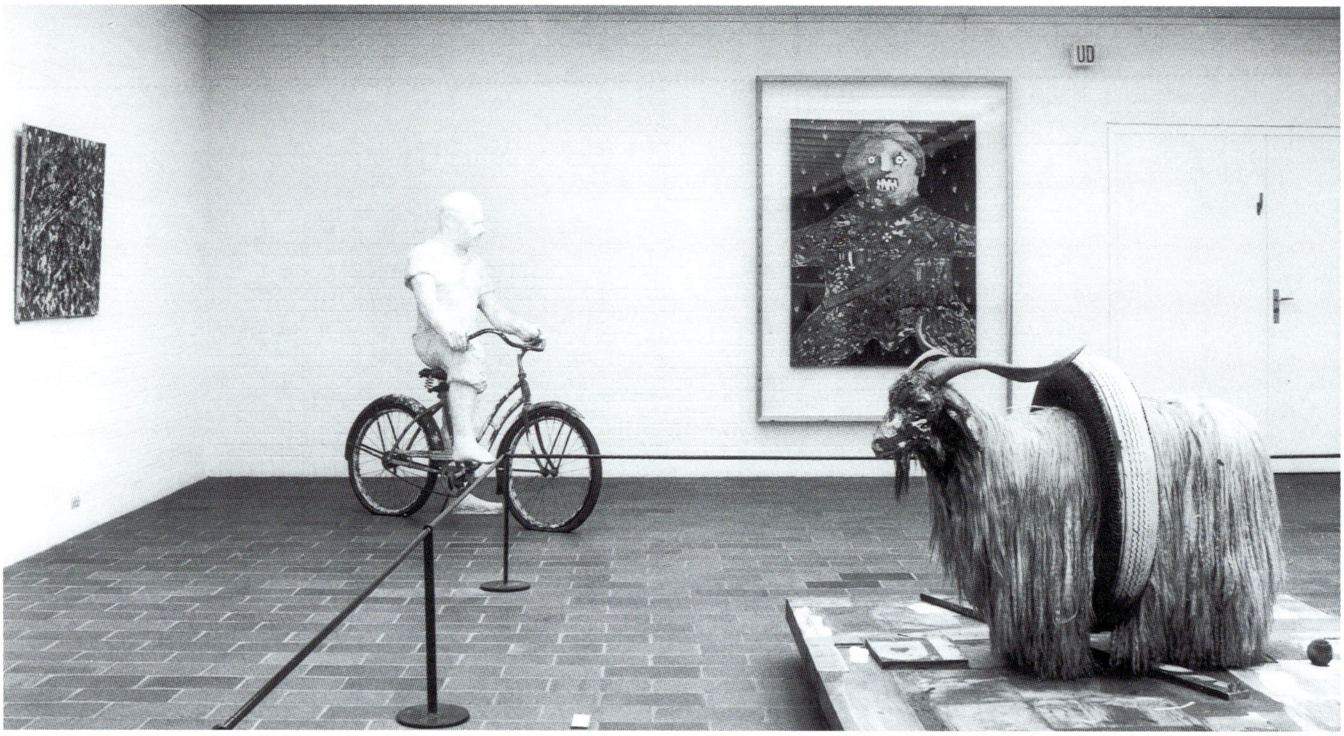

Moderna Museet Visits Louisiana, 1960

The London School: Six Figurative Painters, 1987

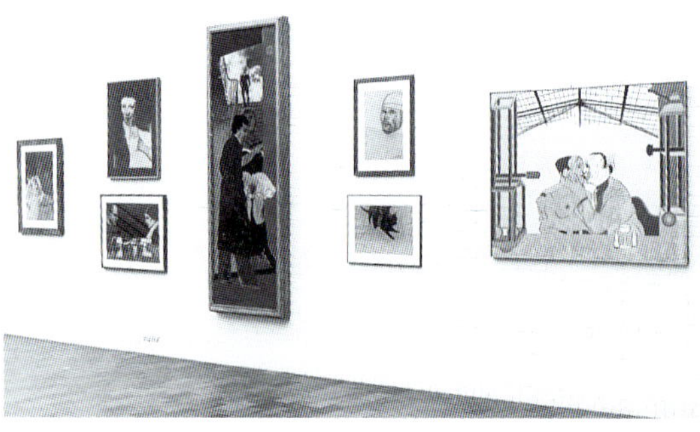

1978 Joseph Beuys and Niels Viggo Bentzon

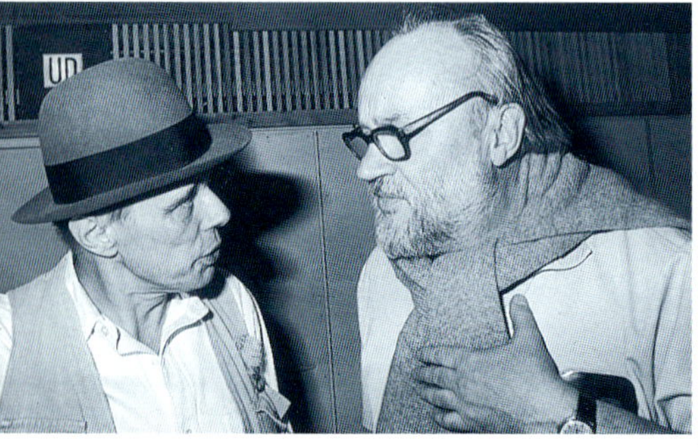

Bread and Puppet Theatre

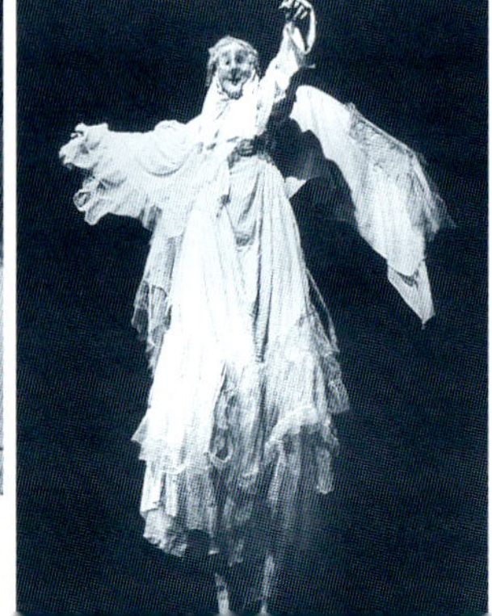

Erik Dietman: Installation in cooperation with schoolchildren from Humlebæk

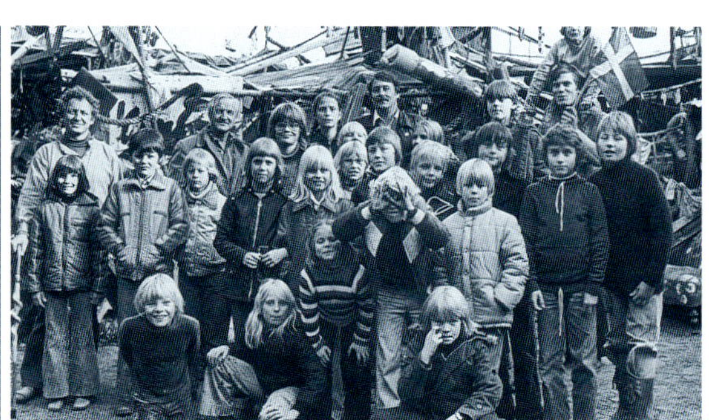

Hans Henrik

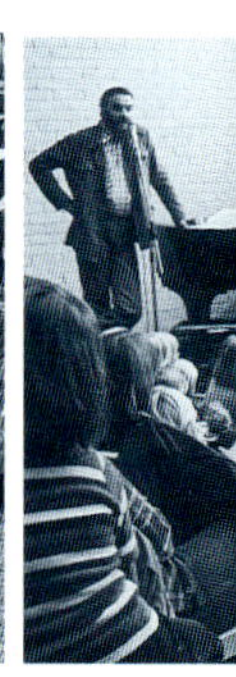

Aftermath: France 1945-54 – New Images of Man, 1982

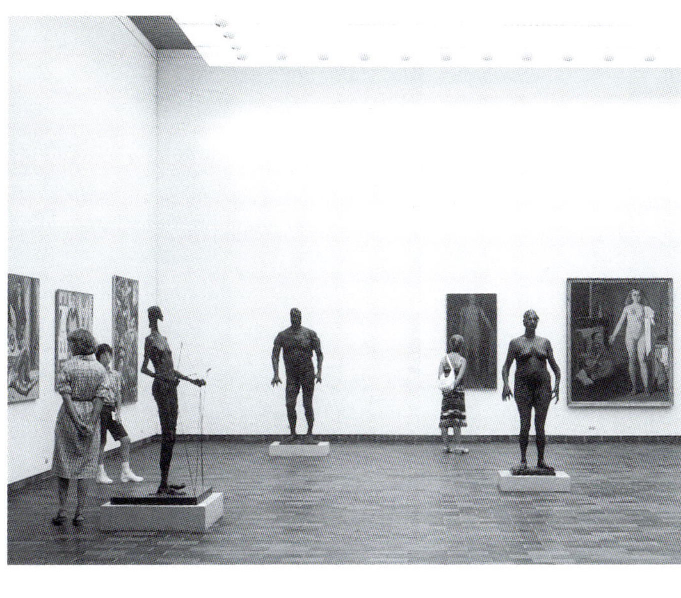

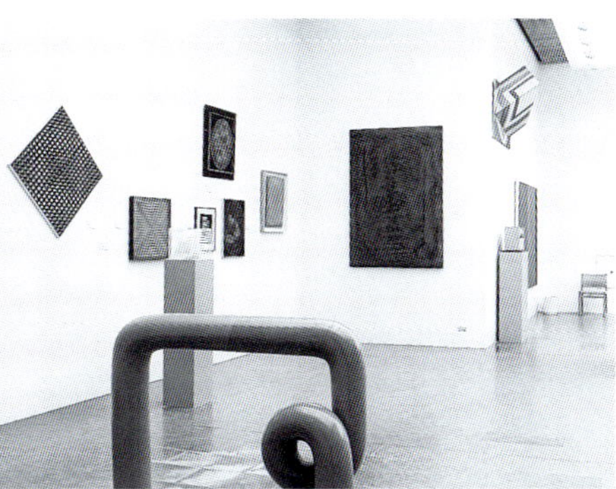

Constructivism in the Louisiana Collection after the Gift from the Riklis-McCrory Collection, 1986

Children Are a People, 1978

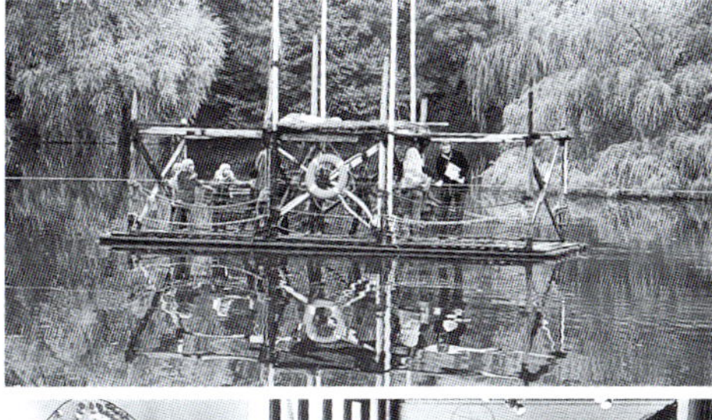

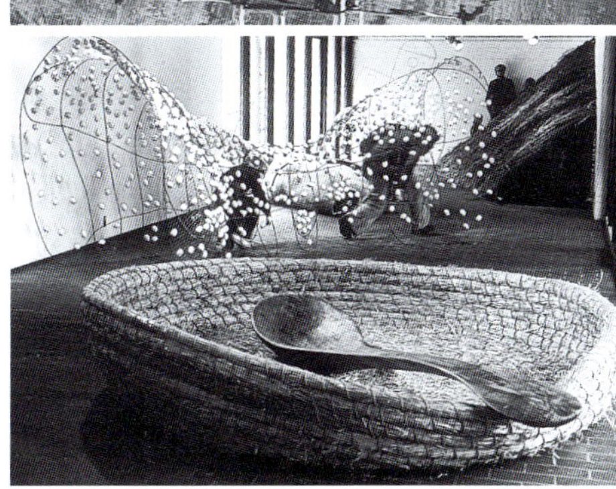

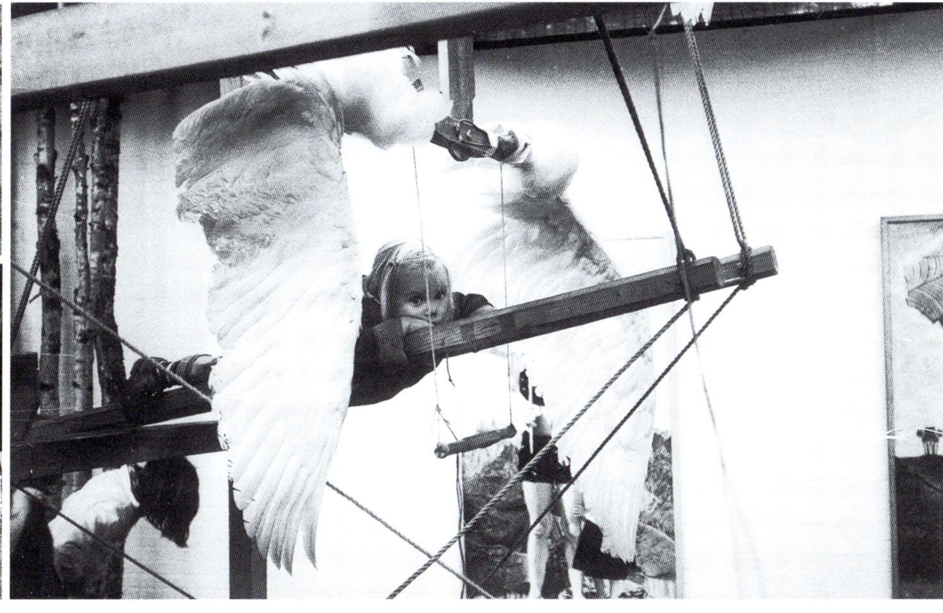

…nd The Danish Wind Quartet

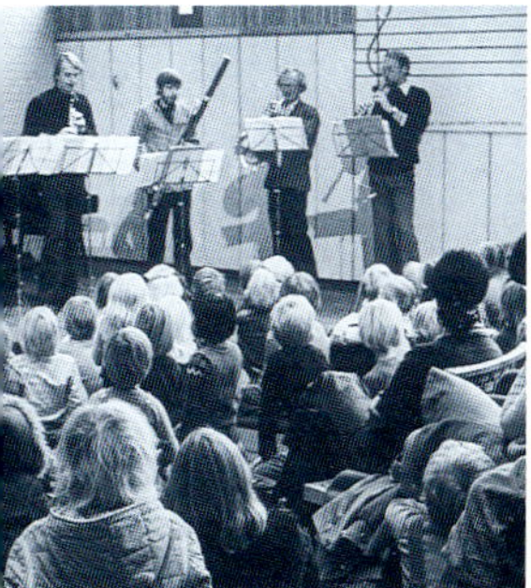

Elsinore Players

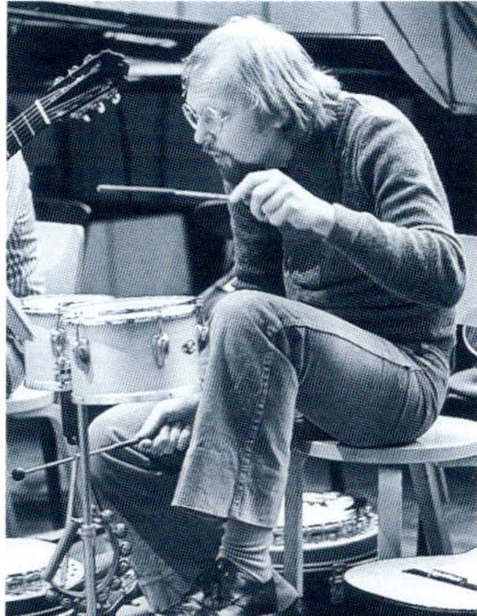

Jesus Raphael Soto and Knud W. Jensen

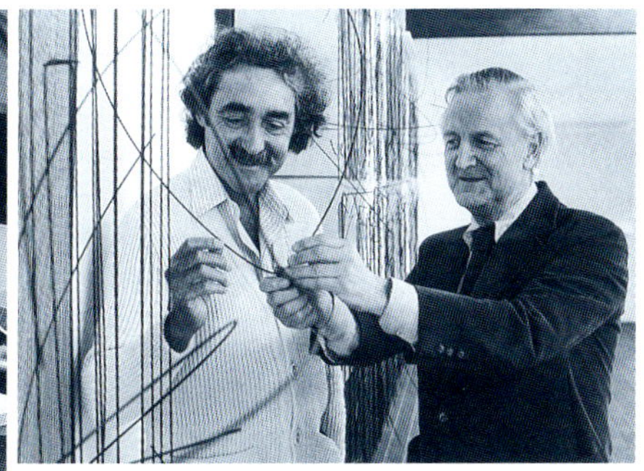

Anton Kontra

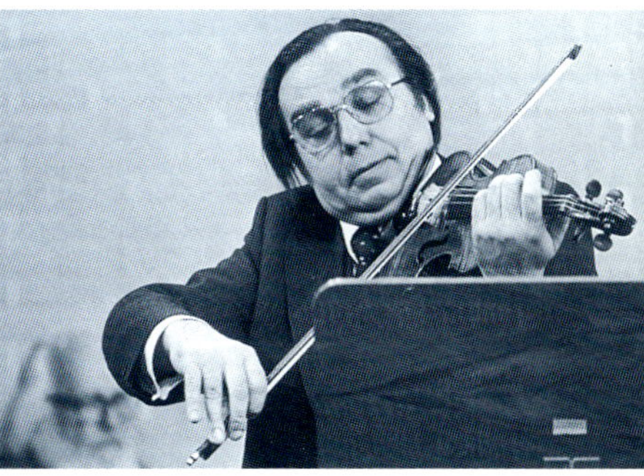

Thematic Exhibitions

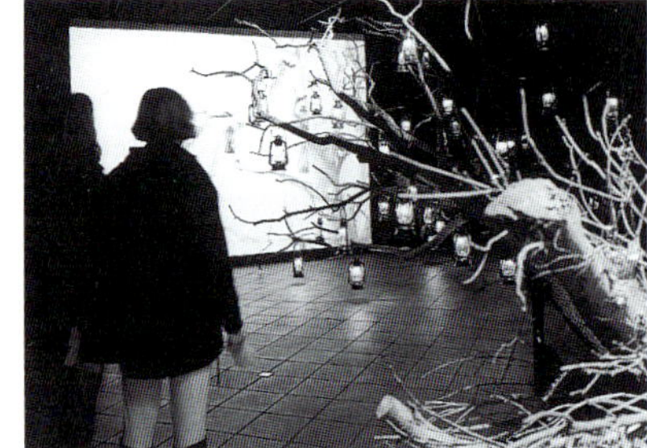

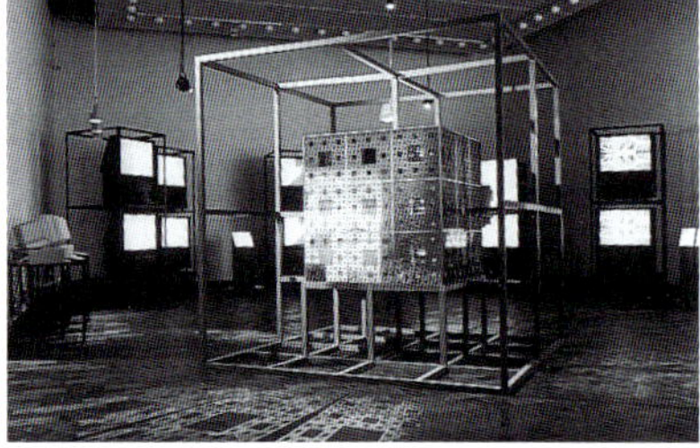

At the Edge of Chaos – New Images of the World, 1993

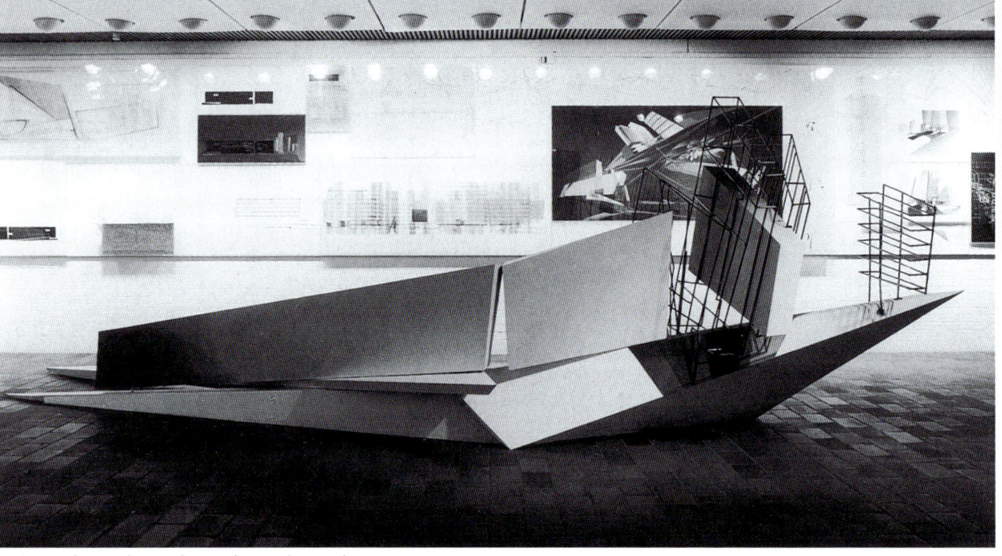

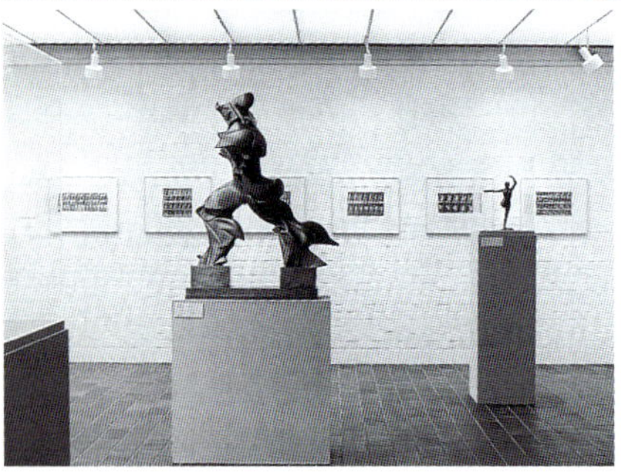

Time – The Fourth Dimension, 1985

Homo Decorans – Man who Decorates, 1985

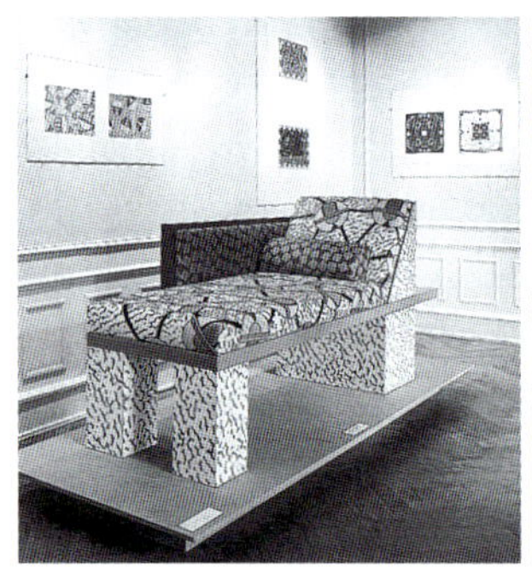

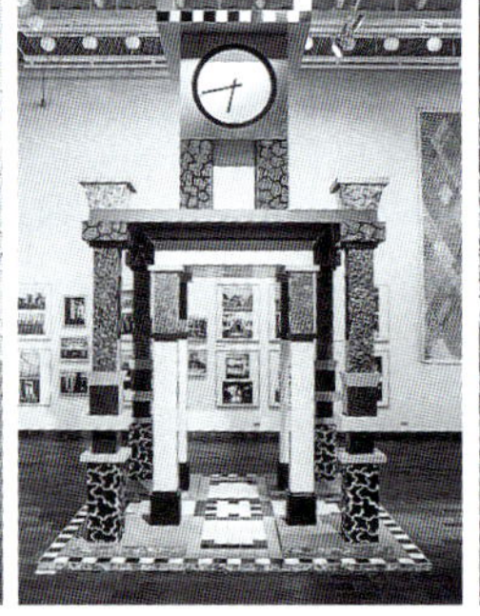

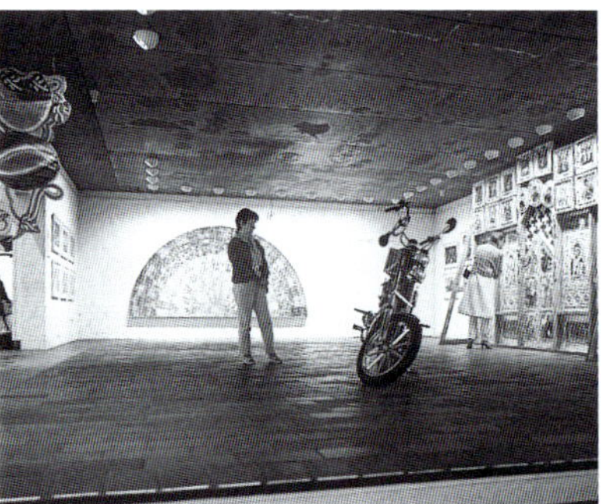

1979 Günter Grass and Per Øhrgaard · Trisha Brown · Odin Theatre · Mary-Claire Chorba – Peter Craig Theatre

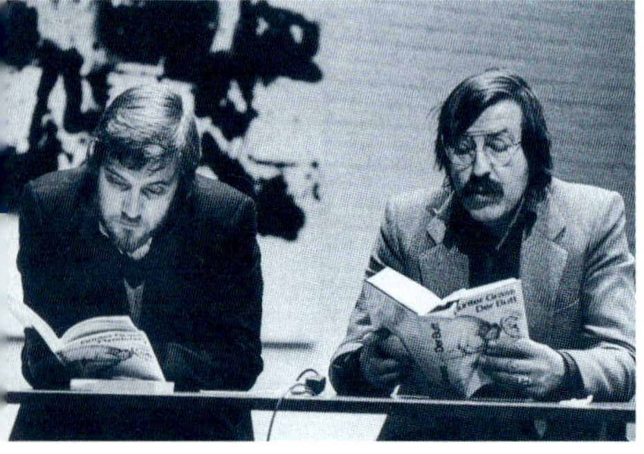

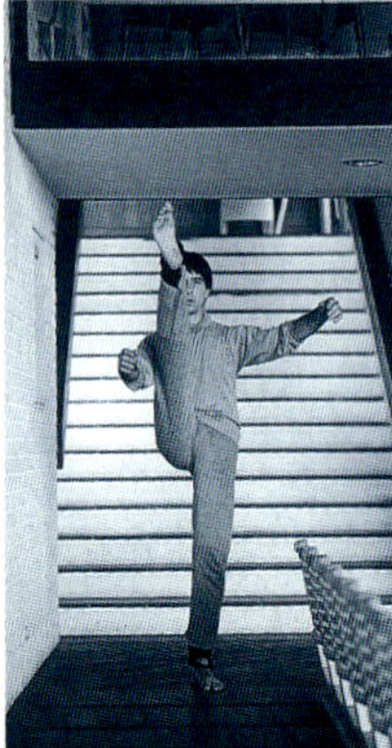

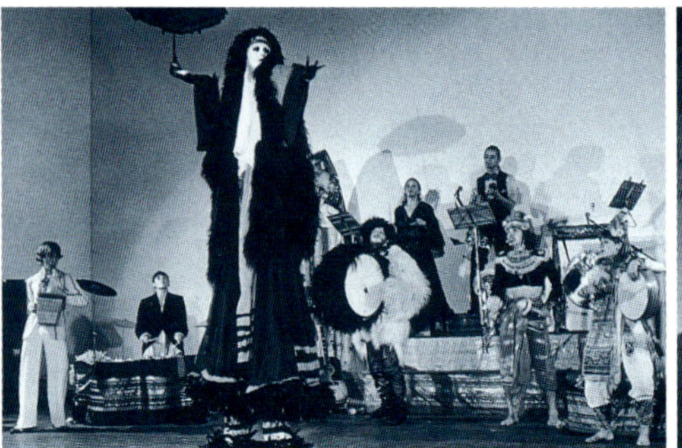

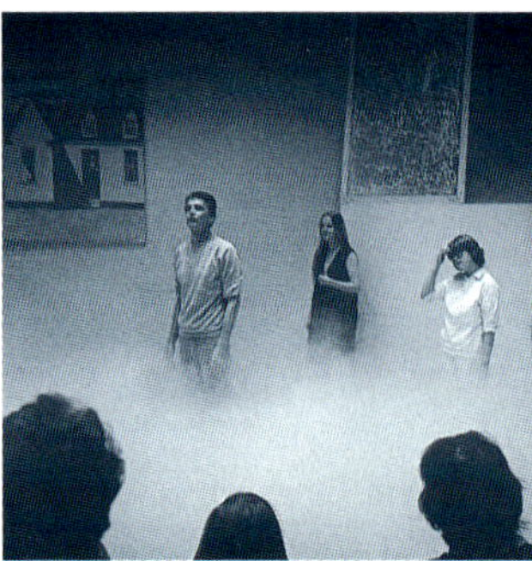

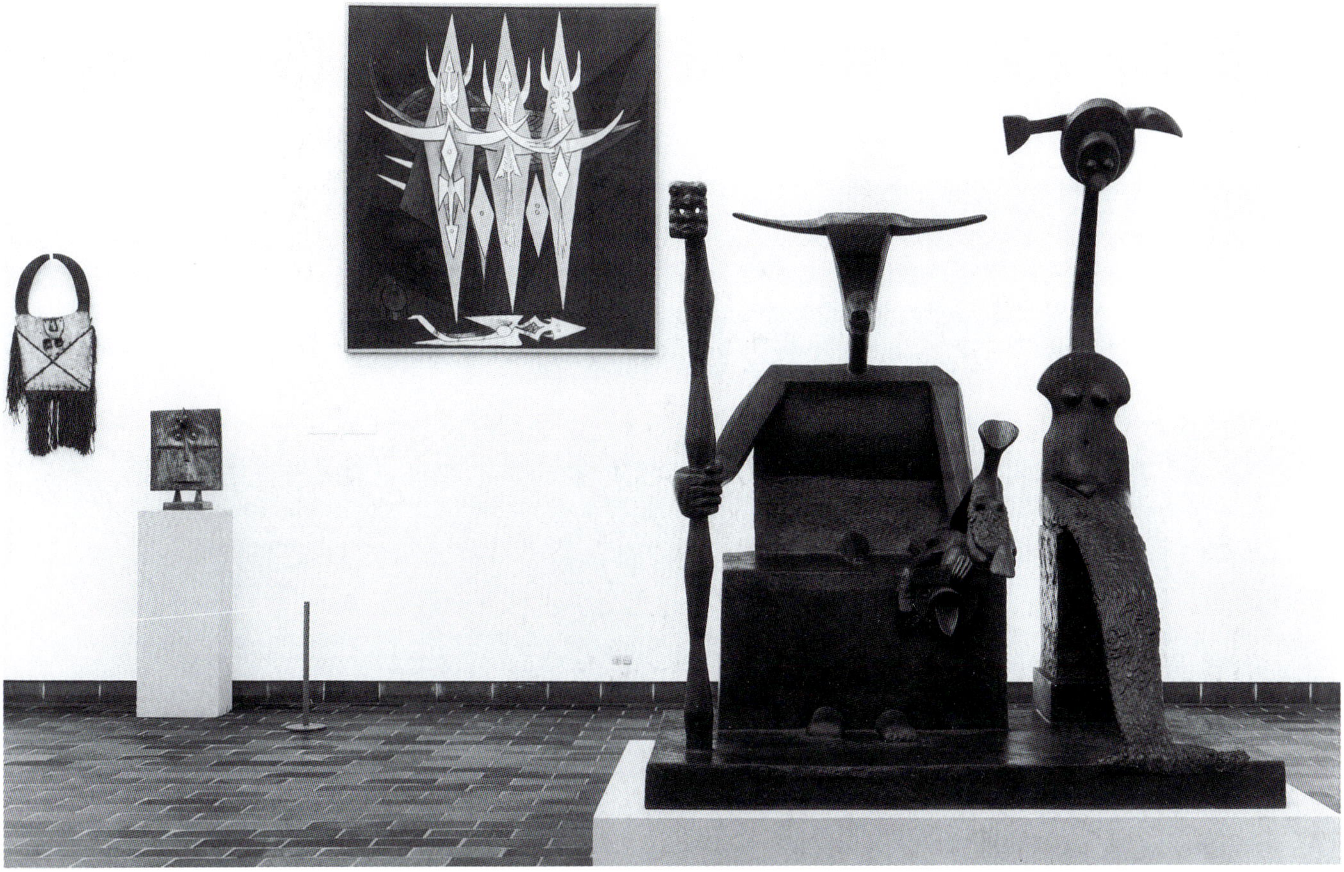

The Global Dialogue – Primitive and Modern Art, 1986

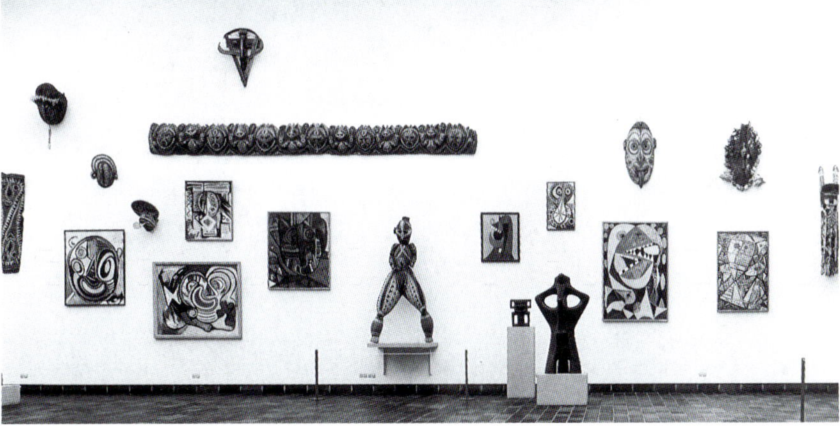

"The Poetry Day"

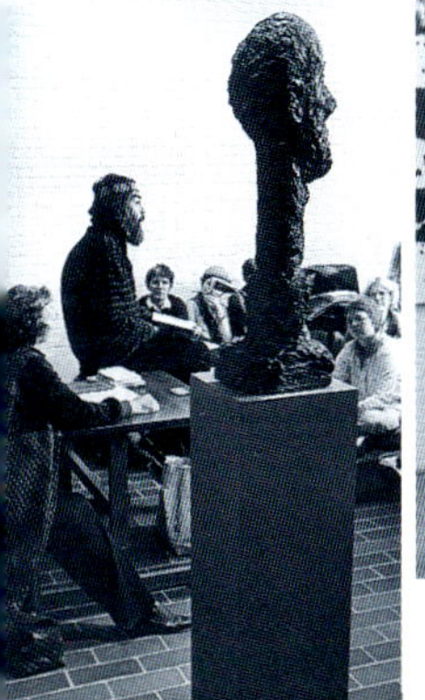

Discussing contemporary history.
Knud W. Jensen, H. P. Clausen and Paul Hammerich

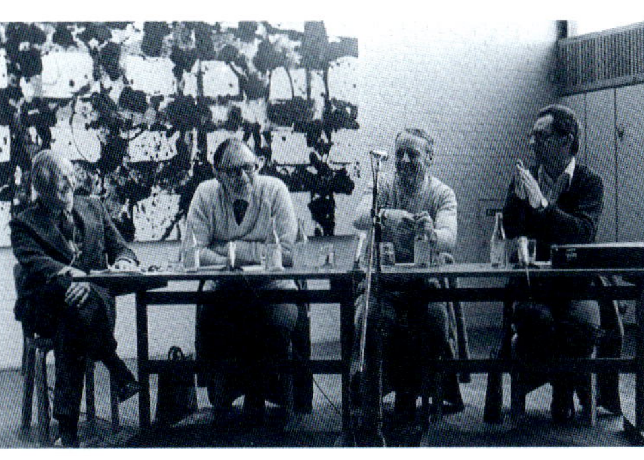

1980 Jørgen Bo and Vilhelm Wohlert

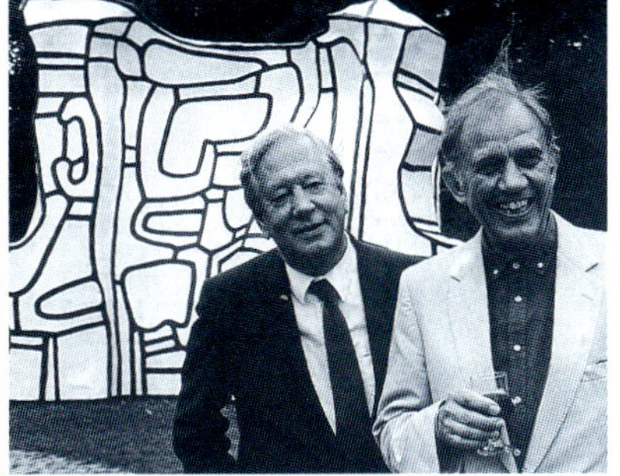

Hans Erik Wallin preparing the exhibition "Treasures of China"

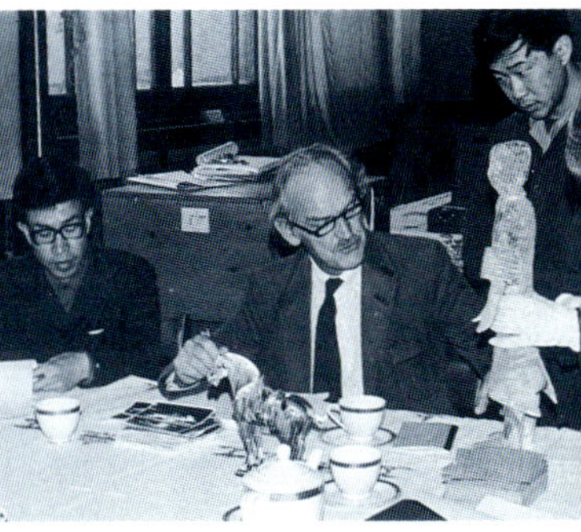

The Postwar Generation

1959	Robert Jacobsen
1960	Lynn Chadwick – Kenneth Armitage
1961	Henry Moore
1962	Pasmore – Paolozzi
1962	Jean Arp
1963	Jackson Pollock
1965	Asger Jorn
1965	James Rosenquist: "F 111"
1965	Olivia Holm-Møller
1966	Cobra 1948-51
1966	Oluf Høst
1966	Robert Jacobsen
1967	Lucio Fontana
1967	"Heerup 60"
1968	Saul Steinberg
1968	Yves Klein
1969	Pierre Alechinsky
1969	Carl-Henning Pedersen
1969	Alexander Calder
1969	Arman
1970	Richard Mortensen
1970	Egill Jacobsen
1972	Robert Indiana
1972	Svend Wiig Hansen
1973	Alfred Jensen
1973	Jean Tinguely
1973	Asger Jorn
1973	Pol Bury
1974	Christian Boltansky
1974	Tàpies
1974	Christo: "Curtain Valley"
1974	Dubuffet
1974	Dewasne
1975	Dario Villalba
1975	Morris Louis
1975	Duane Hanson
1975	Willy Ørskov & Jørgen Haugen Sørensen
1975	Ipousteguy
1976	David Hockney
1976	Henry Moore
1977	Robert Morris
1977	Claes Oldenburg: Drawings
1977	Sam Francis
1978	Christo: "Running Fence"
1978	Soto
1978	Andy Warhol
1979	Ed Kienholz: "Tableaux & Volksempfänger"
1979	Hamilton/Roth: Interfaces
1979	Alechinsky/Appel: Painting with Two Brushes
1980	Robert Rauschenberg
1981	Bram van Velde
1982	Arnulf Rainer
1983	Willem de Kooning
1983	Arnulf Rainer: Hiroshima
1983	Carl-Henning Pedersen: The First Years
1984	Robert Smithson. Sculpture/Drawings
1985	Jan Schoonhoven Drawings and Reliefs
1985	Enzo Cucchi
1986	Richard Serra. Drawings
1986	Jean Tinguely at Louisiana
1986	Sam Francis in the Collection of the Idemitsu Museum in Tokyo
1986	The Prints of Barnett Newman
1988	Mario Merz. Installations and Drawings
1988	Roberto Matta: Paintings
	Germaine Richier: Sculptures
1990	Per Kirkeby
1990	Andy Warhol
1992	Jasper Johns: Graphic Works and Drawings 1960-91 from the Leo Castelli Collection
1993	Baselitz 1990-93
1993	Morris Louis
1995	Asger Jorn
1995	Tony Smith
1995	Alexander Calder
1998	Francis Bacon

Baselitz 1990-93, 1993

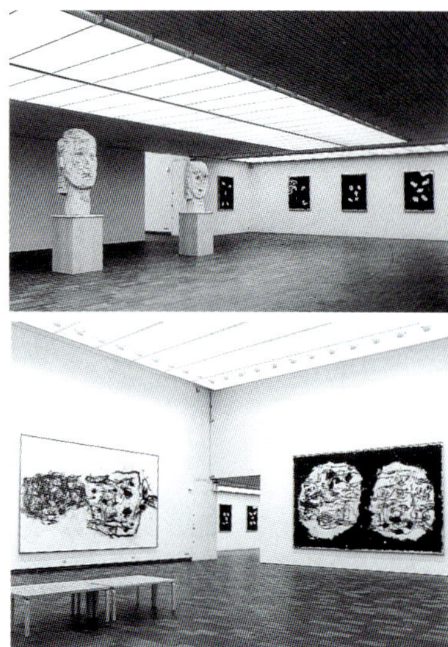

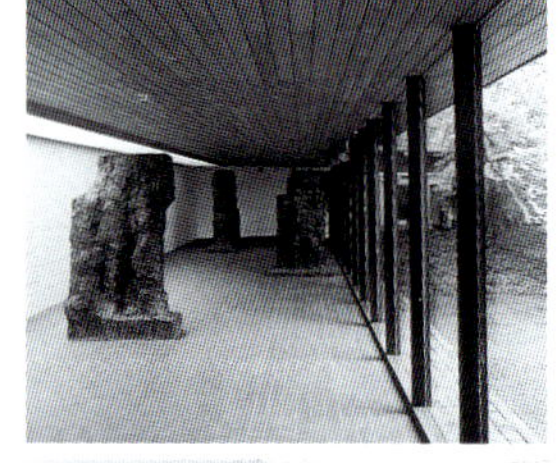

Per Kirkeby, 1990

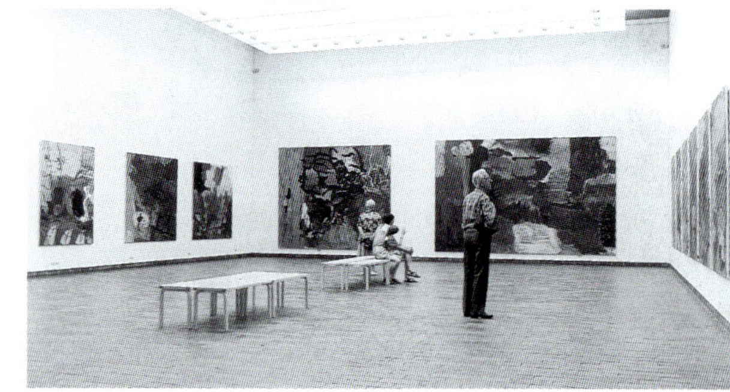

"The Poetry Day"

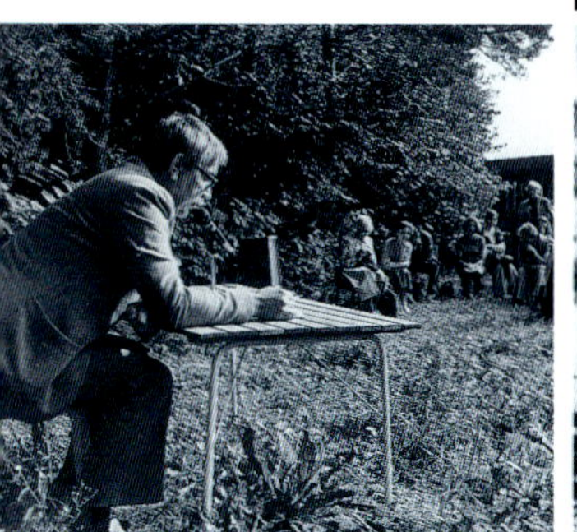

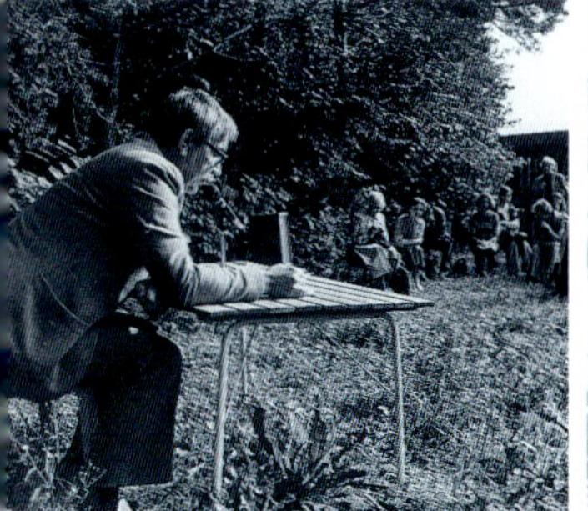

1981 Bent Jørgensen

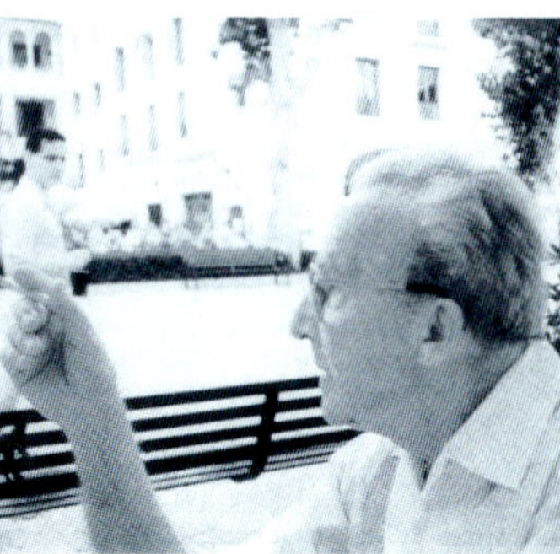

Sam Francis and Knud W. Jensen

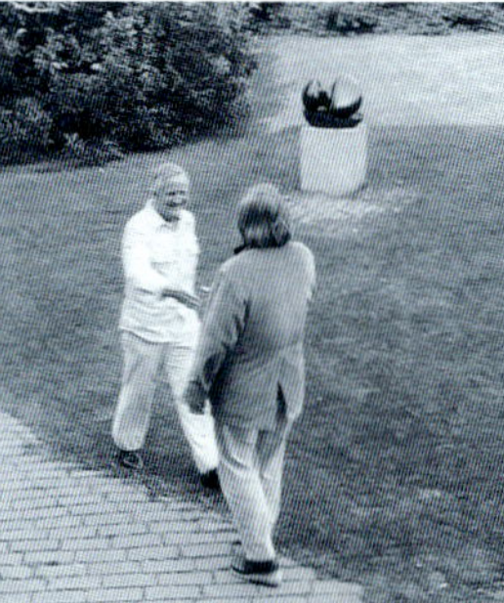

The Dutch ballet group Werkcentrum Dans

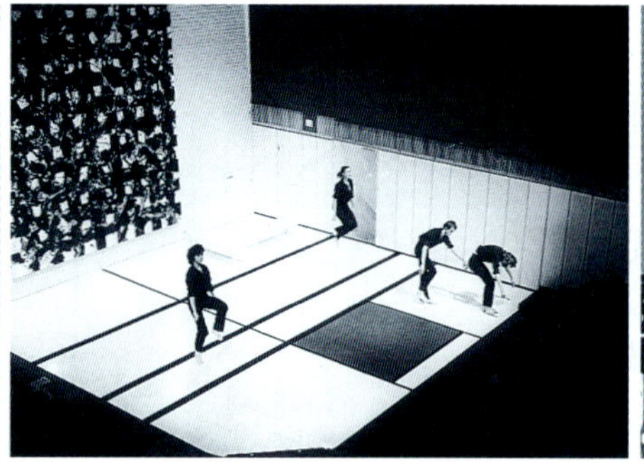

"Danis

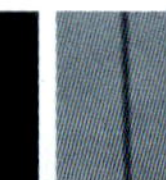

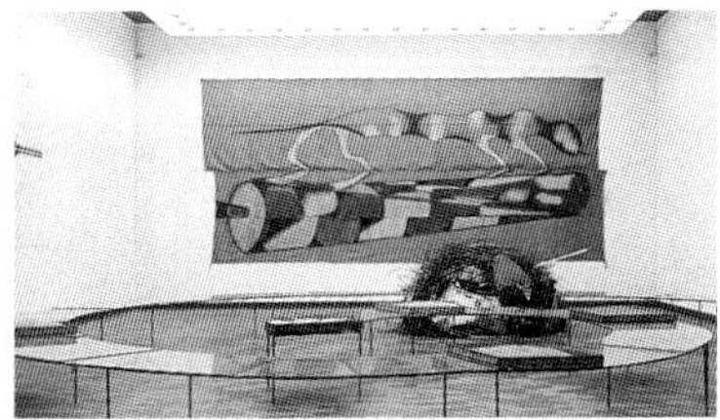

Mario Merz.
Installations and
Drawings, 1988

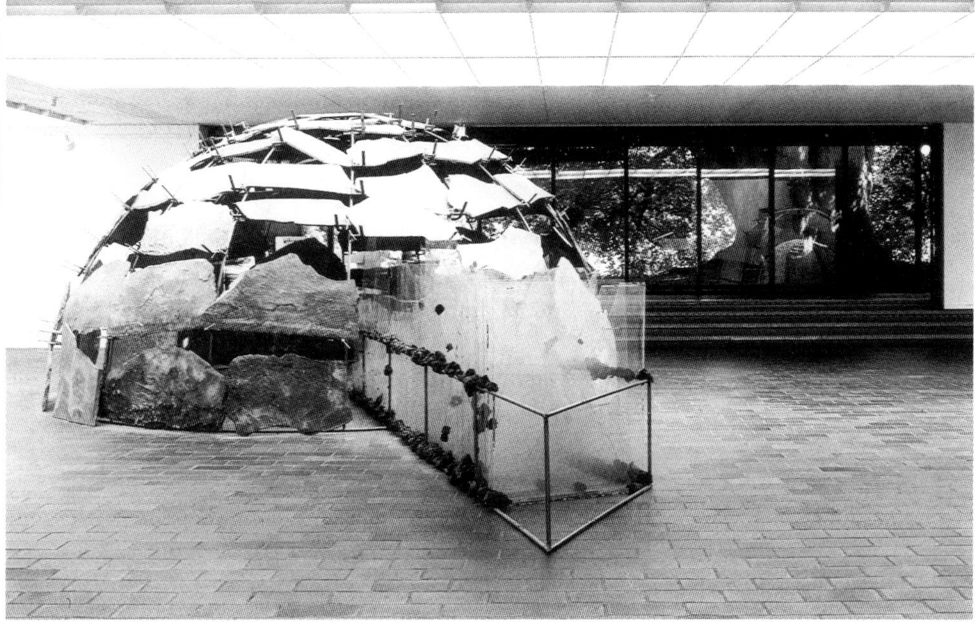

Andy Warhol, 1990

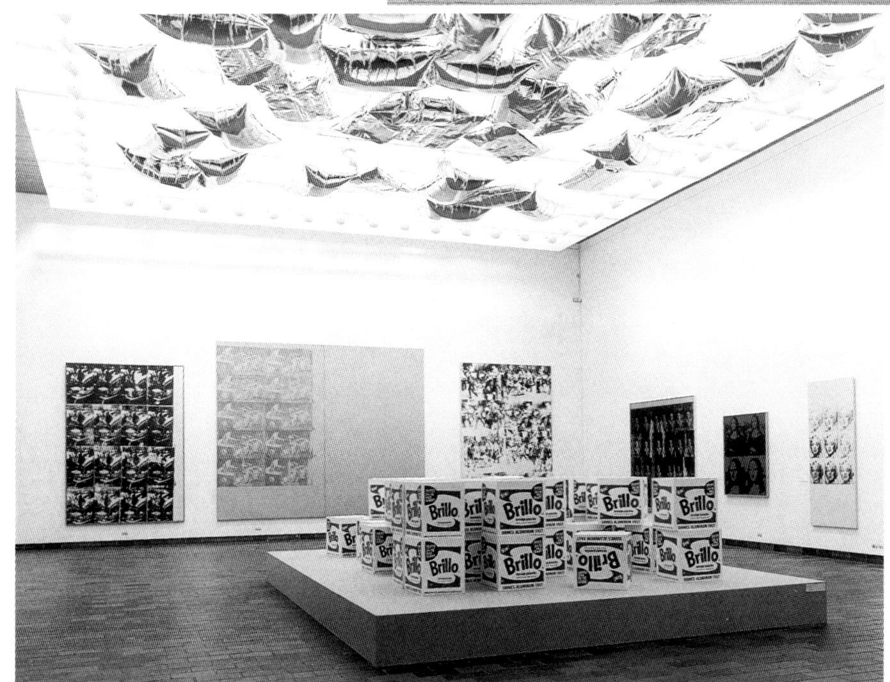

Robert Rauschenberg, 1980

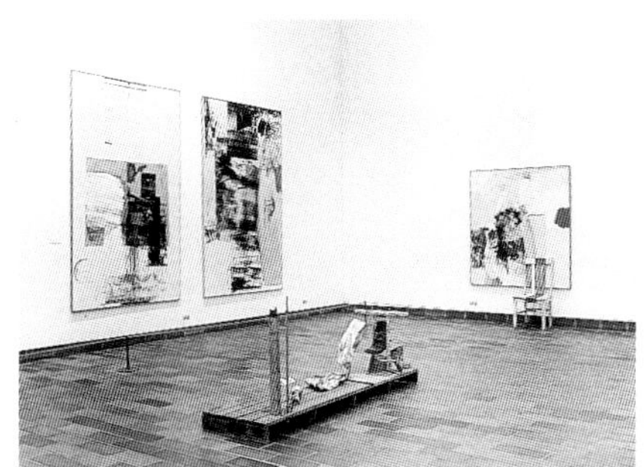

wedish Authors' Meeting"

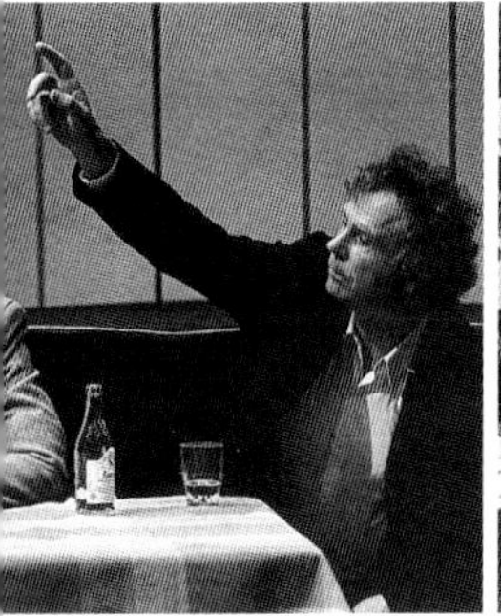

Cultural politics. Hearing at Louisiana

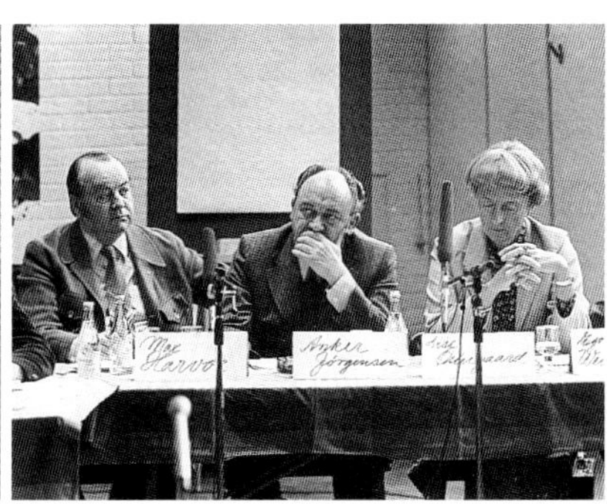

Steingrim Laursen, Richard Serra and Knud W. Jensen

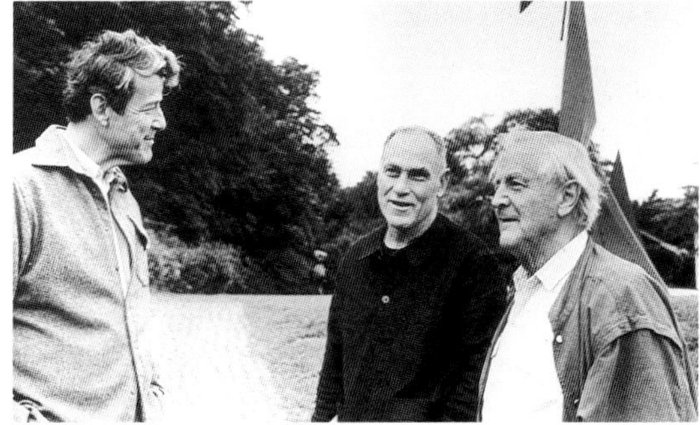

"The Poetry Day".
Thorkild Bjørnvig

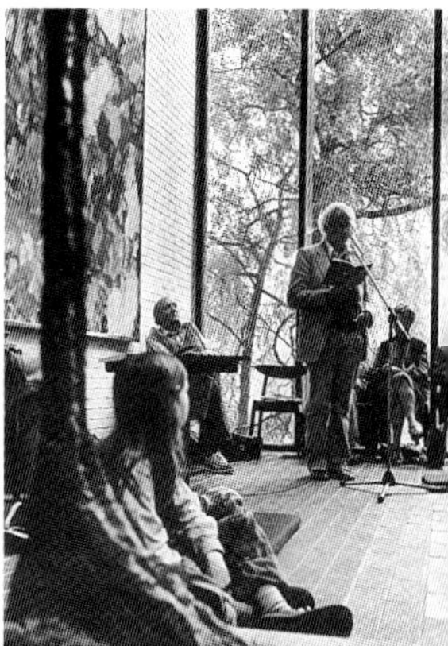

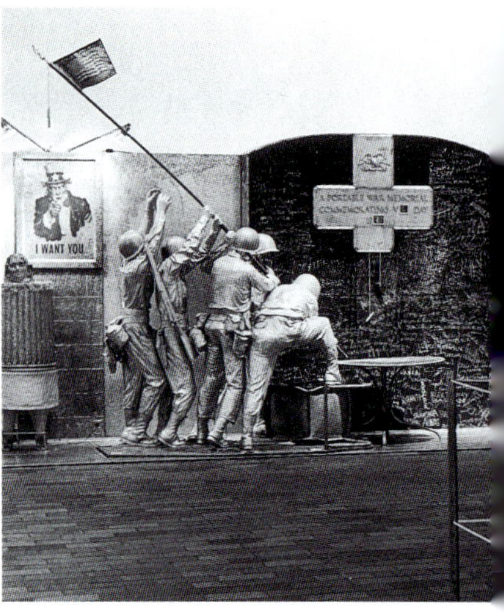

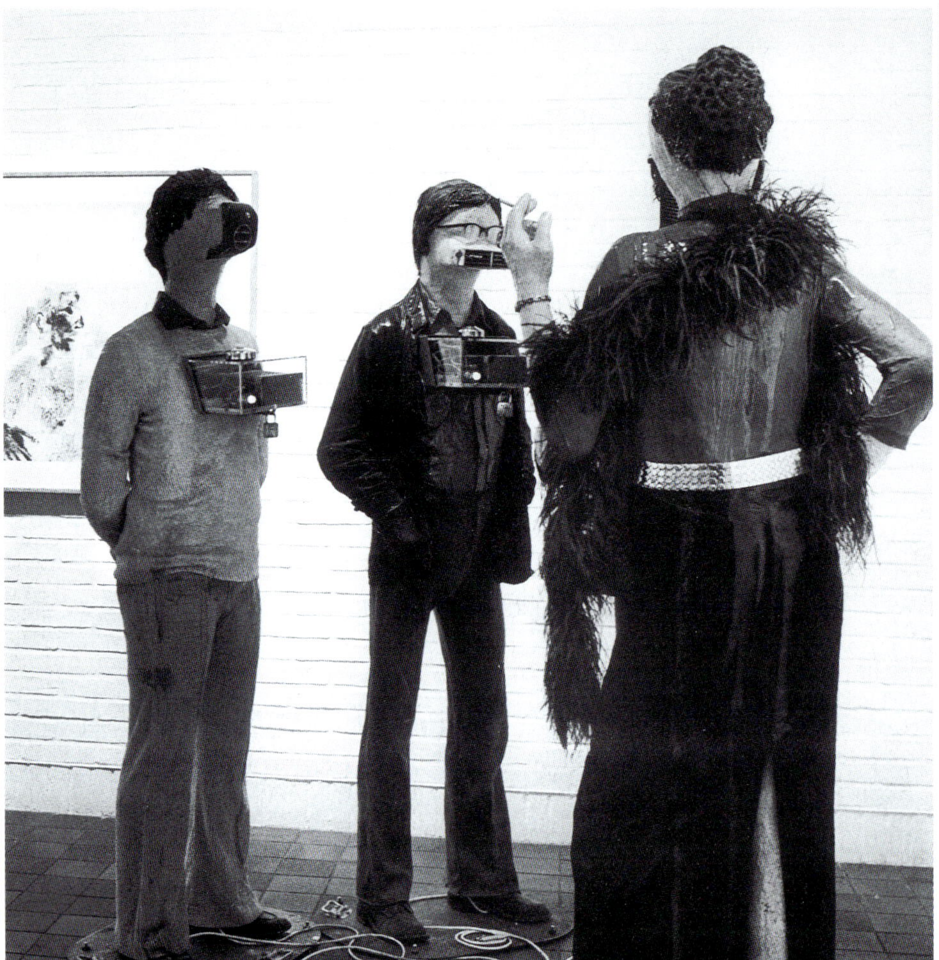

Ed Kienholz: "Tableaux & Volksempfänger", 1979

1981 "War and Man". Billedstofteater

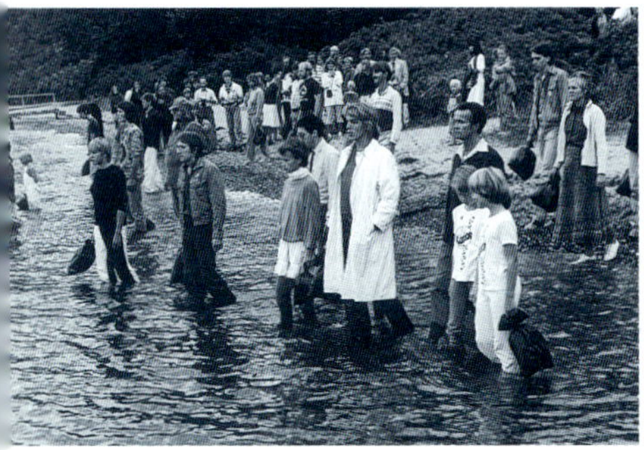

"War and Man". Per Nørgaard conducting the ensemble Sun and Moon

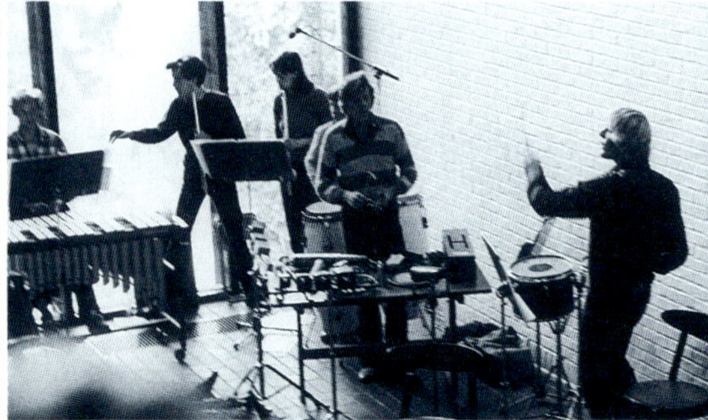

Joseph Beuys and Kjeld Kjeldsen

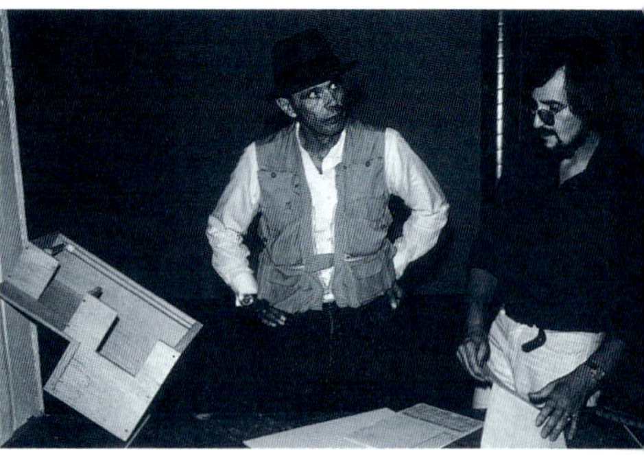

Ed Kienholz: "Tableaux & Volksempfänger", 1979

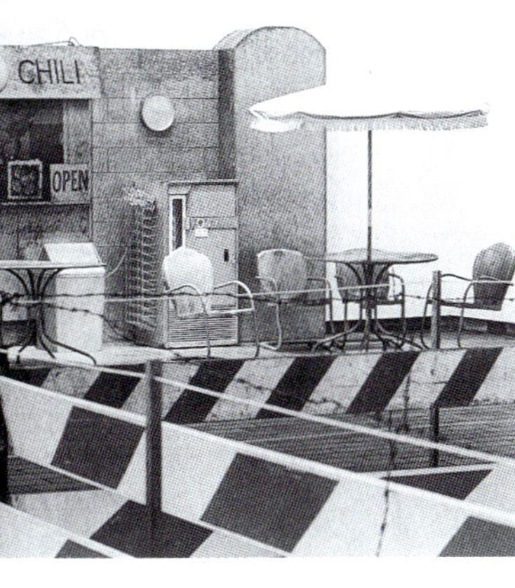

Francis Bacon, 1998

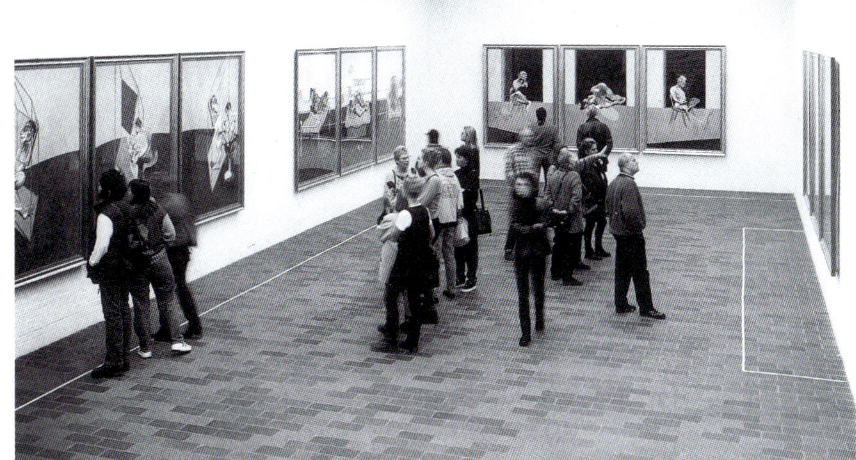

Jean Tinguely at Louisiana, 1986

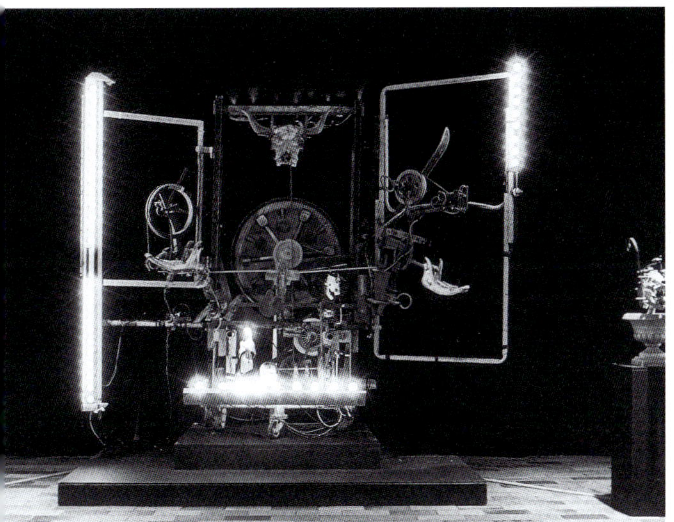

1982 The Jutland Opera performing Leif Thybo's opera "The Immortal Story"

Teatro de la Claca

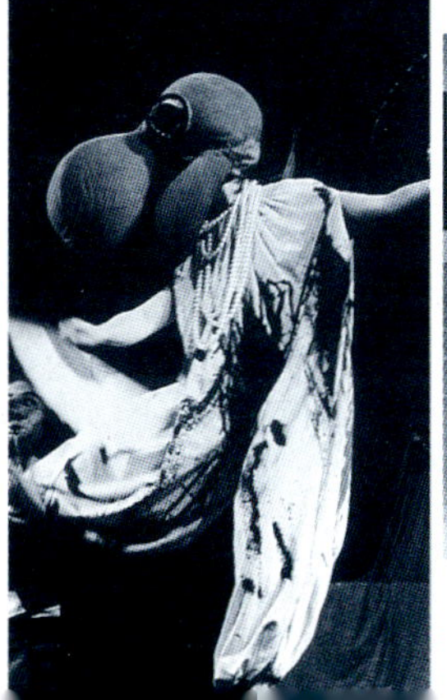

The inauguration of the South Wing

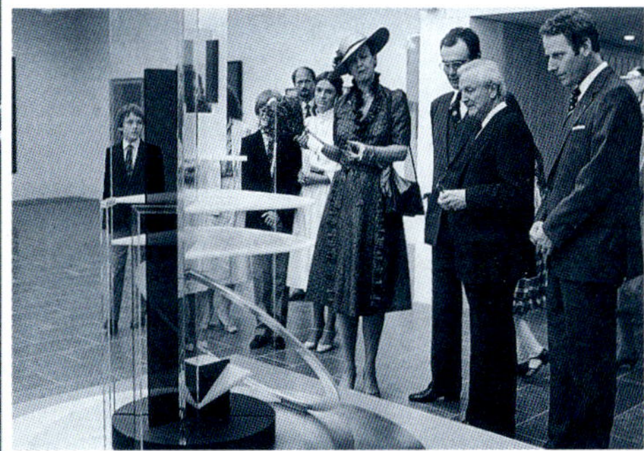

1983 "Peace and Man". Billedstofteater

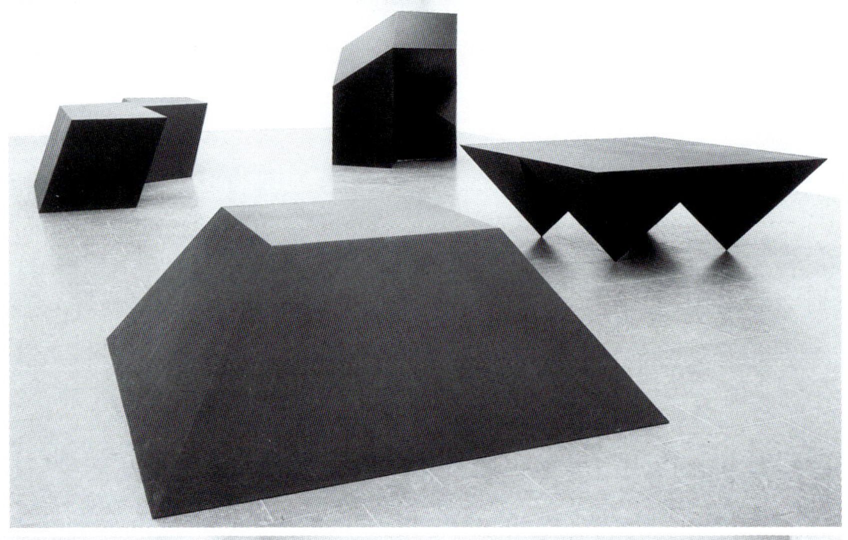

Tony Smith, 1995

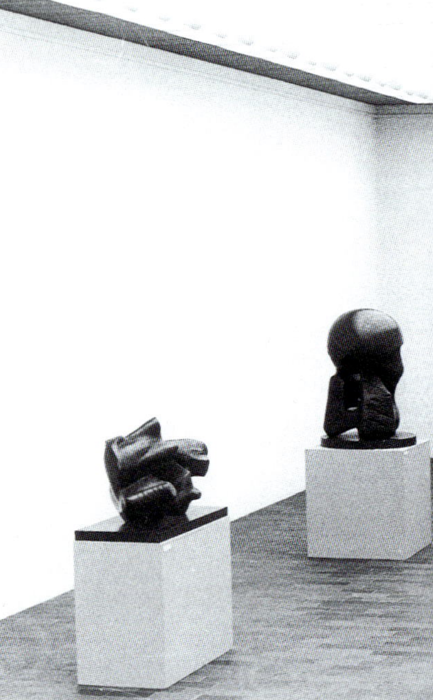

Henry Moore, 1961

Alexander Calder, 1995

Almost Big Band

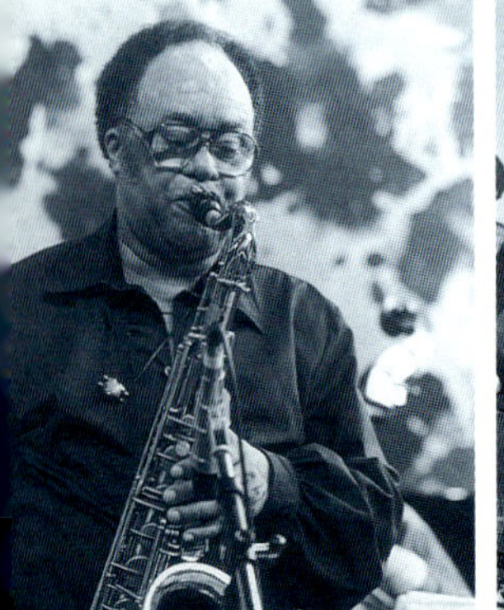

Tukak Theatre

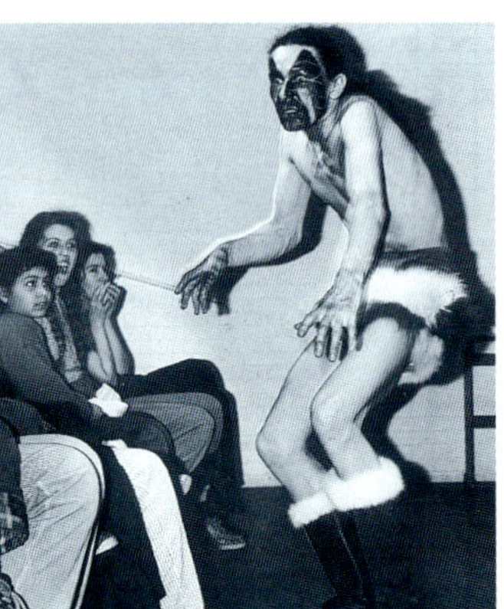

Jesper Klein and the Chamber Orchestra

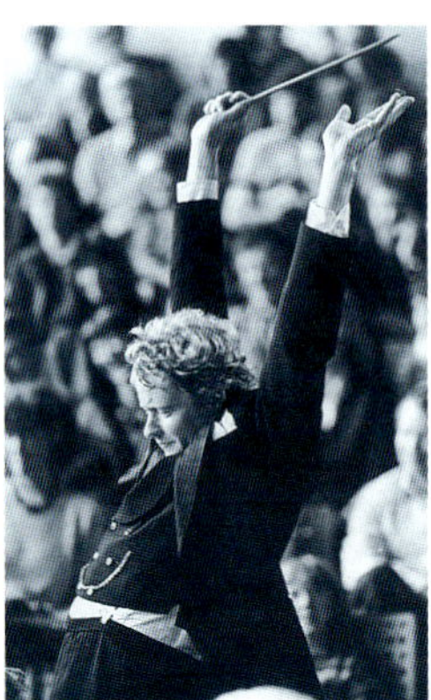

1984 Isaac Stern at Louisiana. Violin Master Class

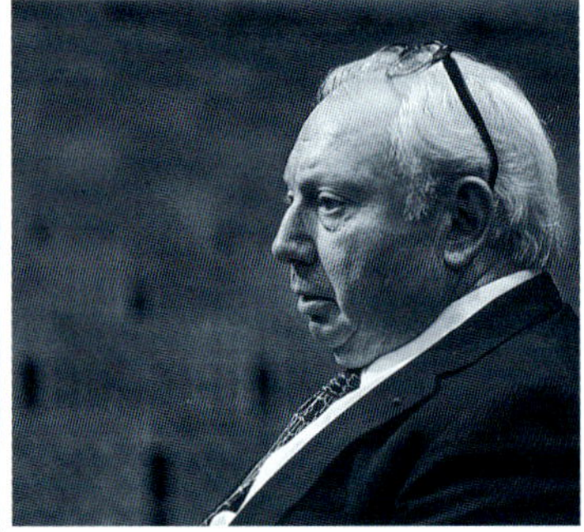

Children's weekend

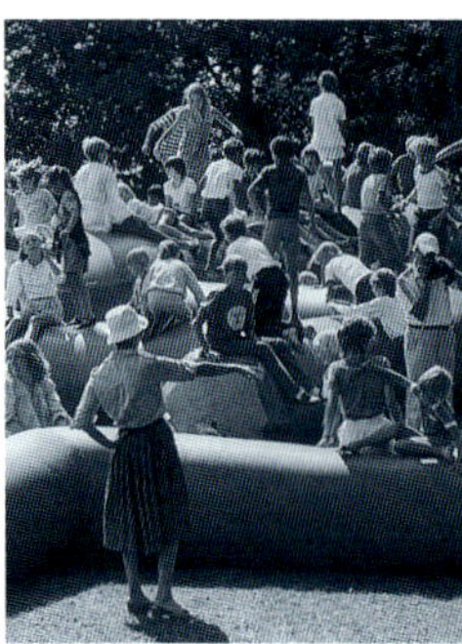

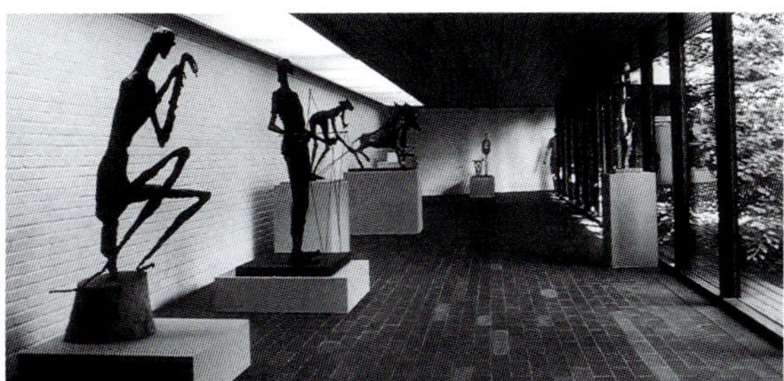

Roberto Matta: Paintings
Germaine Richier: Sculptures, 1988

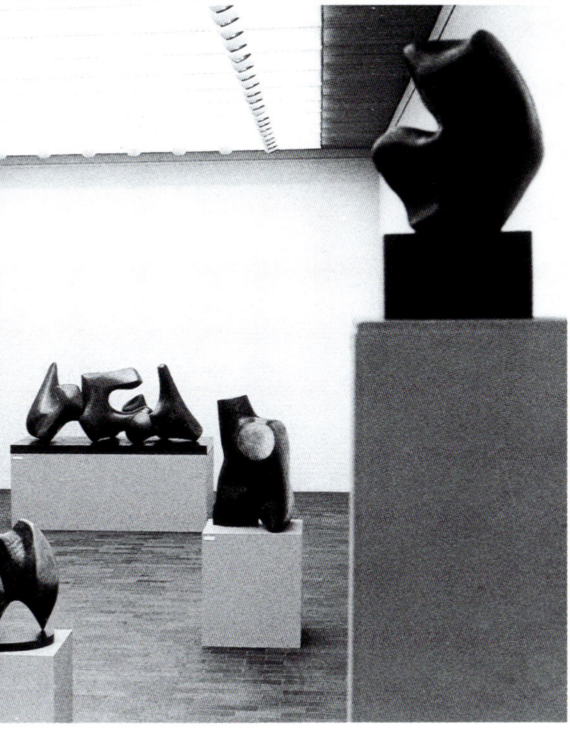

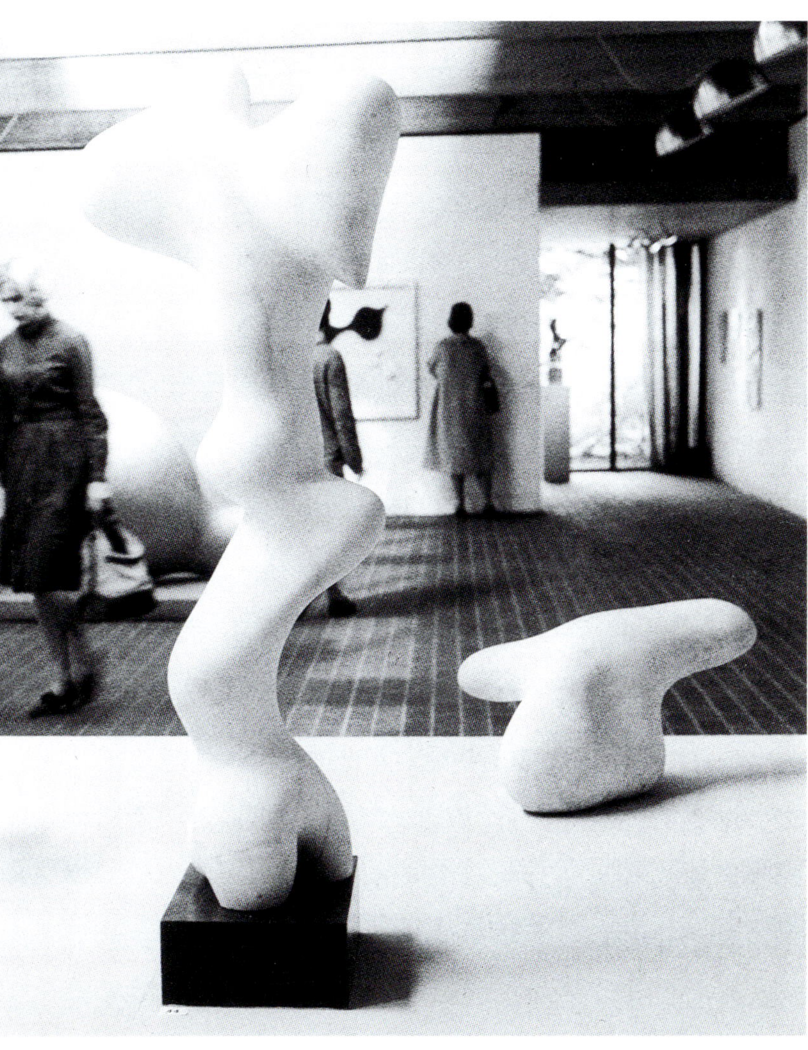

Jean Arp, 1962

Conductor Ken Takasei and the Louisiana Chamber Orchestra

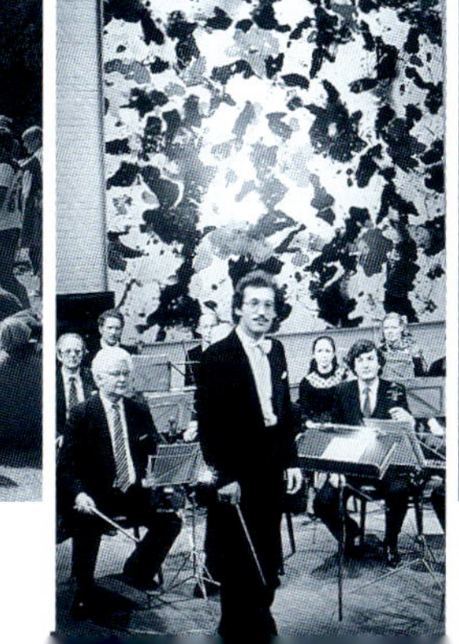

Knud W. Jensen honorary doctor at Lund University

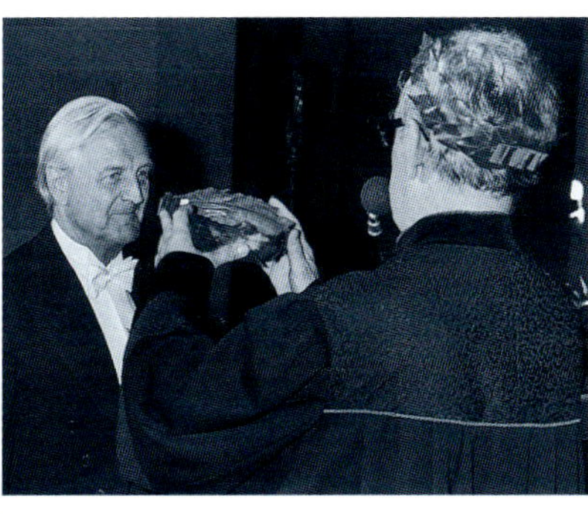

Anna Wahlgreen and her eight children

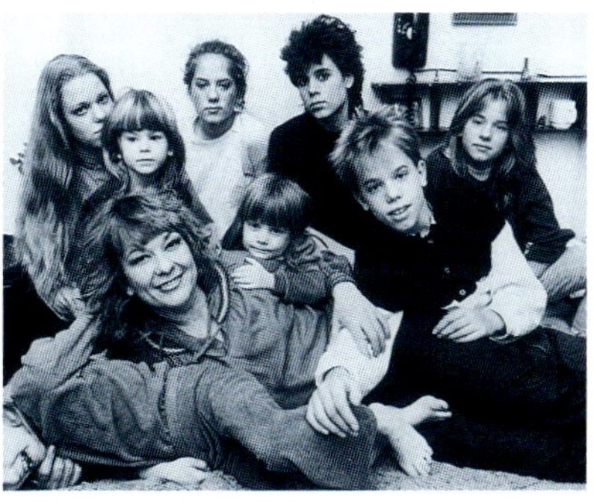

1985 "Young Danish Poets". Pia Tafdrup and F. P. Jac

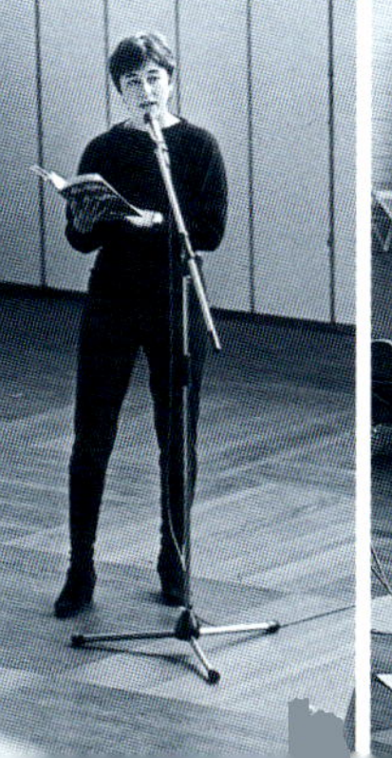

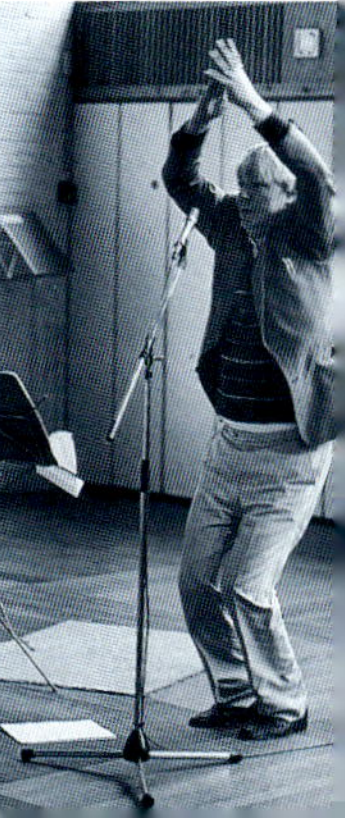

Contemporary Art Thematic and solo exhibitions

1959 Works from Documenta II
1964 Four Sculptors
1964 American Pop Art
1964 Contemporary British Painting
1965 The Marzotto Prize, 1964
1965 Arnaldo and Gio Pomodoro
1965 Young Danish Art
1966 "Bearings 66"
1966 Scandinavian Youth Biennial
1967 The Marzotto Prize, 1966
1968 Spanish Art of Today
1968 Works from Documenta IV
1970 Tabernakel
1971 Swedish Alternative
1972 Hasior – Beres
1972 Young Danish Art
1973 Extreme Realism
1975 Jan Groth
1975 Jacques Monory
1975 Bernhard Luginbühl
1976 Latin American Art from CAYC, Buenos Aires
1976 Elementary Forms in Dutch Art
1976 Nouvelle peinture française
1976 Louis Cane
1976 "Let's Mix All Feelings Together"
1976 Soho Downtown Manhattan
1977 Ten Artists from Israel
1977 Aspects of German Art
1978 Hantai
1978 Nobuo Sekine & Le U Fan
1979 Art of the 70s from the Crex Collection
1979 Günter Grass: Etchings
1979 Mark Boyle
1980 André, Dibbets, Long, Ryman
1980 Nature-Art/Art-Nature
1981 Canadian Art from the 70s
1981 Drawing Distinctions: American Drawing in the 70s
1982 Neil Jenney
1982 Robert Moskowitz, Susan Rothenberg, Julian Schnabel
1982 Mimmo Paladino
1982 Olle Kåks
1982 Robert Irwin
1983 Chia – Clemente – Cucchi
1983 German Painting about 1980
1984 Jonathan Borofsky, Tony Cragg, Cindy Sherman
1984 New York Graffiti
1986 Sculpture – 9 Artists from Great Britain
1986 Jan Groth – Drawings 1975-85
1987 Sitings: Alice Aycock, Richard Fleishner, Mary Miss, George Trakas
1988 Michael Buthe – Environments
1988 Enzo Cucchi – Drawings
1988 Whitney Biennial Video
1989 Antony Gormley – Sculpture
1989 12 Contemporary Artists from Switzerland
1989 Borealis 4 – Installations in Space
1989 Erik Levine – Sculpture
1990 Joel Shapiro – Sculpture
1990 Stephan von Huene Sound – Sculpture – Installation
1990 Marina Abramovic/Ulay "The Lovers – The Great Walk"
1991 Jenny Holzer – The Venice Installation
1991 Eric Fischl
1993 Jana Sterbak
1993 Mistaken Identities
1994 Kiki Smith
1996 NowHere
1997 Cai Guo Qiang
1997 The Louisiana Exhibition 1997. New Art from Denmark and Scania
1998 Sam Taylor-Wood

NowHere, 1996

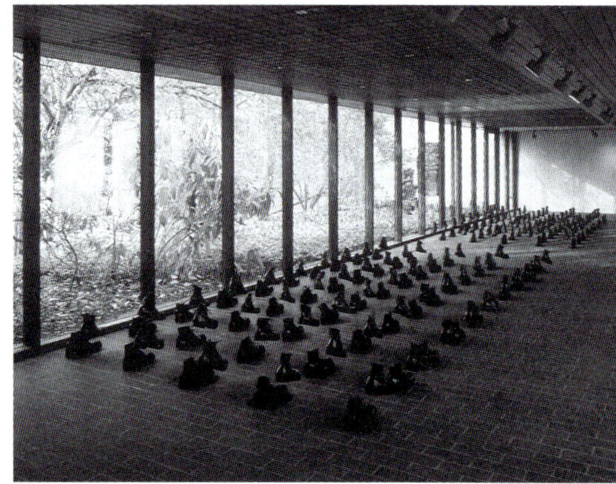

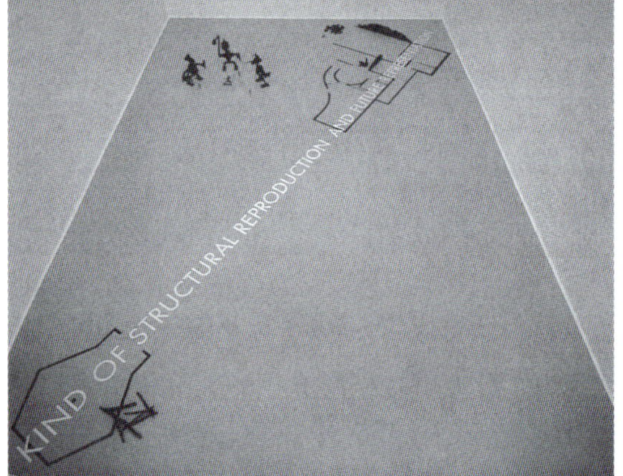

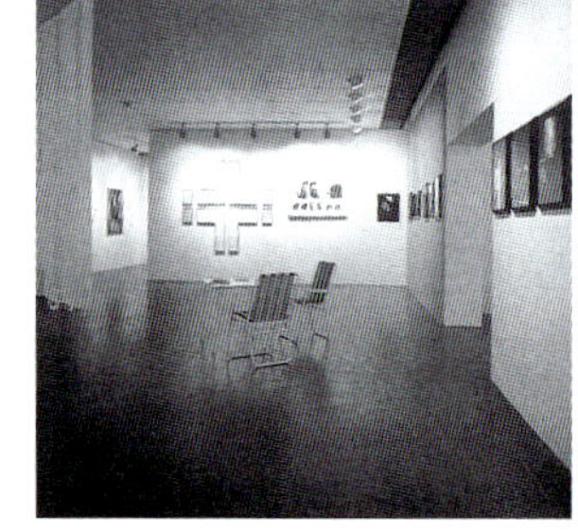

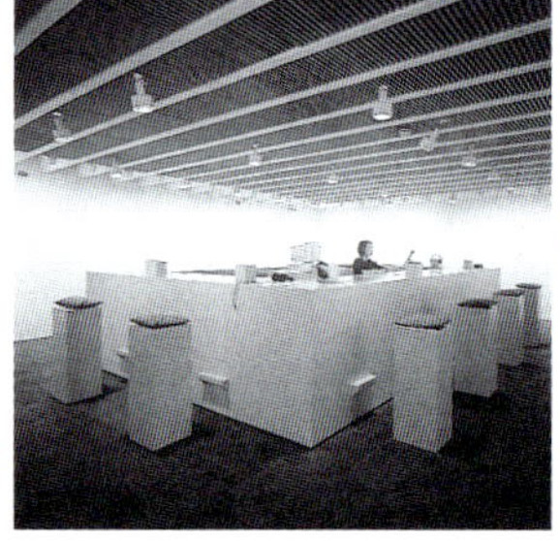

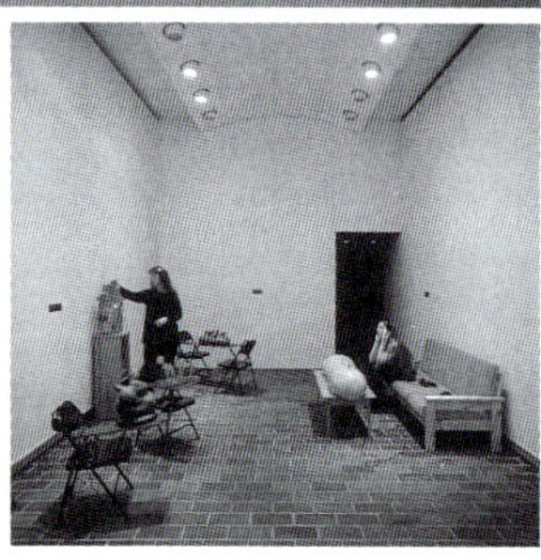

"What is Postmodernism"

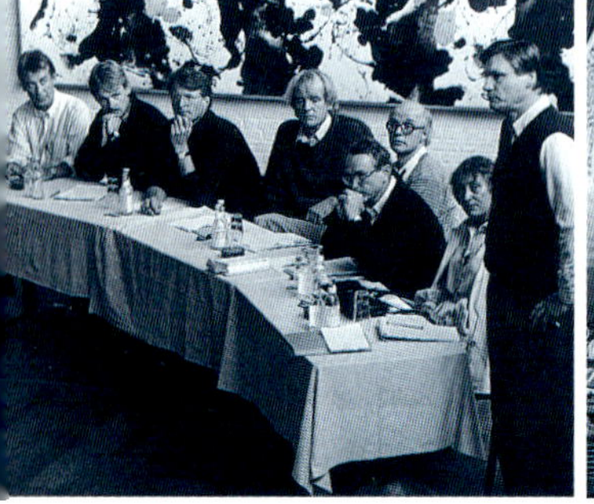

"Homo Decorans". Keith Haring painting

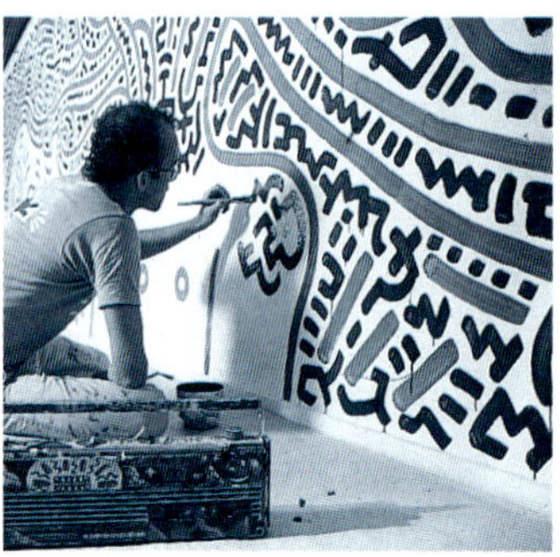

1986 Isabel Allende together with Knud W. Jensen and his daughter Sanne Bertram

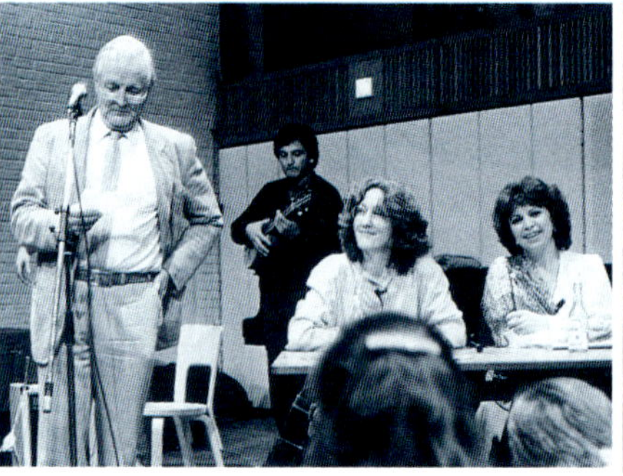

Chinese Dance

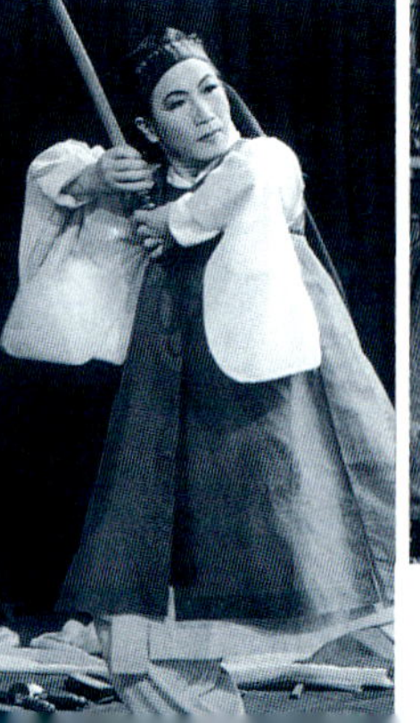

Jean Tinguely

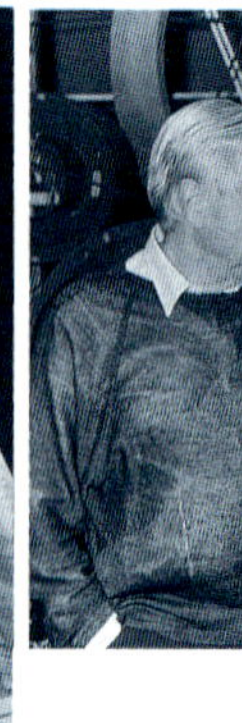

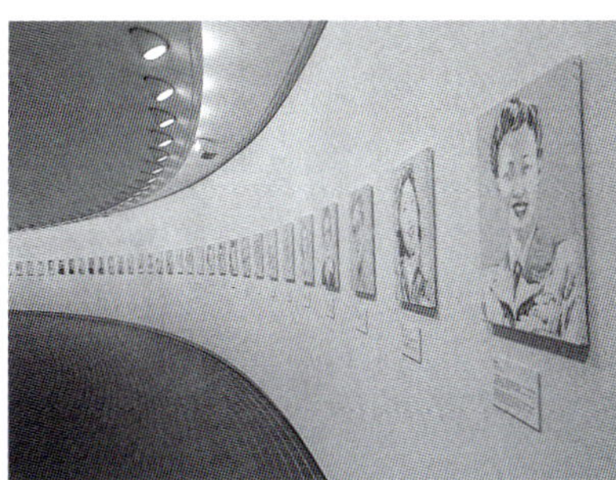

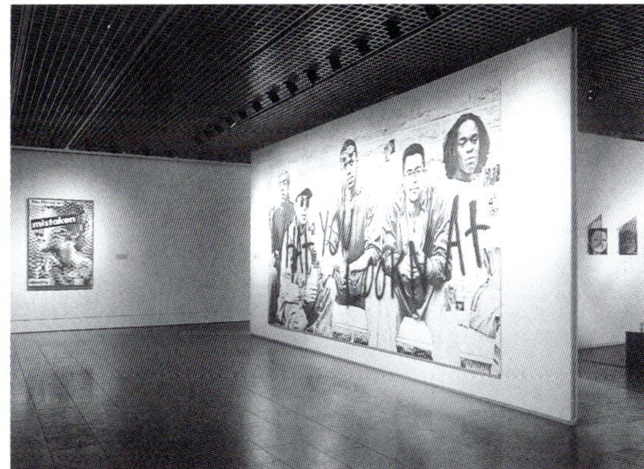

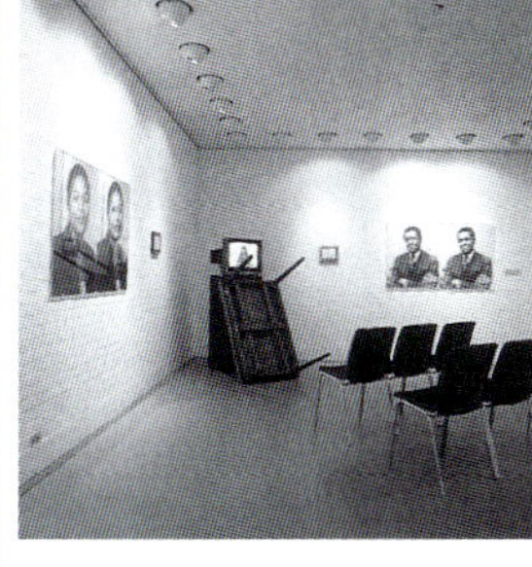

Mistaken Identities, 1993

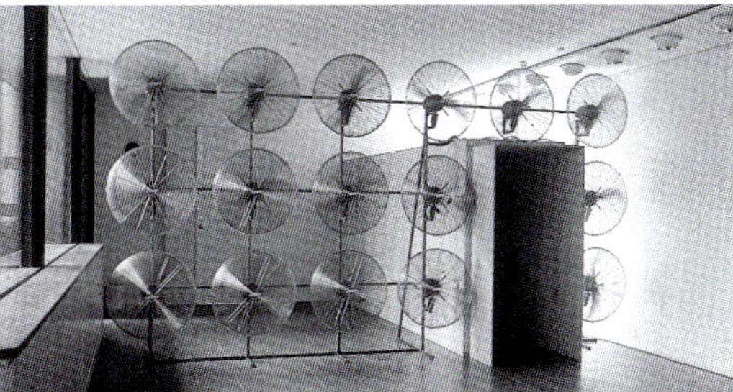

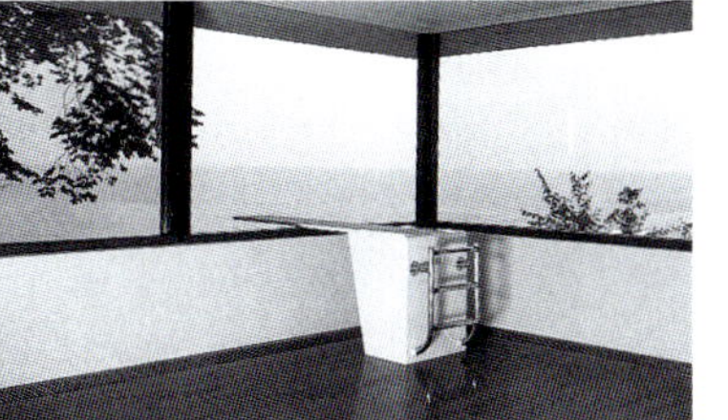

The Louisiana Exhibition 1997. New Art from Denmark and Scania, 1997

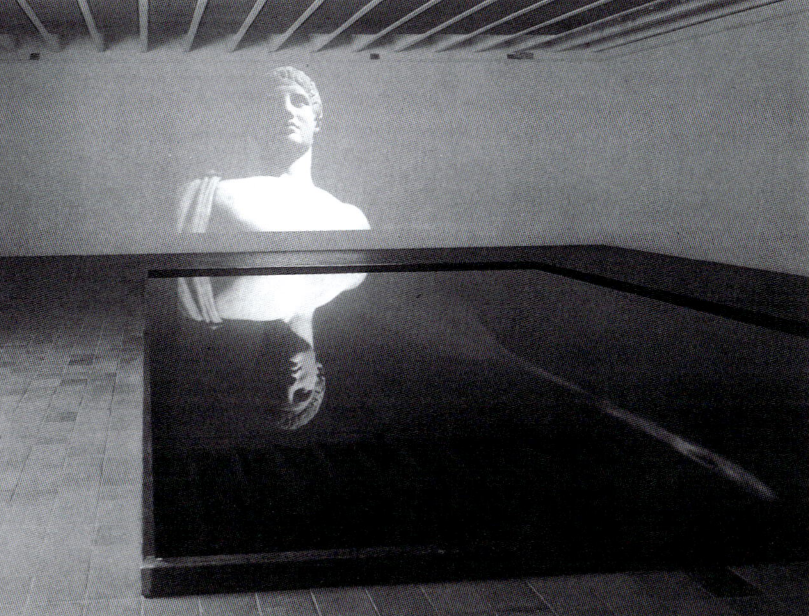

Borealis 4 – Installations in Space, 1989

Knud W. Jensen | 1987 "Camps"

A weekend for peace. Hearing with a. o. Nina Hagen

1988 Mario Merz

"Literature and Perestroika". Andrei Siniavski, Jury Afanasev and Fazil Iskander

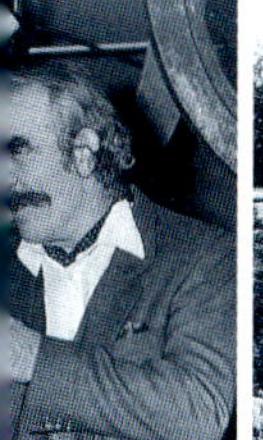

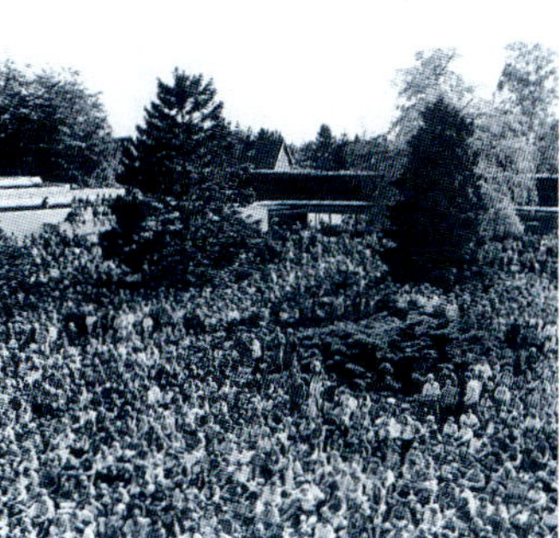

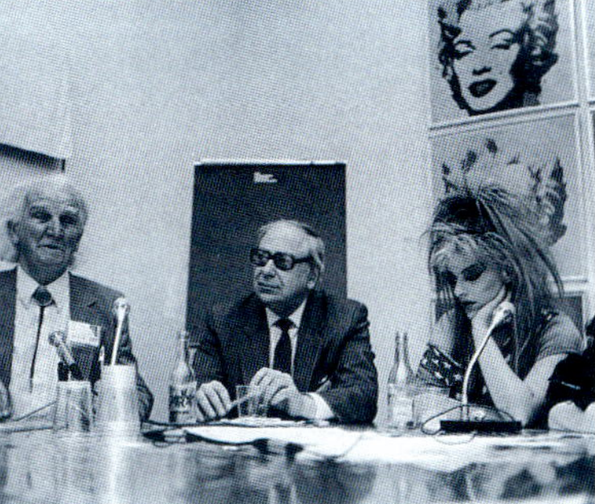

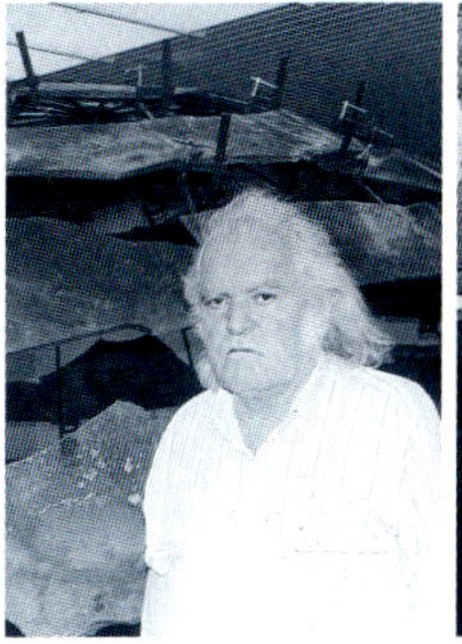

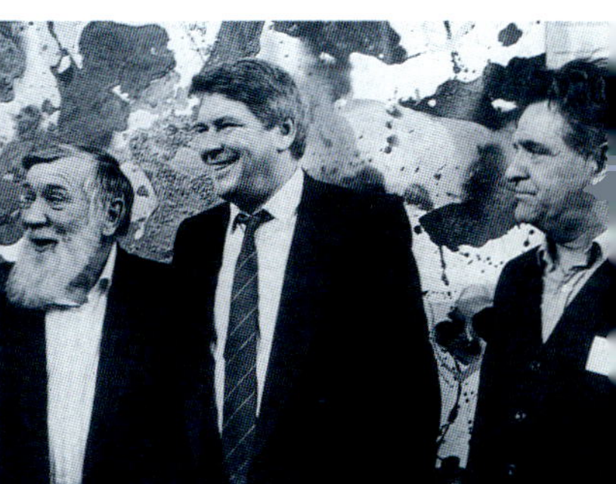

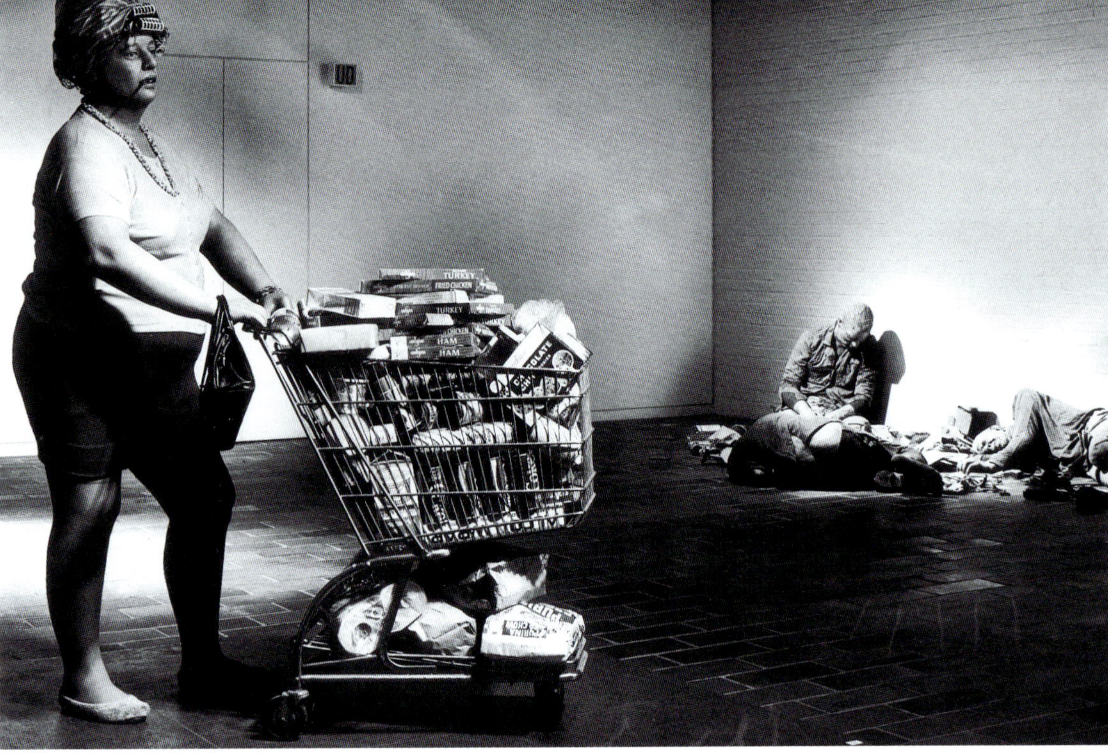
Extreme Realism, 1973

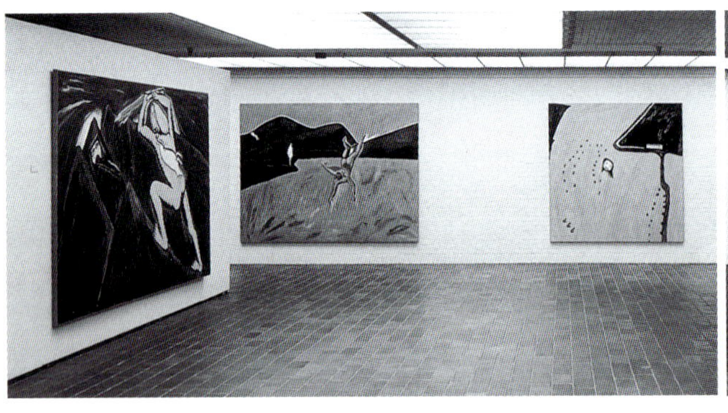
Chia – Clemente – Cucchi, 1983

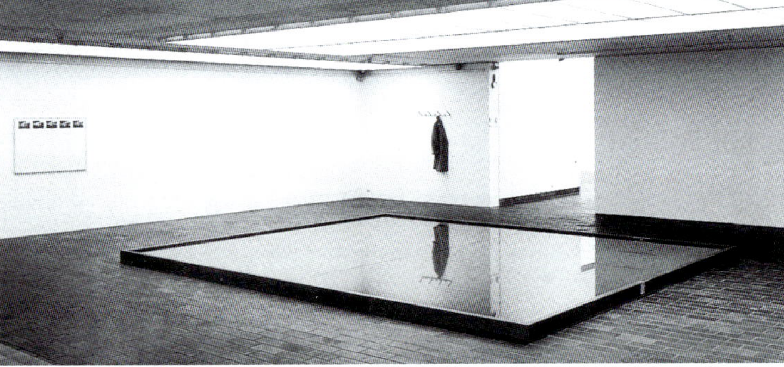
12 Contemporary Artists from Switzerland, 1989

1989 "Festival of Contemporary Music"

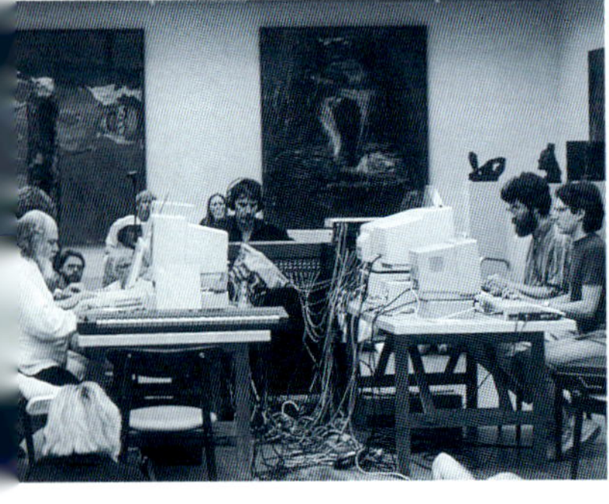

"New Art from Switzerland". Da Moto's Performance

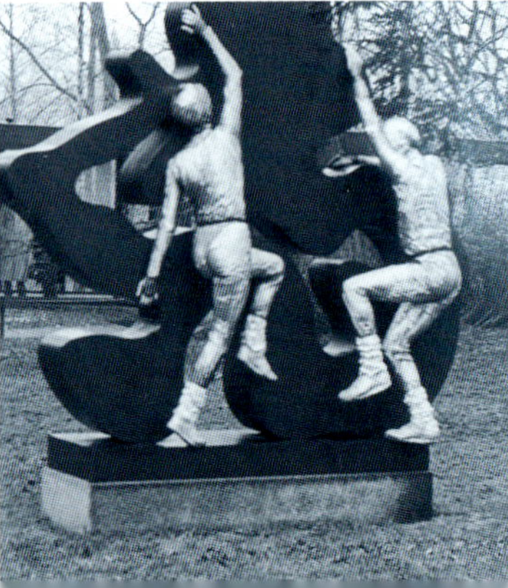

1990 The seminar "The Scandinavian Way and Perestroika"

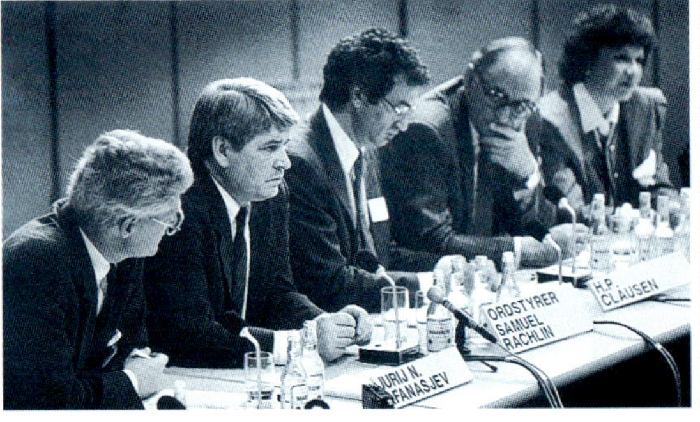

1991 Ib Michael

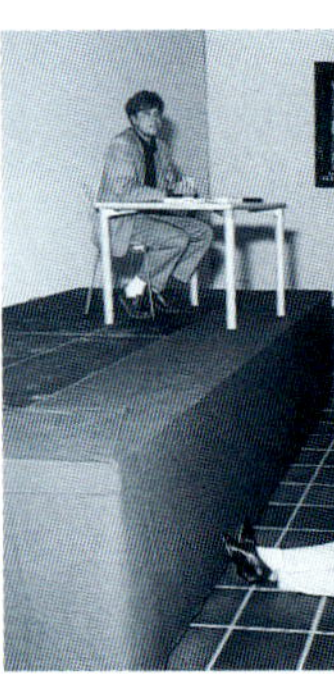

Erik Levine – Sculpture, 1989

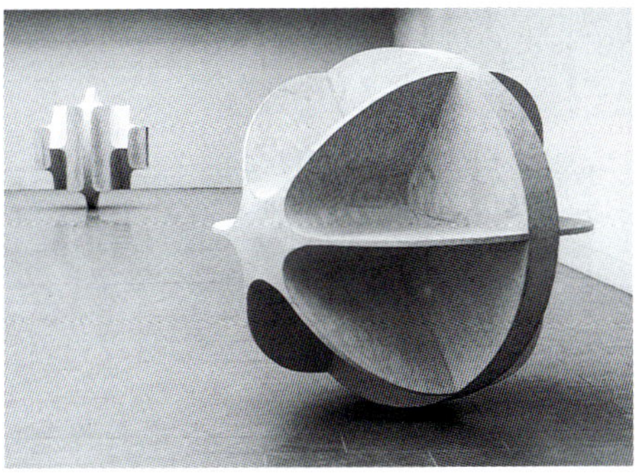

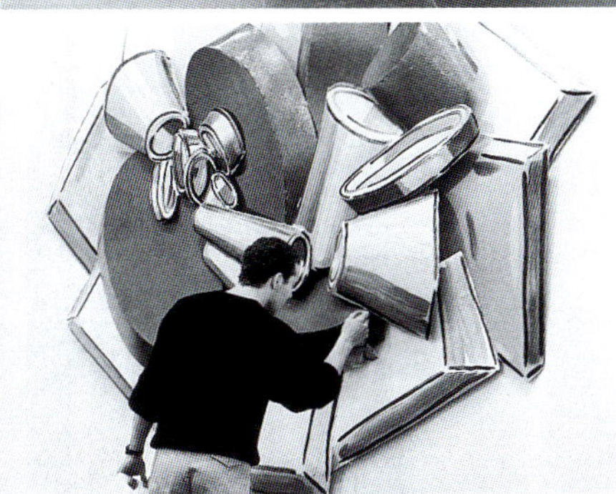

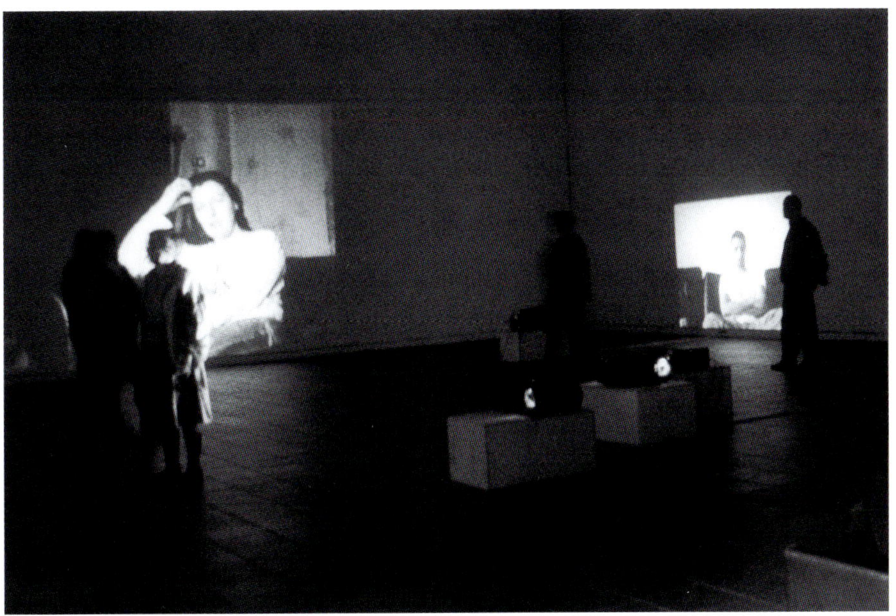

Sam Taylor-Wood, 1998

Sculpture – 9 Artists from Great Britain, 1986

New York Graffiti, 1984

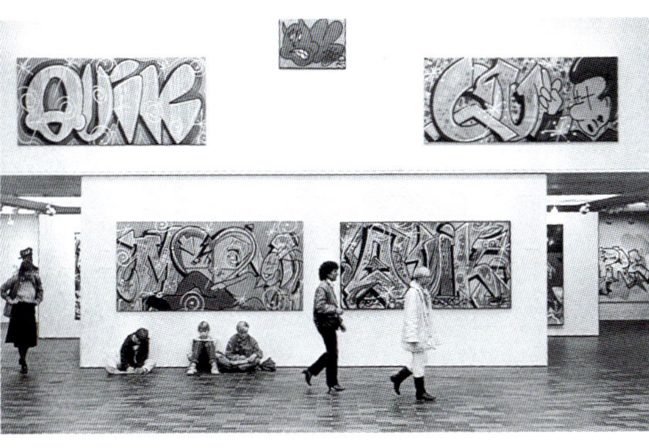

Enzo Cucchi – Drawings, 1988

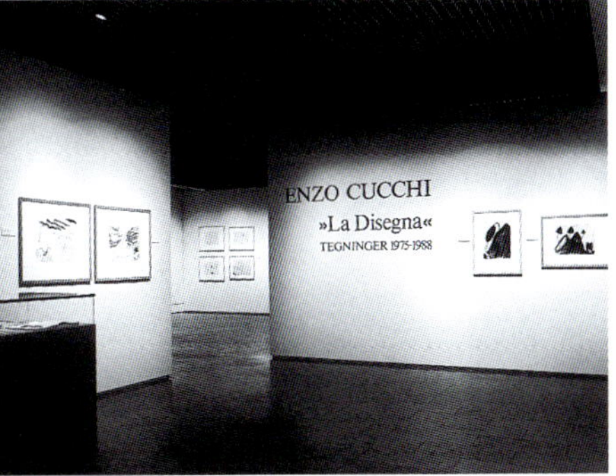

The inauguration of the Graphics Wing. Herbert Pundik and Kurt Fromberg

1992 "Authors' Meeting". Tage Skou Hansen "My Balcony Flower Box". Children's theatre

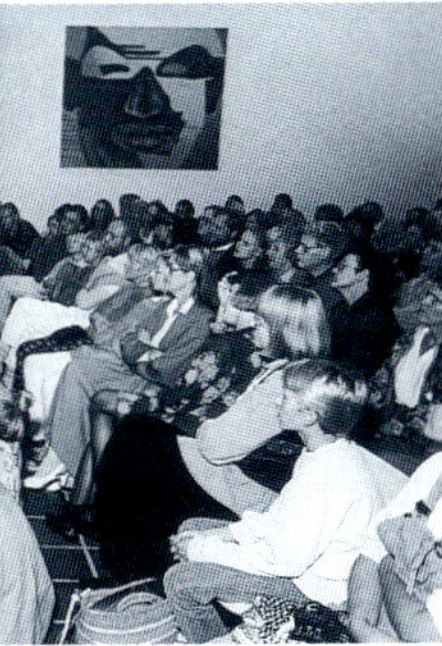

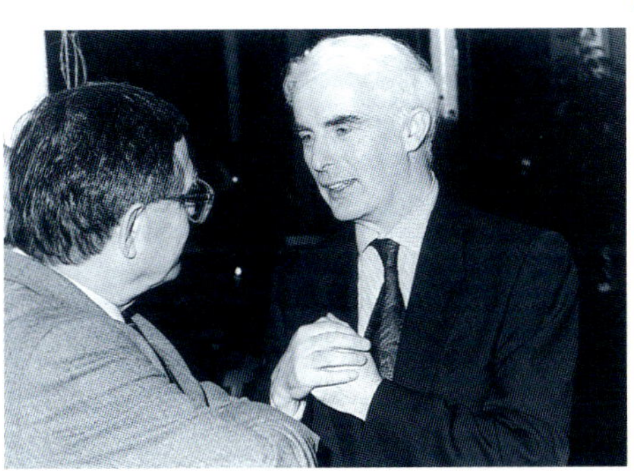

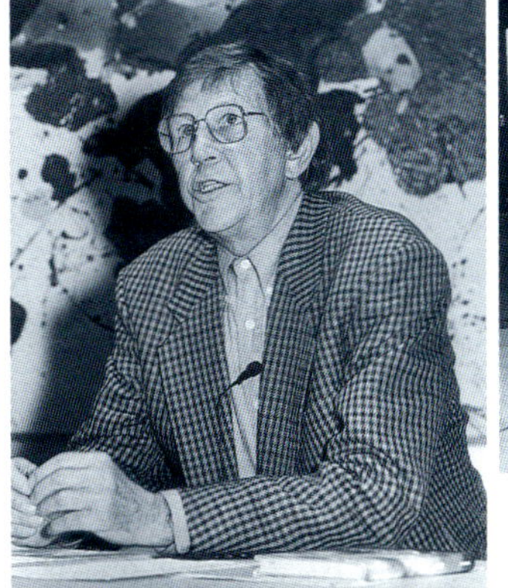

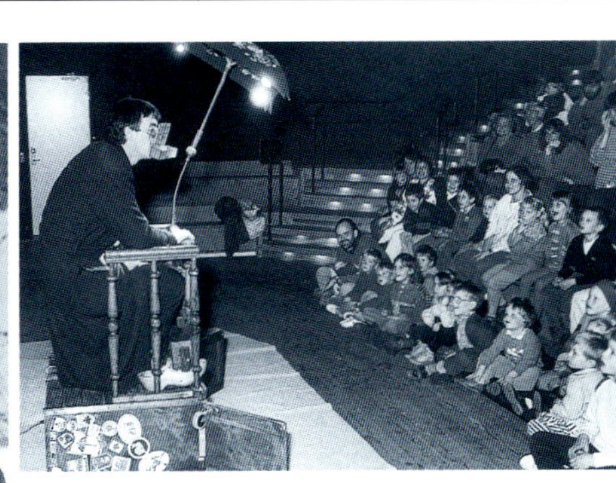

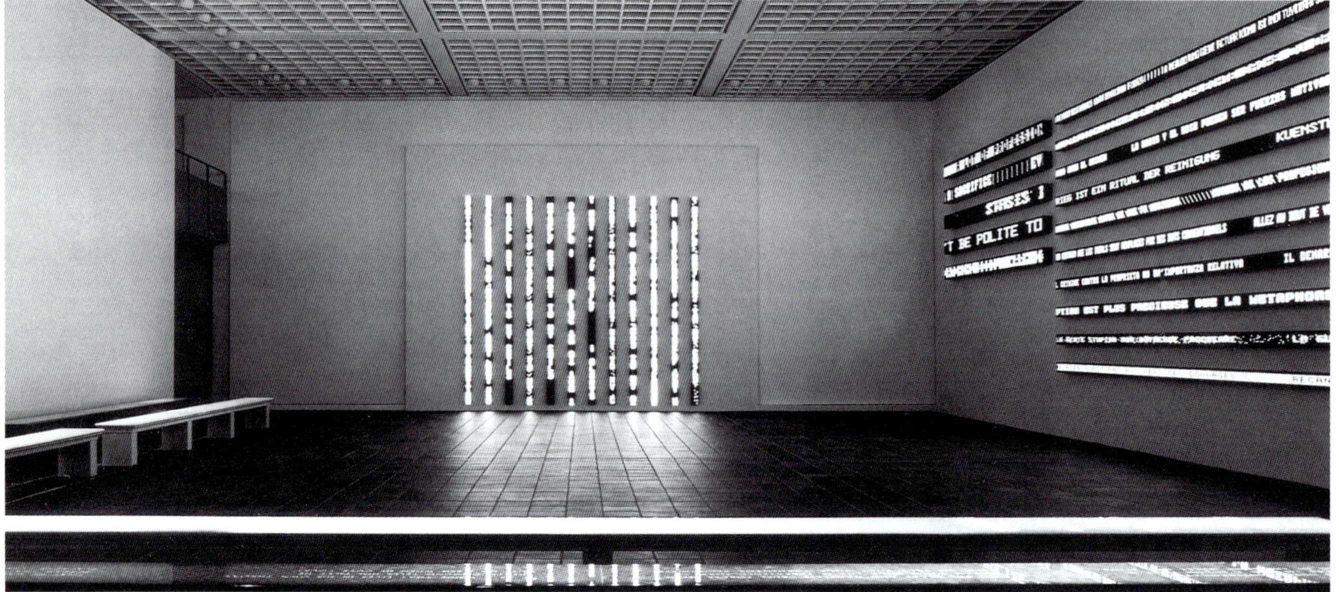

Jenny Holzer – The Venice Installation, 1991

Robert Irwin, 1982

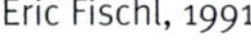

Eric Fischl, 1991

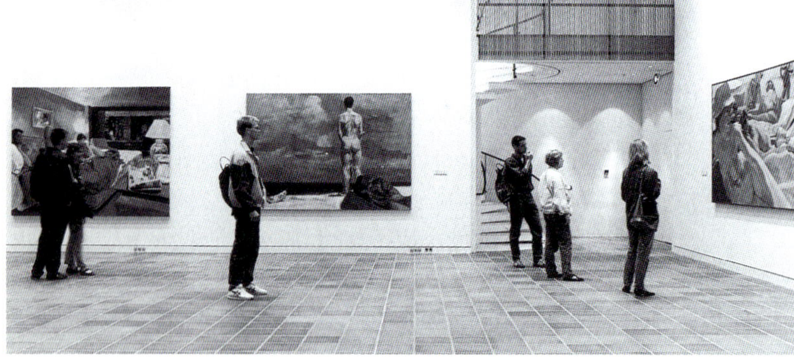

President Mario Soares, Mrs. Soares and Steingrim Laursen

Meeting in the museum's Boat House. Salman Rushdie

1993 The symposium "Art and Advertising" including a. o. Jeff Koons

Midsummer Night. Suzanne Brøgger

The Paul Hammerich

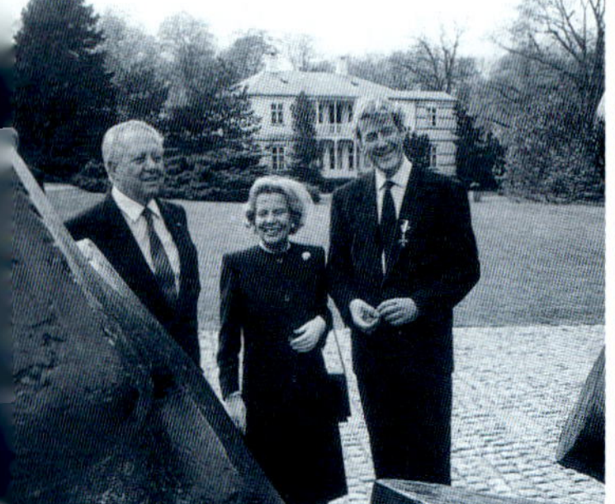

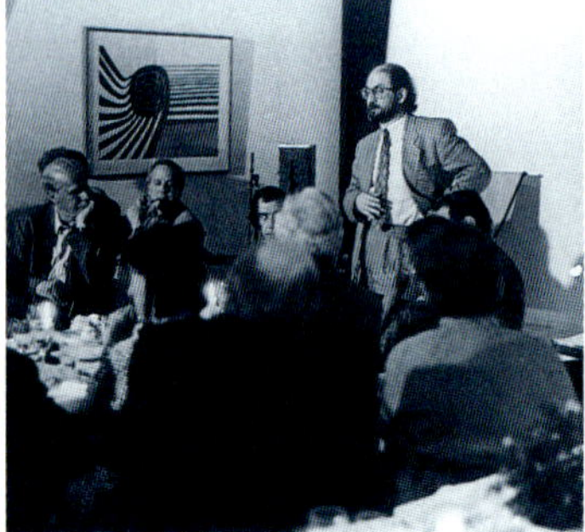

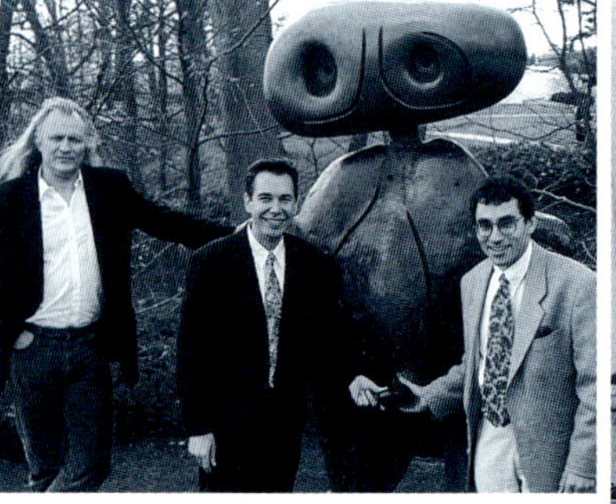

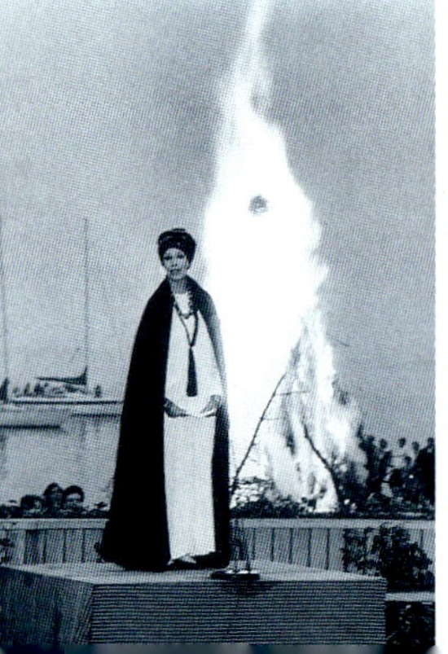

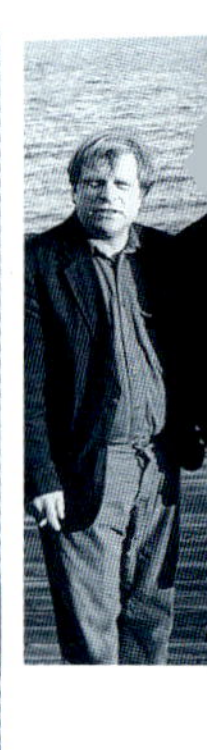

Jana Sterbak, 1993

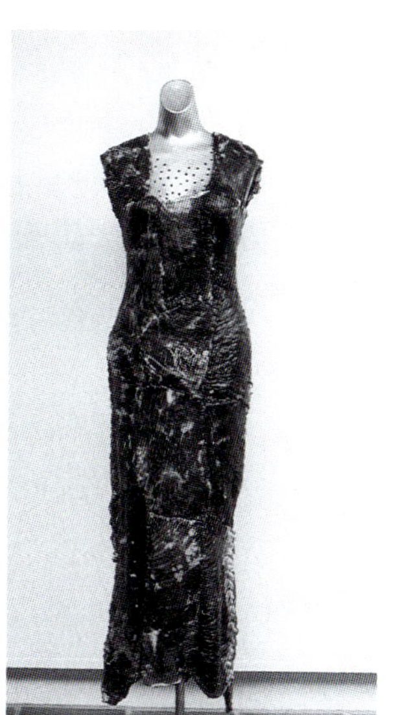

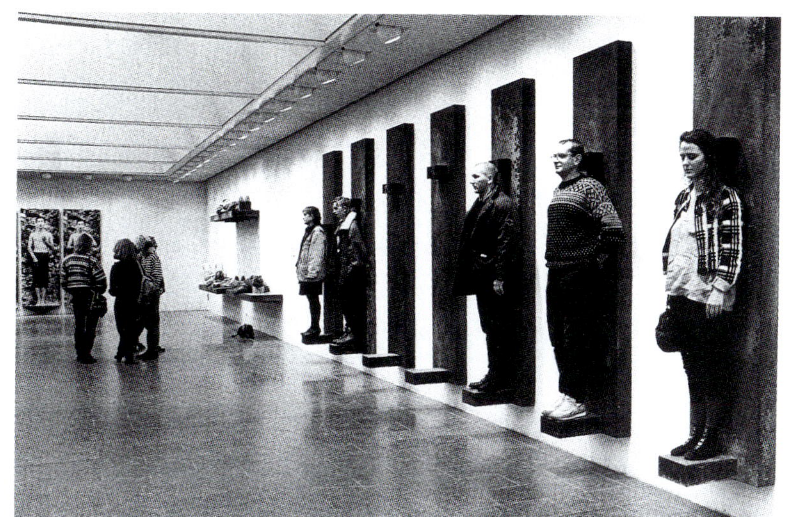

Marina Abramovic/Ulay "The Lovers – The Great Walk", 1990

Antony Gormley – Sculpture, 1989

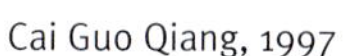

Cai Guo Qiang, 1997

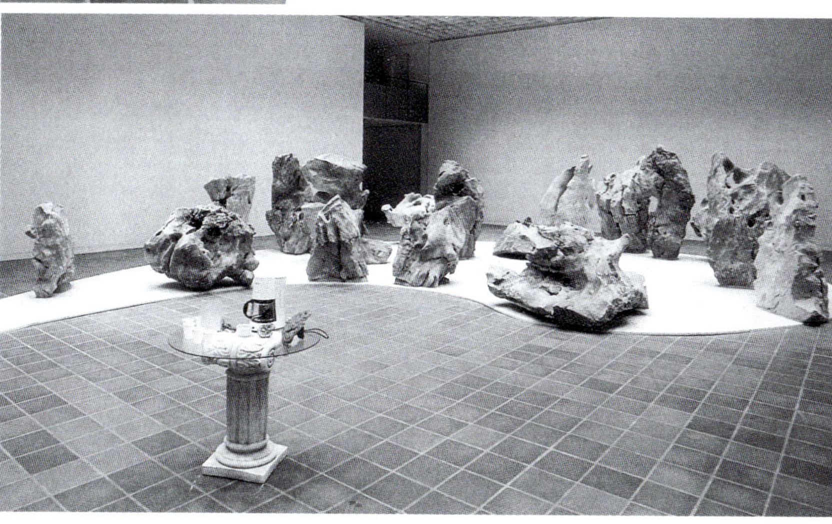

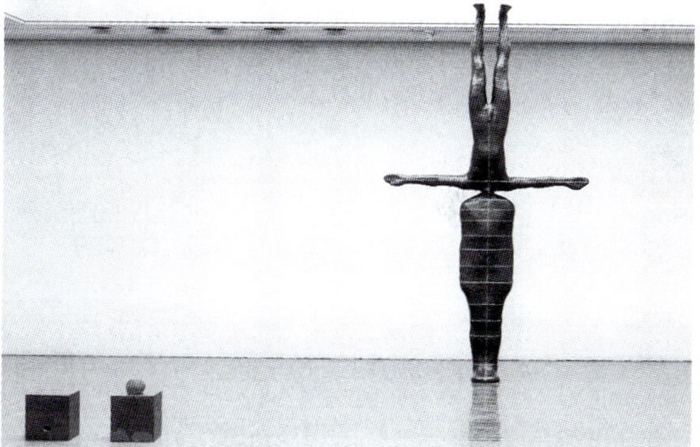

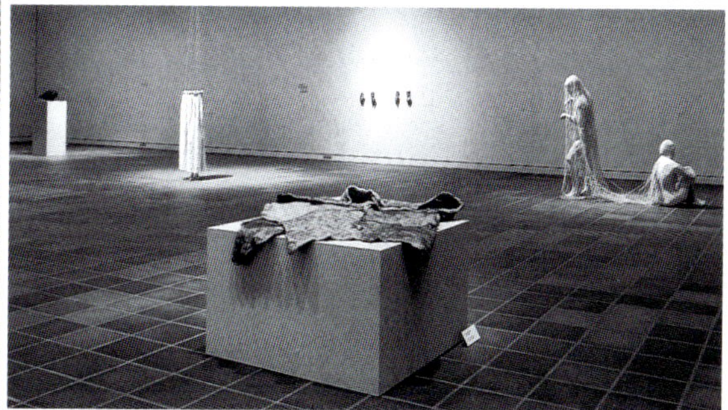

Kiki Smith, 1994

Award to Suzanne Brøgger

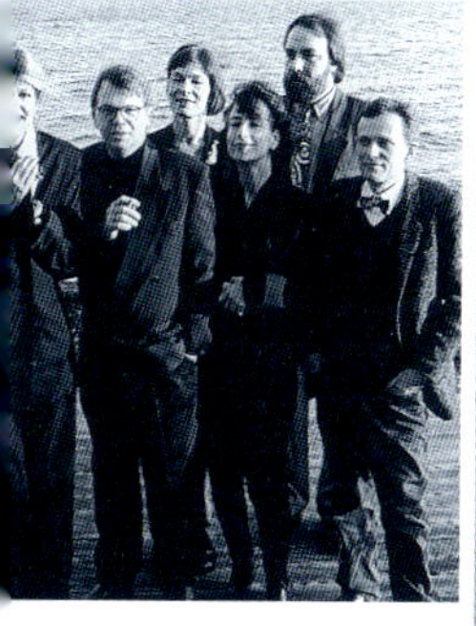

Germaine Greer

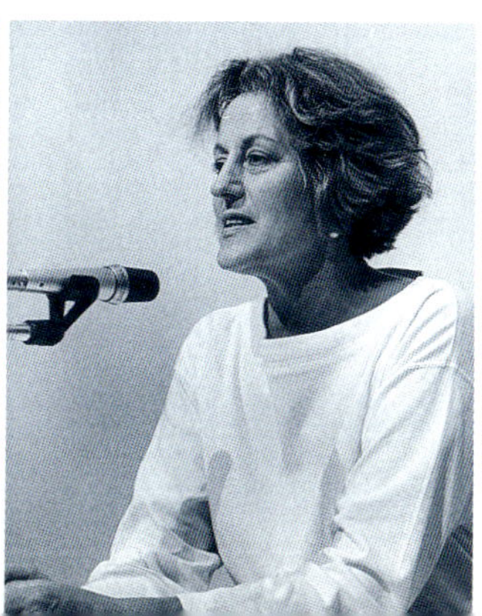

1994 Kiki Smith

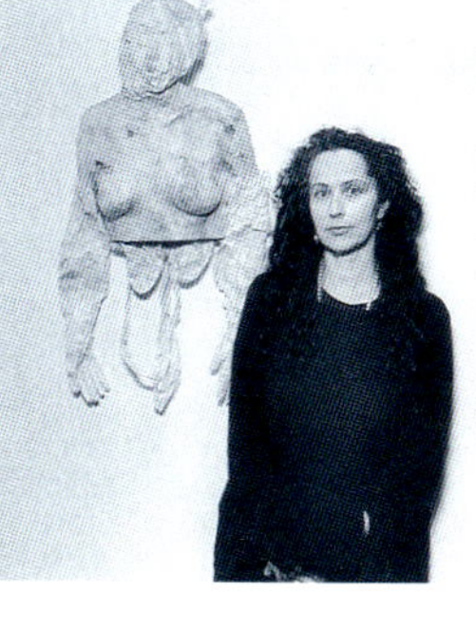

Allan Philip

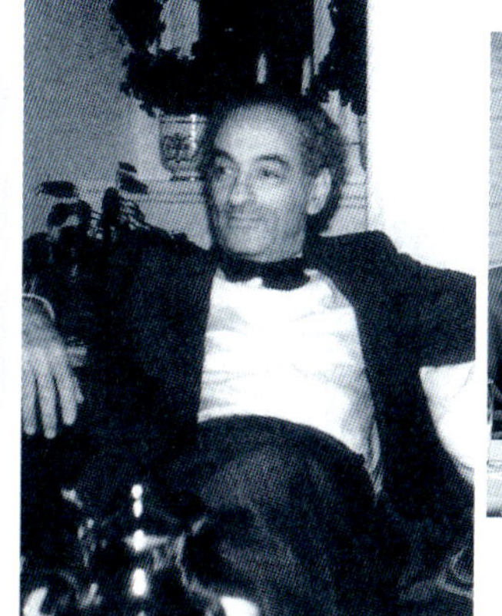

Isabel Allende and Bille August

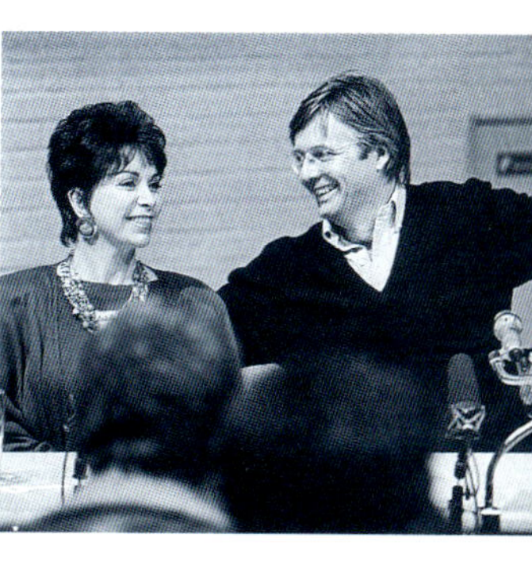

Architecture & Design

1961	"The Glass"
1964	Visionary Architecture
	Danish Architecture Abroad
1969	Architecture without Architects
1973	Public Design in Holland
1974	Anonymous Design
1977	Alternative Architecture
1979	Italian Design
1980	Meet the Architects
1980	The Architect as Designer
1981	The House as Image
1982	Poul Kjærholm 1950-80
1990	Innovation via Design
	The ID Prize 25 Years
1996	Design and Identity
	– Aspects of European Design

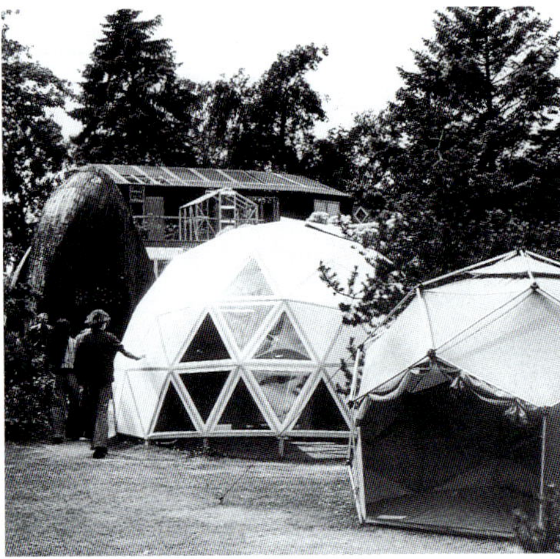

Alternative Architecture, 1977

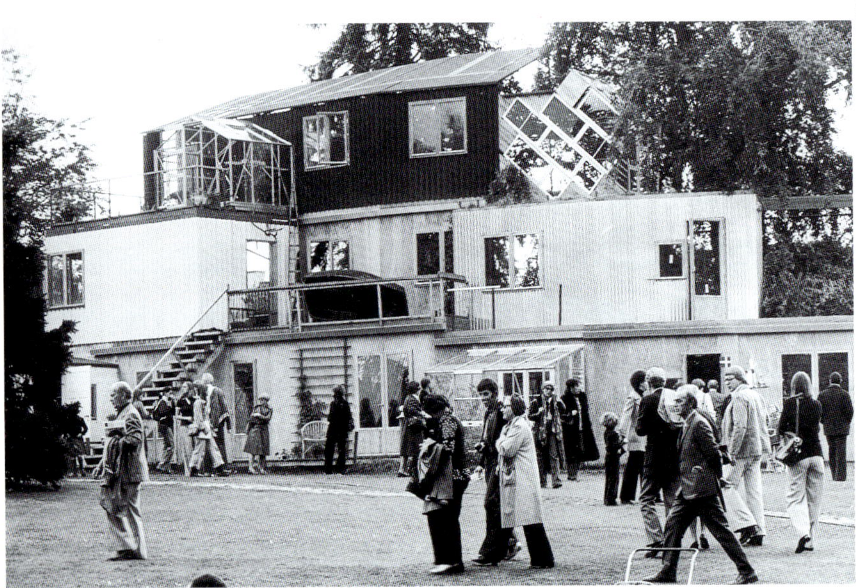

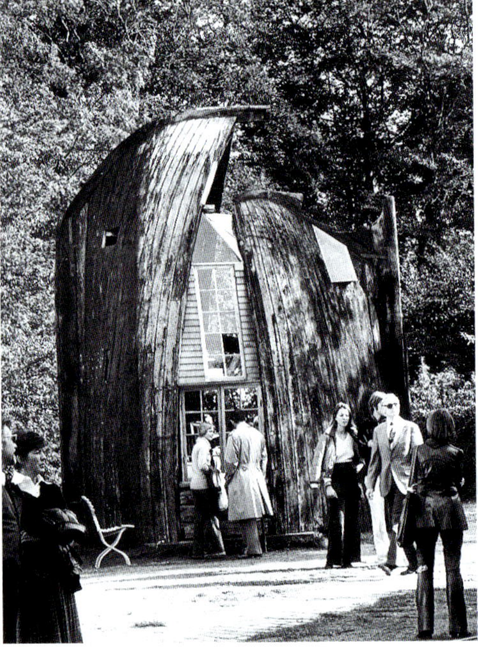

"To be or not to be European" – symposium. Øystein Hjort, Robert Storr, Peter Schjeldahl and Per Kirkeby

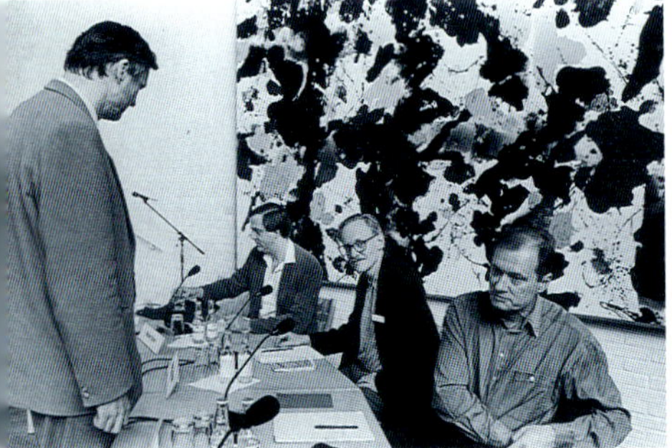

Gavin Jantjes and Lars Nittve

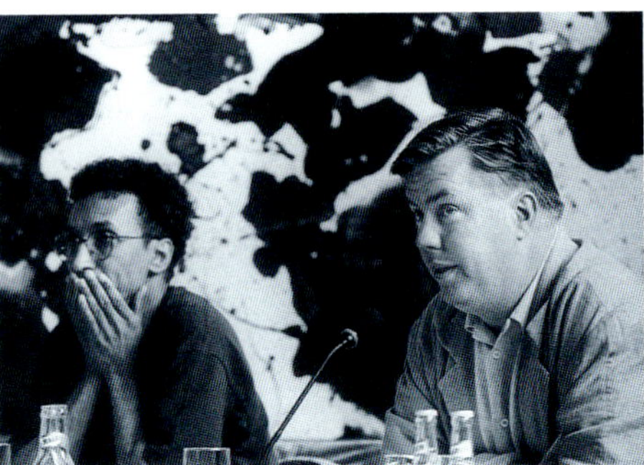

Knud W. Jensen

Erik Holm

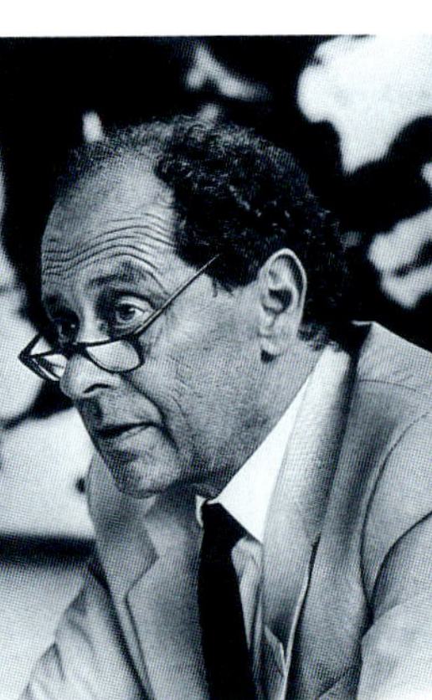

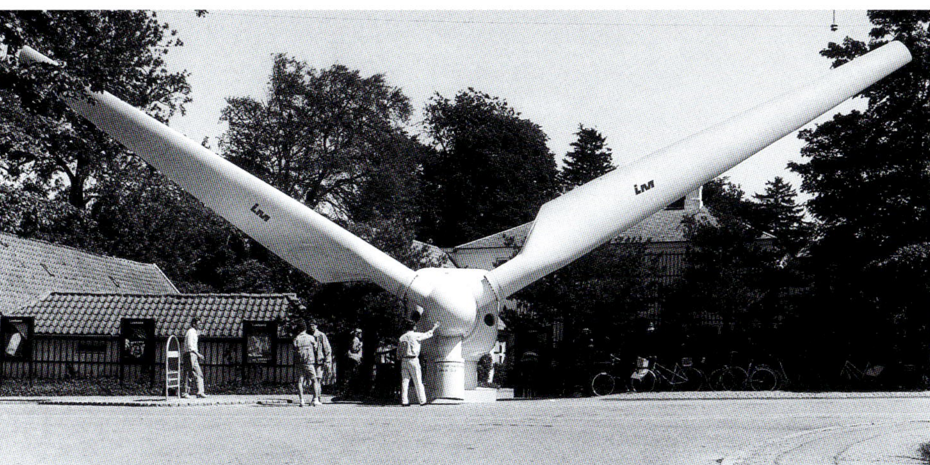

Innovation via Design
The ID Prize 25 Years, 1990

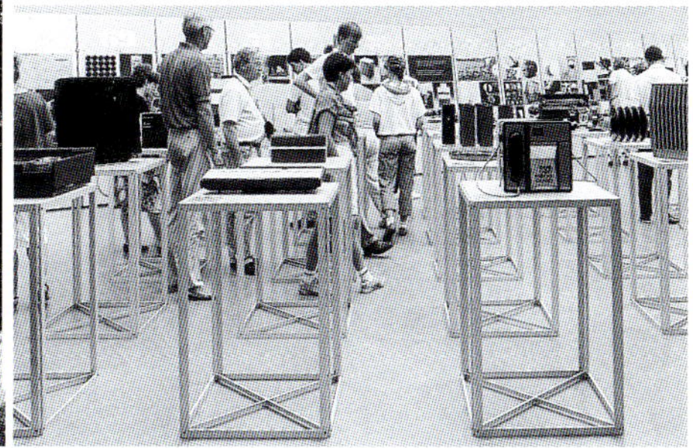

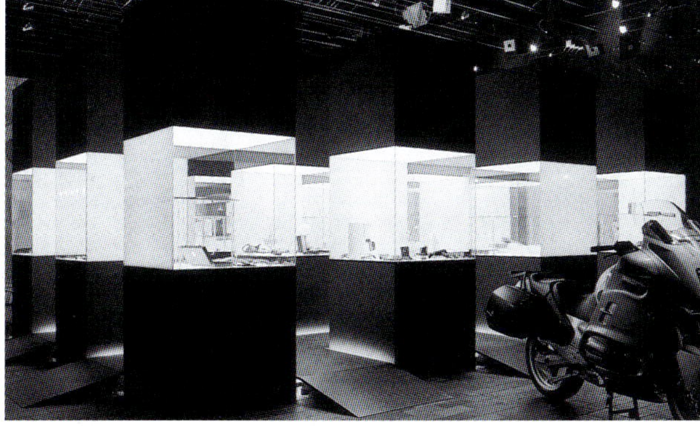

Design and Identity
– Aspects of European Design, 1996

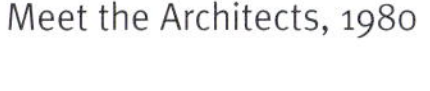

Meet the Architects, 1980

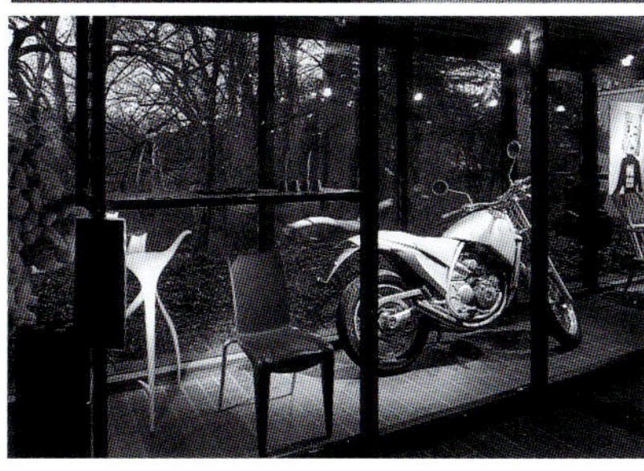

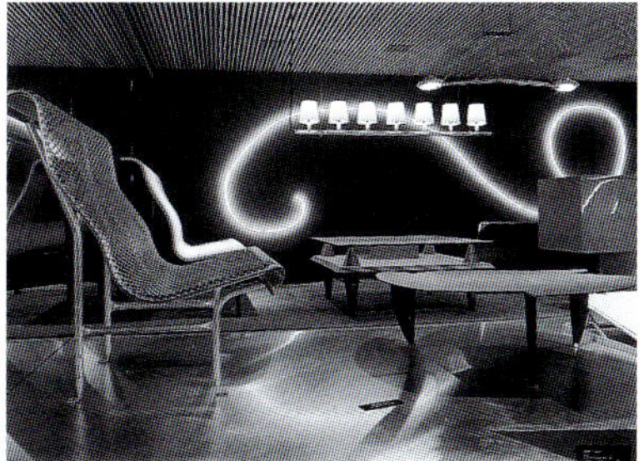

Inauguration of the Children's Wing

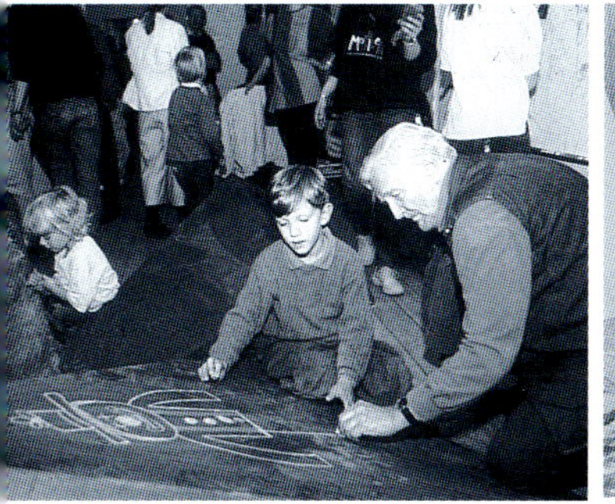

Workshop in the Children's Wing with Bjørn Nørgaard

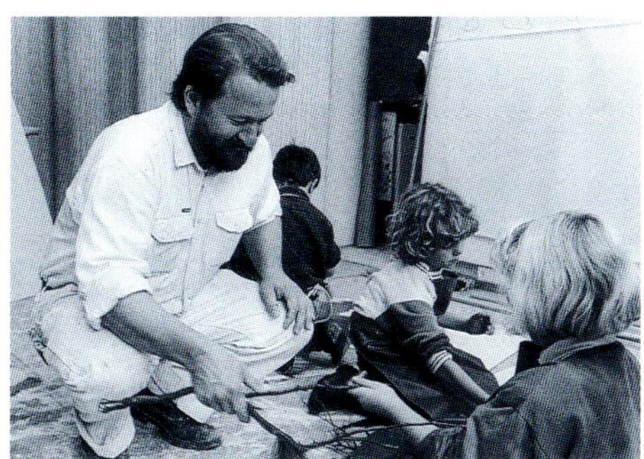

Jana Sterbak, Anneli Fuchs and Steingrim Laursen

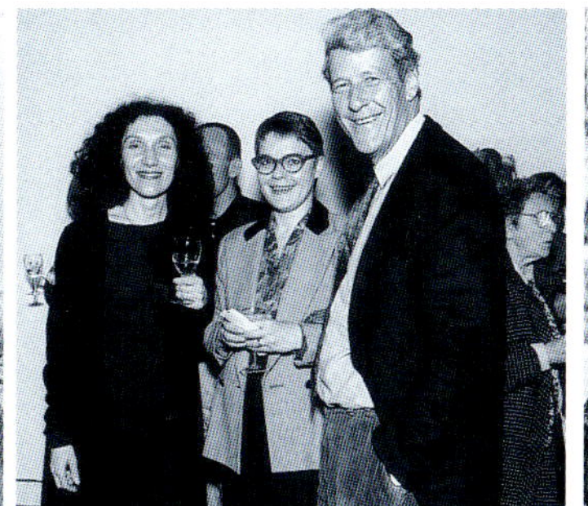

1995 Hugo Arne Buch

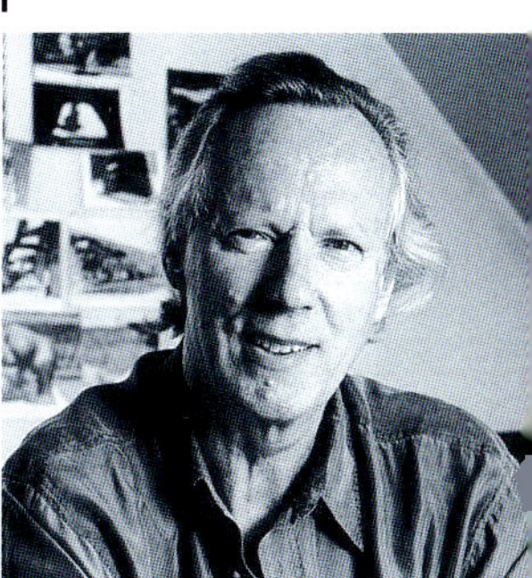

Architecture & Design

The House as Image, 1981

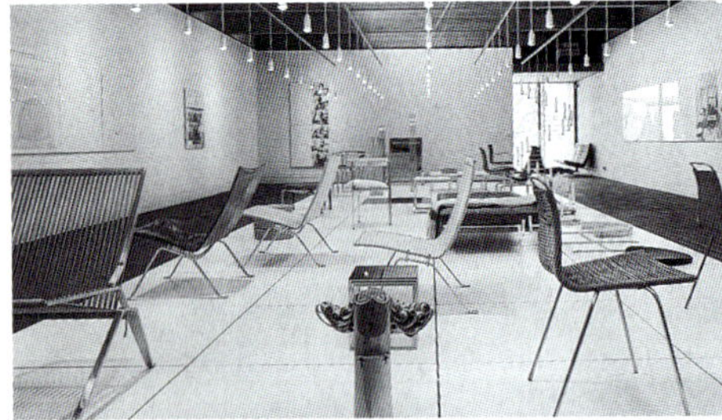

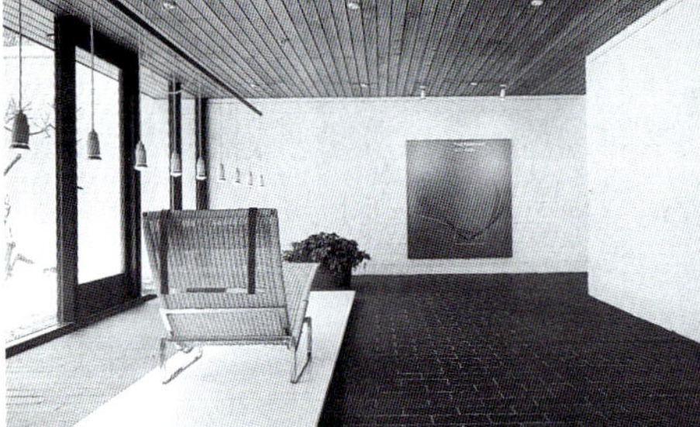

Poul Kjærholm 1950-80, 1982

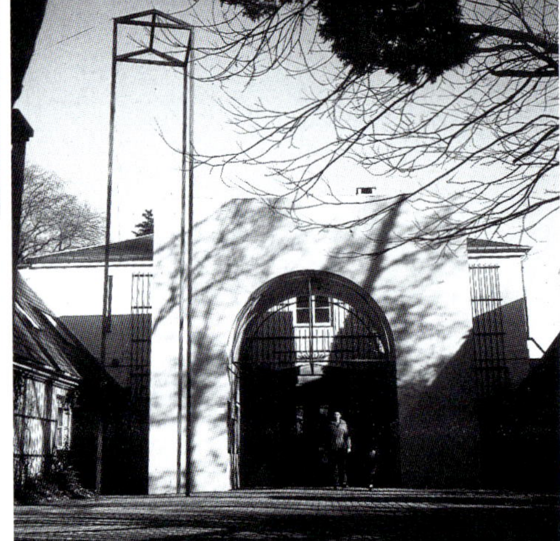

The House as Image, 1981

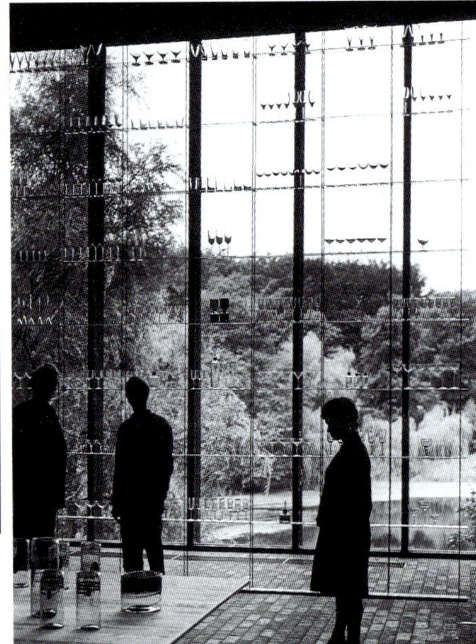

"The Glass", 1961

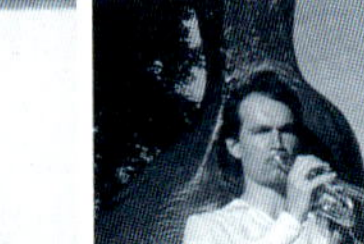

Ivry Gitlis

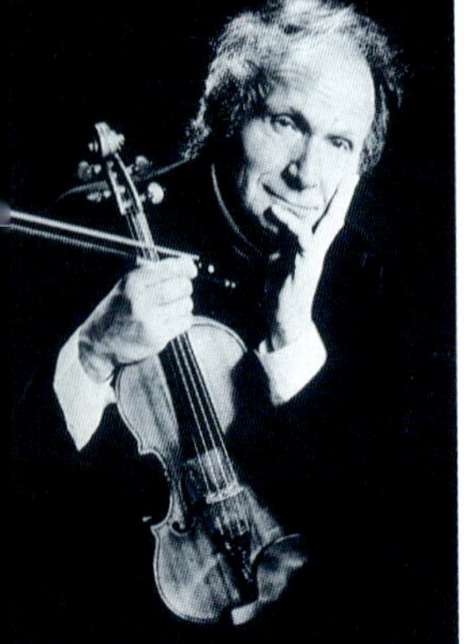

Presenting the Paul Hammerich Award.
Klaus Rifbjerg and Knud W. Jensen

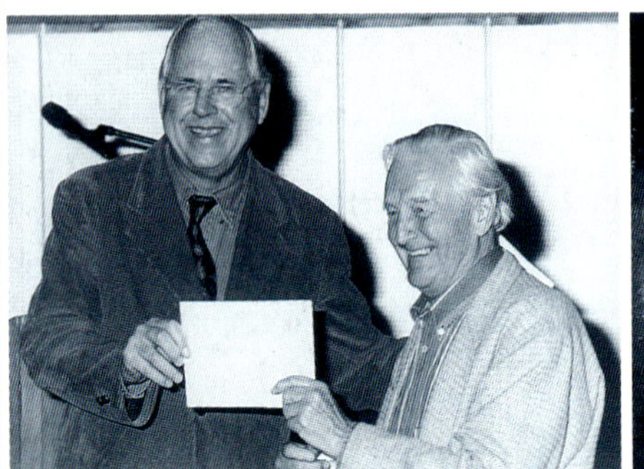

Marcus Stockhausen and Die Michaels Trompeter

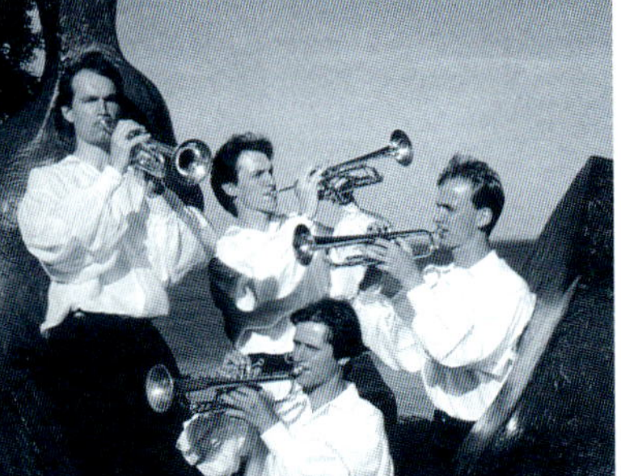

1996 Louisiana Museum Art Ensemble

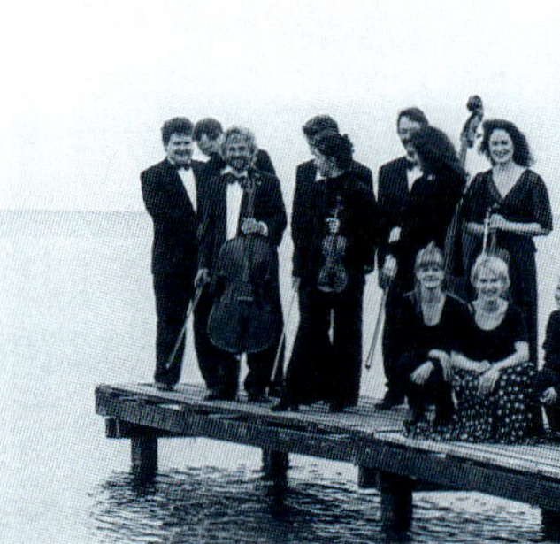

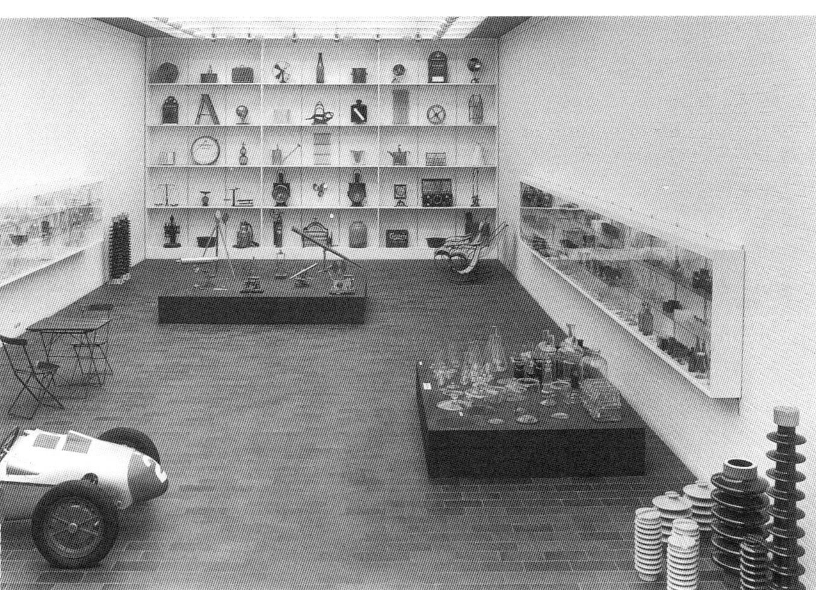

Anonymous Design, 1974

The Architect as Designer, 1980

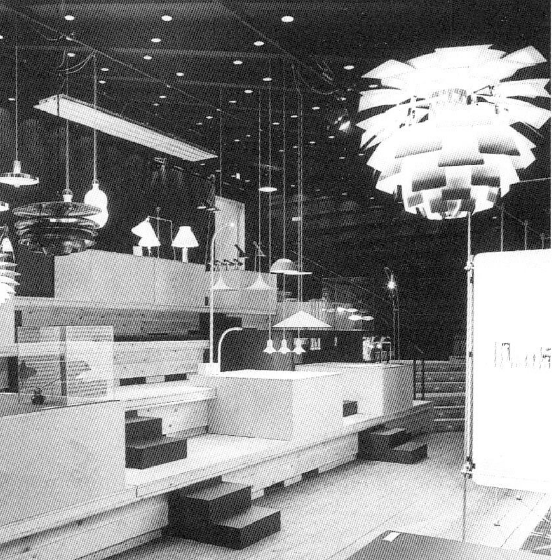

Anonymous Design, 1974

Italian Design, 1979

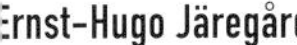

Ernst-Hugo Järegård

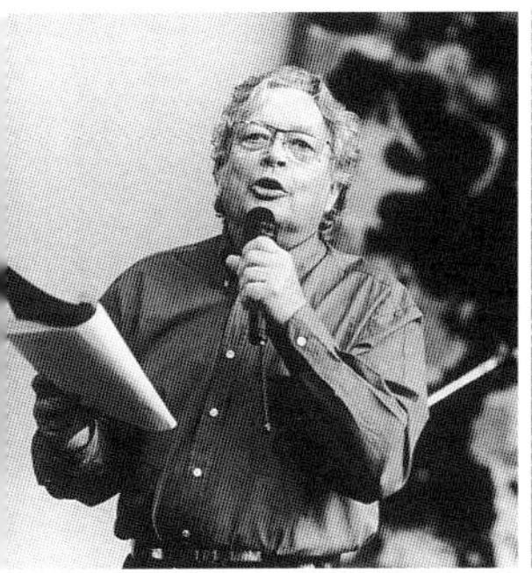

The Paul Hammerich Award. Bodil Kjær

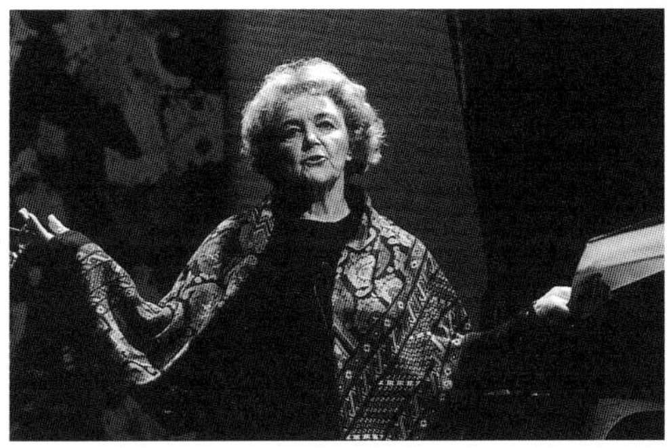

Morten Sabroe and Herbert Pundik at the presentation of the Paul Hammerich Award

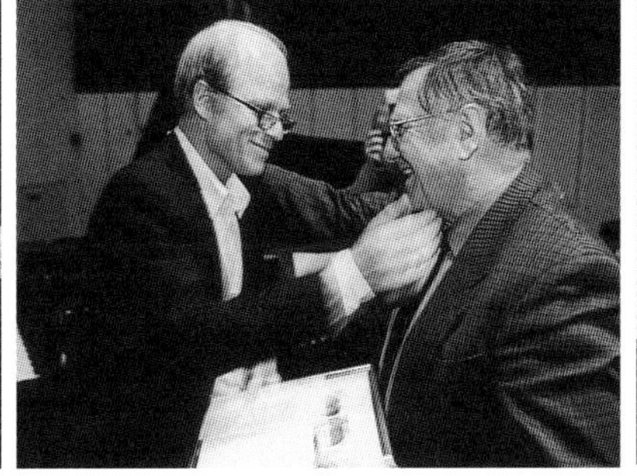

"NowHere". The team of curators with Lars Nittve in the front row

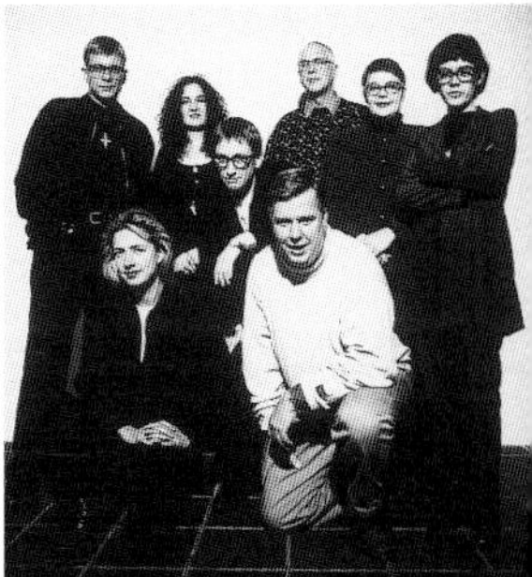

Photography

1964 Photographs: "What is Man?"
1967 Portrait of Carl Th. Dreyer
1972 "Projection"
1972 Asta Nielsen
1973 Eisenstein
1973 Visible-Invisible
New Scientific Photography
1973 Lennart Nilsson
1974 Fellini
1980 American Photography 1920-40
1981 Mirrors and Windows:
American Photography after 1960
1983 Henri Cartier-Bresson, Photographer
1984 The Frozen Image
– Scandinavian Photography
1985 Lucas Samaras:
Polaroid Photographs 1969-1983
1985 Georg Oddner
– Photographic Pictures 1955-85
1986 Yoshiaki Tono: Aquademic Photographs
1987 ¡Tierra y Libertad! Photographs of
Mexico 1900-1935
1988 Irving Penn – Photography
1988 Robert Capa – A Retrospective
1988 Blow Up
1989 Master Photographers 1959-88
1989 Yousuf Karsh
1990 Poetry and Reality – Post-Revolution
Soviet Photography
1990 Walker Evans: American Photographs
1991 Imogen Cunningham/Frontiers
– Photographs 1906-76
1991 The World as Seen by
Magnum Photographers
1992 Robert Mapplethorpe
– A Retrospective
1992 Jeff Wall
1992 William Eggleston
– Ancient and Modern.
Colour Photographs
1993 Wim Wenders: Film and Photo
1994 BILD
Photography in Contemporary
German Art
1994 Duane Michals
Photography and Reality
1995 Lewis Baltz
1995 Borealis 7 – Desire
1997 FLAMINGO
Robert Frank Photographs 1948-96

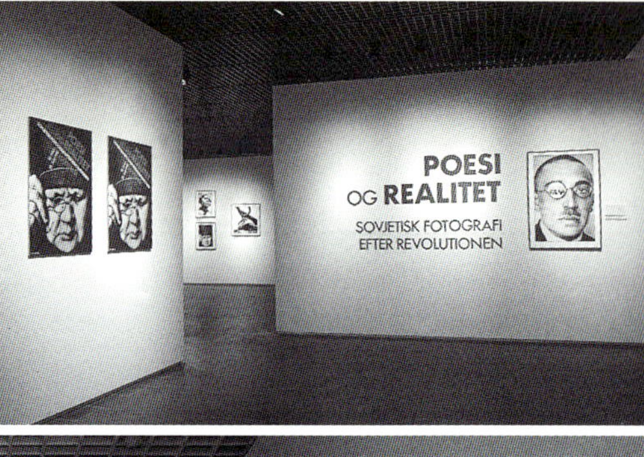

Poetry and Reality – Post-Revolution Soviet Photography, 1990

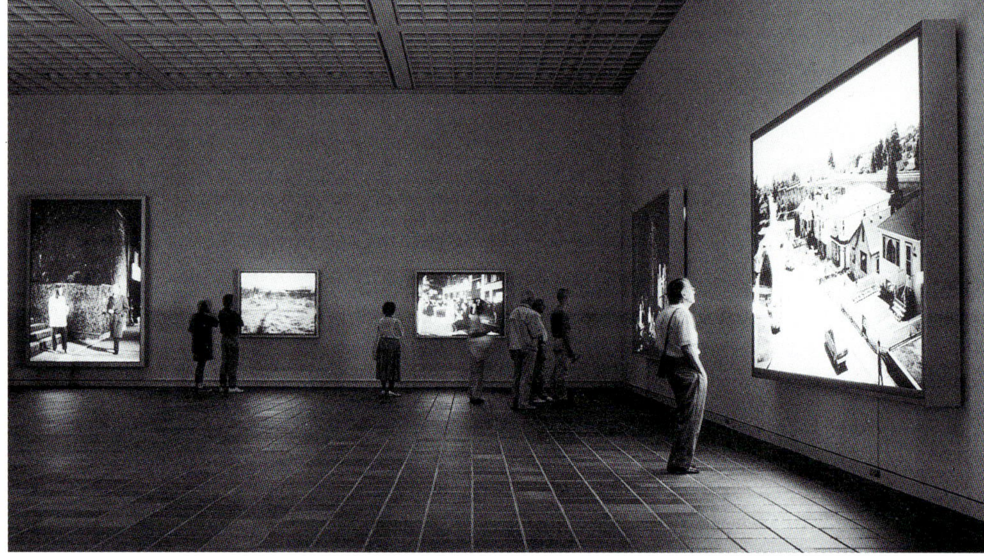
Jeff Wall, 1992

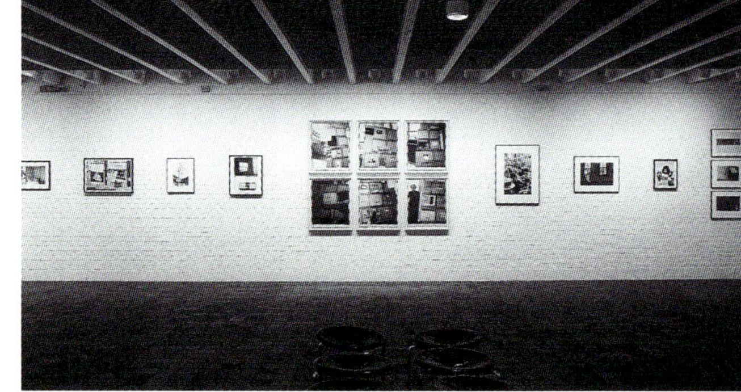
FLAMINGO. Robert Frank Photographs 1948-96, 1997

Cristina Lage Hansen

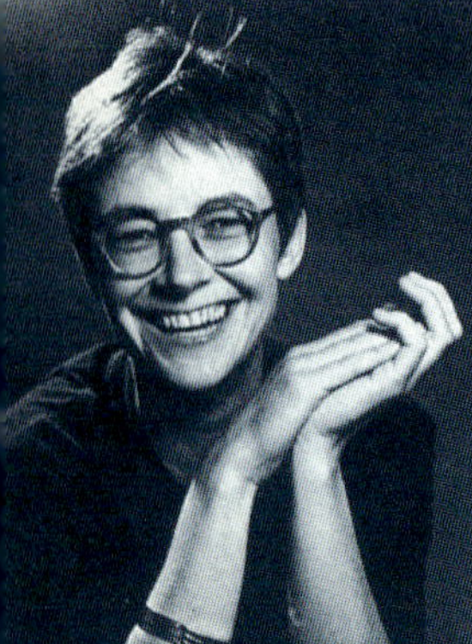

From the exhibition "NowHere", section "Get Lost"

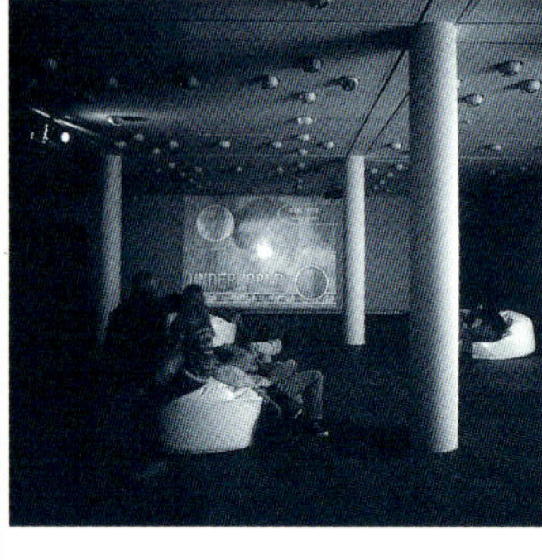

1997 The violoncellist Ralph Kirshbaum. Master Class

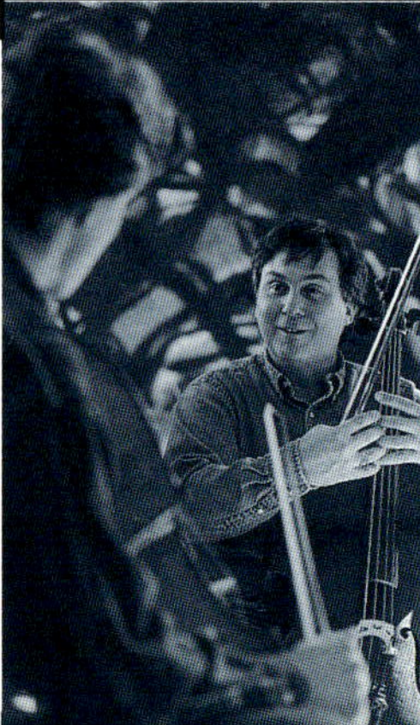

Dr. Roger Goepper and Kjeld Kjeldsen in Beijing

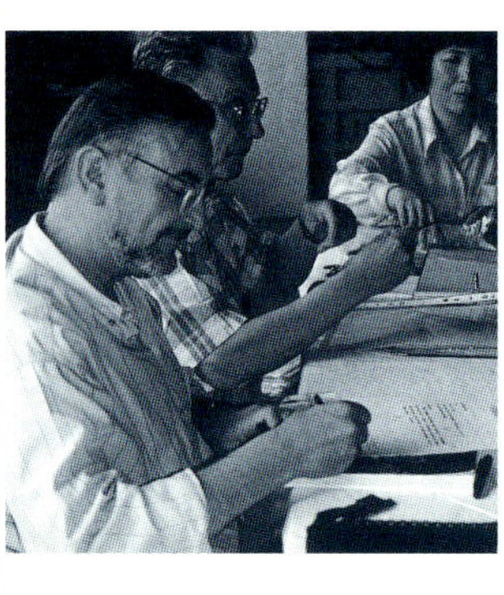

Lars Nittve

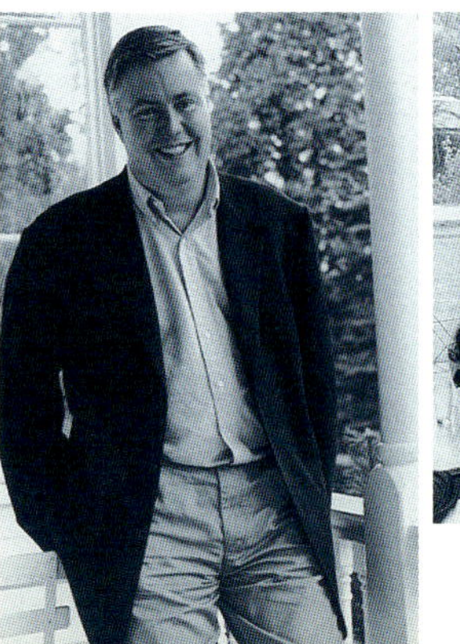

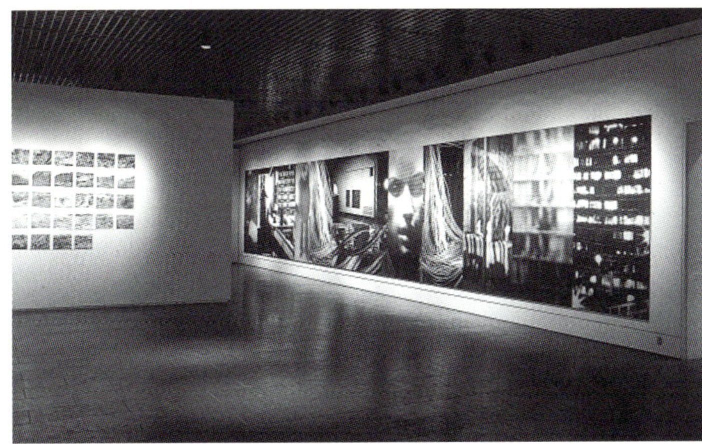

Lewis Baltz, 1995

BILD. Photography in Contemporary German Art, 1994

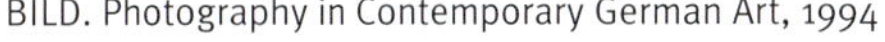

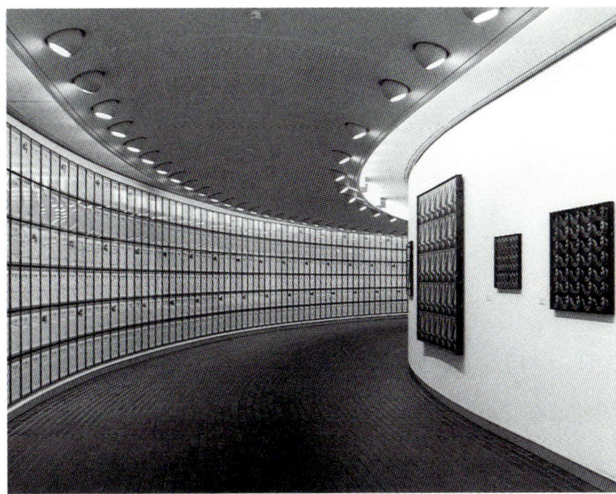

Robert Mapplethorpe – A Retrospective, 1992

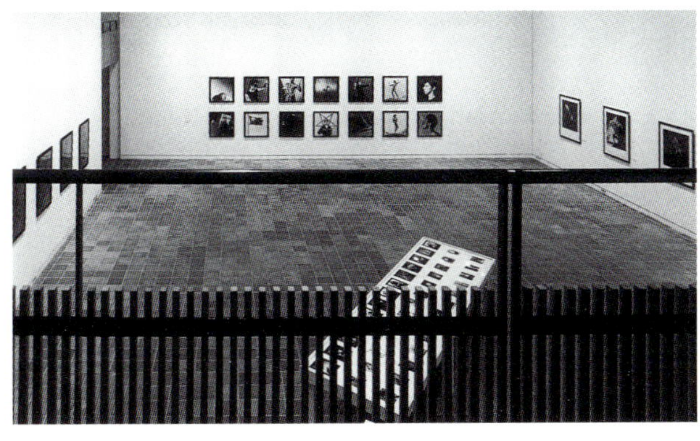

BILD. Photography in Contemporary German Art, 1994

"Sunshine & Noir. Art in L. A. 1960-1997". Opening

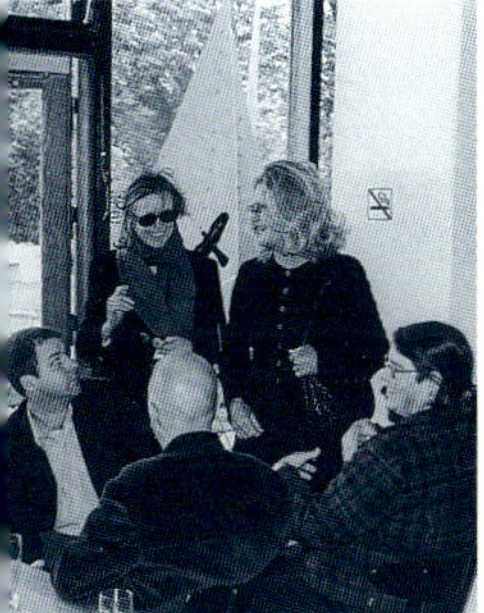

Jim Isermann and Helle Crenzien

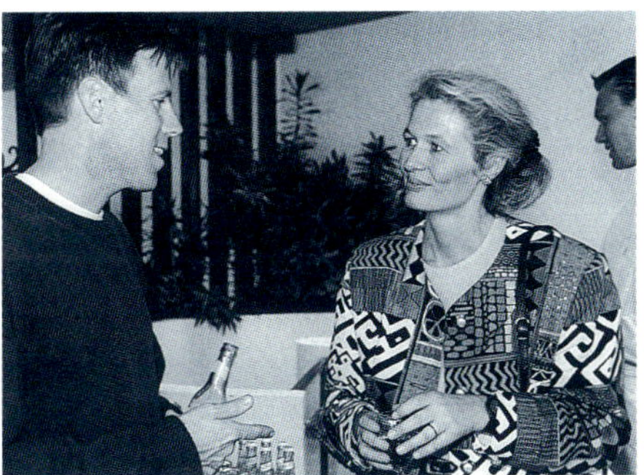

The Louisiana Exhibition 1997. New Art from Denmark and Scania. Tone O. Nielsen, Lars Grambye and Åsa Nacking

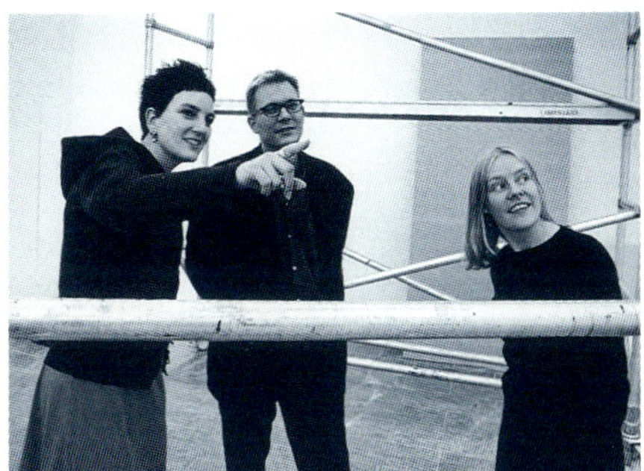

1998 "Sam Taylor-Wood". Opening

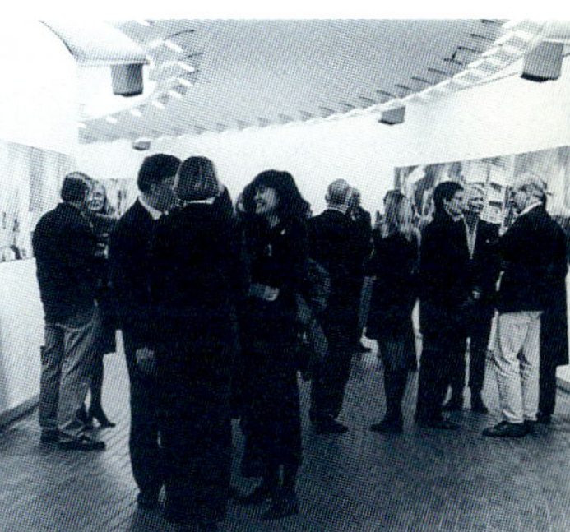

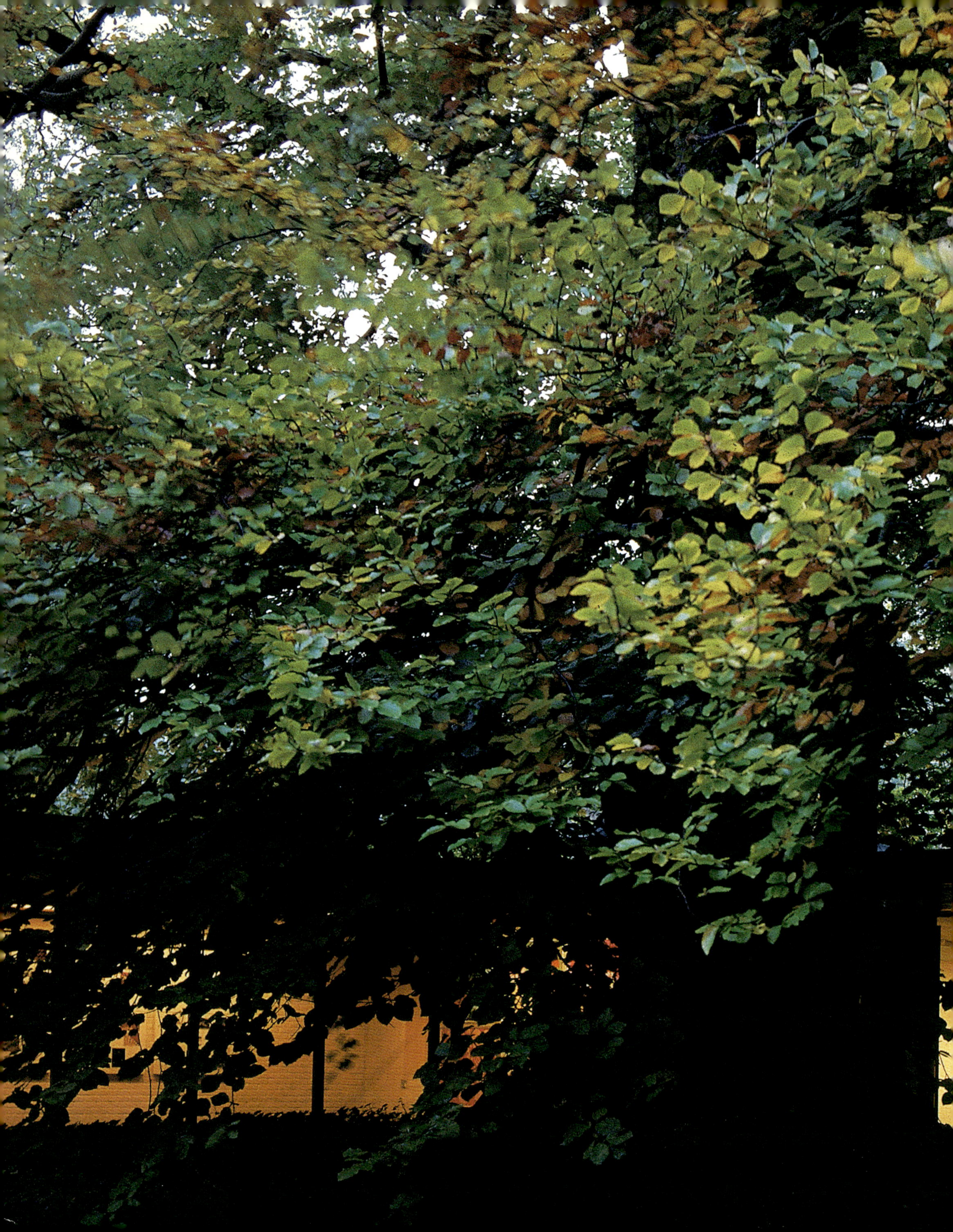

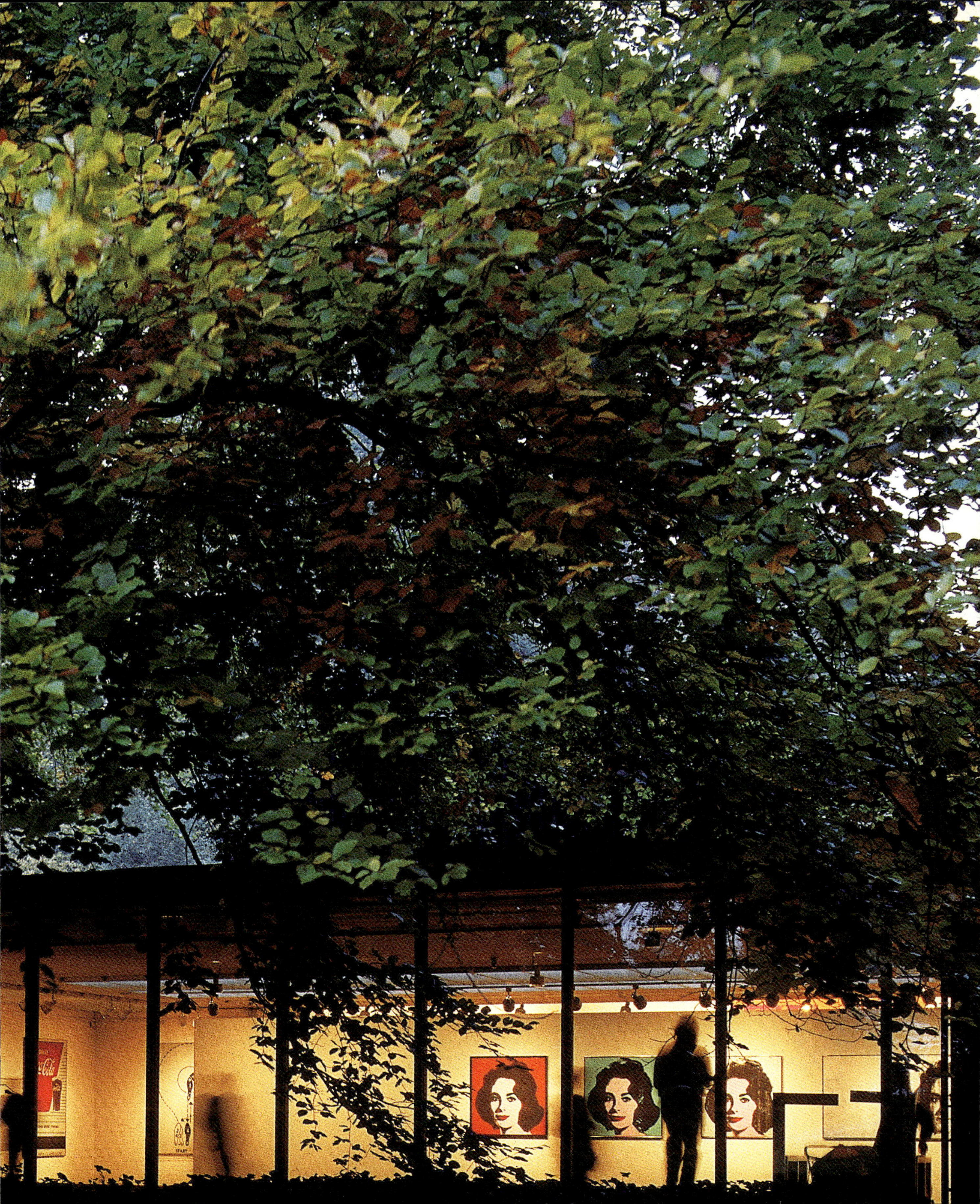
START

Louisiana 'on location'

Poul Erik Tøjner

Louisiana is not only an art museum and an art collection; it is also a view of art. Naturally you can easily go to Humlebæk and wander around the long corridors, having a look at this and that in order to end up in the café and sit there enjoying the interaction of the many different impressions, the view over the Sound and whatever prospects there might lie in a bite to eat. Not a word against this, or the food either! But if you want to experience the place as more than a conglomeration of art, some reflection on the view of art underlying it hardly comes amiss. Not least because, like the architecture, certain parts of the collection gain their significance from the totality to which they contribute.

Ever since Knud W. Jensen opened his Louisiana in 1958 it has been a 'work in progress'. 1966, 1971, 1976, 1982 and 1991 have been years of expansion as far as the building is concerned, and with the inauguration of the Children's Wing in 1994 and the extension of the museum shop in 1998 the museum is now finally complete, both as building and idea. The latter has been the guiding principle for the former, because an understanding of Louisiana as an architectural project requires being able to perceive the idea of art that the place has made its own. Right from the start two preconditions have determined the architecture for which Jørgen Bo and Vilhelm Wohlert have been responsible throughout the years: continuity and care. Where continuity is the feeling of being led along through something originally from the old villa to the old bastion on the edge of the Sound. This concept, combined with the aim to preserve the natural beauty of the surroundings, has created the course of the building through the landscape. The big windows bring the park into contact with the rooms; as a pedestrian visitor you feel you are really out for a walk. Whereas previously the way back from the bastion was through the park and its numerous sculptures, the erection of the Graphics Wing has now transformed the straight course into a round trip. This has several advantages, not least the fact that the café is no longer so immodestly the tour's goal but just a station on the way.

Over these two architectural preconditions finally soars the view of art that binds the whole project together. Louisiana constitutes a break with the traditional museum institution: It offers no inevitably chronological or educational exhibition, but aims to present culture as a relatively free project. Culture in the widest sense of the word – the numerous lectures, concerts, debate days, conferences and ethnographic exhibitions etc. lie like rings around a concept of culture that is characterised by spreading itself. It never shuts anything up in rooms for experts or the elite, but aims quite concretely – again architecturally mediated – to place art as symbol or experience precisely at a point between outside and inside,

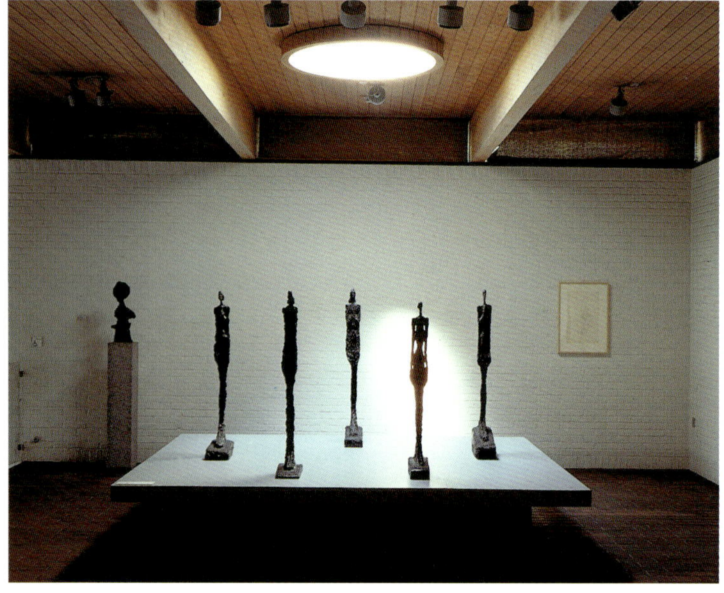

Alberto Giacometti's "Venice Women", 1956

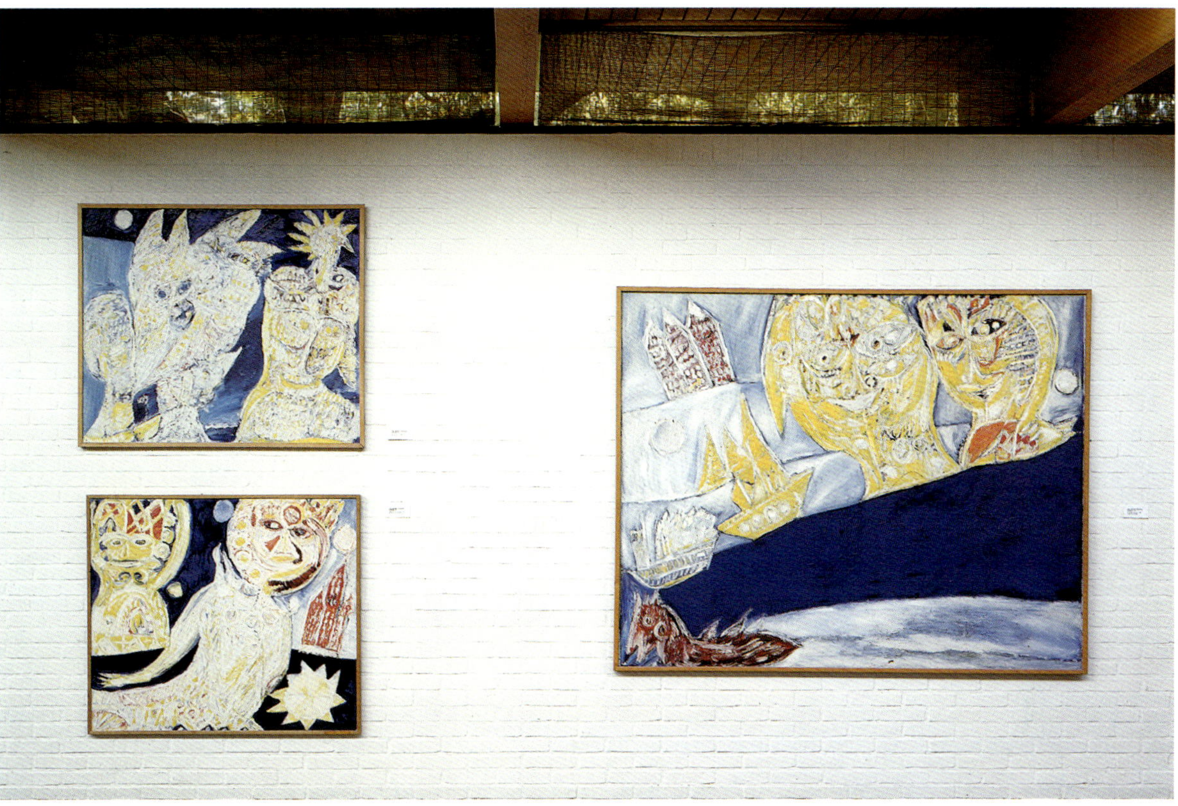

The first lantern room in the North Wing with works by Carl-Henning Pedersen

between us and nature and history. A world within the surrounding world.

A number of artists and art groups seem quite naturally to be in line with the view of art characterising the Louisiana idea, which basically is a view of human nature. Thus Heerup, Cobra with Jorn, Bille, Egill Jacobsen and Carl-Henning Pedersen are prominent Danish artists in a tradition that acknowledges the existential roots of art. Especially fine is Louisiana's collection of Carl-Henning Pedersen's paintings (not least when you consider how many inferior blue birds the man has let fly during the course of time). These are from a period when Carl-Henning Pedersen's imaginative worlds vibrated with energy and mysticism. And at Louisiana you can follow him out of the colours and into vibrant black-and-white in the Graphics Wing. There are some fine examples of Bille; amongst others you can take a walk with his *Spadserende form* ("Walking Form"). Heerup has his own little work-place here in Humlebæk, a sublime junk shop with the sculpture or assemblage *Døden høster* ("Death Reaping") from 1943 and the painting that describes a period in Rembrandt's life, *Rembrandt-fantasi* ("Rembrandt Fantasy"), 1956, as main works. In Cobra's foreign section Louisiana has been more fortunate than so many other places – there are some fine works of Pierre Alechinsky, including a good self-portrait, *Autoportrait sans traits* ("Self-Portrait without Features") from 1965.

Two sculptors who really had nothing to do with Cobra nevertheless shared the preoccupation with the human condition that characterised many of the Cobra painters. This was first and foremost Alberto Giacometti, of whose strikingly original sculptures the museum has an exceptional collection. Giacometti constitutes the pivotal point of the older part of the collection. Germaine Richier also joined the community

It is a question of creating a few focal points, which give the individual museum its distinctive character. Sometimes modern museums are criticised for interesting themselves in the same names. Their collections are said to become too uniform, all composed according to the same recipe. This is an unfair accusation, because the same names may well recur, but in different settings with the emphasis now in one movement and now in the other.

Knud W. Jensen: Mit Louisiana-liv ("My Louisiana Life"), *Copenhagen, 1993*

Louisiana ought unconditionally to make its name as a place for sculpture. The museum's setting in the park beside the Sound was a clear challenge and gave us a special position. Few other museums could offer the artist such conditions.
The ever-bigger semicircle the buildings formed among the big groups of trees created the possibility for isolated garden spaces where the sculptures could be erected in close interplay with the architecture.

Knud W. Jensen: Mit Louisiana-liv ("My Louisiana Life"), *Copenhagen, 1993*

with sculptures devoted to the metamorphosis of the body and fantasy.

The conception of the painting or sculpture as a possible dialogue about the basic human condition is partially repeated in Louisiana's interest in late post-war German art, as represented by Anselm Kiefer and Georg Baselitz. In them both we find the insistence on painting as a language from which emotional and historical insight can still be wormed. Most grandiose and constructed in Kiefer, and more of a primitive gesture in Baselitz, whom Louisiana not only displays as a painter, but also and in considerably better form as a graphic artist. In a number of state proofs we can follow Baselitz change slightly from print to print. Regarded separately you can scarcely talk about pictures, but regarded as a whole something arises that is more than the sum of all the small scribbles.

The museum also has a large collection of Per Kirkeby, who belongs to the same generation, with chief emphasis on his painting and sculpture from the 1980s, a period that reveals more differences than similarities between him and Jorn and his companions, a connection otherwise often assumed. In a few of Kirkeby's paintings the figure, a body-like shape, may well be present, but it is always related to a space that opens out backwards like a cave or grotto. Thus the landscape, the earth as a geological formation, is central in quite a different sense than it ever became in the Cobra generation's paintings, which were more concerned with the relationship between painting and fantasy than between painting and nature.

However, the human being, nature, history, fantasy, melancholy, existentialist stopping places and the basic human condition are only one side of Louisiana's great collection of modern Danish and international art. In contrast to the whole spiritual circus there are two very big and broadly represented art trends: Pop Art and a spectrum of

The first exhibition room in the South Wing with Naum Gabo's *Column* from 1923/75. Also works by Jean Dubuffet, Francis Bacon, Antonio Tàpies and Germaine Richier

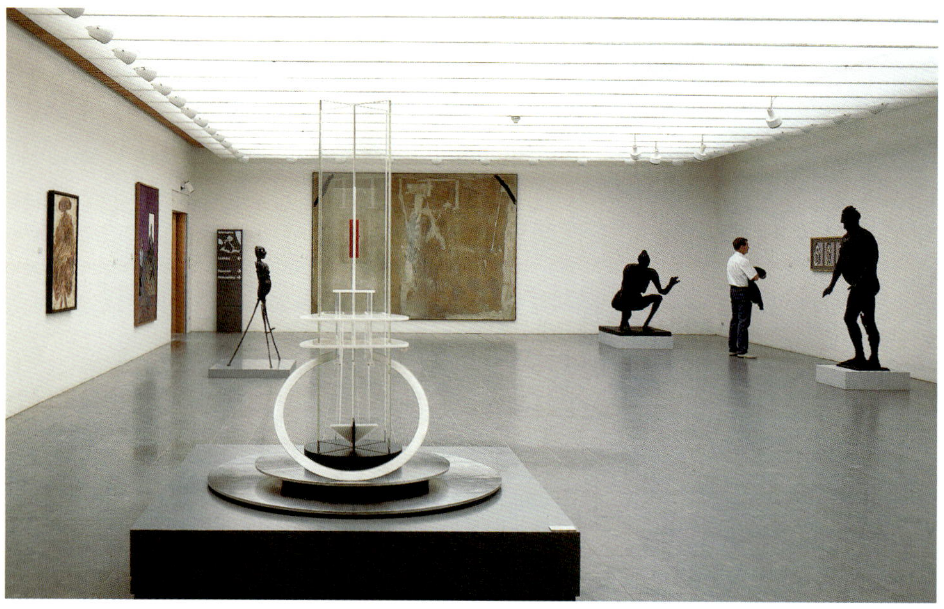

works to do with Constructivism and Concrete movements in art. Each moves in its own direction, as far as temperament is concerned. In all its intentionally banal emptiness Pop Art almost cannot be big enough. In Humlebæk there are 'billboards' by the usual comic-strip team Roy Lichtenstein and Andy Warhol. On the other hand, some of the Constructive art almost cannot be small and subdued enough – a niche with works on paper from the Joseph and Celia Ascher Collection makes an admirable little breathing-space among the many square metres. However, there is more breadth and height when we reach the period around the Second World War, with our Danish Richard Mortensen as the shining talent among them all. From time to time his huge *Opus Normandie* from 1956 is brought out and hung – the painting is nine metres long. Robert Jacobsen, too, belongs here with his sculptures from the 1950s and what sculptures! Louisiana has two of the best he has ever made – *Bevægelses-problem* ("Problem of Motion"), from 1955, and *Sculpture en fer forgé* ("Sculpture in Wrought Iron") from 1959. Brilliant little chamber ballets in iron.

The Constructive art may seem to be in stark contrast all along the line to, for example, Cobra's colour-speckled and colour-spitting fantasies. But if you go behind the pictures the contrast is not so great. It is a question of two different attempts to make a kind of pure picture; they merely differ as to what it is that makes a picture pure. 'Spontaneity and the emancipation of fantasy', the spontaneous artists might answer. Whereas the Constructivists might say 'discipline and abstract geometrical order', referring to the fact that by almost withdrawing from the picture they make room for the picture's own laws. These are two conceptions of the world which can meet here in a common endeavour.

Louisiana is not only inside, it is to a great extent also outside. And we have hereby reached an art form that is one of Louisiana's strong points, namely sculpture. Henry Moore and Jean Arp are ready to be embraced; that is to say, in the case of Moore it is the viewer that falls into the sculpture's arms rather than the opposite. Both Arp's and Moore's organic idiom appeals to the sense of touch, almost to physical contact with the sculptures. With Moore and Arp we are liberated from isolation; Giacometti's lonely mass human beings stand somewhere in the building, crying lead tears and longing for Moore's motherly rendezvous in the park on the edge of the Sound. Max Ernst's figures provide a more bizarre and imaginative element, as they stand watching a bus-full of Swedish surrealists. Even Henri Laurens, who was always overshadowed by Picasso, has taken up residence here under the trees, while the Constructivists likewise have their representative out here in the shape of Alexander Calder. The most important of the Danish sculptors is Willy Ørskov; Louisiana has three big bronze statues to document the man's originality.

Pop Art in the South Wing
with works by Andy Warhol,
Roy Lichtenstein and others

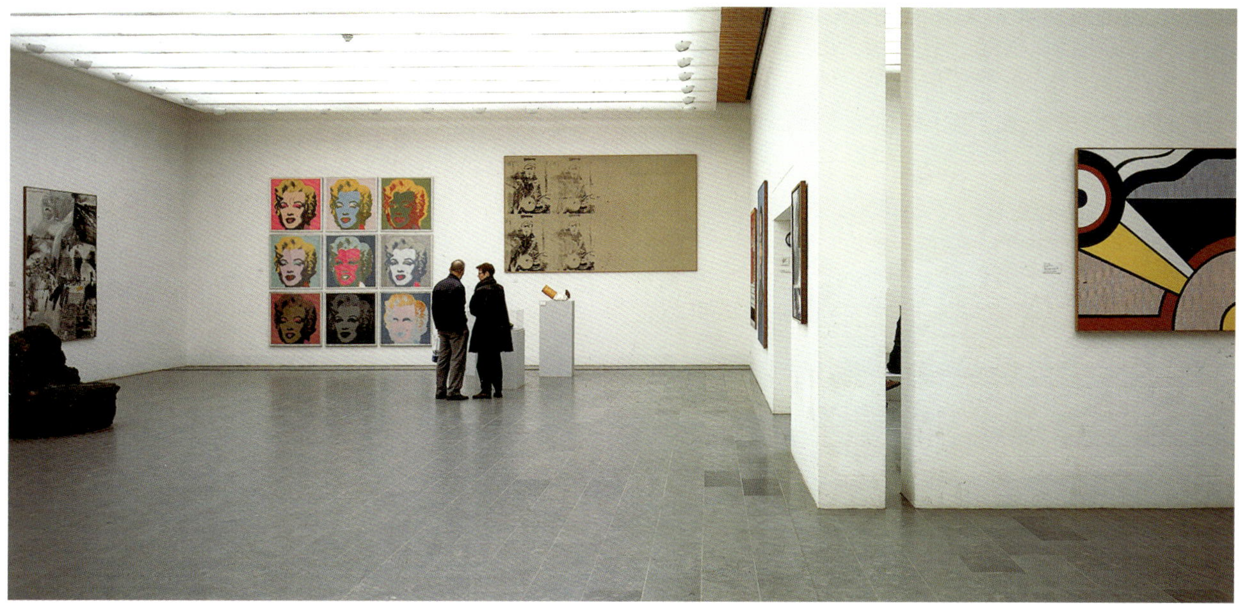

Our main task is to create a meaningful totality in each room or park area, so that the works illuminate specific artistic situations in the different decades since 1950. We endeavour to make these exhibitions increasingly perfect by way of new purchases, in order thereby to cultivate the special nature of the collection.

Knud W. Jensen: Mit Louisiana-liv ("My Louisiana Life"), *Copenhagen, 1993*

He developed greatly as a sculptor, using materials and concepts derived from widely different fields and cultural layers, and this can in fact be observed in the sculptures at Louisiana. At first glance the classic compositions resemble a cross between something monumentally geometric and something organic, but on closer inspection they seem to possess far more associations. They are almost reminiscent of a kind of arm chair with the impressions of peculiar beings, not to say the remains of bodies, still sitting in them.

Louisiana is not to be captured on a few pages with the aid of three or four concepts or art-historical periods. The collection has its lines, but it has also reproduced itself by gemmation. Thus Sam Francis assumes a great and dominating role, though it is probably more dominating than great. In fact Francis apparently seldom paints in formats less than the size of a badminton court, and Louisiana does indeed have a couple of such courts on display. It naturally possesses smaller works too, but one of the points about Francis is that he doesn't really come off until he can be measured in metres. On the one hand, Francis paints his pure painting without giving a thought to narrative, motif or content, and on the other hand, he does in fact merge well with the environment when he enters into it mostly as decoration. As previously mentioned, one of the points of Humlebæk is that it is not a sin for art to be able to enter into something bigger, a place, an environment, a society. That is, as decoration, or something that functions in a totality in a cultural totality, of life and art.

Finally, two places where one ought to stop for a while should be mentioned, mentioned precisely because one has a tendency to move on. One of them is in the old villa where Louisiana began – the villa was simply called Louisiana. Here hangs a small selection of the slightly older Danish art to be found in the Humlebæk collections. There is Lundstrøm, one of whose famous packing box pictures is owned by Louisiana. There is Jerichau, there is Karl Isakson, but there are first and foremost a number of magnificent pictures by Erik Hoppe. The latter is famous for his paintings from Søndermarken, where he painted the light and the trees and the grass and the earth again and again. But in the 1930s he also painted Copenhagen, with a sense for the weightiness of the architecture, for the monumentality of the houses, which he never, however, depicted as sinister but almost comfortingly massive. Erik Hoppe at his best is one of the very best artists in that decade of Danish art. As a rule one is pushed through the old villa, either by the crowds from behind or by the slightly irritating creak of the parquet floor, but one ought to stand firm and stay a while.

The other place that also demands a brief halt consists of just a single work. It is a kind of installation or little sculptural machine entitled *Attempt to Raise Hell*, and is from 1974 by Dennis Oppenheim. It consists of a little man cast in metal and clad in a corduroy suit; he is sitting on a base in front of a metal bell suspended from the ceiling. From time to time he butts the church bell with full force and the metal sings out in the room. The problem is that it is apparently impossible to calculate the interval at which he does this. I have been trying for many years, but have never yet succeeded. You stand there waiting, all tensed up, but nothing happens; you finally relax, and then he bangs it. Boingggg!

English translation by Paula Hostrup-Jessen

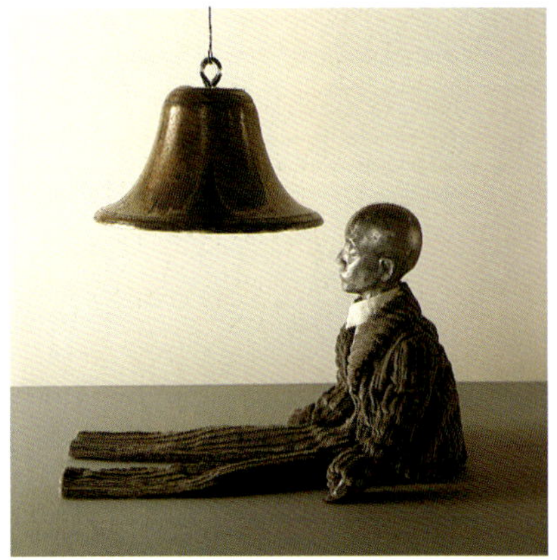

628
Dennis Oppenheim:
Attempt to Raise Hell, 1974

Note:
"Louisiana on location" is a slightly revised edition of an article previously printed in *Poul Erik Tøjner:* Museernes bedste billeder, 2 ("The Museums' Best Pictures, 2"), *published by Palle Fogtdal, 1992*

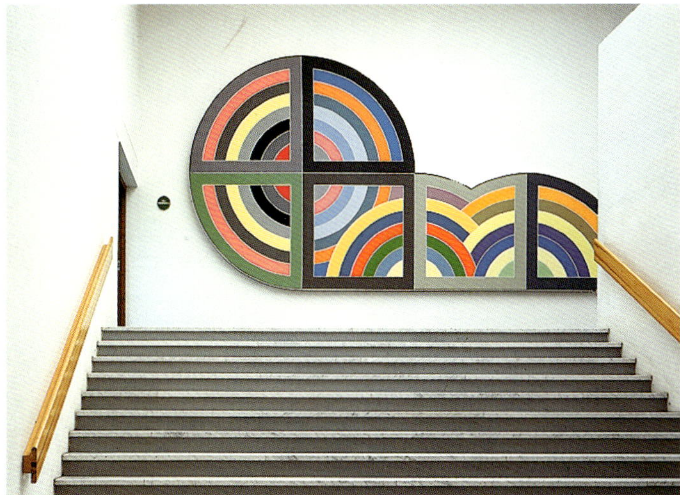

The flight of steps in the South Wing with Frank Stella's painting *Ctesiphon II* from 1967

The high-ceilinged exhibition room in the South Wing with works by Anselm Kiefer and Per Kirkeby

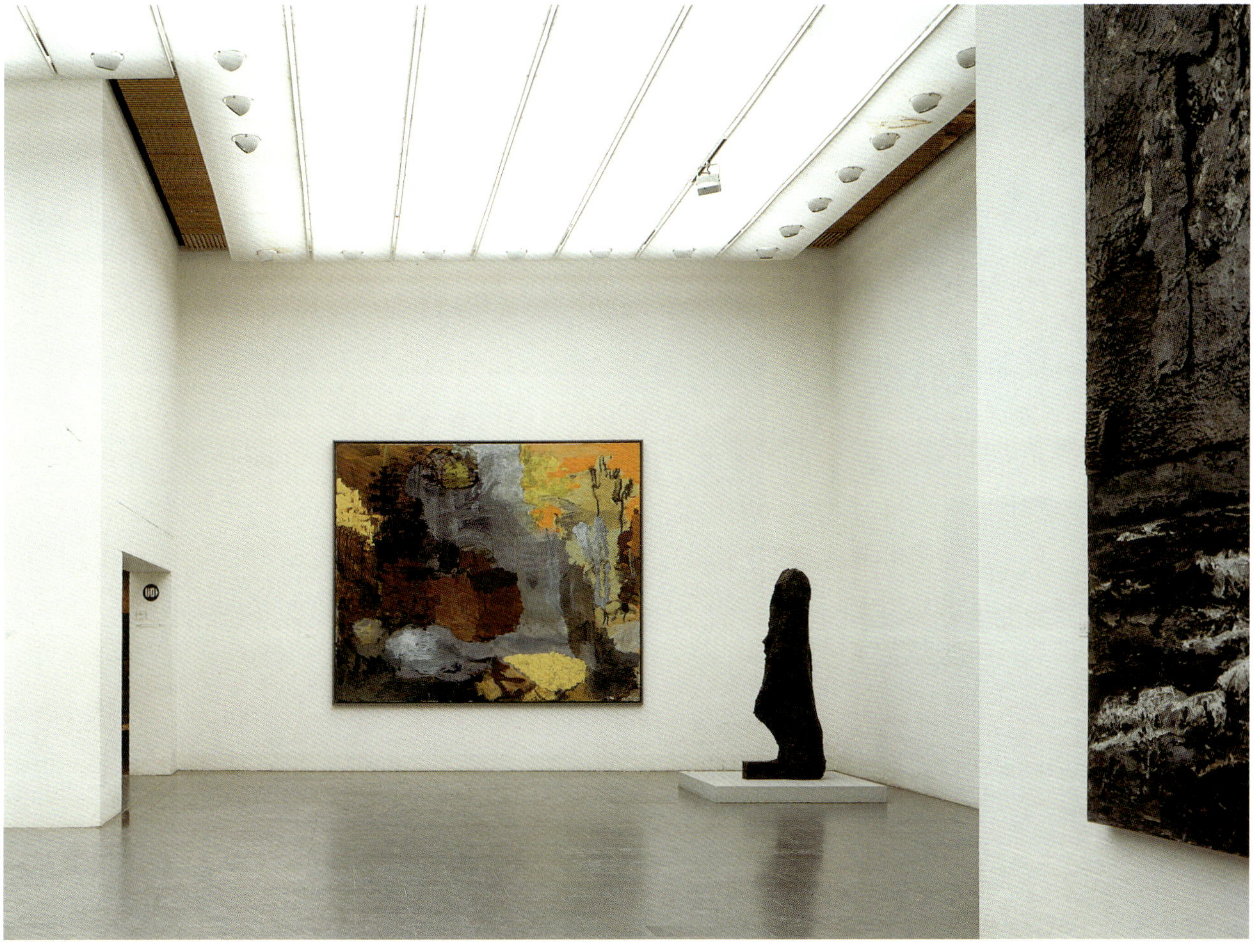

Early Danish Modernism

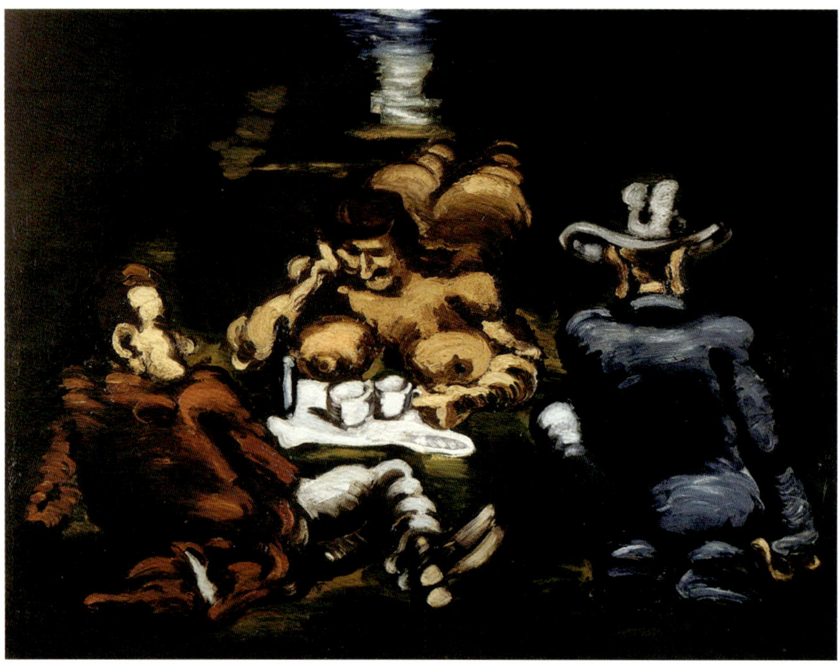

534
Vilhelm Lundstrøm:
Le Déjeuner sur l'herbe, 1920

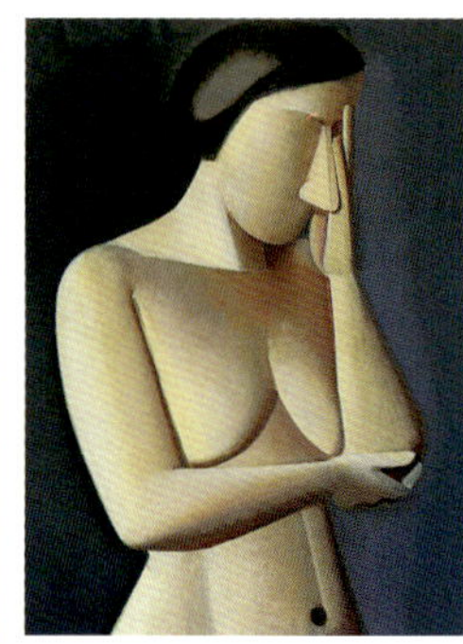

539
Vilhelm Lundstrøm:
Nude, 1930

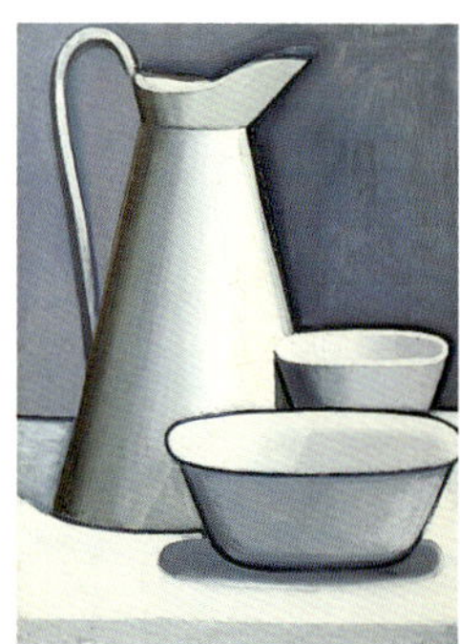

535
Vilhelm Lundstrøm:
Still Life with Pitcher, 1925

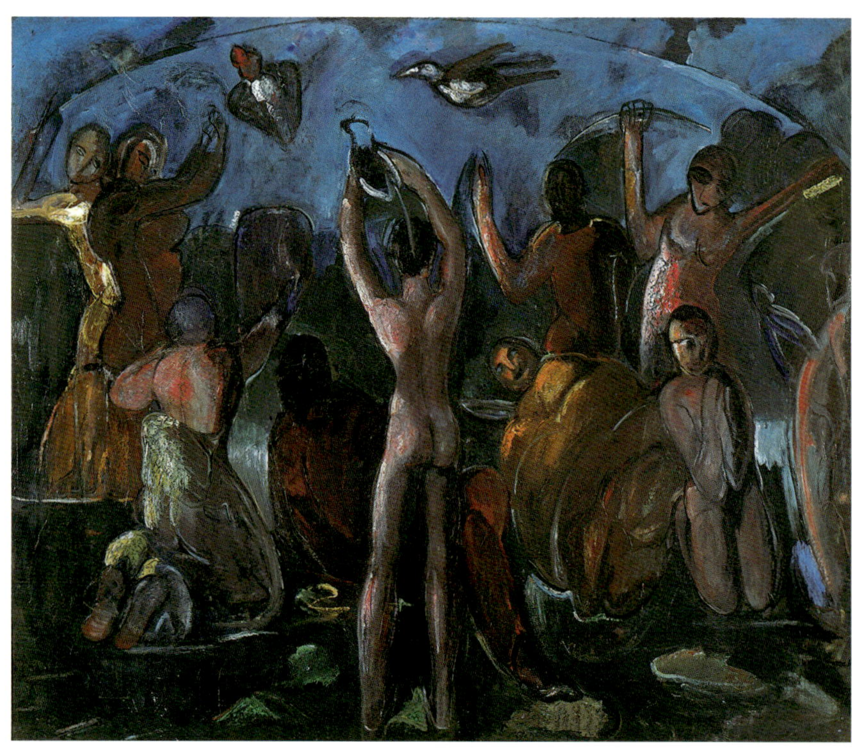

401
Jens Adolf Jerichau:
People in Search of Omens III, 1915

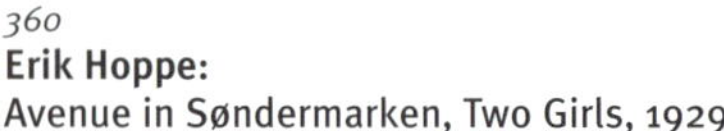

360
Erik Hoppe:
Avenue in Søndermarken, Two Girls, 1929

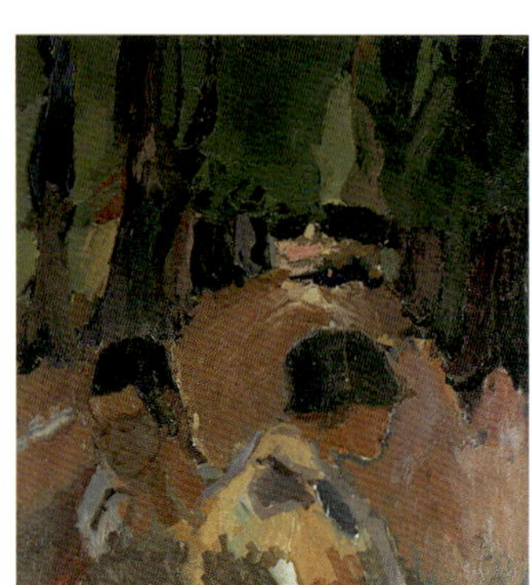

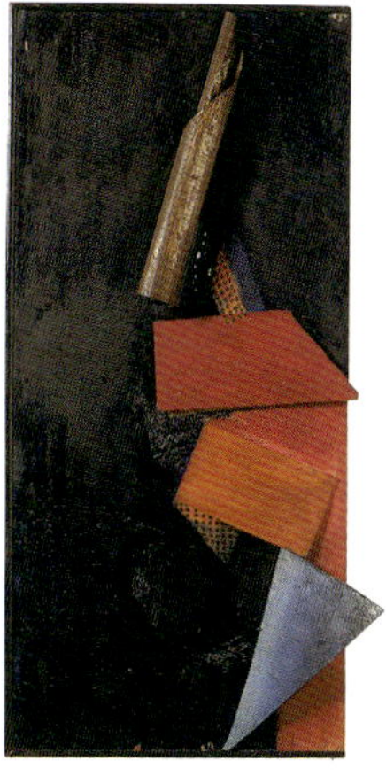

533
Vilhelm Lundstrøm:
Packing Box Picture (The Morning After), c. 1917

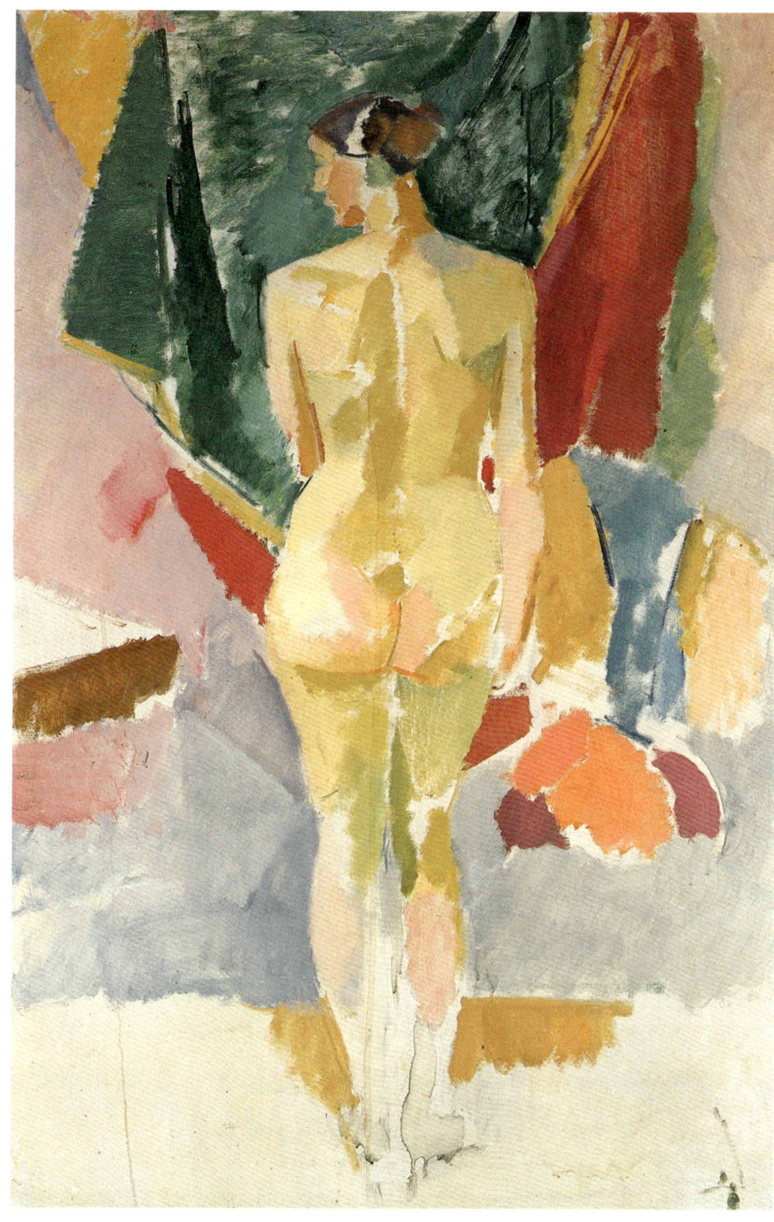

375
Karl Isakson:
Standing Nude from the Back, 1918-20

240
Harald Giersing:
The Churchyard in Svanninge, 1925

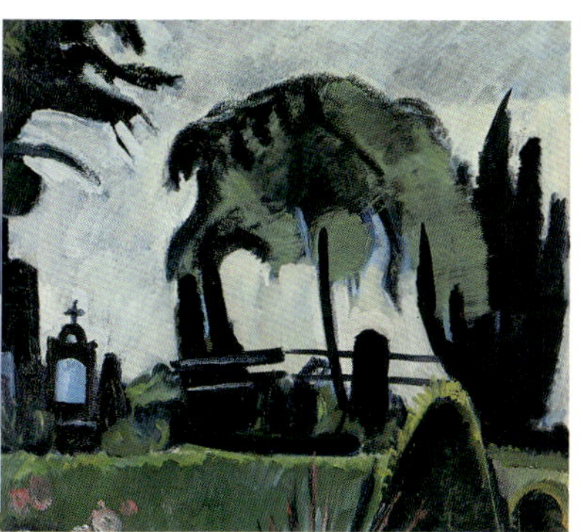

852
Niels Larsen Stevns:
View to Bokul, Gudhjem, 1929

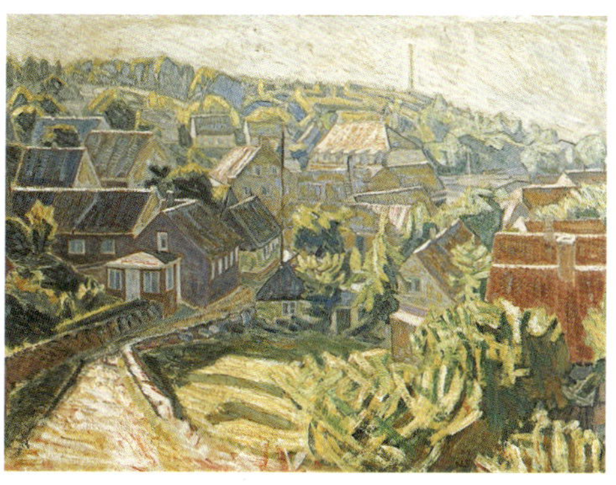

167
Adam Fischer:
French Soldier, 1918

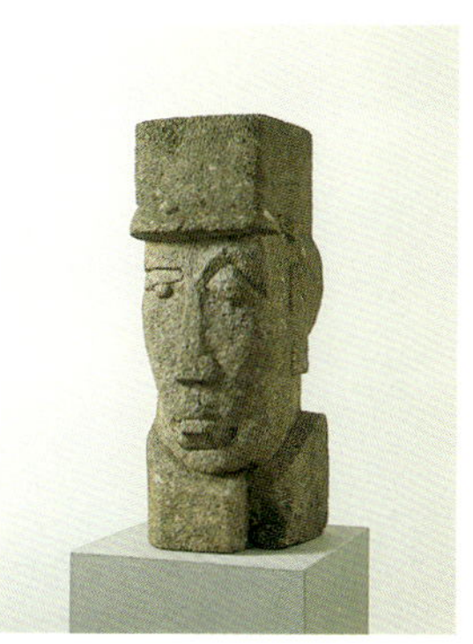

European Art of the 50s and 60s

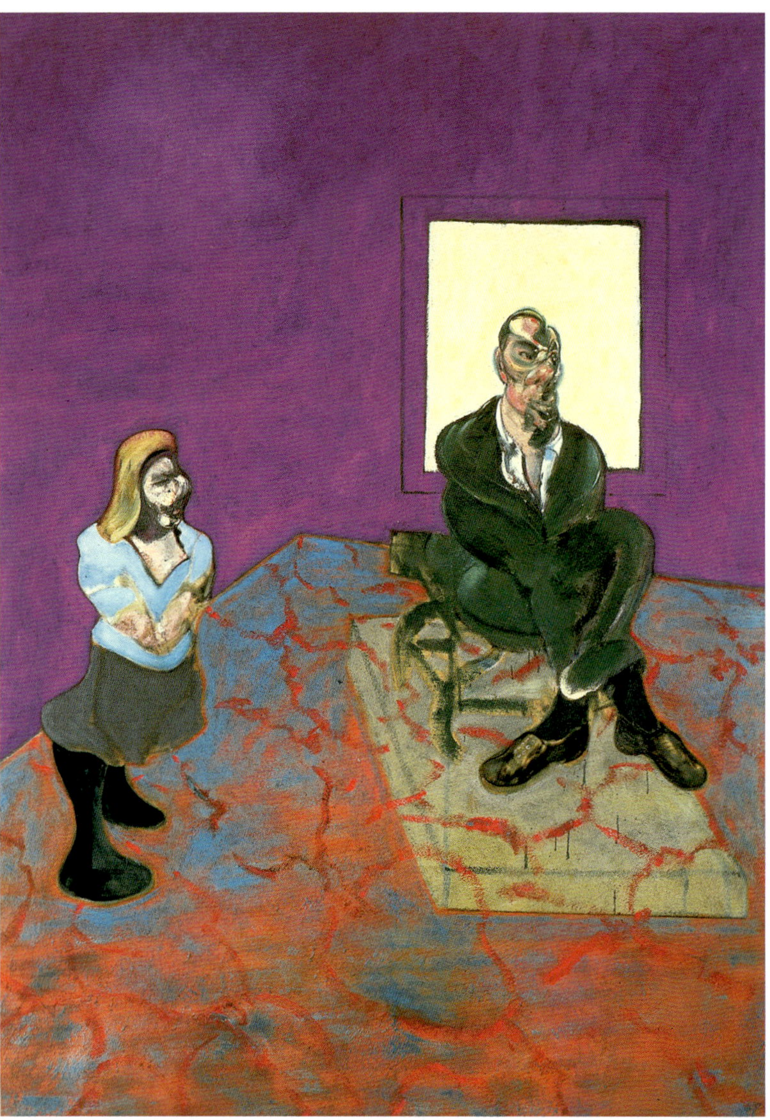

50
Francis Bacon:
Man and Child, 1963

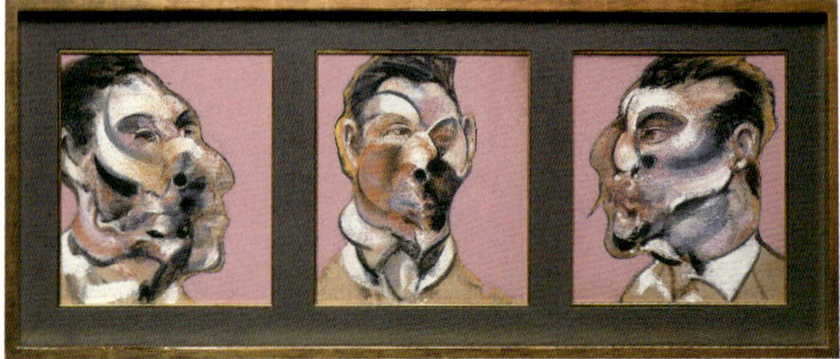

51
Francis Bacon:
Three Studies of George Dyer, 1969

143, 141
Jean Dubuffet:
Beard Orient, 1959
The Uncertain (Female Figure), 1950

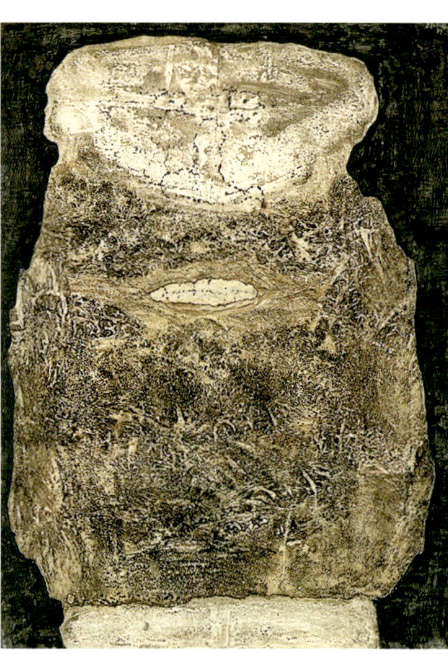

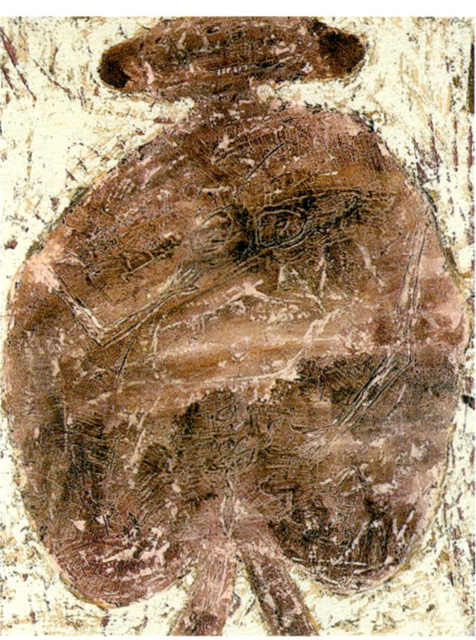

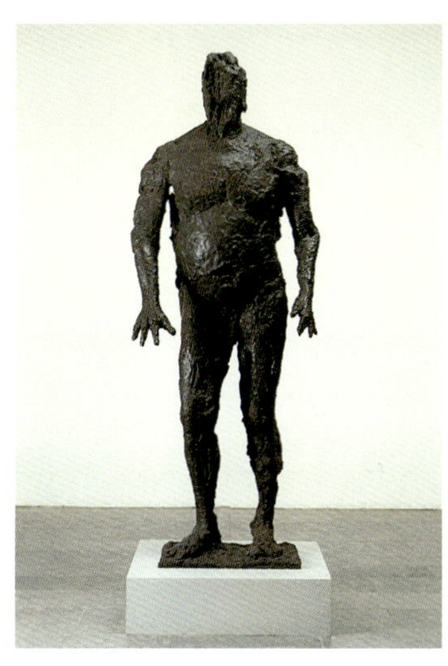

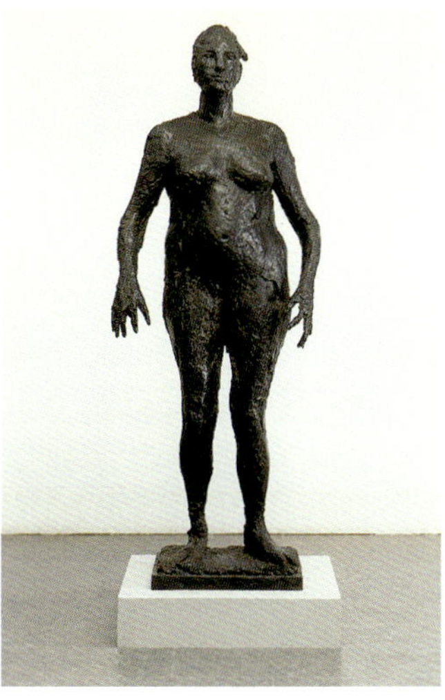

779, 780
Germaine Richier:
Storm, 1947-48 (left)
Hurricane, 1948-49 (right)

737
Pablo Picasso:
Le Déjeuner sur l'herbe, 1961

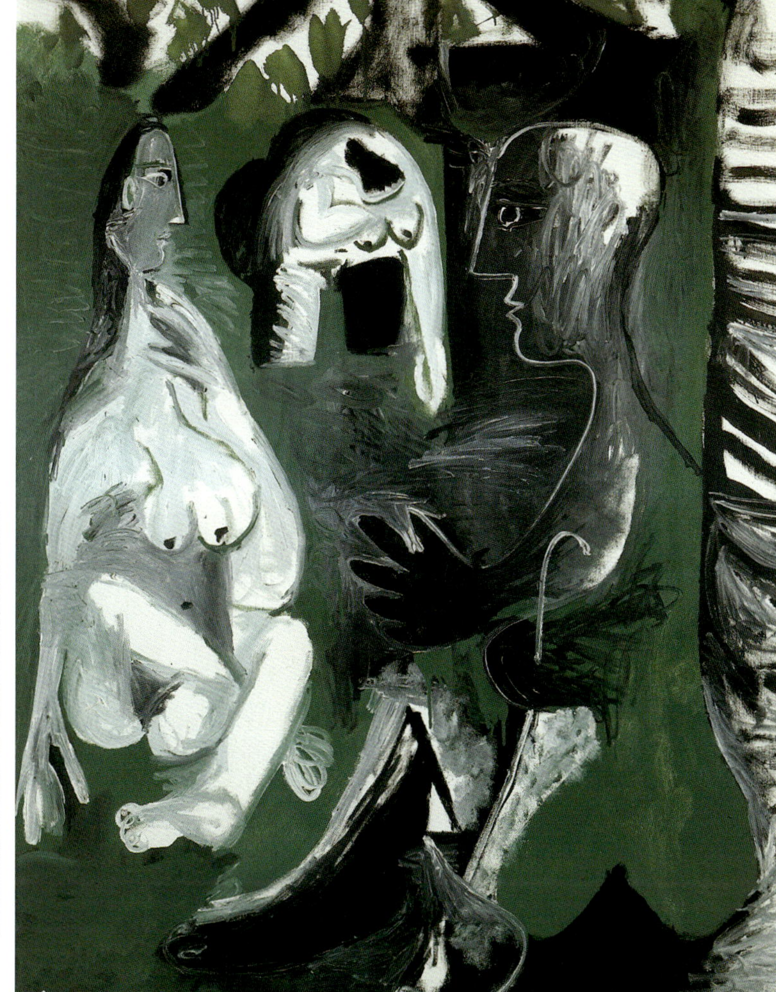

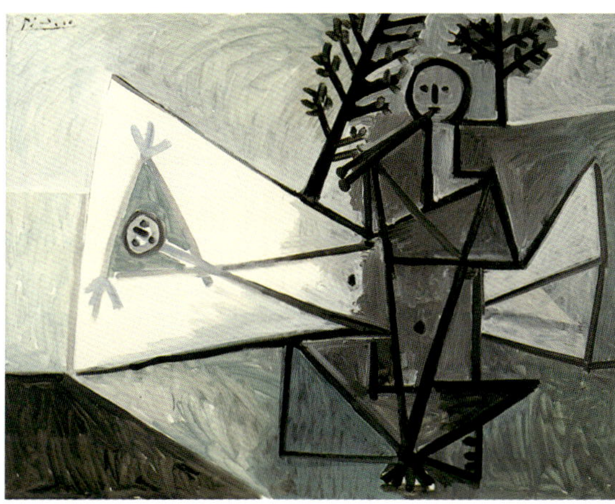

736
Pablo Picasso:
Woman and Flute Player III, 1956

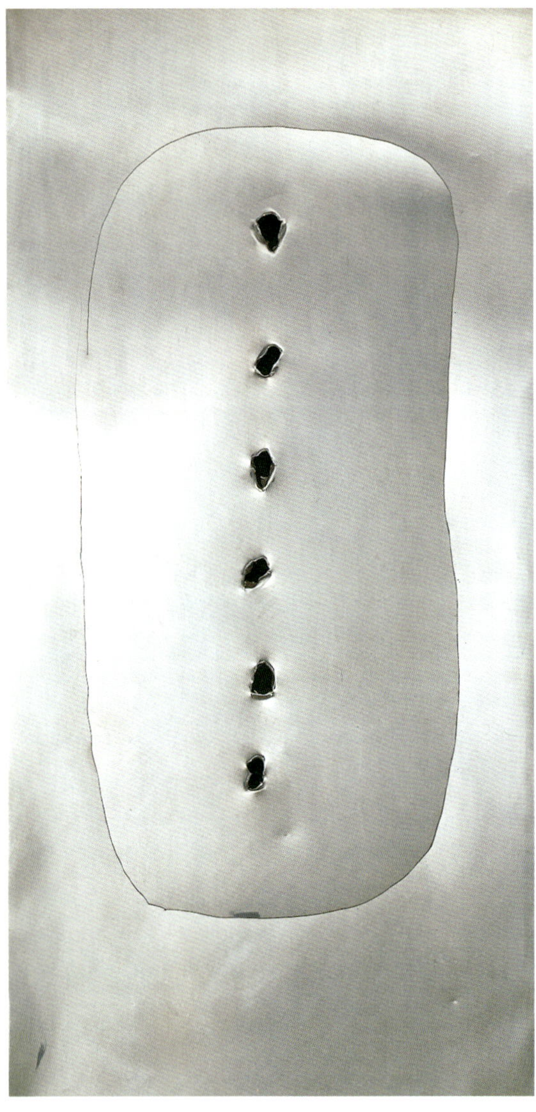

176
Lucio Fontana: New York, 1962

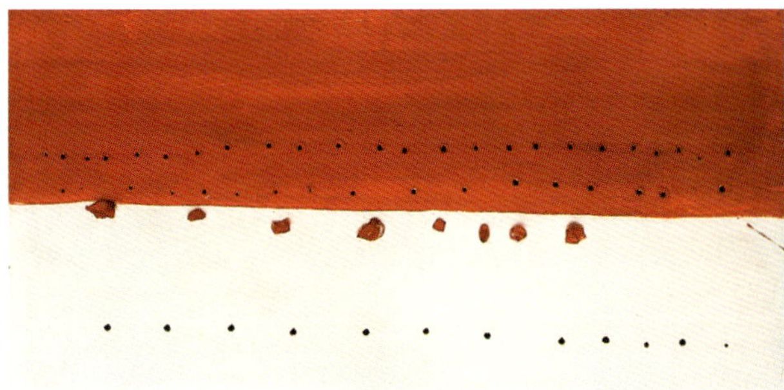

174
Lucio Fontana:
Spatial Concept, 1950

473, 472, 471
Yves Klein:
Monopink (MP 16), 1960
Monogold (MG 17), 1960
Monoblue (IKB 75), 1960

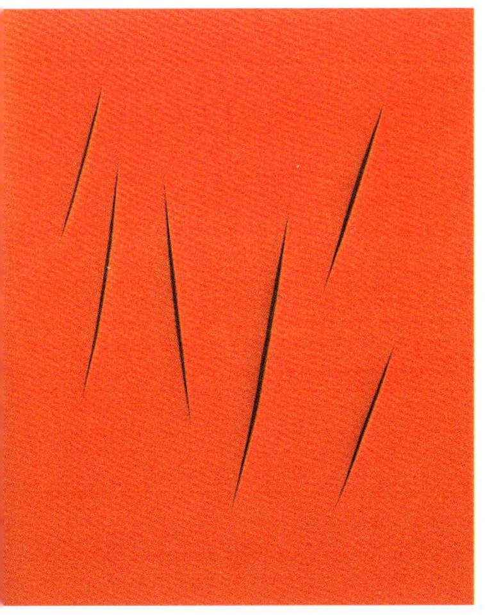

178
Lucio Fontana:
Spatial Concept, Waiting, 1967

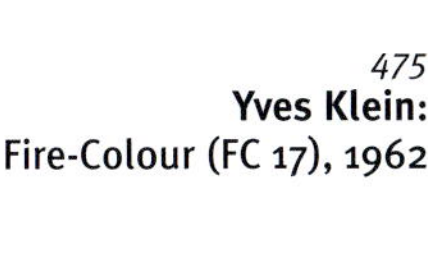

475
Yves Klein:
Fire-Colour (FC 17), 1962

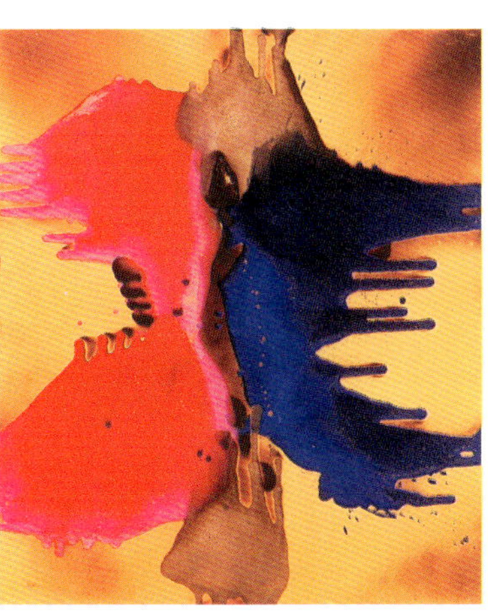

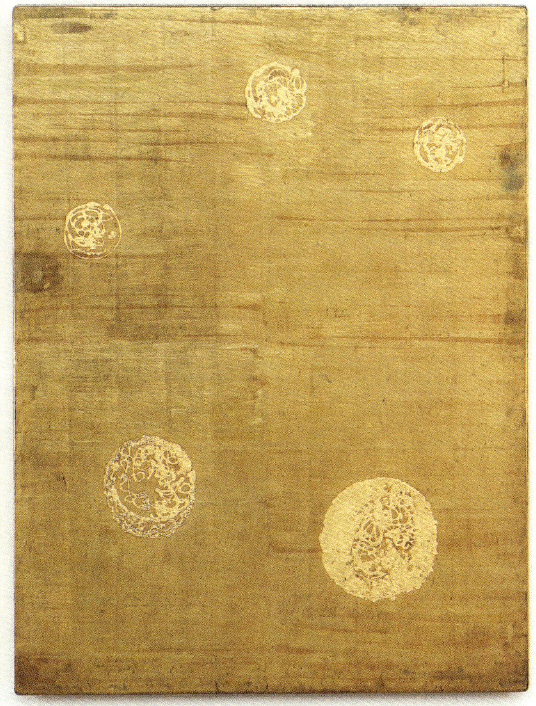

Alberto Giacometti

225-229
Venice Women, 1956

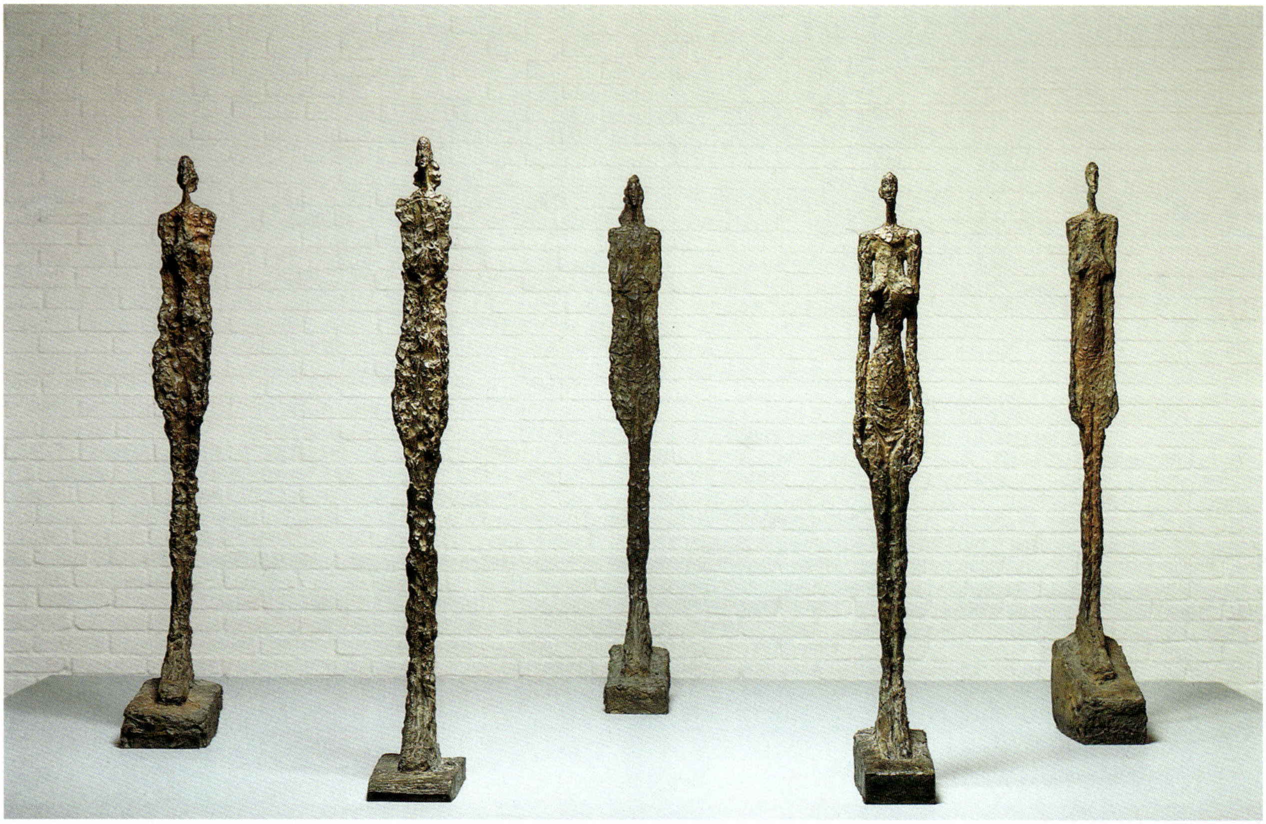

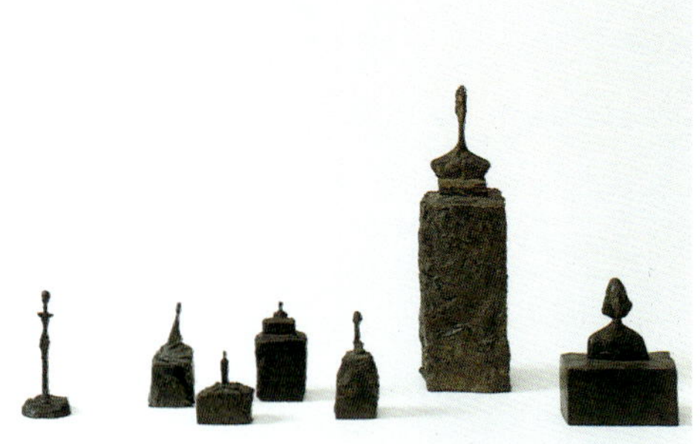

233, 219, 218, 217, 216, 221, 220
Small figure and small busts, 1940-1962

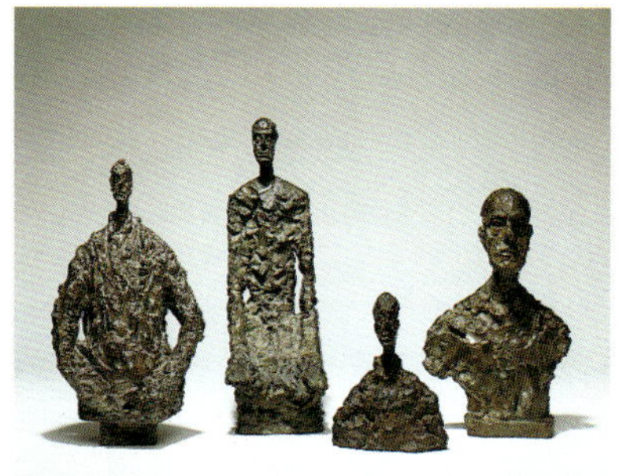

223, 236, 224, 234
Busts of Diego, 1953-1965

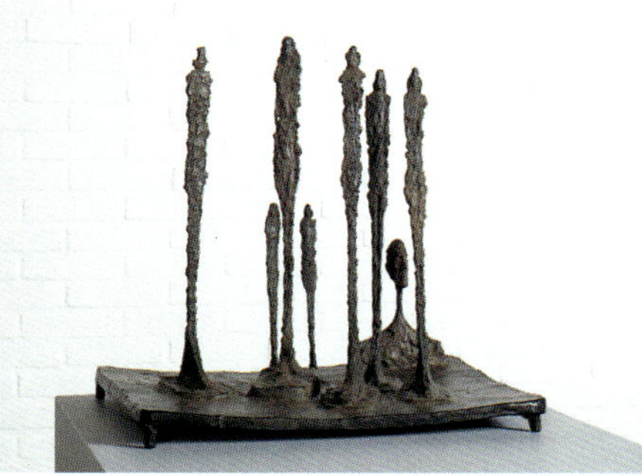

222
Forest, 1950

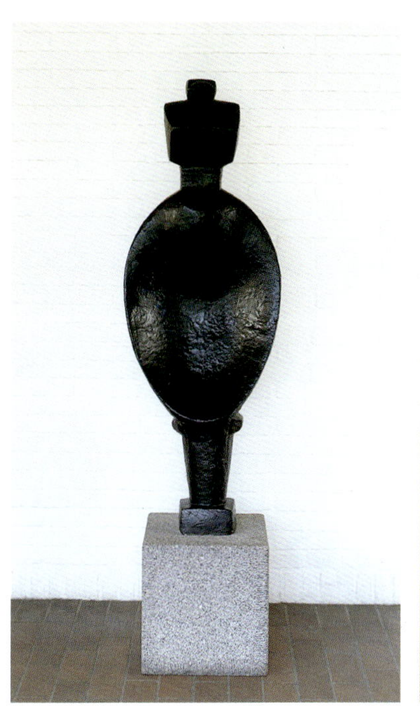

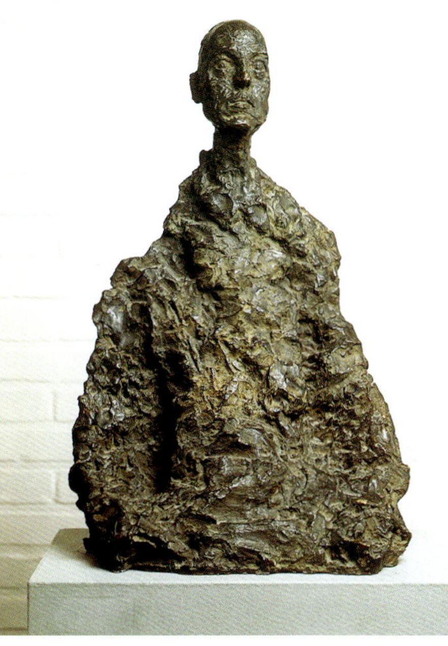

214, 237
Spoon-Woman, 1926 (left)
Bust of Elie Lotar, 1965 (right)

231, 232, 230
Walking Man, 1960
Standing Woman IV, 1960
Big Head, 1959-60

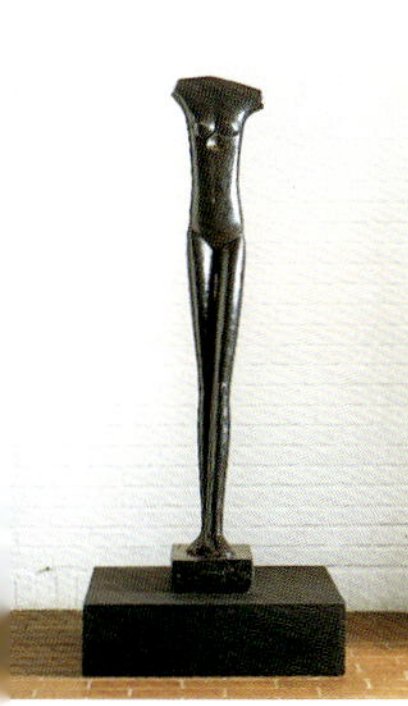

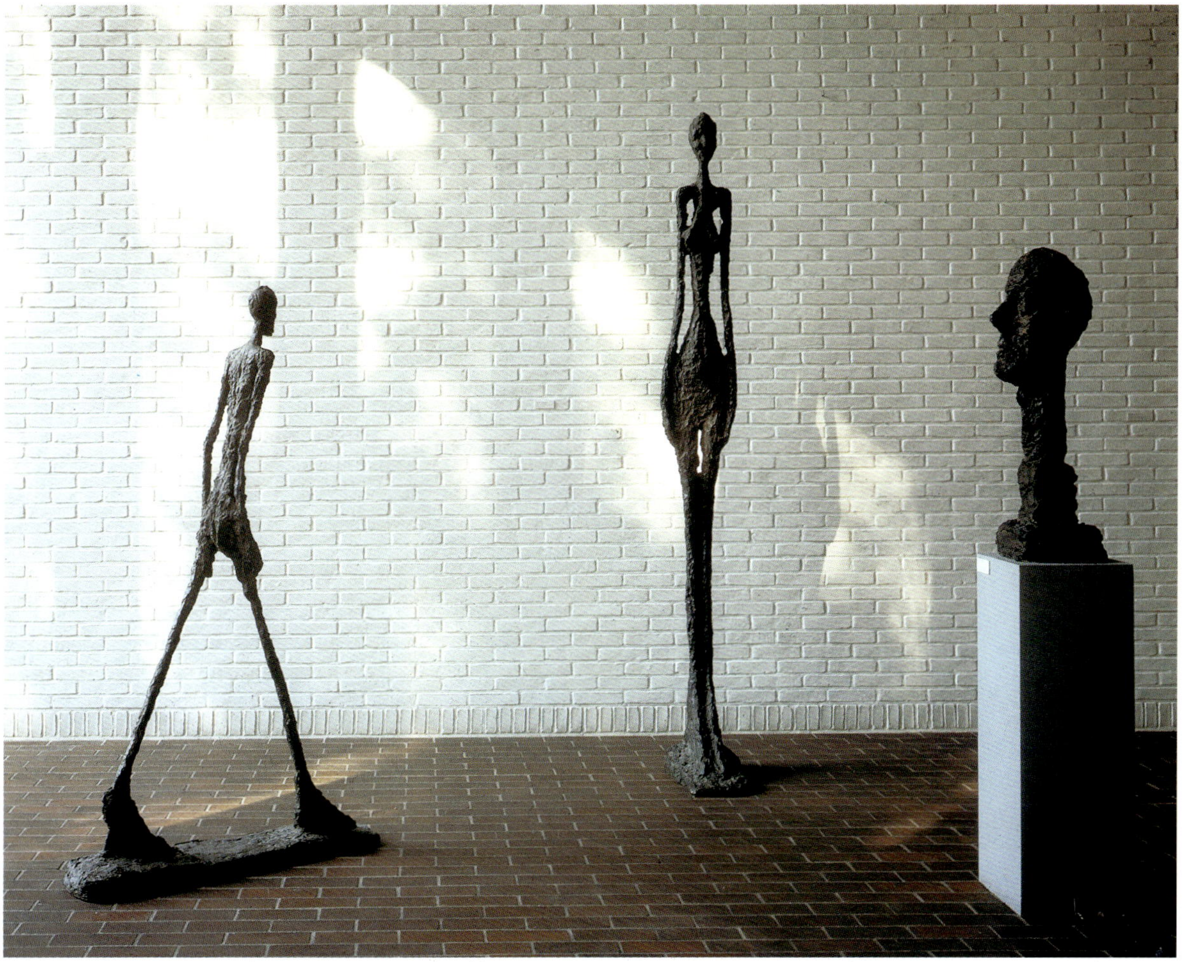

215
Walking Woman, 1932-34

Cobra

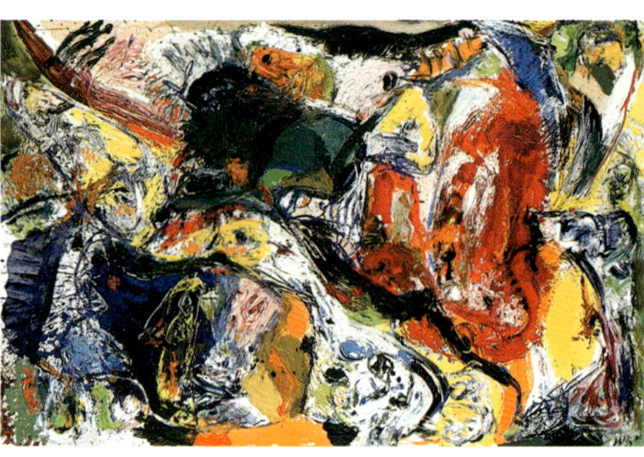

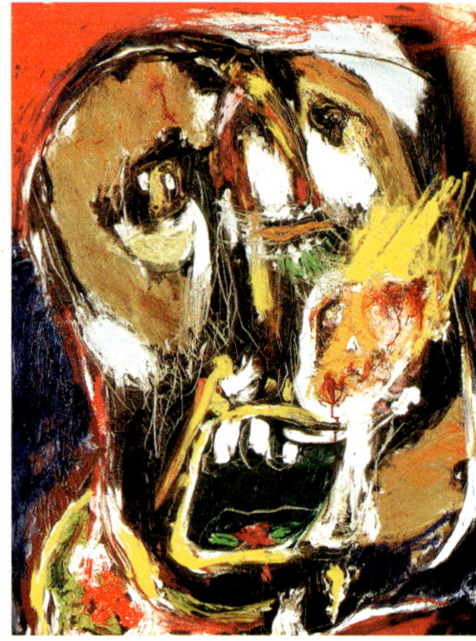

412, 413
Asger Jorn:
Dead Drunk Danes, 1960 (left)
Double Face, 1960 (right)

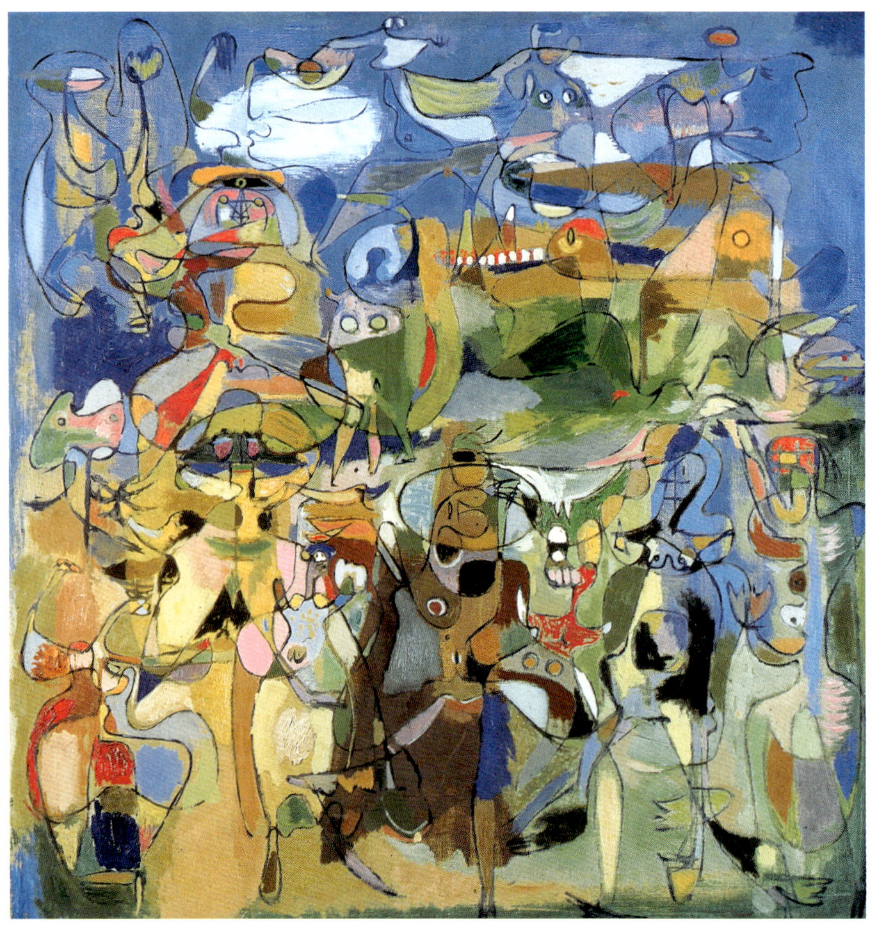

407
Asger Jorn: Titania II, 1940-41

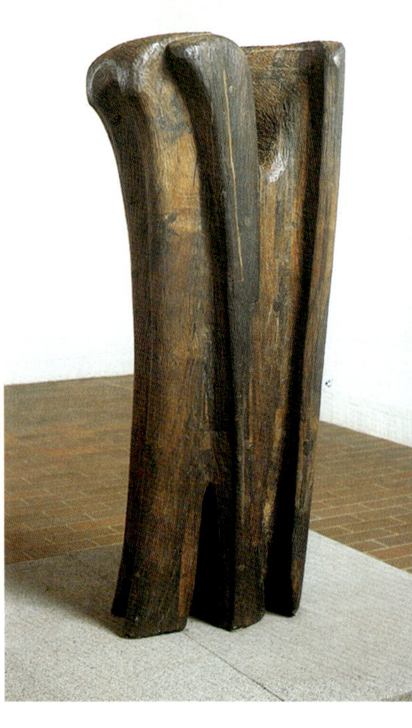

880
Erik Thommesen: Woman, 1960

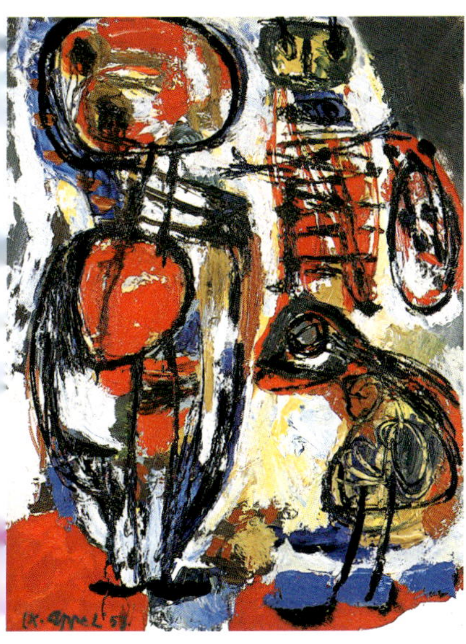

39
Karel Appel: Street Life, 1953

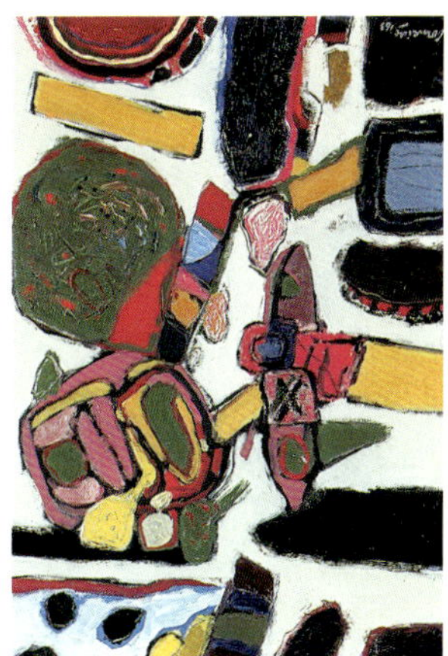

112
Guillaume Corneille: Small Opening in the Sky over a Green Meadow, 1963

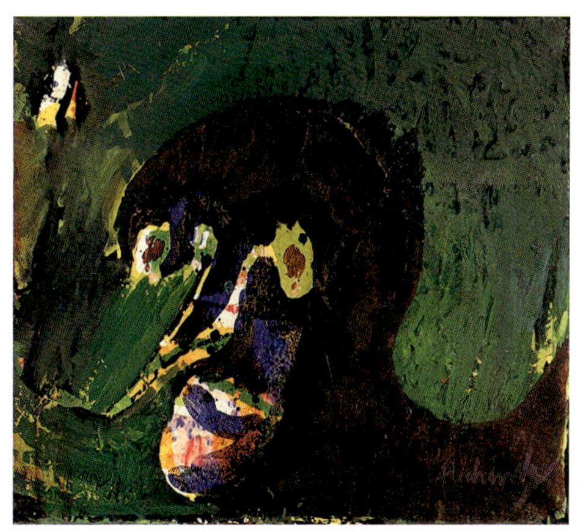

9
Pierre Alechinsky: Self-Portrait without Features, 1965

10
Pierre Alechinsky: Doubt, 1968

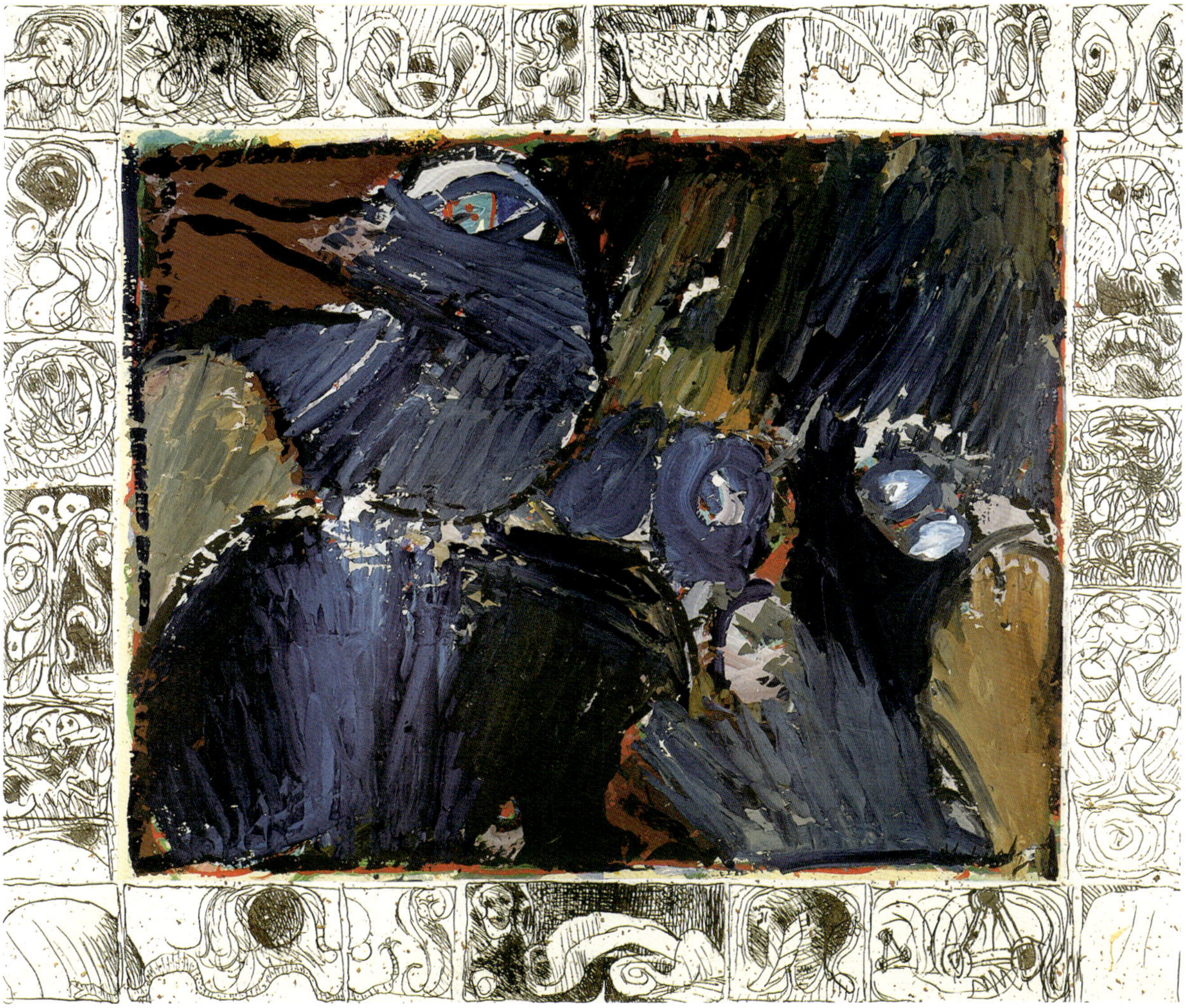

334, 321, 311
Henry Heerup:
Mask, 1955
Death Reaping, 1943
The Horn of Fertility, 1935

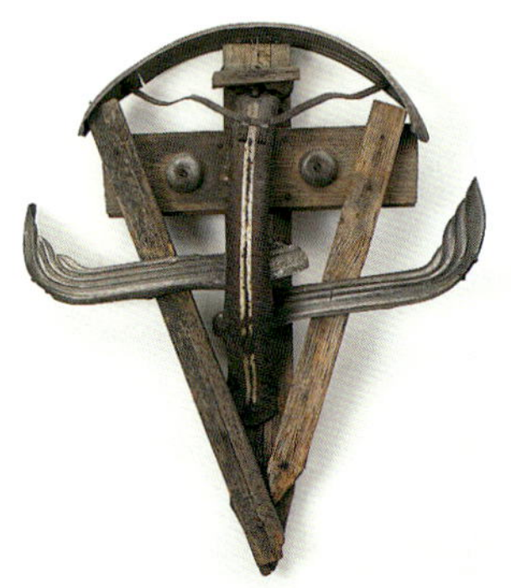

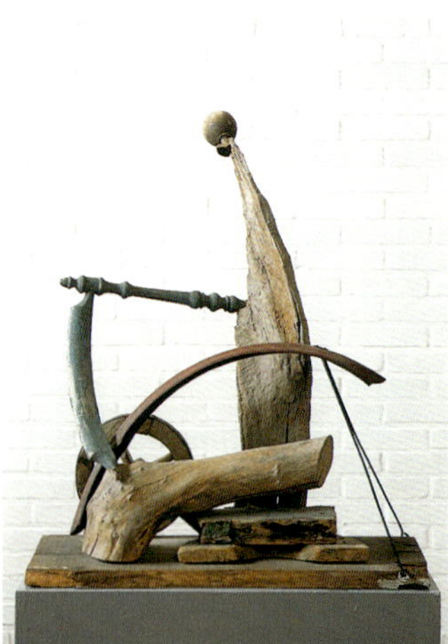

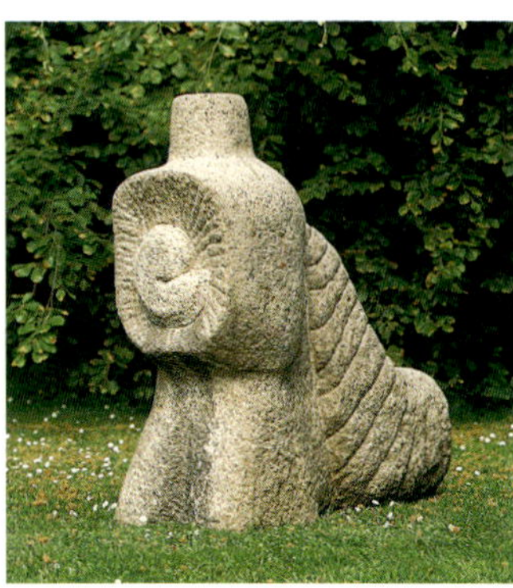

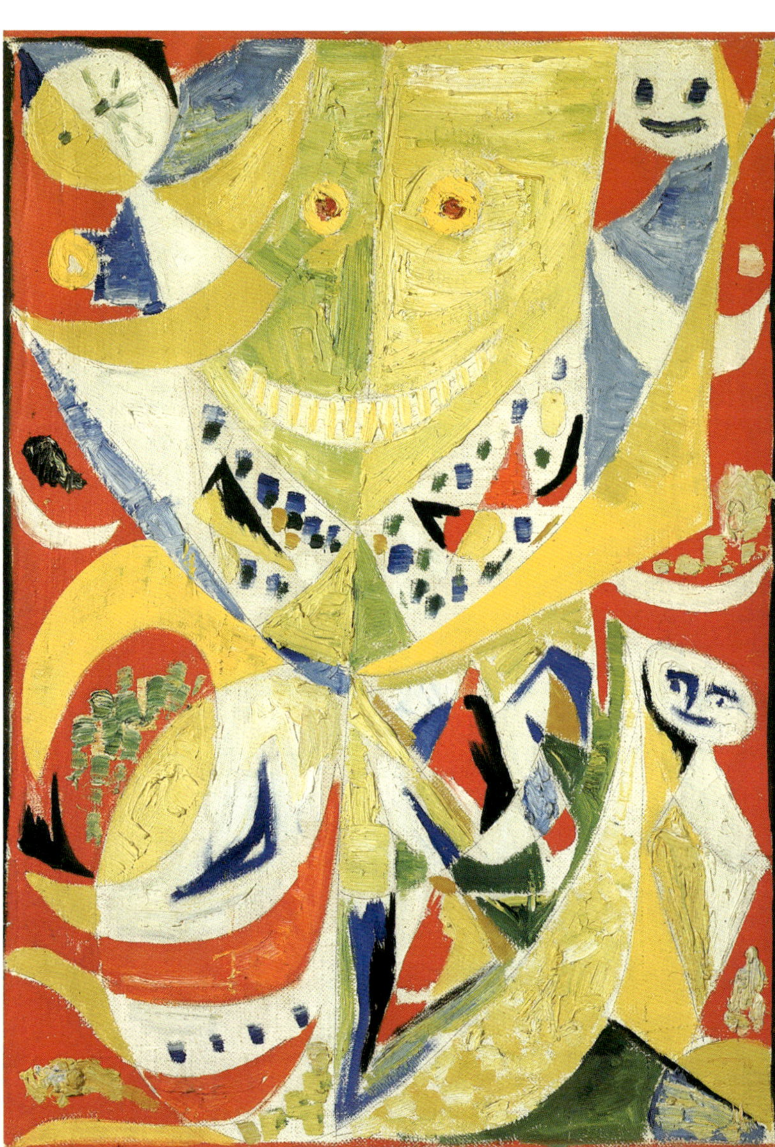

383
Egill Jacobsen: Mask, 1945

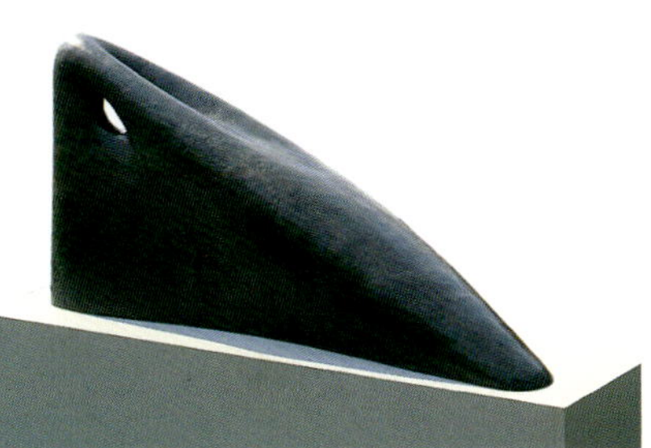

549
Sonja Ferlov Mancoba:
Sculpture, 1940-46

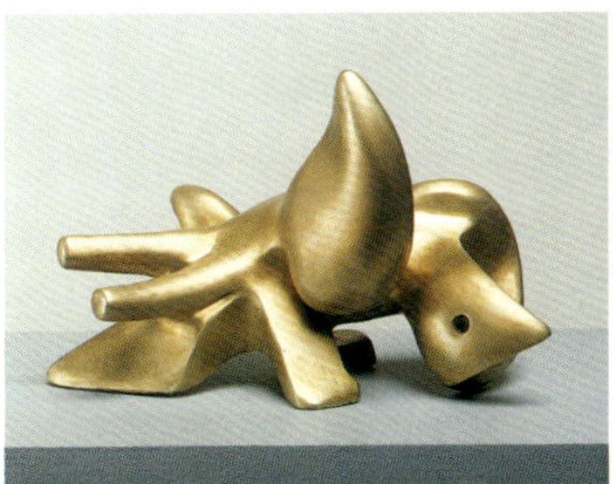

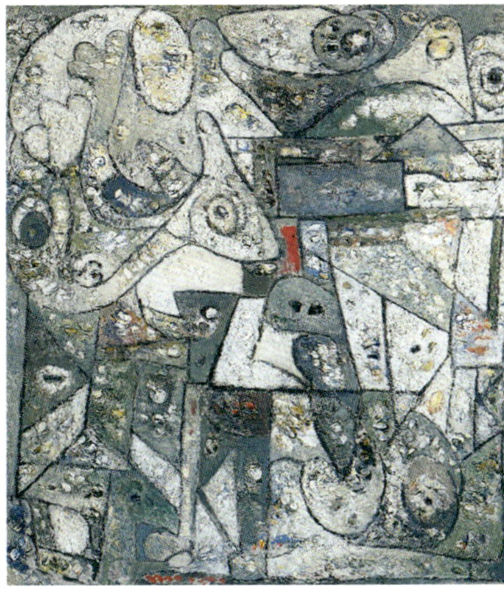

76, 72
Ejler Bille:
Tricky Bird, 1933 (left)
White, Blue, Green
with Red Dominant, 1960 (right)

650
Carl-Henning Pedersen:
People and the Sea I, 1949

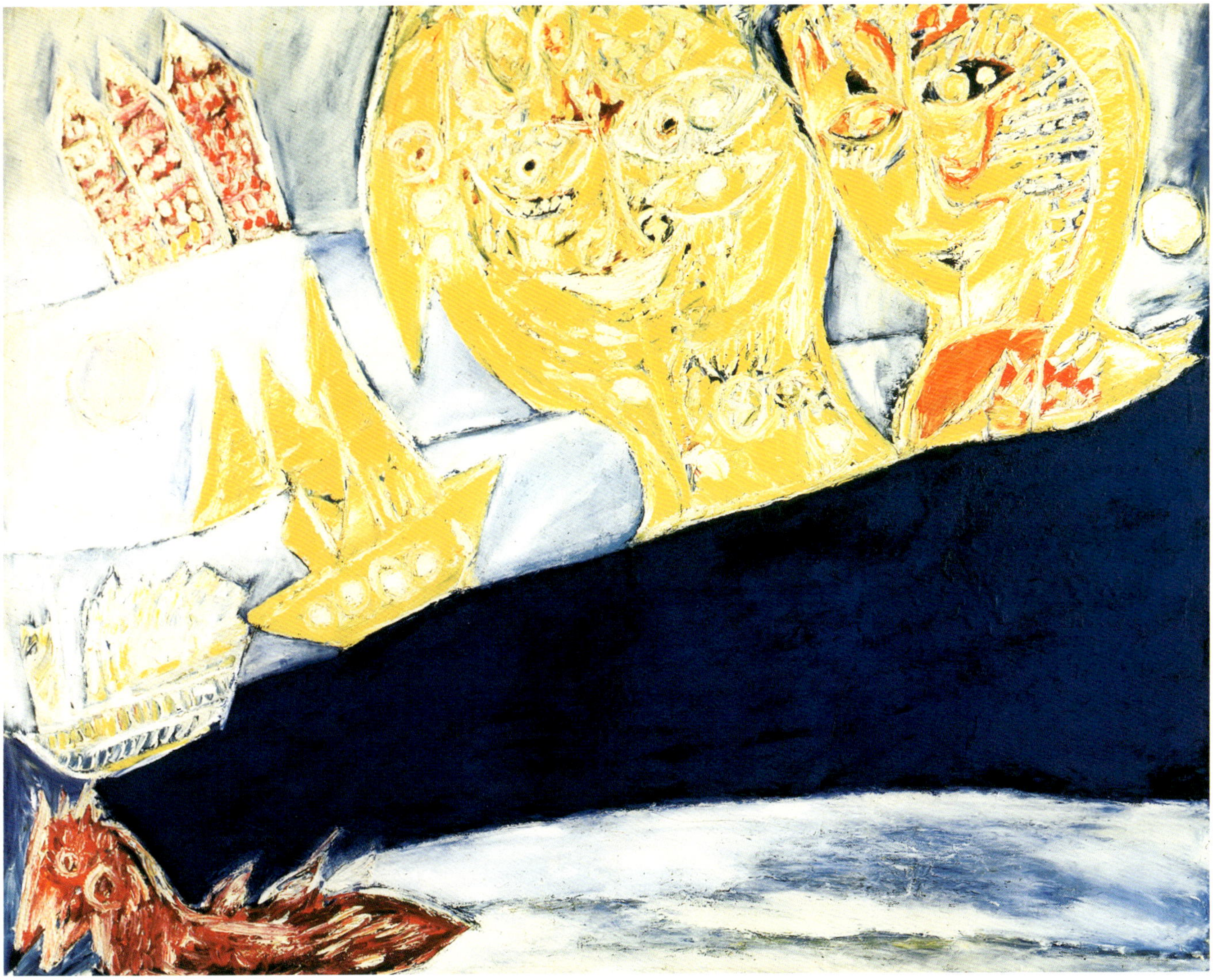

Constructivism and Concrete Art

5
Josef Albers: Homage to the Square: Yellow Climate, 1961

104
Eduardo Chillida: Erabaki, 1968

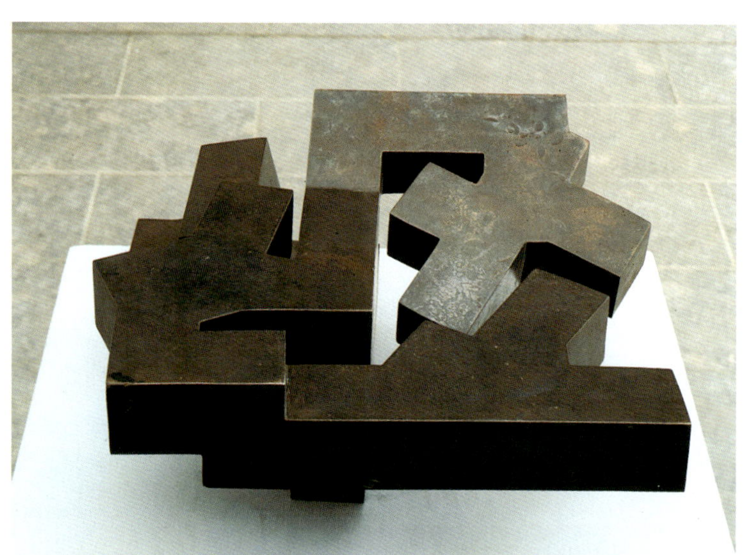

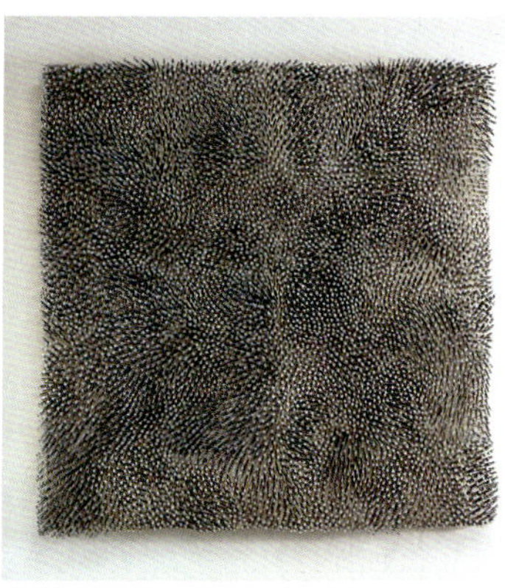

902
Günther Uecker: White Field, 1983

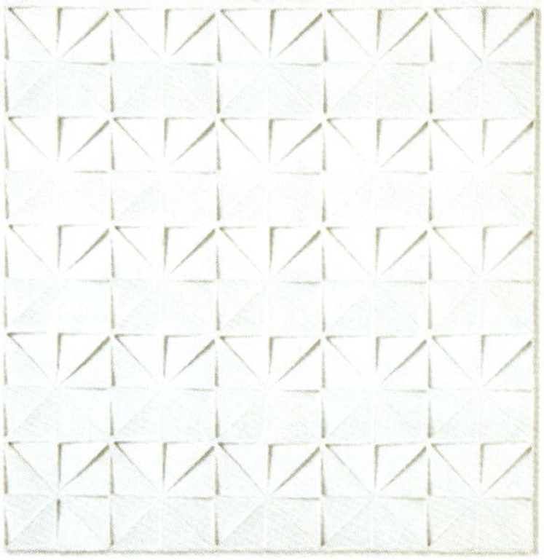

813
Jan Schoonhoven: R-69.3, 1969

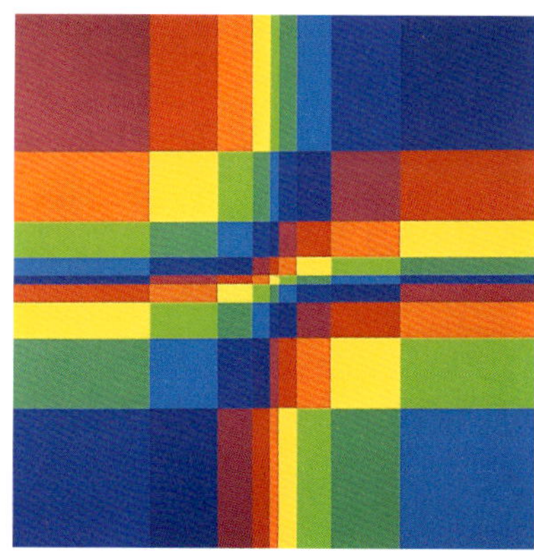

513
Richard Paul Lohse: Nine Horizontal and Nine Vertical Colour Rows, 1950-83

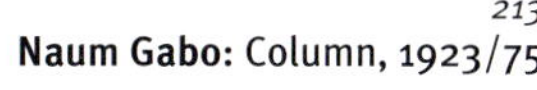

213
Naum Gabo: Column, 1923/75

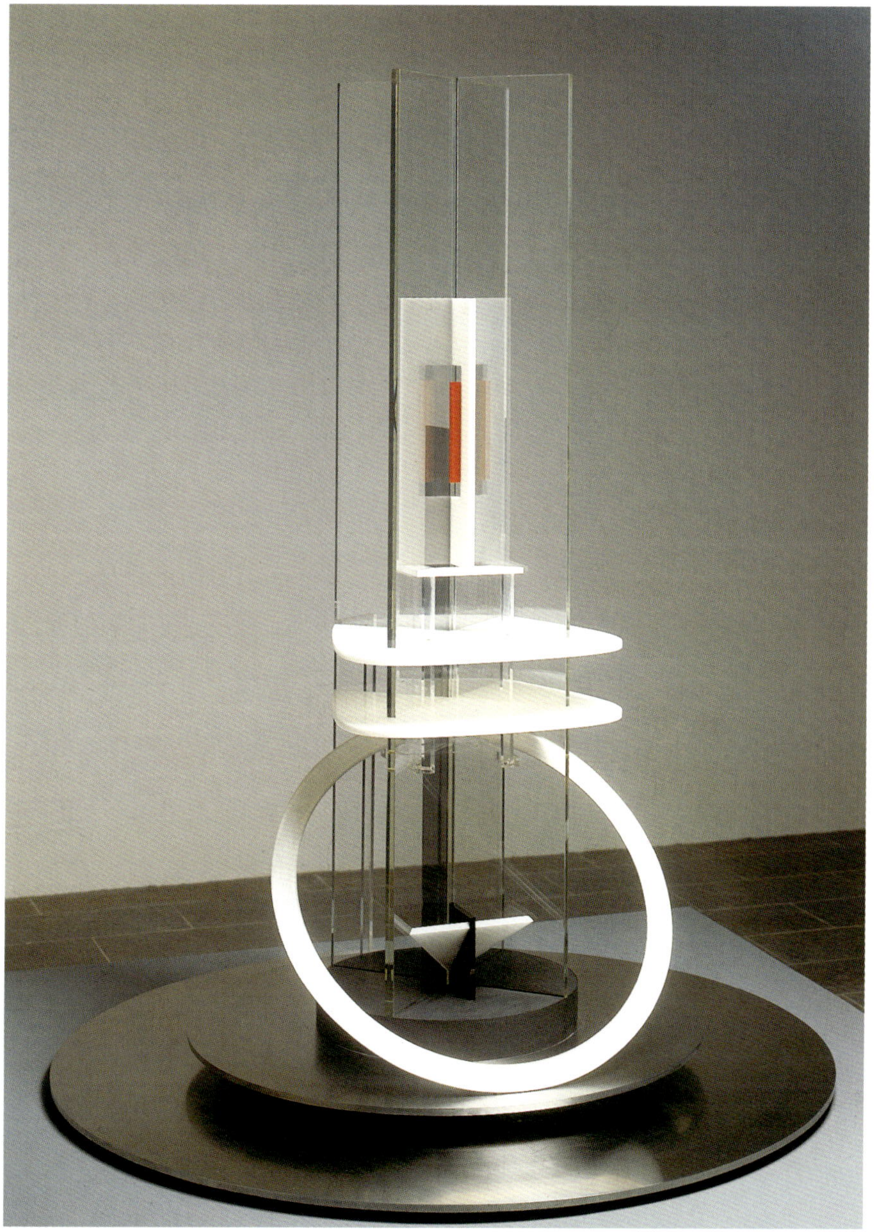

840
Jesus Rafael Soto:
The Big Blue, 1964

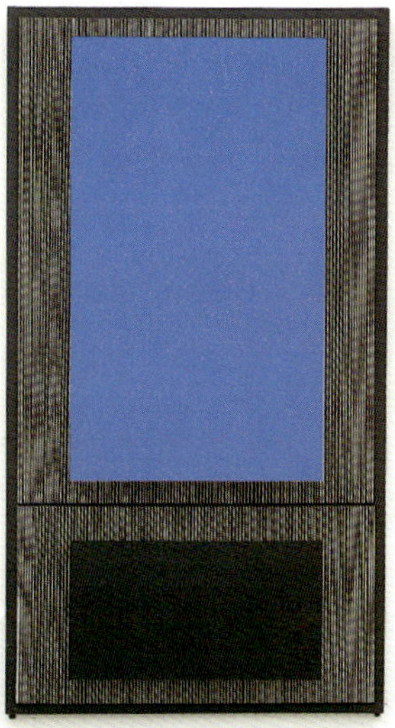

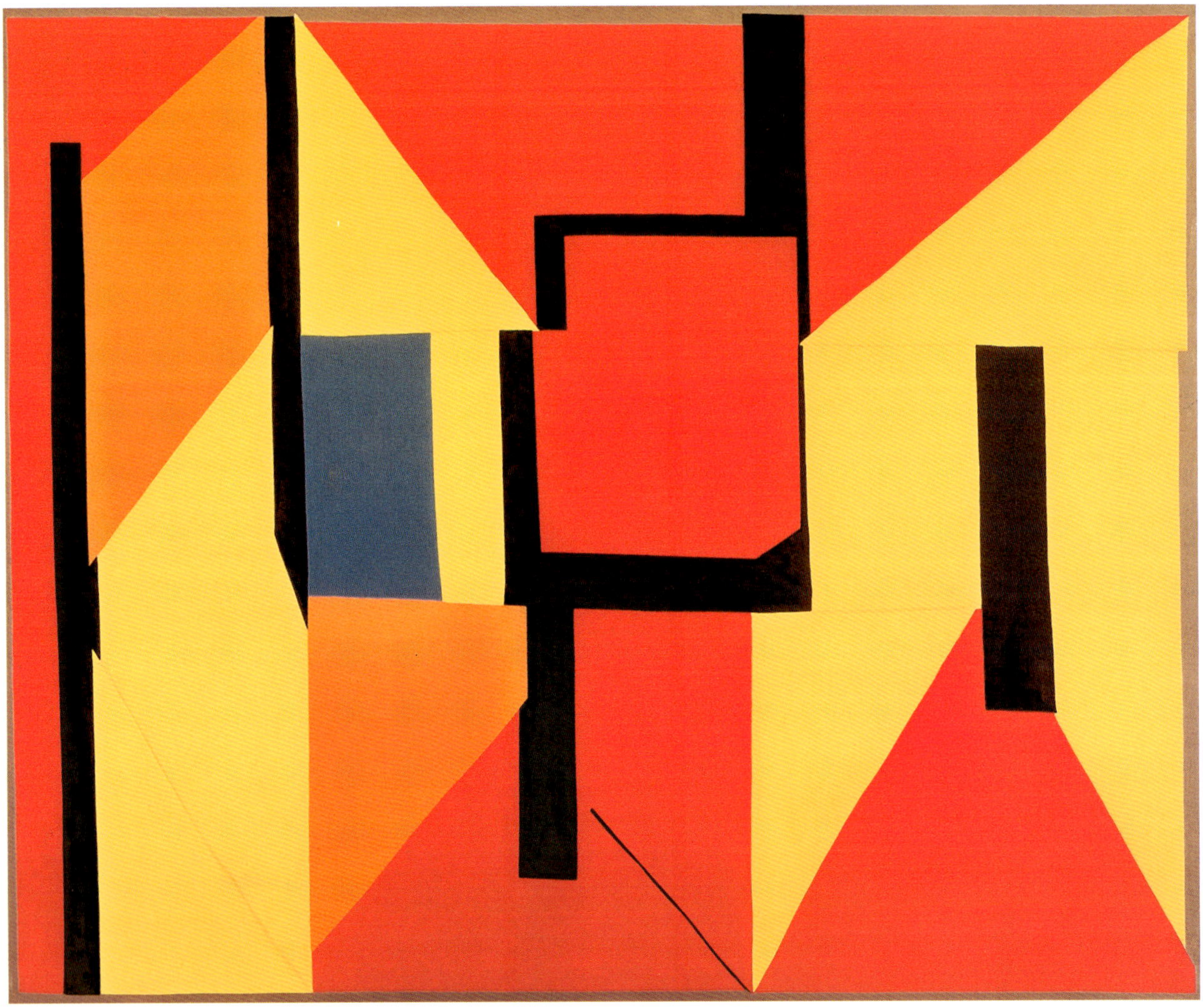

608
Richard Mortensen: South, 1956

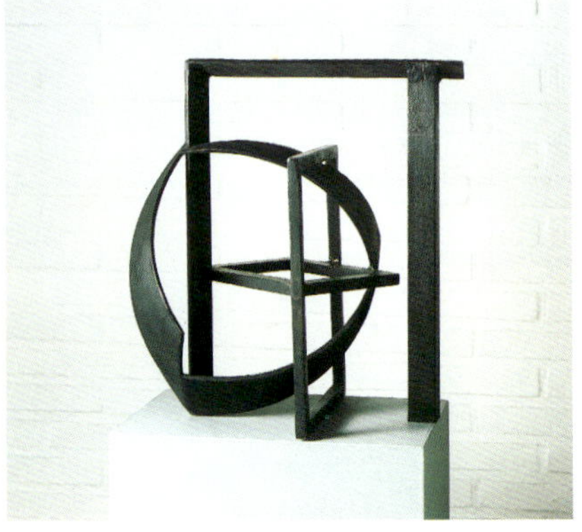

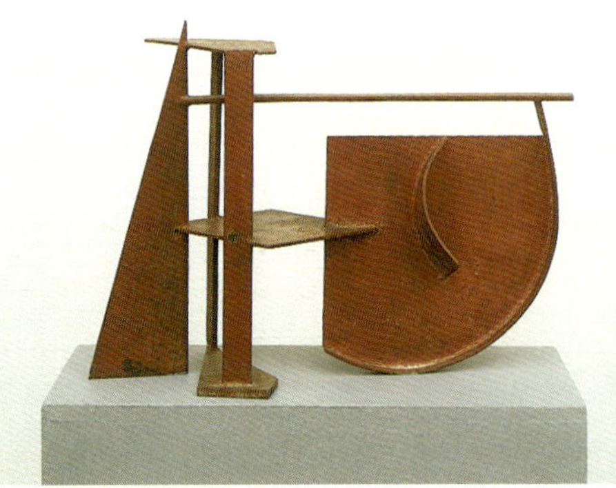

395, 388
Robert Jacobsen:
Sculpture in Wrought Iron, 1959 (left)
Problem of Motion, 1955 (right)

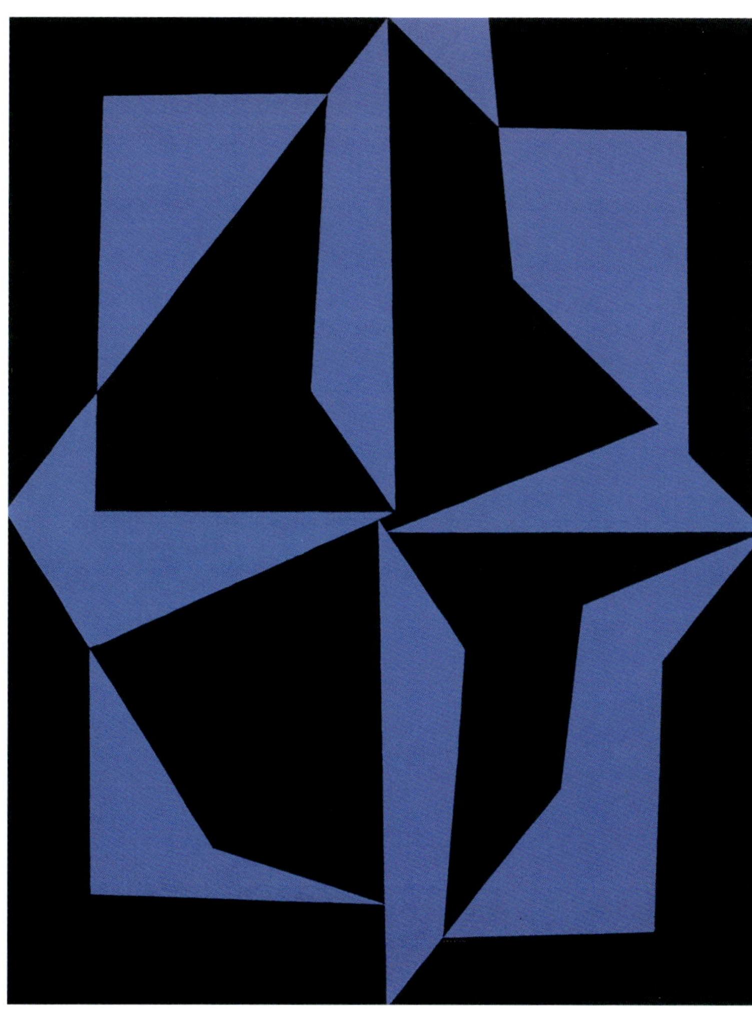

907
Victor Vasarely: Zilah, 1957

52
Olle Baertling: Ogri, 1959

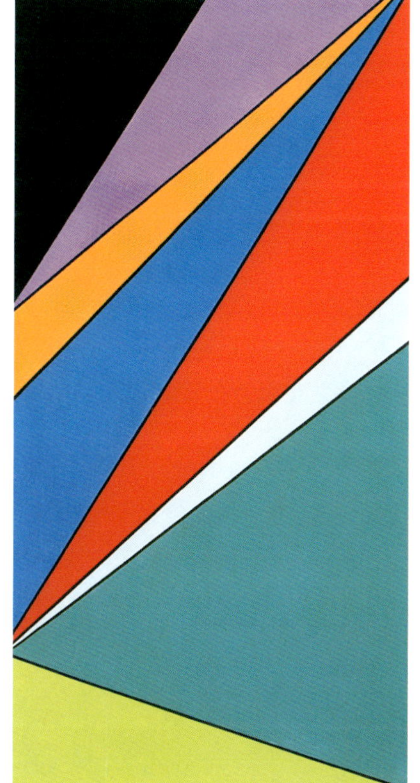

349
Auguste Herbin: Yellow, 1946

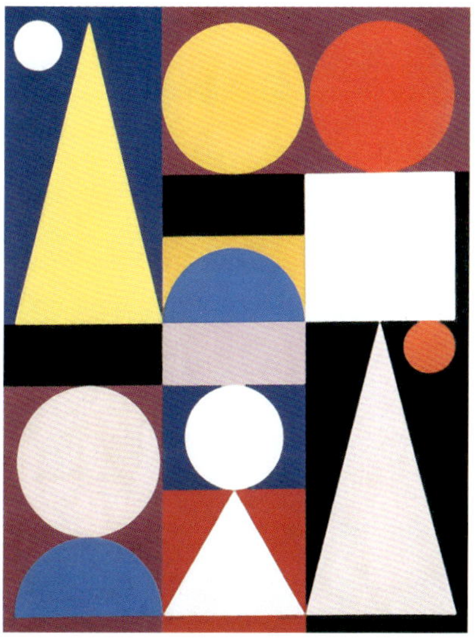

Recent Danish Art

922
Willy Ørskov:
Untitled, 1979-80

276, 273
Svend Wiig Hansen:
Delos, 1962
People in Metamorphosis III:
The Celestial Child, 1963

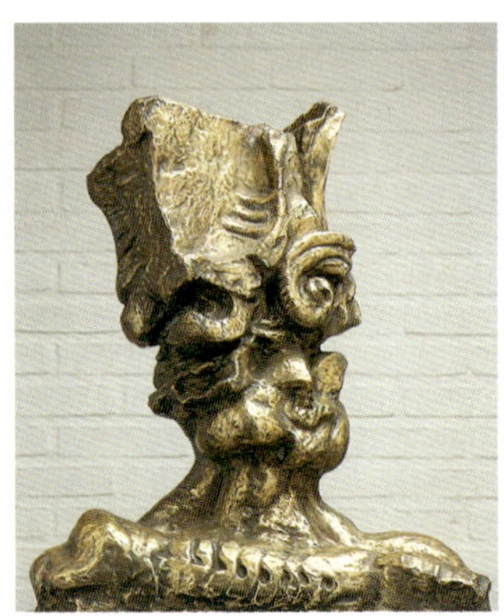

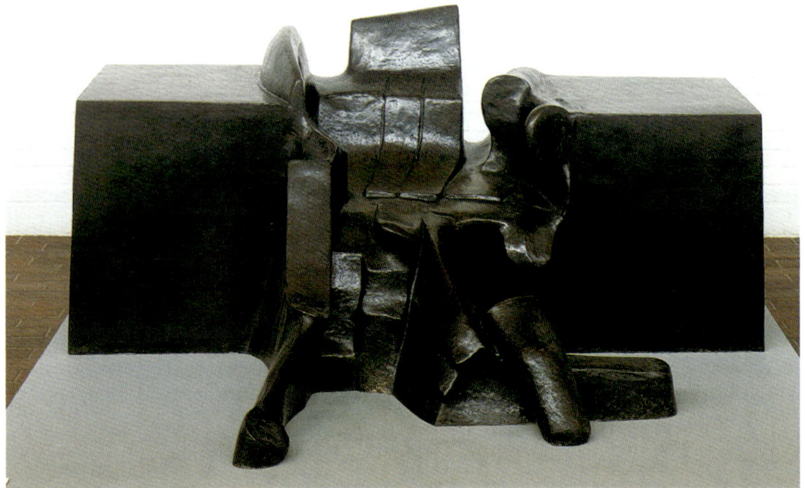

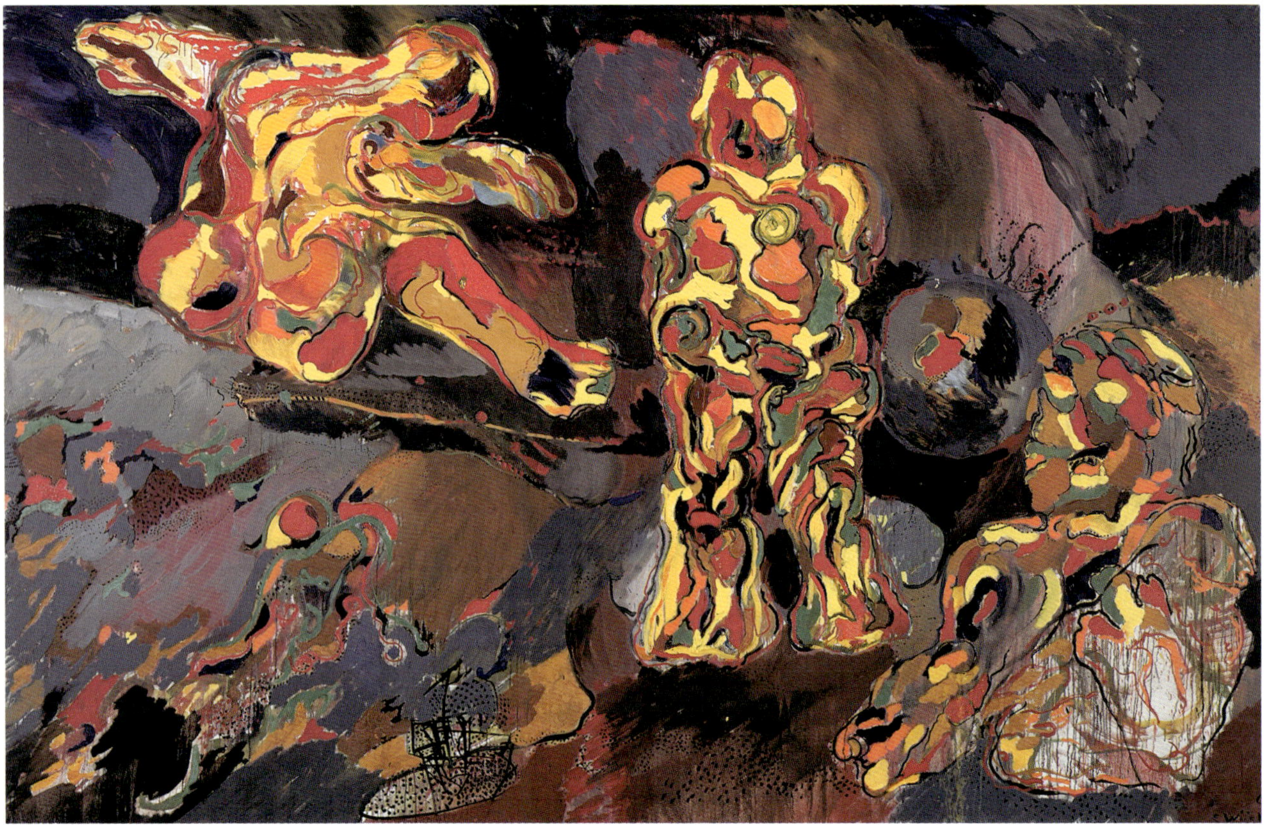

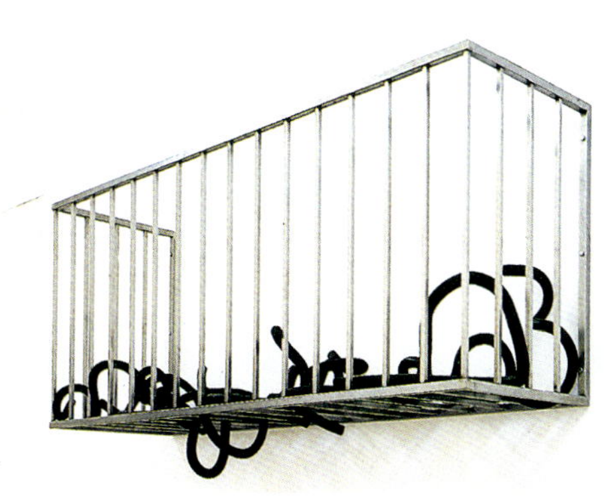

635
Kirsten Ortwed: B4, 1997

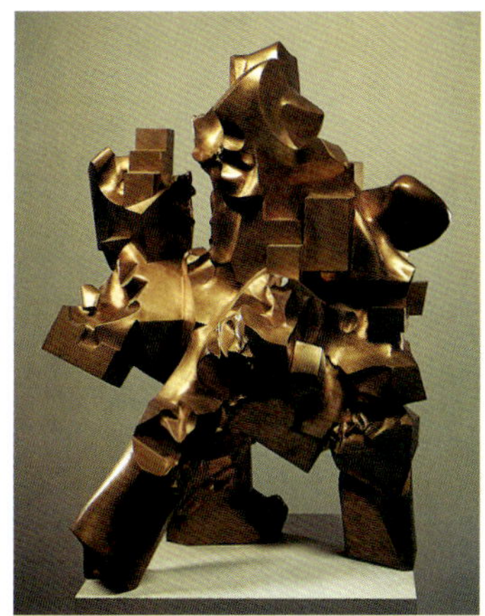

347
Hein Heinsen: Untitled, 1989

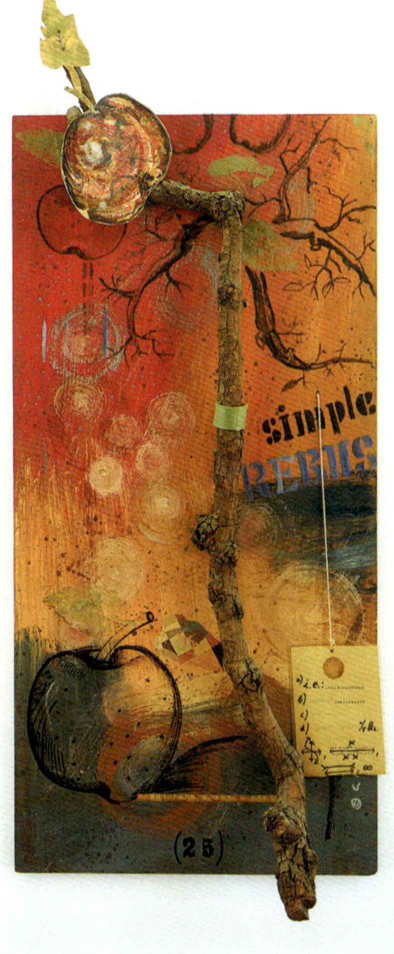

492
Arthur Köpcke: Picture Puzzle: Like Father, Like Son, 1964

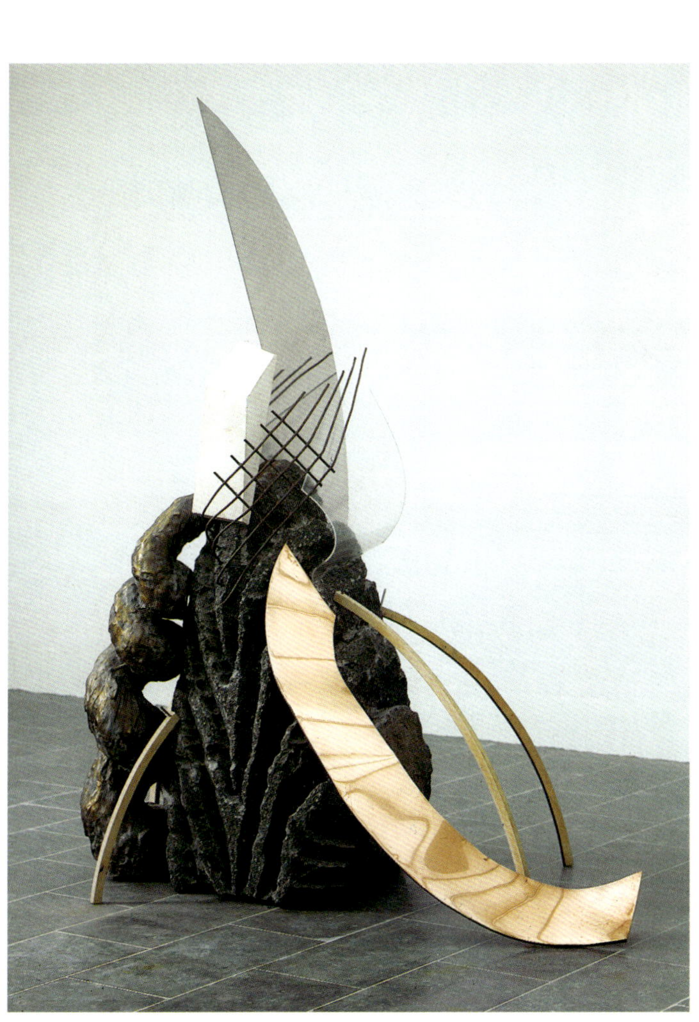

622
Bjørn Nørgaard: The Spiral, 1980

Neo-Dada and Pop Art

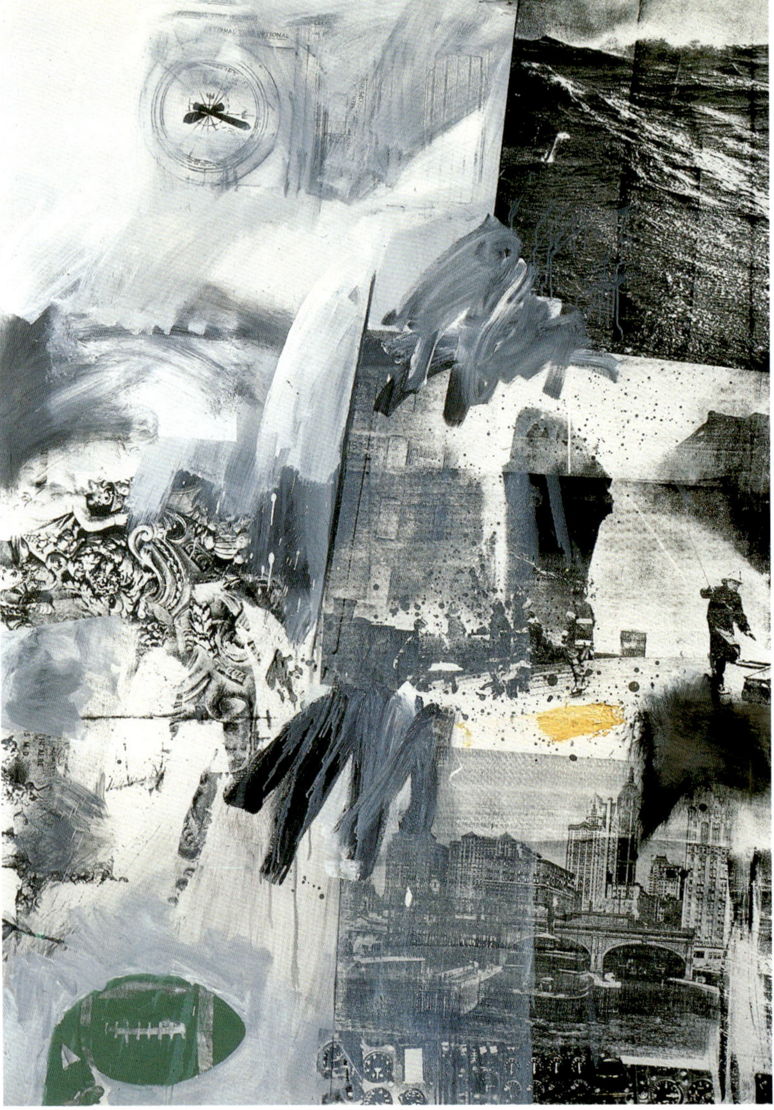

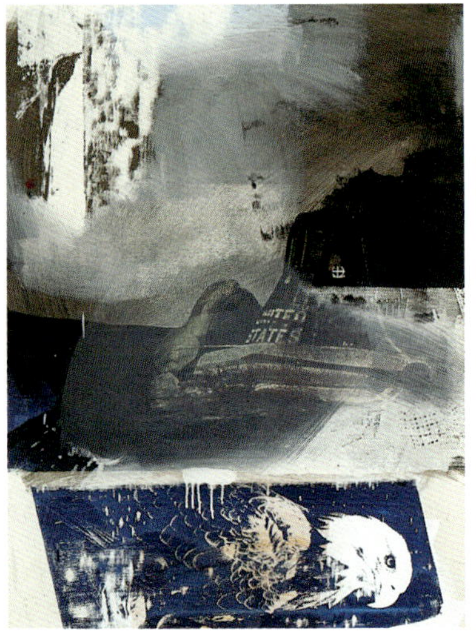

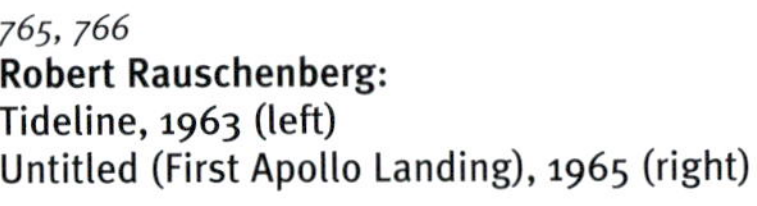

765, 766
Robert Rauschenberg:
Tideline, 1963 (left)
Untitled (First Apollo Landing), 1965 (right)

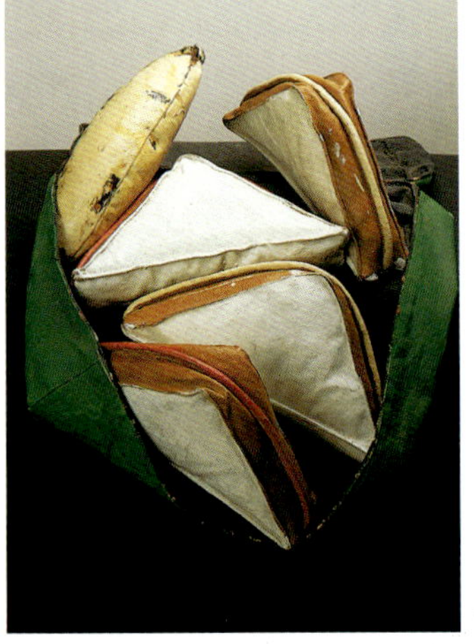

402, 624
Jasper Johns: Green Target, 1957
Claes Oldenburg: Lunch-Box, 1961

911, 914
Andy Warhol:
Close Cover before Striking, 1962 (left)
Mao, 1972 (right)

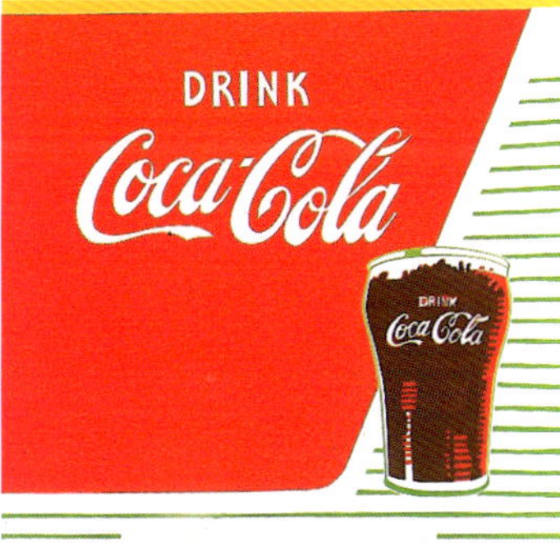

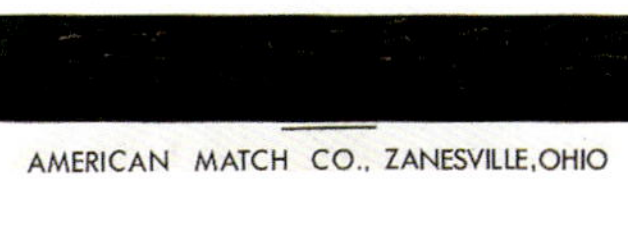

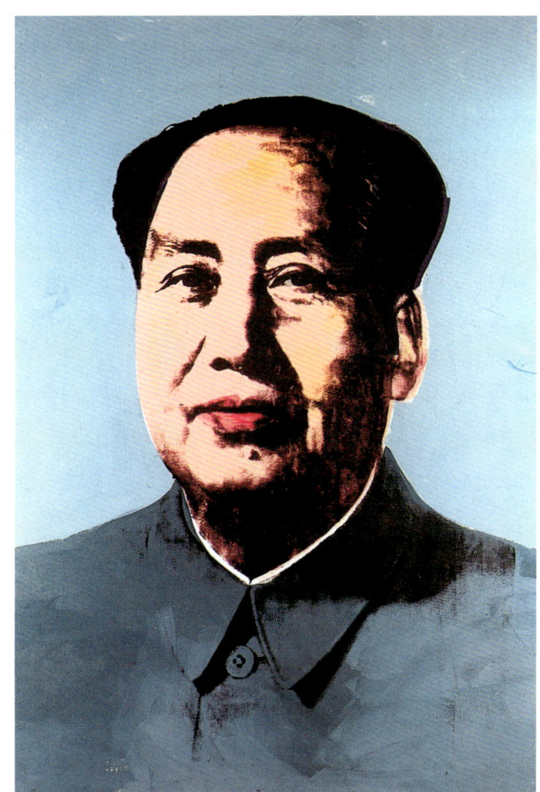

136
Jim Dine: White Bathroom, 1962

511
Roy Lichtenstein:
Figures in Landscape, 1977

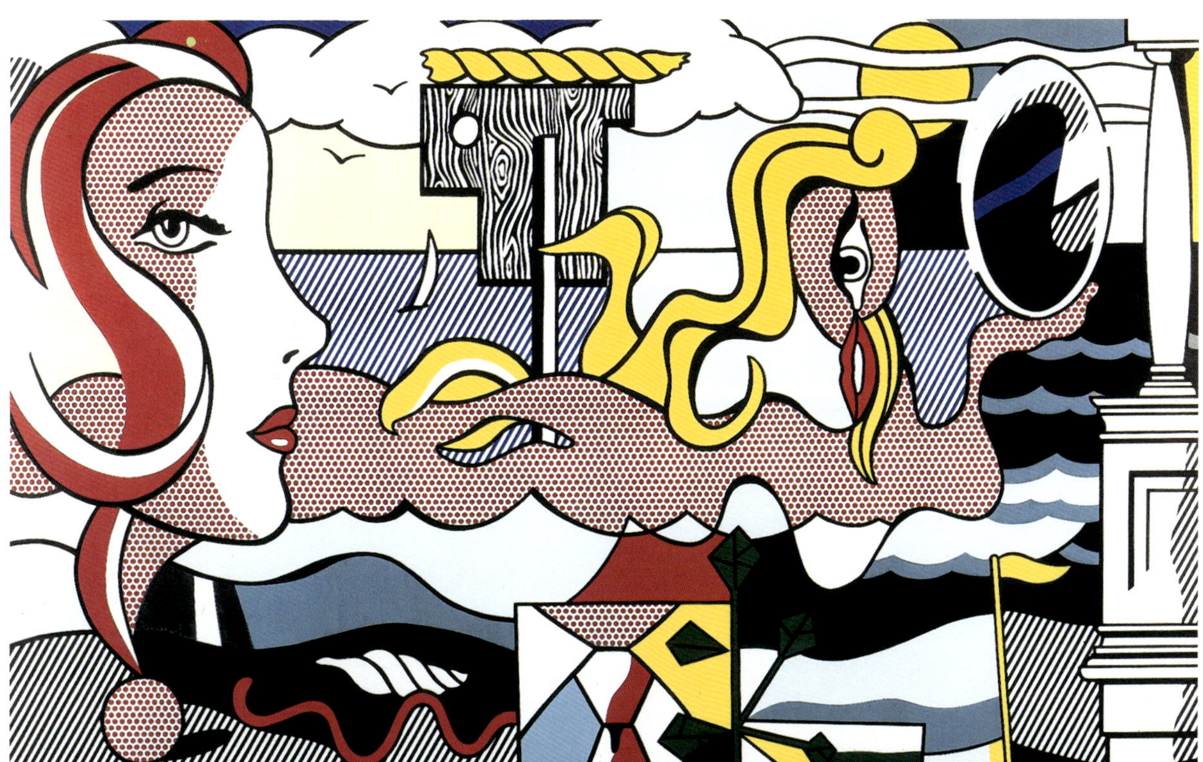

Nouveau Réalisme

770, 771
Martial Raysse:
Do You Remember Tahiti in September 61, 1963 (left)
Young Venetian Girl, 1963 (right)

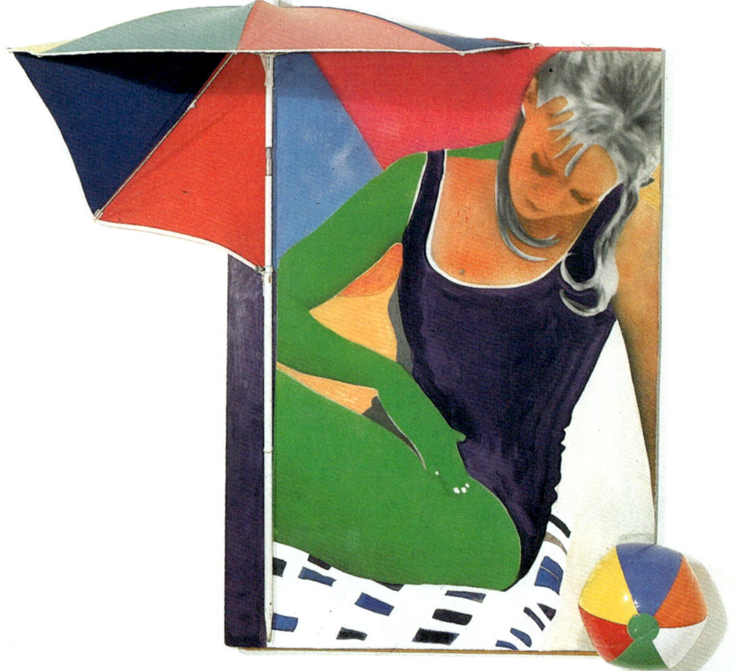

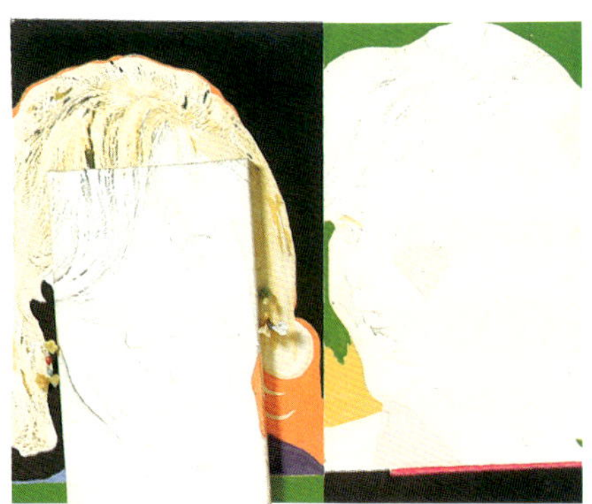

883, 884
Jean Tinguely:
Green Baluba, 1962 (left)
Seesaw, 1965 (right)

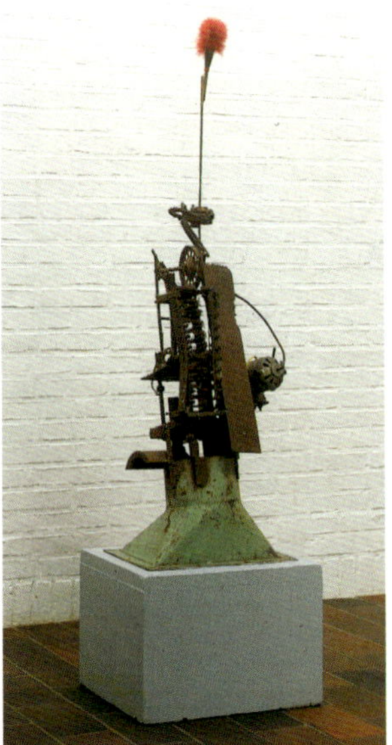

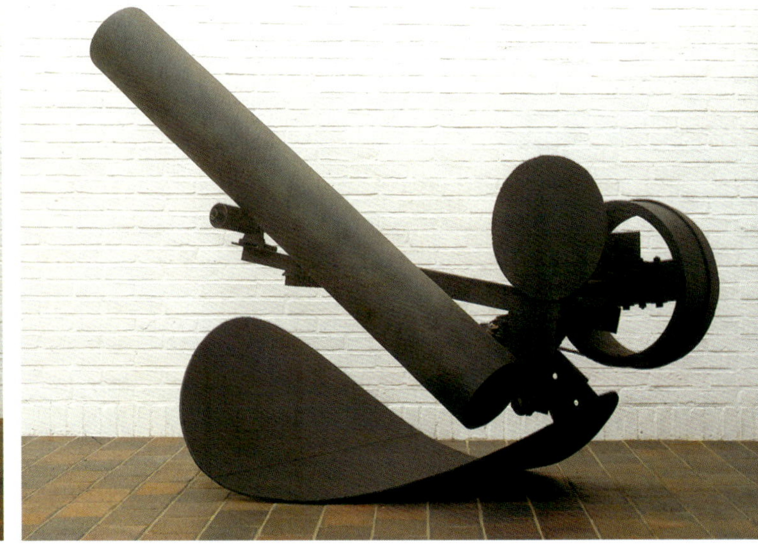

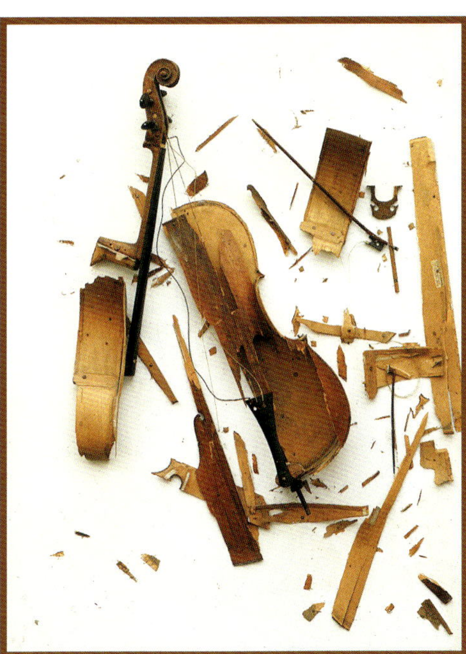

44
Arman: Munich Concert No. 1 "Violoncello Anger", 1963

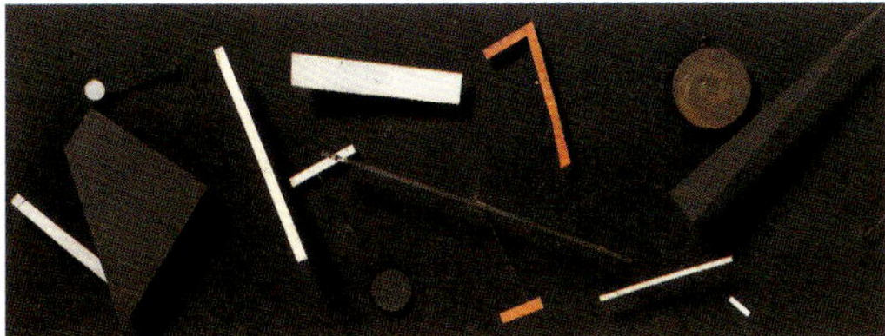

881
Jean Tinguely:
Metamechanical Relief, 1956

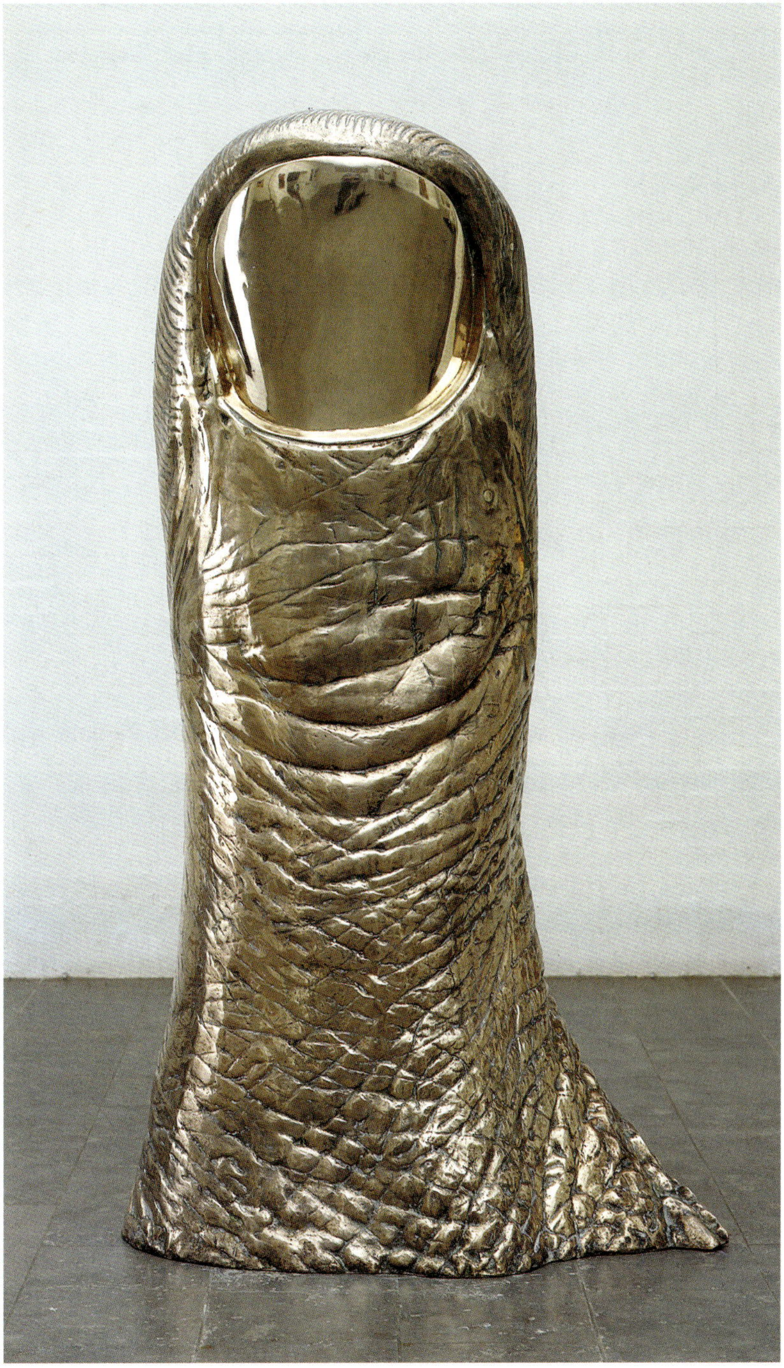

102
César: The Big Thumb, 1968

Morris Louis

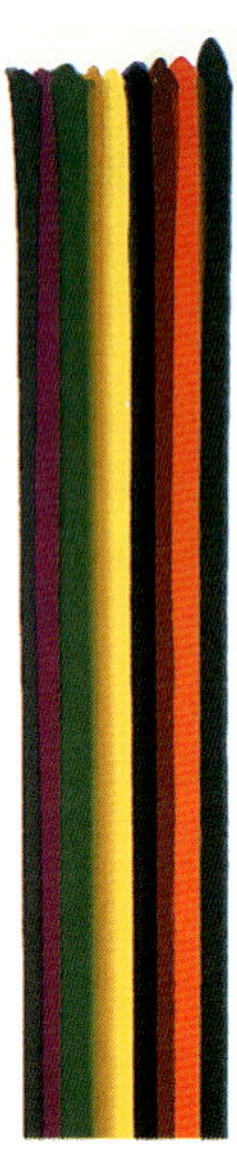

531
Happy Friday, 1962

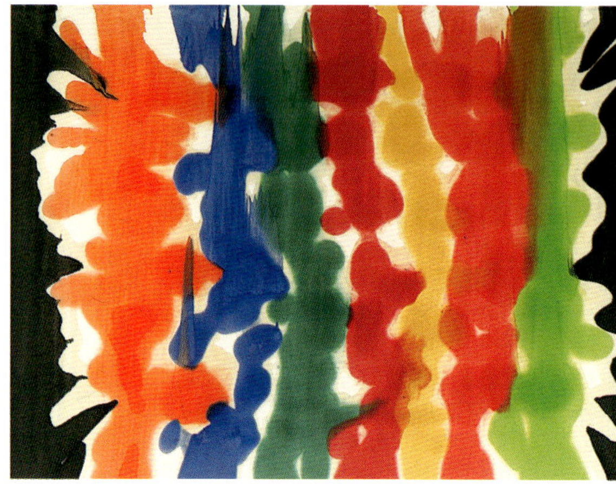

526
Para No. 1, 1959

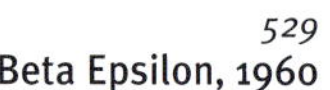

529
Beta Epsilon, 1960

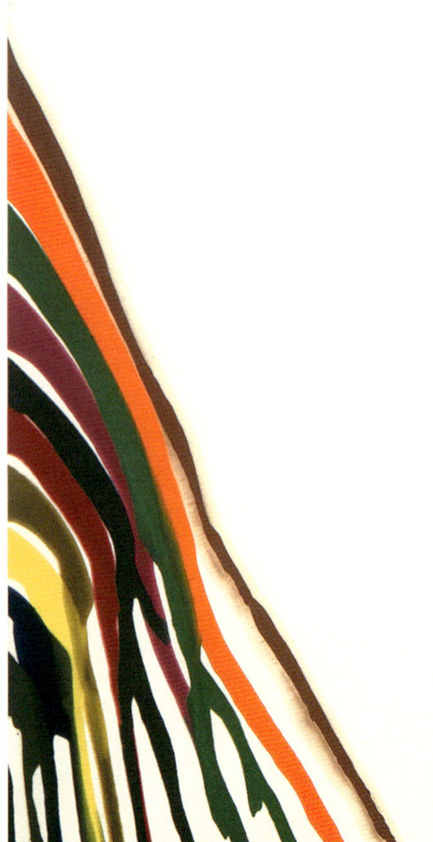

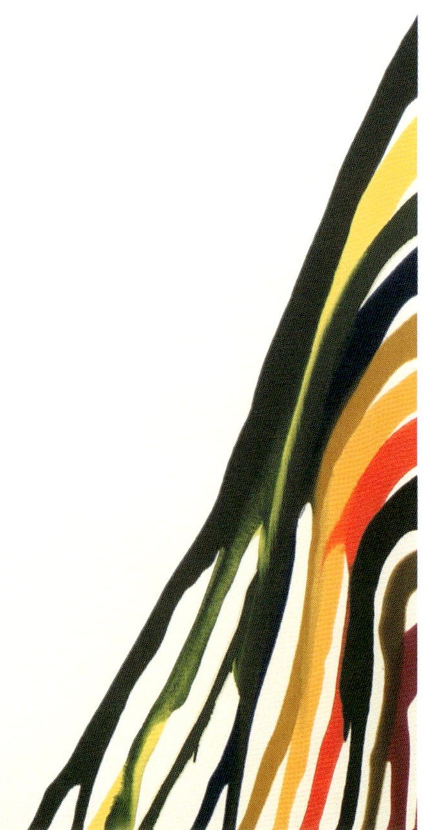

528
Omega IV, 1959-60

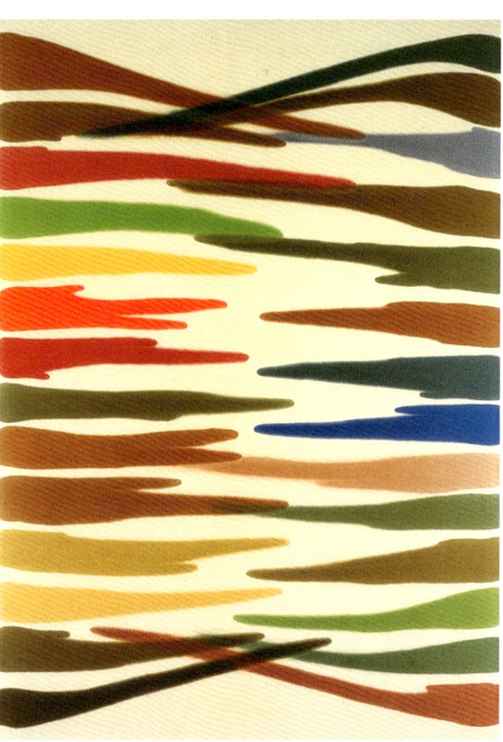

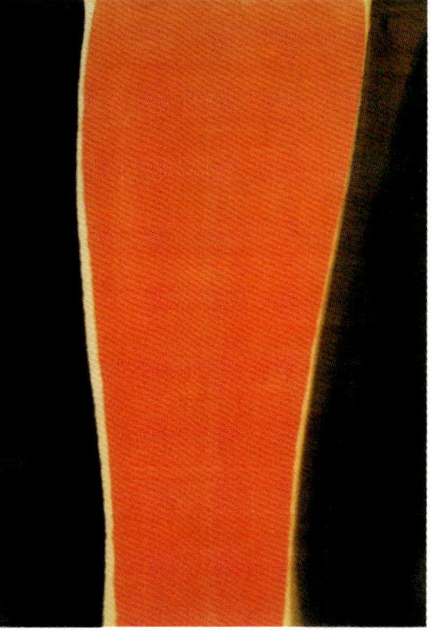

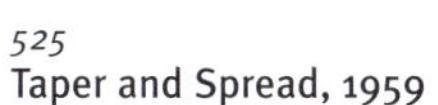

525
Taper and Spread, 1959

523
Dalet Nun, 1958

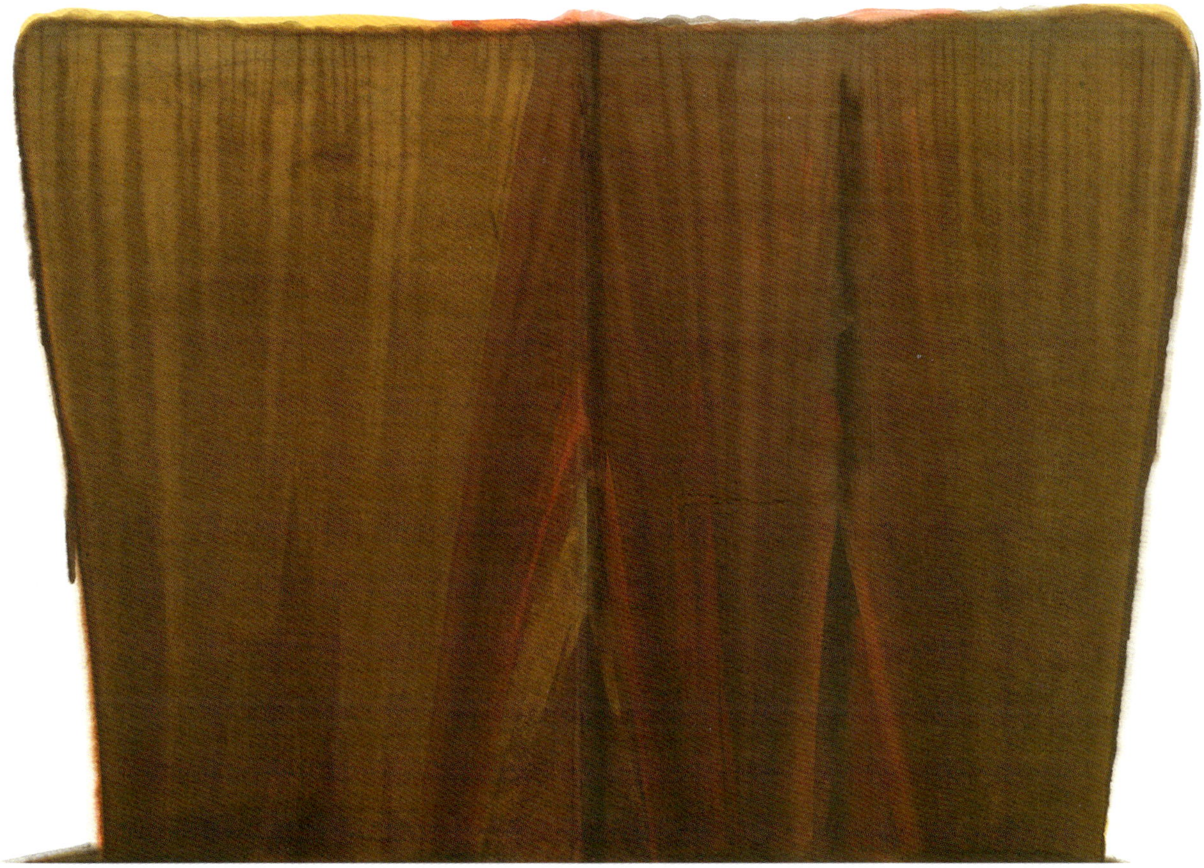

Sam Francis

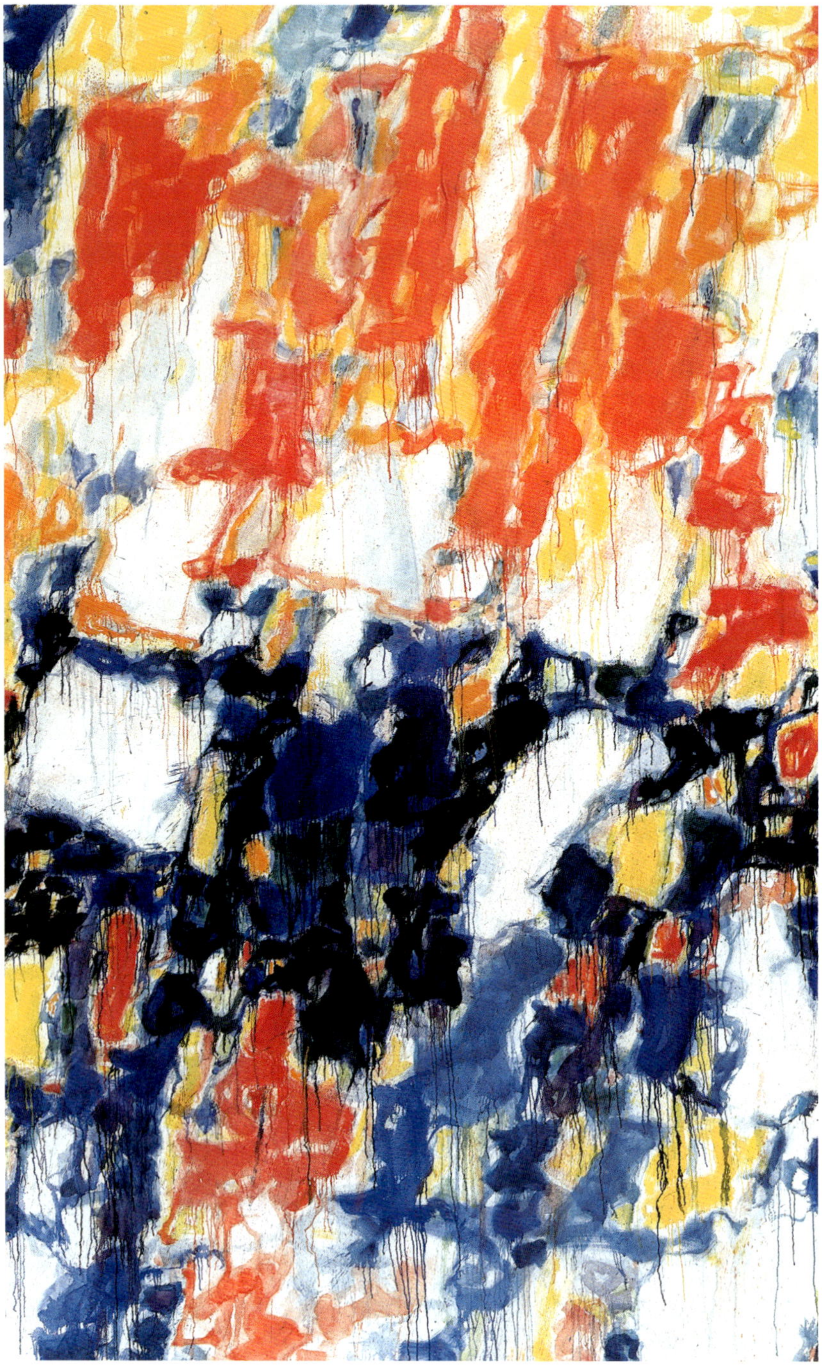

180
Untitled, 1956

191
Untitled (Edge Painting), 1966

182
Untitled, 1958

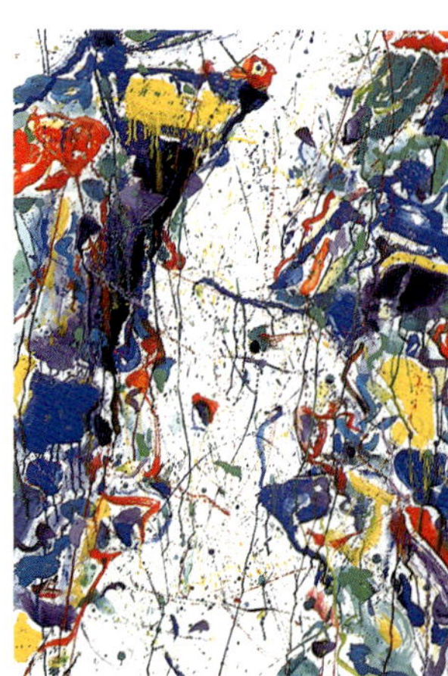

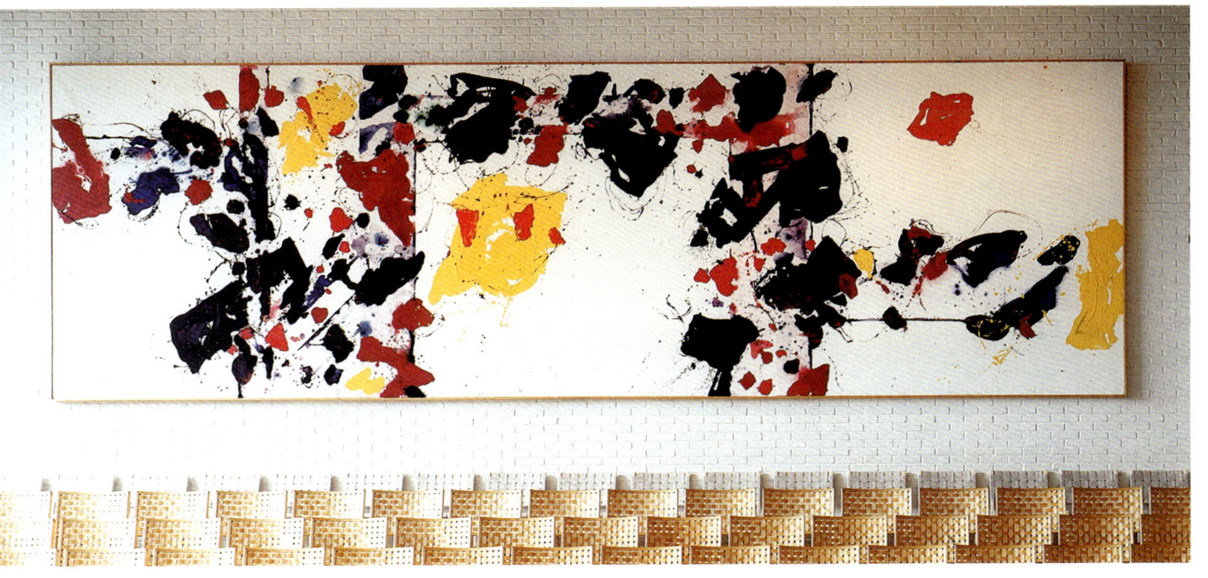

203
Untitled, 1981-83

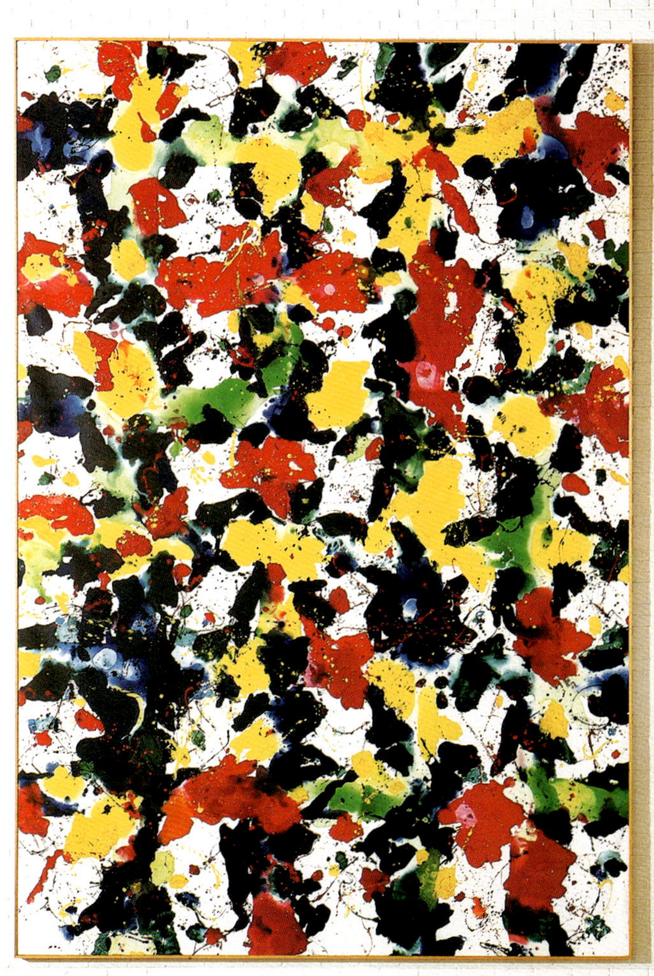

181
Untitled, 1957

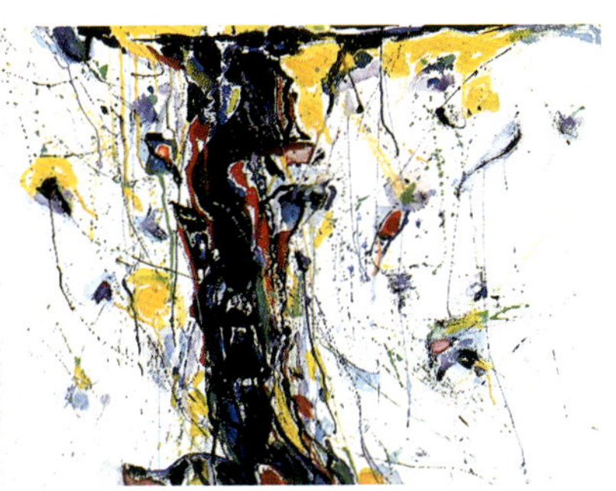

199
Big Red II, 1979

Minimalism and Shaped Canvas

418
Donald Judd:
Untitled, 1969

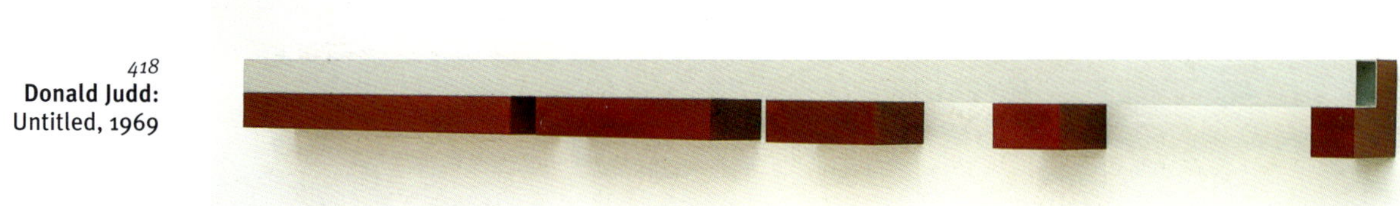

808
Robert Ryman:
Untitled, 1961

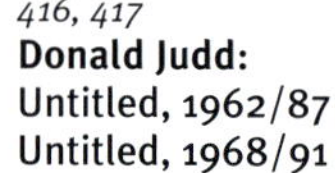

416, 417
Donald Judd:
Untitled, 1962/87
Untitled, 1968/91

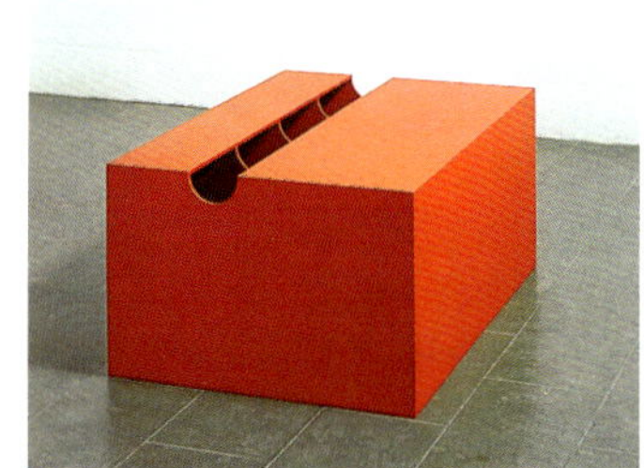

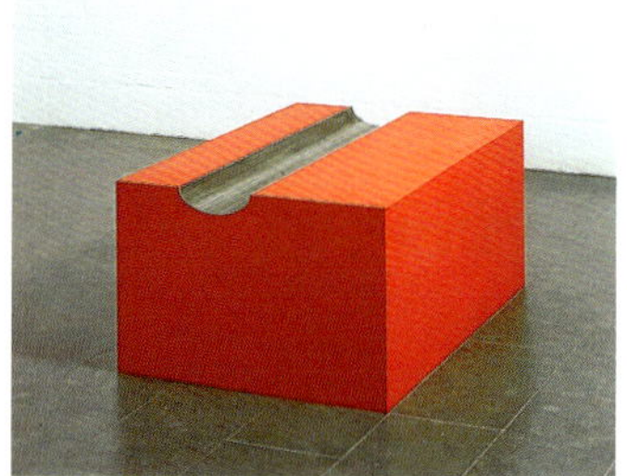

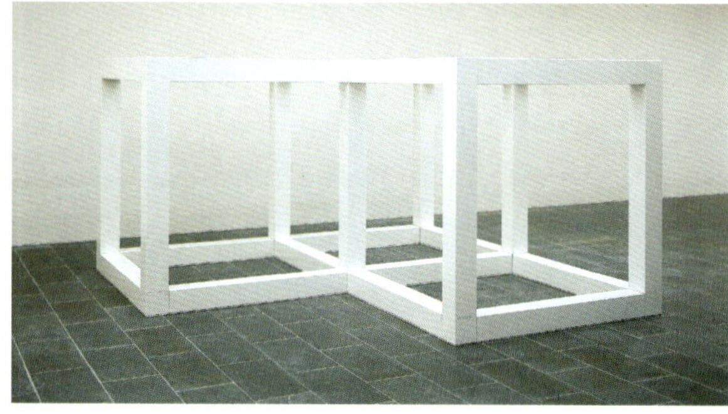

508
Sol Lewitt:
Three Cubes (Angle), 1969

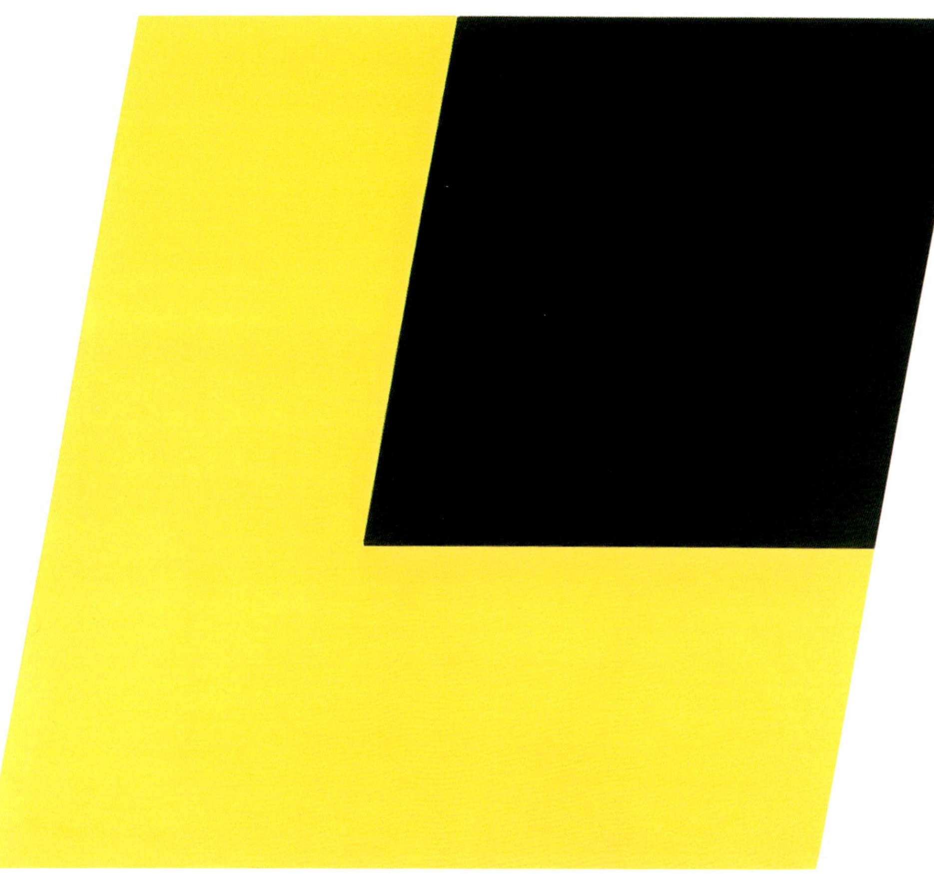

430
Ellsworth Kelly: Yellow Black, 1968

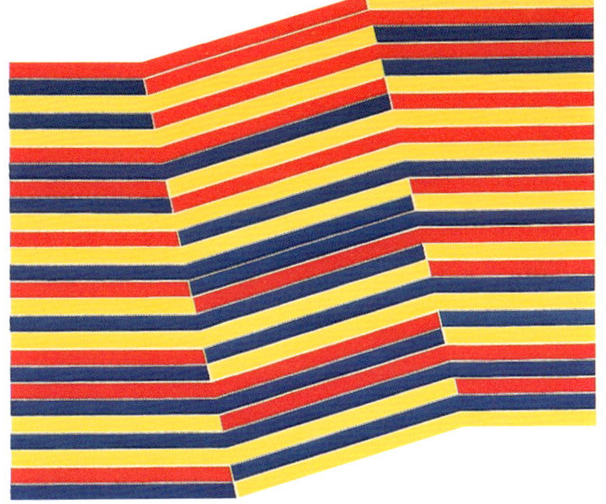

846
Frank Stella: Bam, 1966

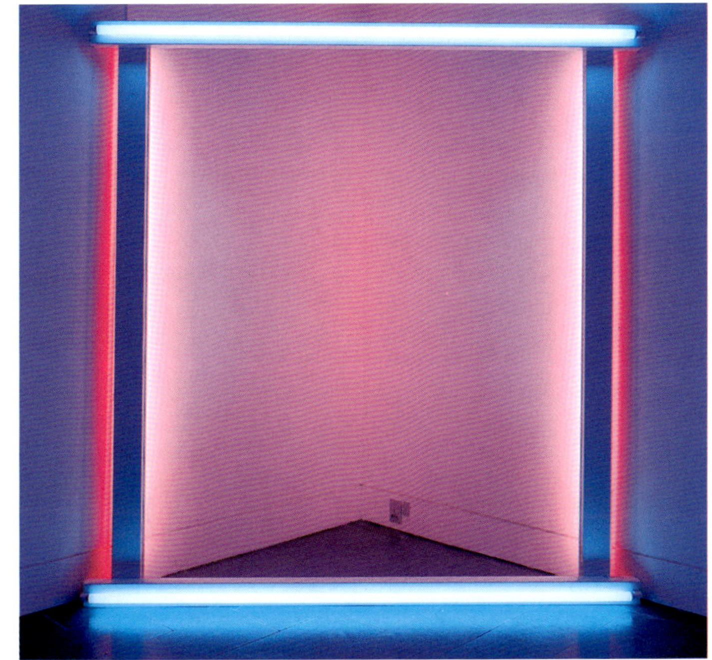

173
Dan Flavin: Untitled
(to Barbara Lipper), 1973

Late Picasso/Late Dubuffet

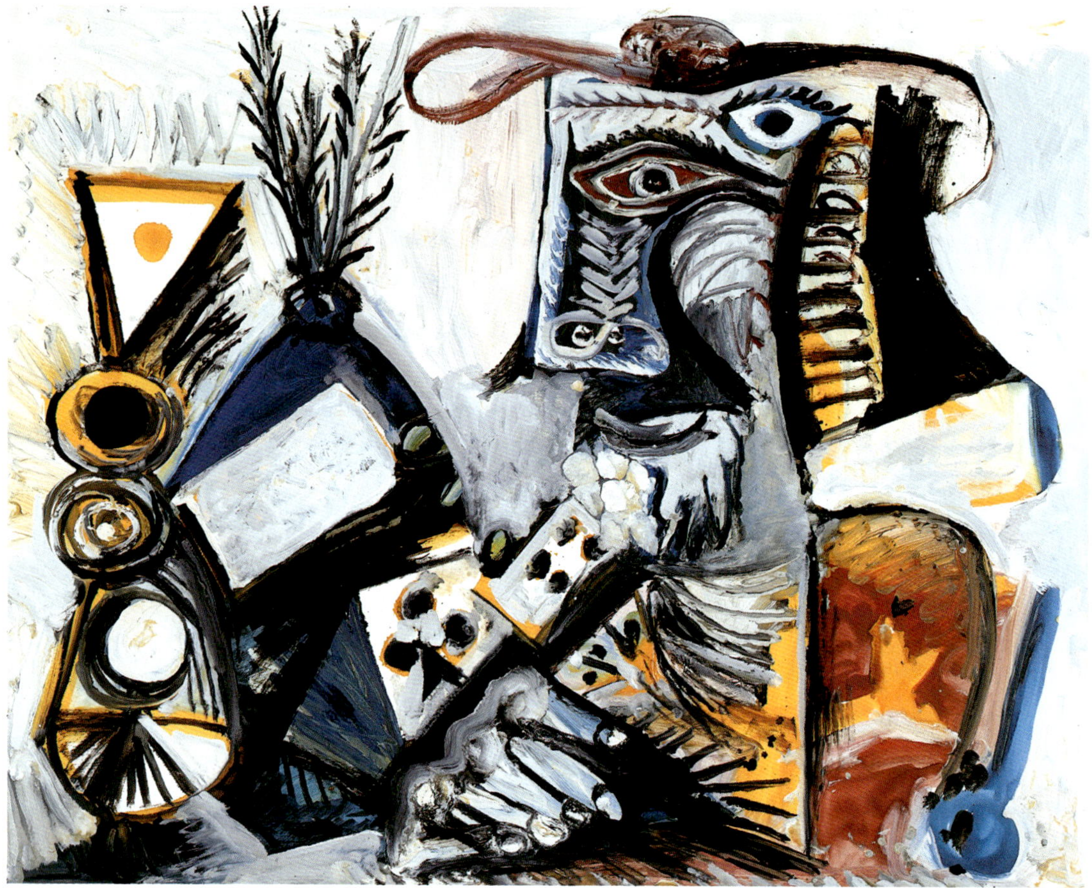

738
Pablo Picasso:
The Card Player II, 1971

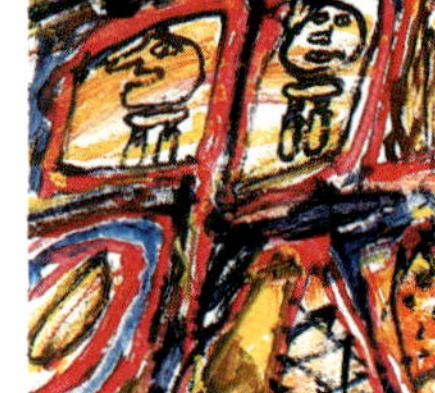
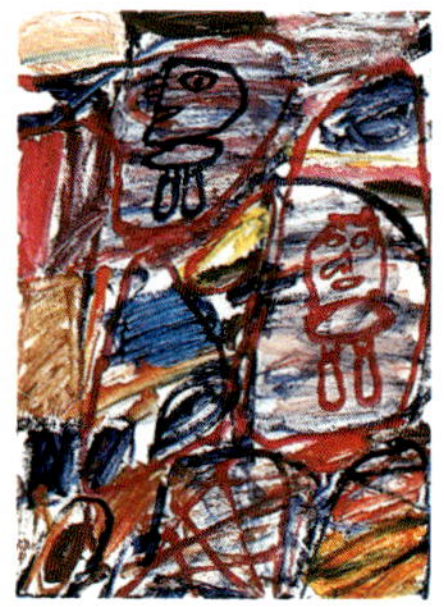
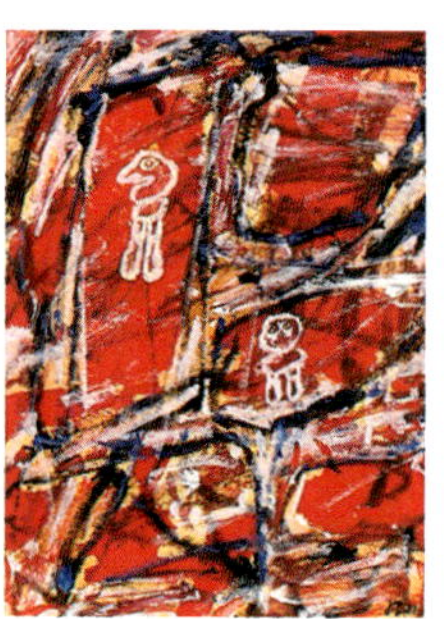
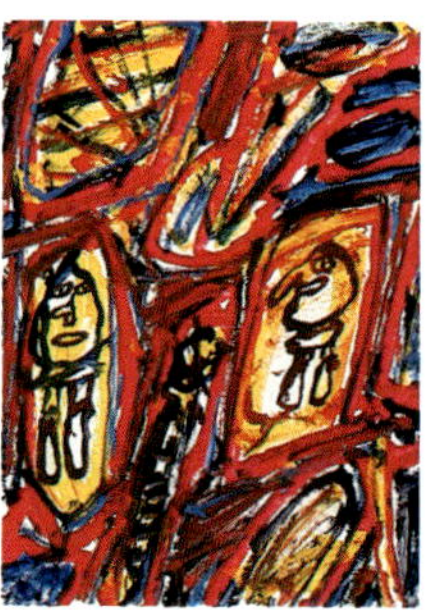

145-148
Jean Dubuffet:
Sites with figures, 1981

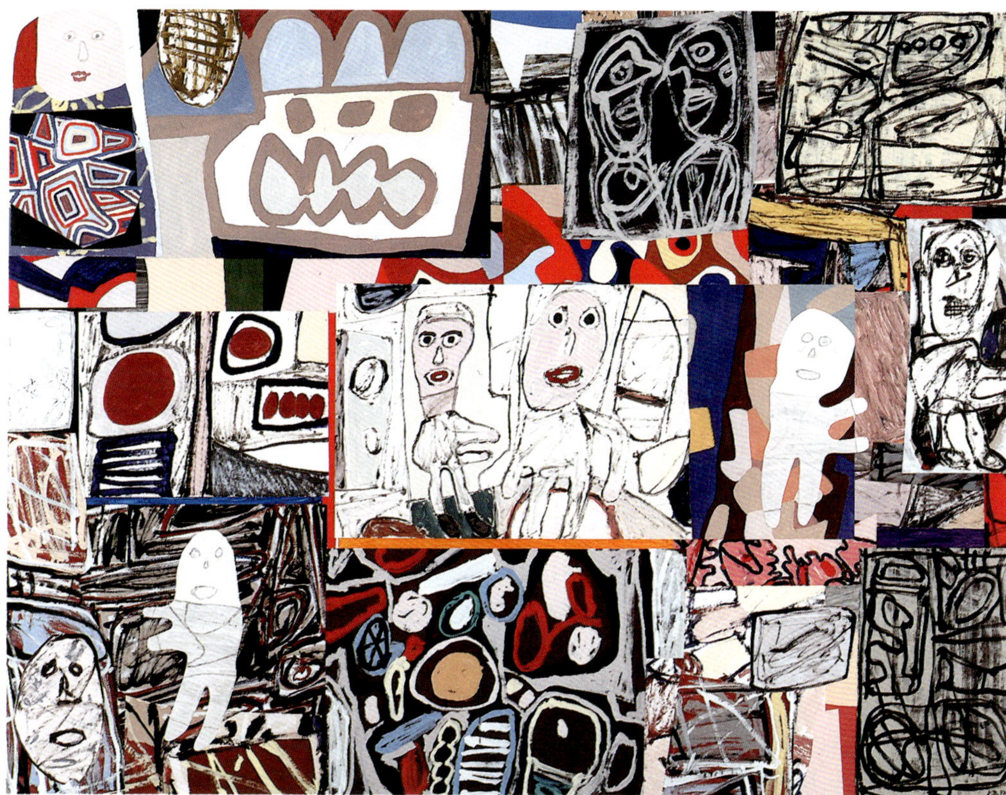

144
Jean Dubuffet:
The Daily
Implications, 1977

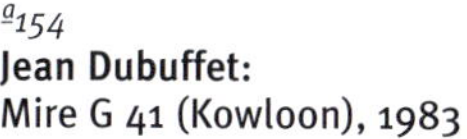

154
Jean Dubuffet:
Mire G 41 (Kowloon), 1983

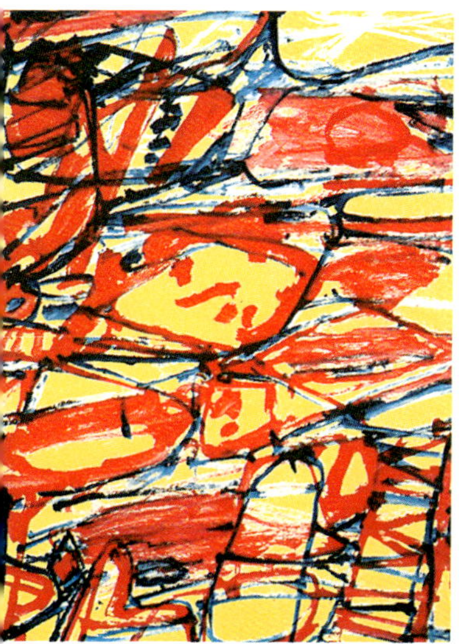

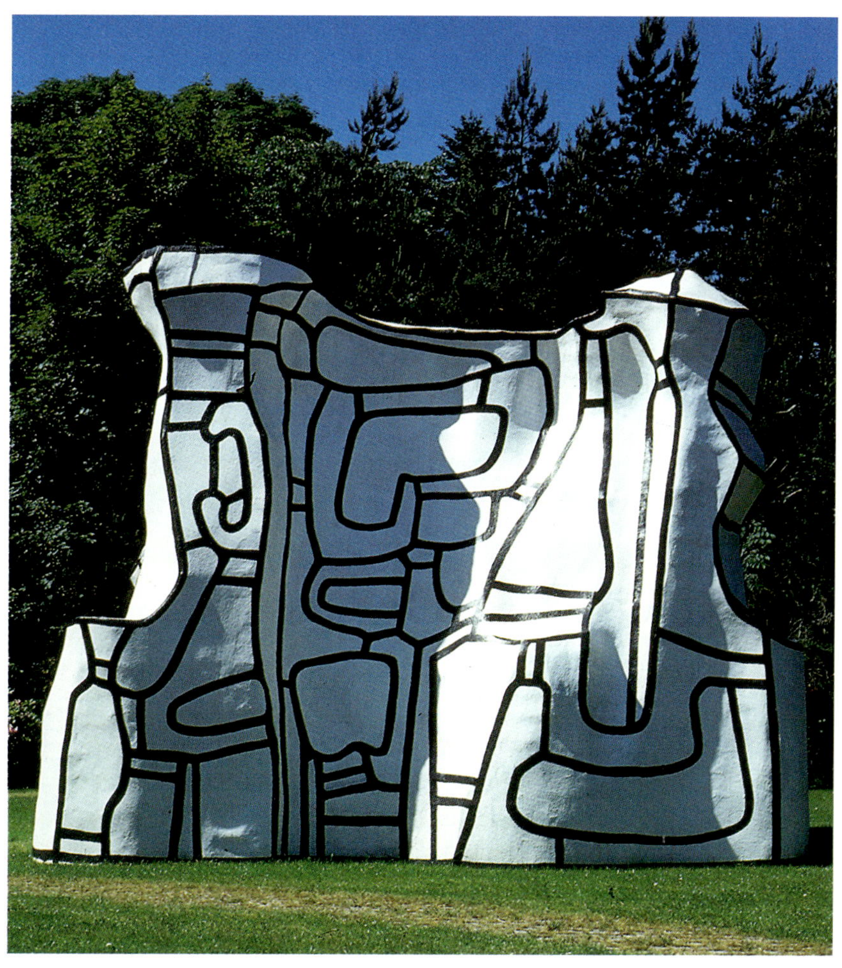

155
Jean Dubuffet:
Dynamic Manor, 1969/82

American Art after 1970

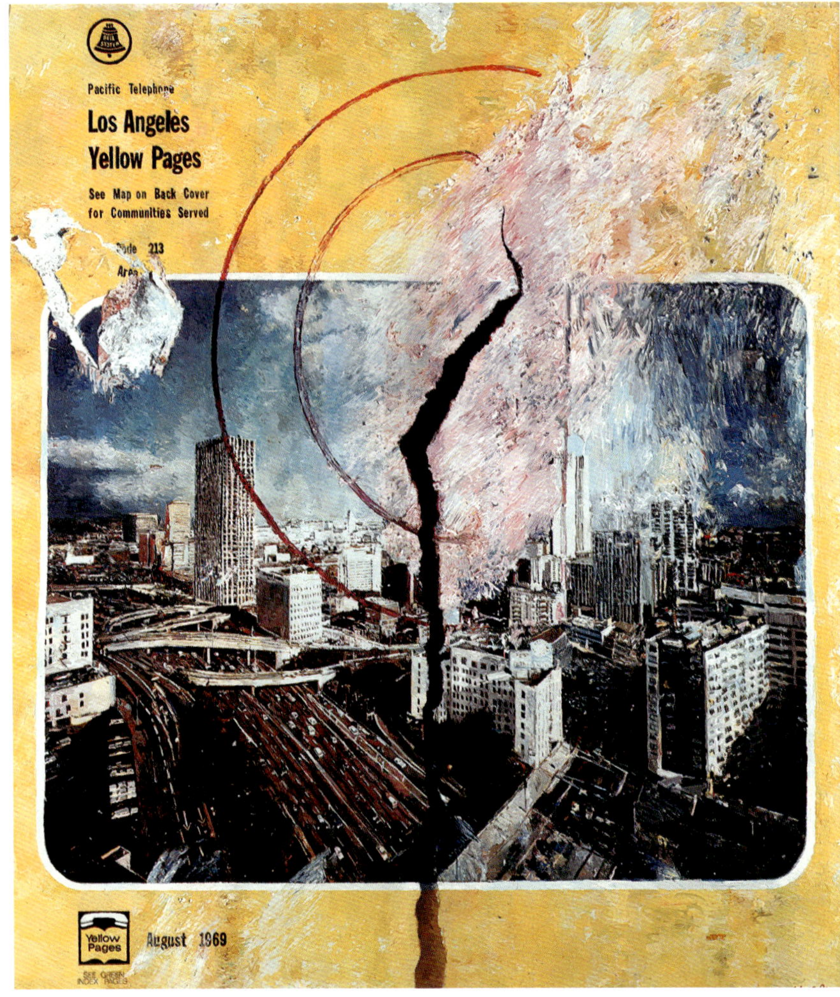

598
Malcolm Morley:
Pacific Telephone
– Los Angeles Yellow Pages, 1971

243
Robert Gober:
Double Sink, 1985

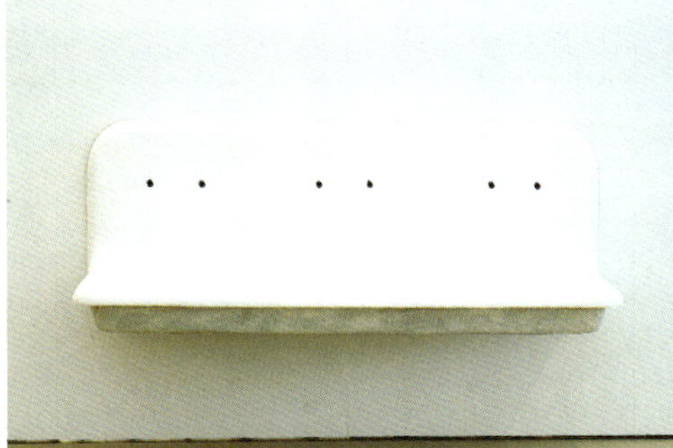

397
Neil Jenney:
Swimmer-Reflection, 1970

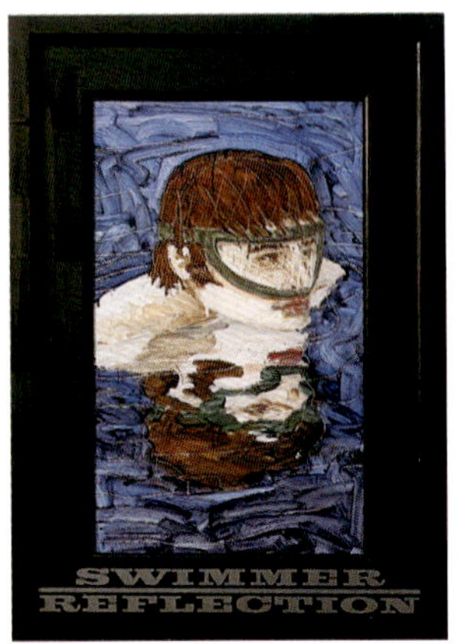

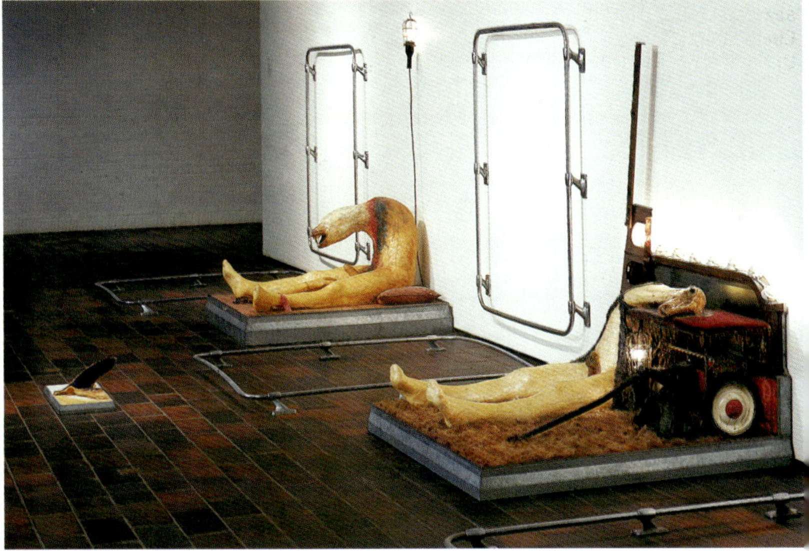

438
Edward Kienholz:
The Middle Islands, 1972

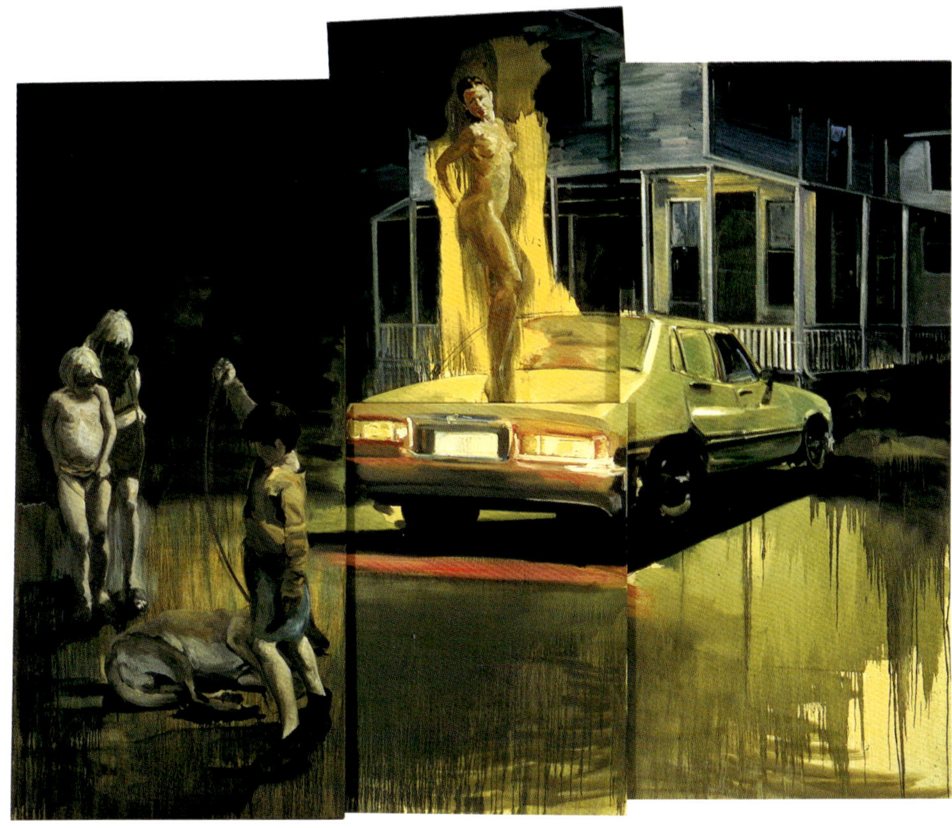

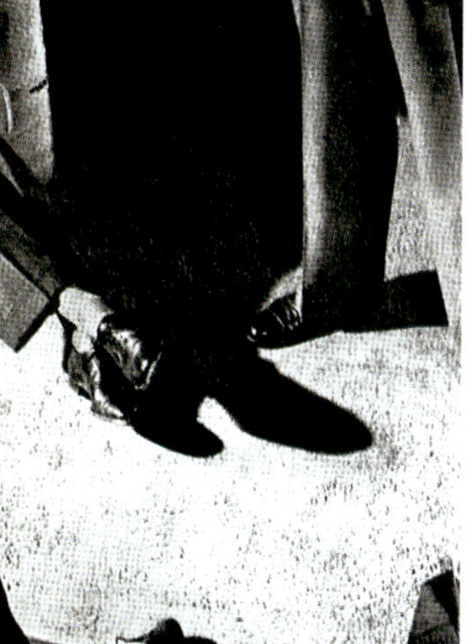

170
Eric Fischl: Birth of Love (Second Version), 1987

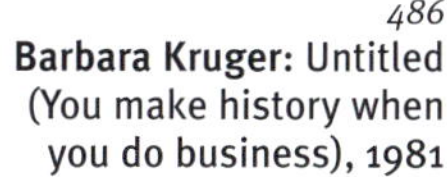

486
Barbara Kruger: Untitled (You make history when you do business), 1981

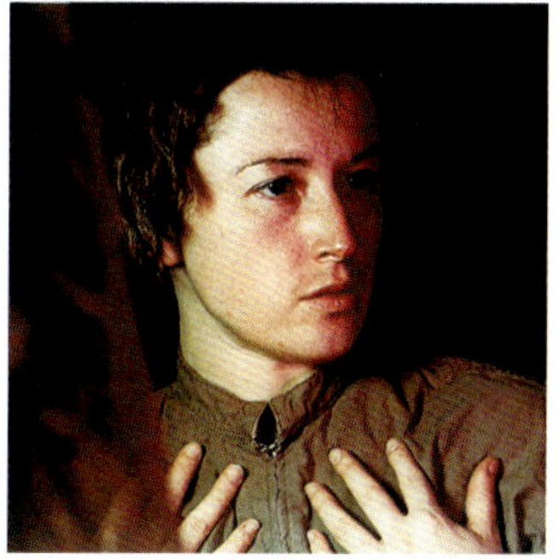

827
Cindy Sherman:
Untitled # 109, 1982

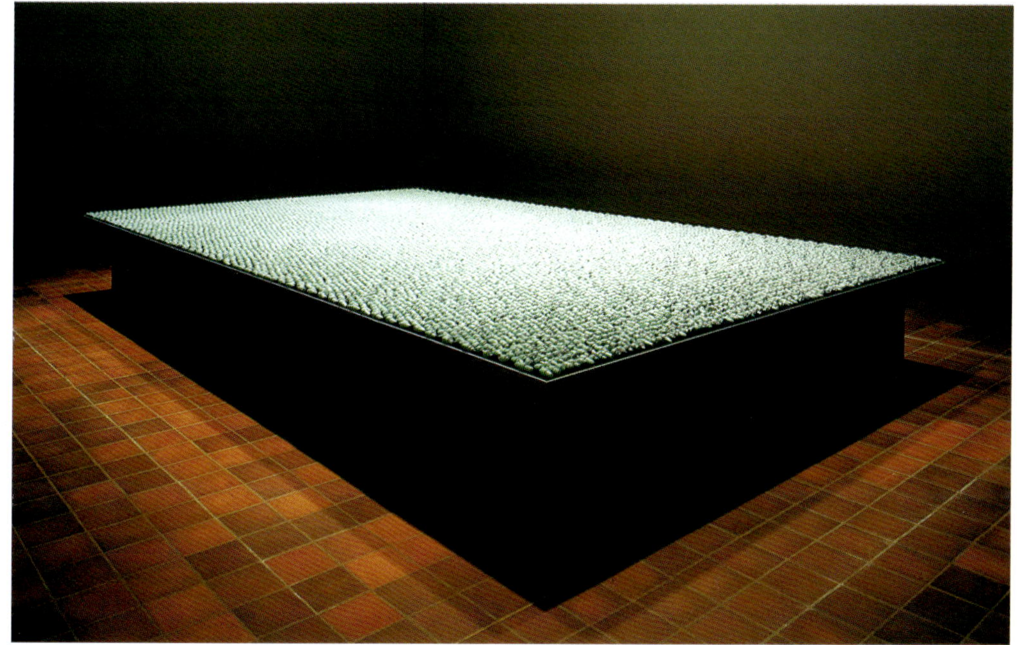

568
Allan McCollum: Over 10.000 Individual Works, 1987-89

European Art after 1970

Joseph Beuys installing the Honey Pump at the Documenta 6, Kassel, 1977

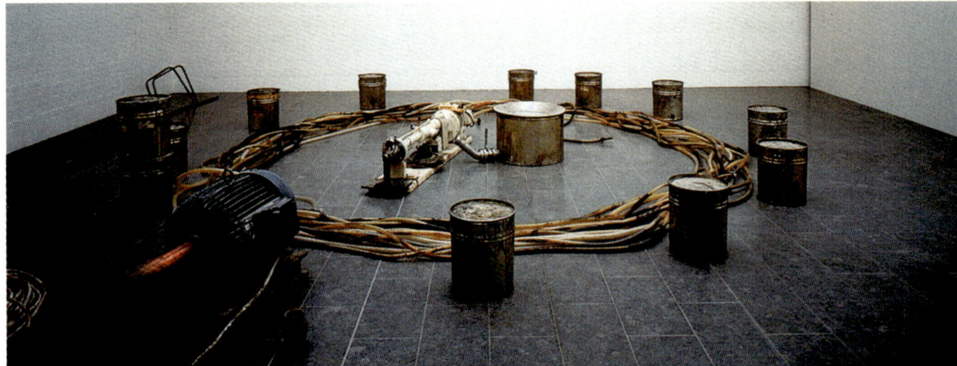

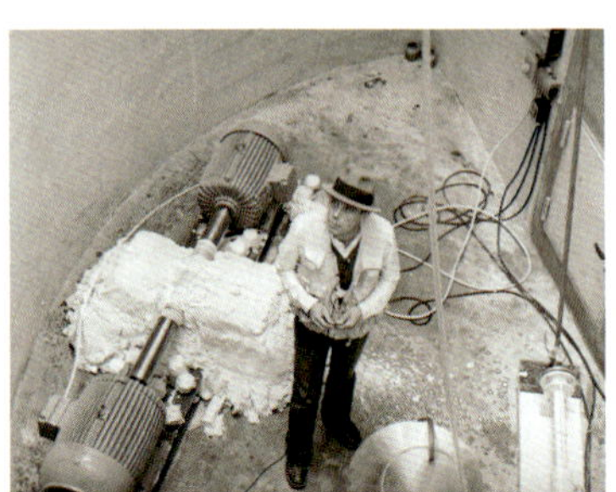

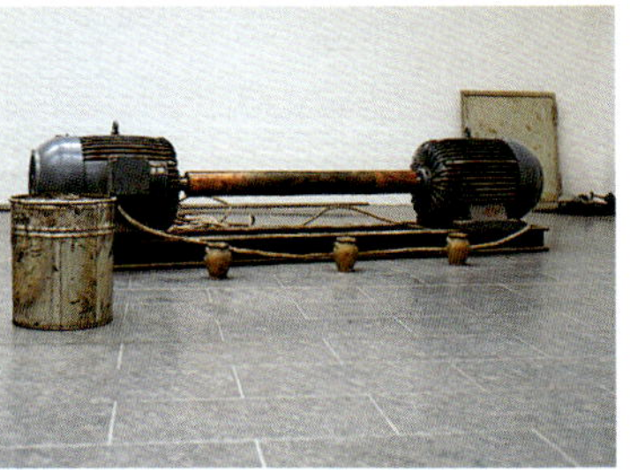

66
Joseph Beuys: Honey Pump in the Workplace, 1974-77

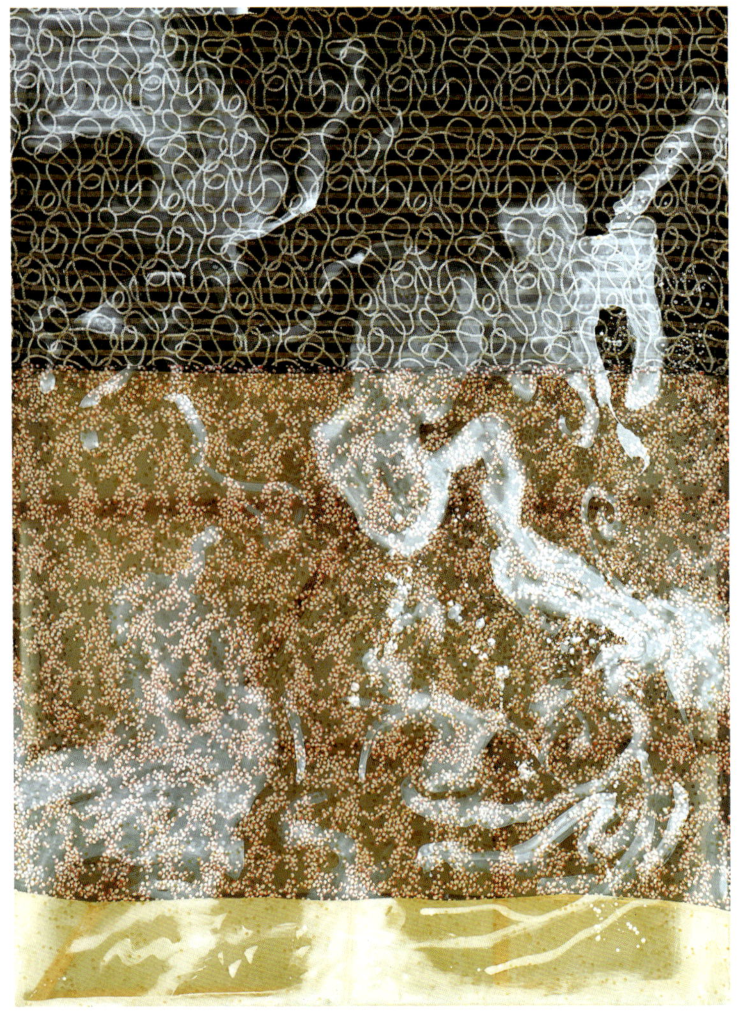

754
Sigmar Polke: Strings of Pearls, 1988

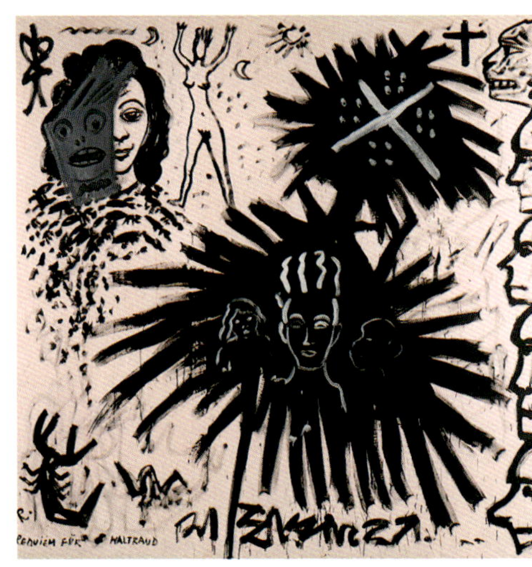

729
A.R. Penck: Requiem for Waltraud (N-Complex), 1976

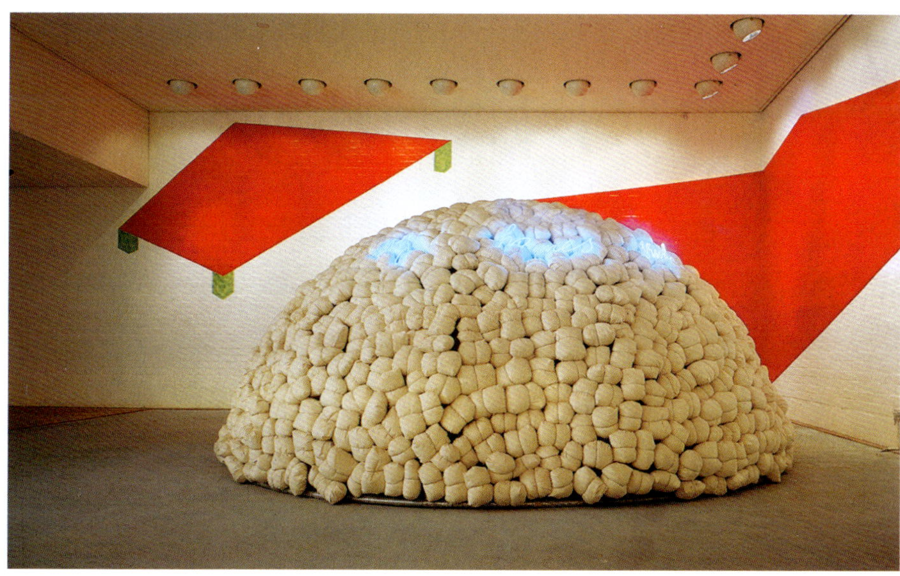

582
Mario Merz: My Home's Wind and Fibonacci Tables, 1969/82

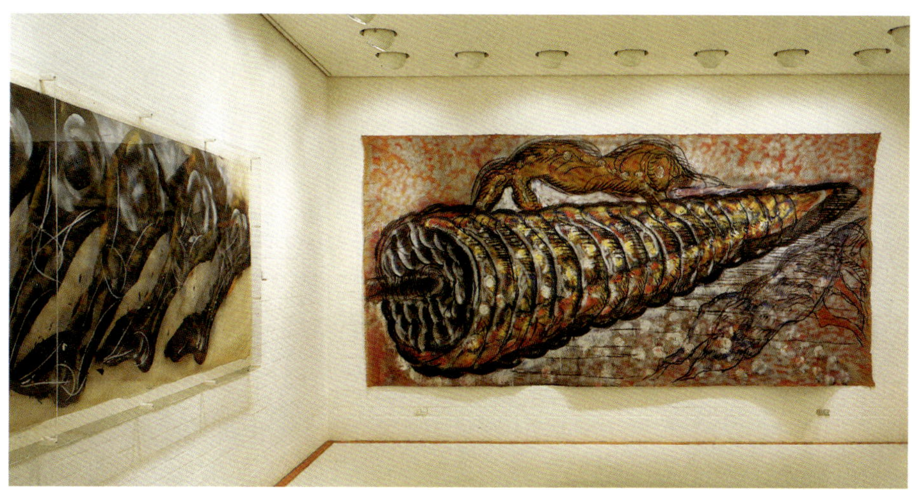

583
Mario Merz:
Spiral Shell, 1981-82

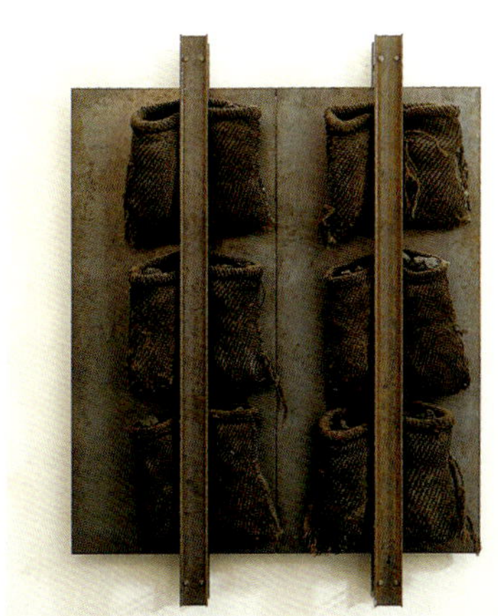

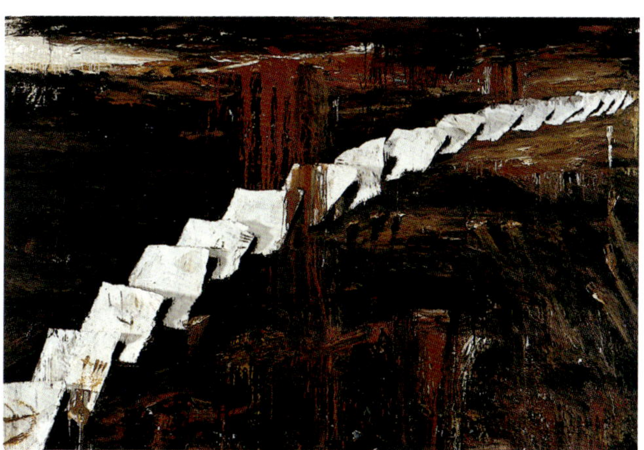

484, 118
Jannis Kounellis:
Untitled, 1988 (left)
Enzo Cucchi:
Untitled, 1985 (right)

Georg Baselitz/Per Kirkeby

452
Per Kirkeby:
Much Later, 1992

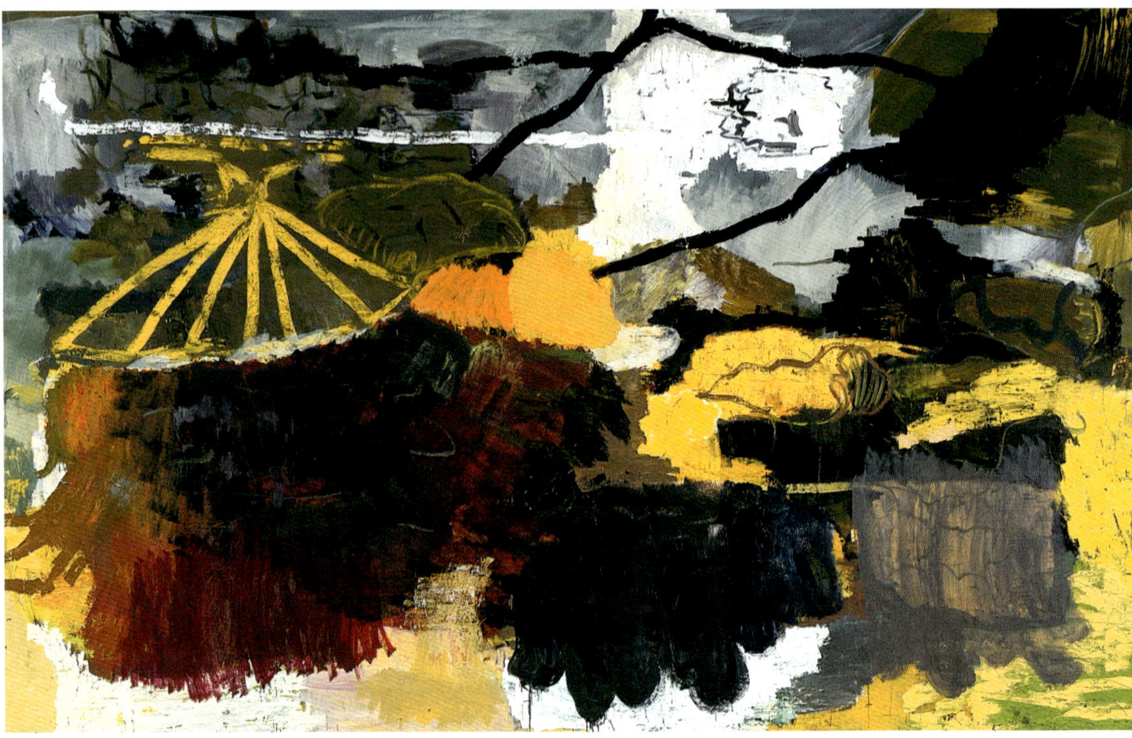

59
Georg Baselitz:
The Women from Dresden: Heath, 1990

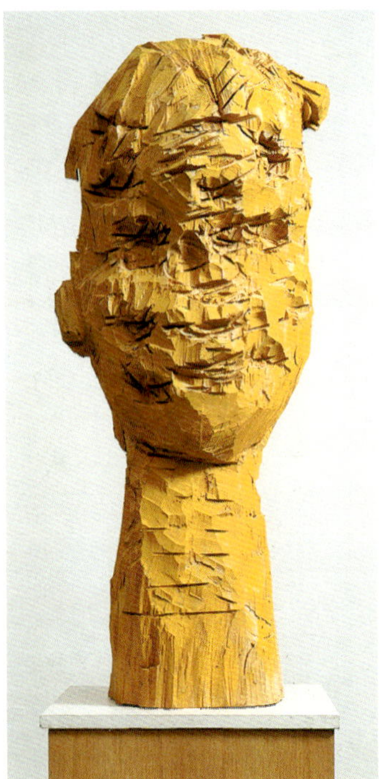

57, 56
Georg Baselitz:
The Loving Couple, 1984 (left)
The Abgar Head, 1984 (right)

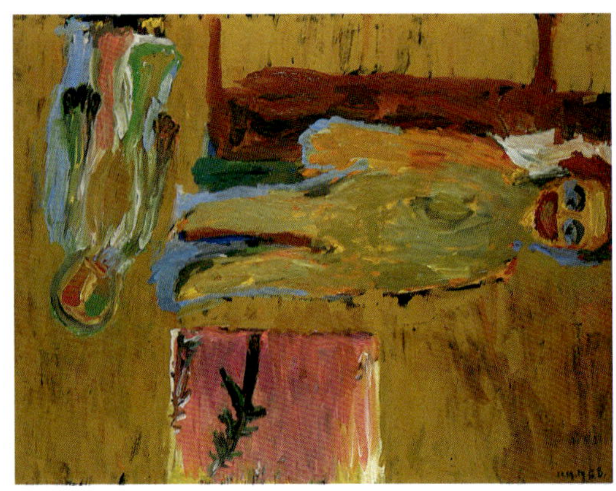

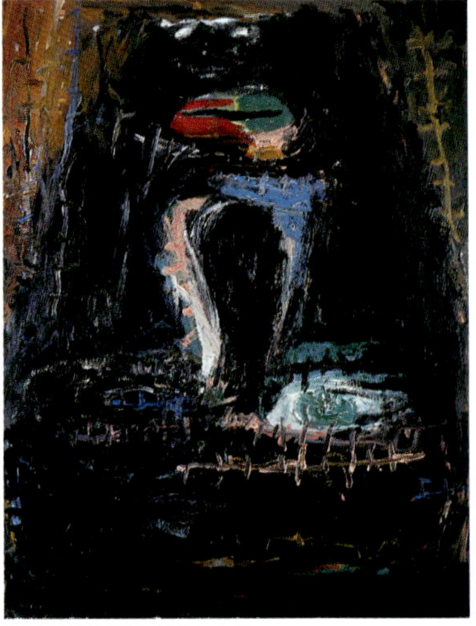

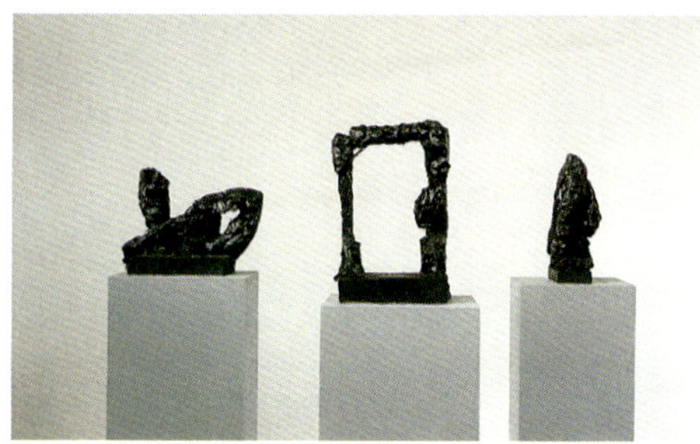

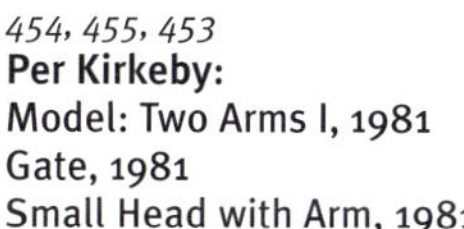

454, 455, 453
Per Kirkeby:
Model: Two Arms I, 1981
Gate, 1981
Small Head with Arm, 1981

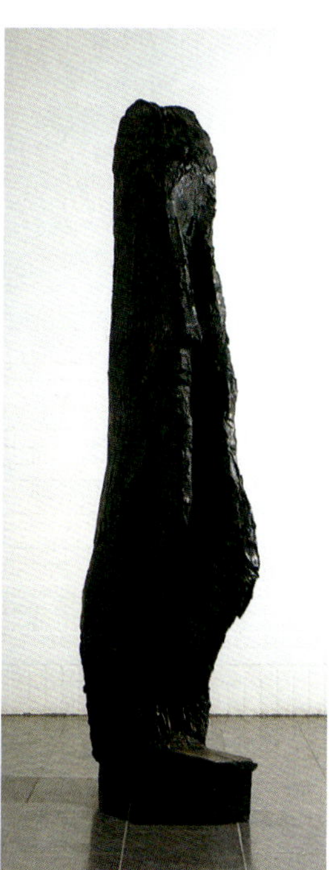

456
Per Kirkeby:
The Big Head with Arm, 1983

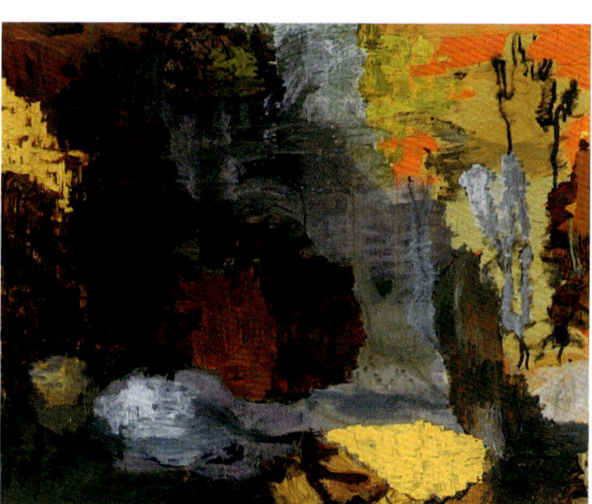

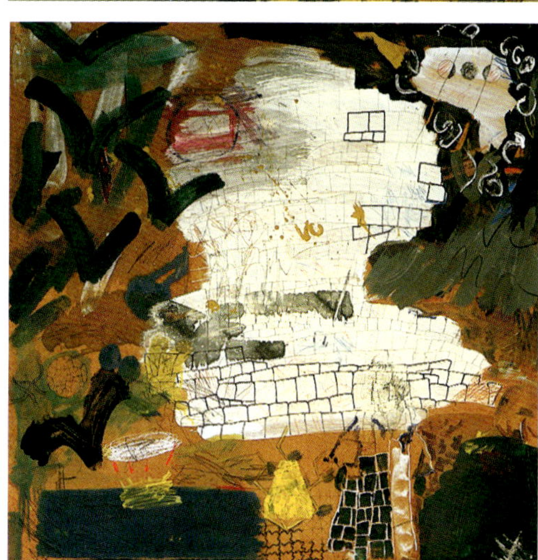

440, 451
Per Kirkeby:
Beatus-Apokalypse, 1989
The Temple of the Sun, 1969

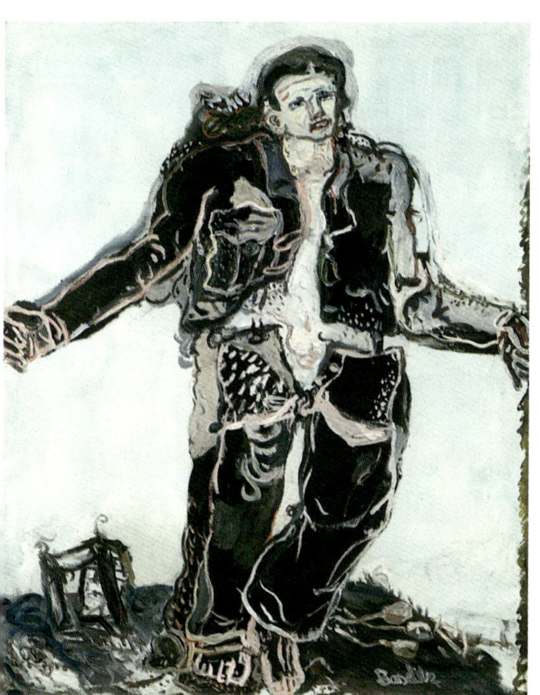

55
Georg Baselitz:
The New Type, 1966

Anselm Kiefer

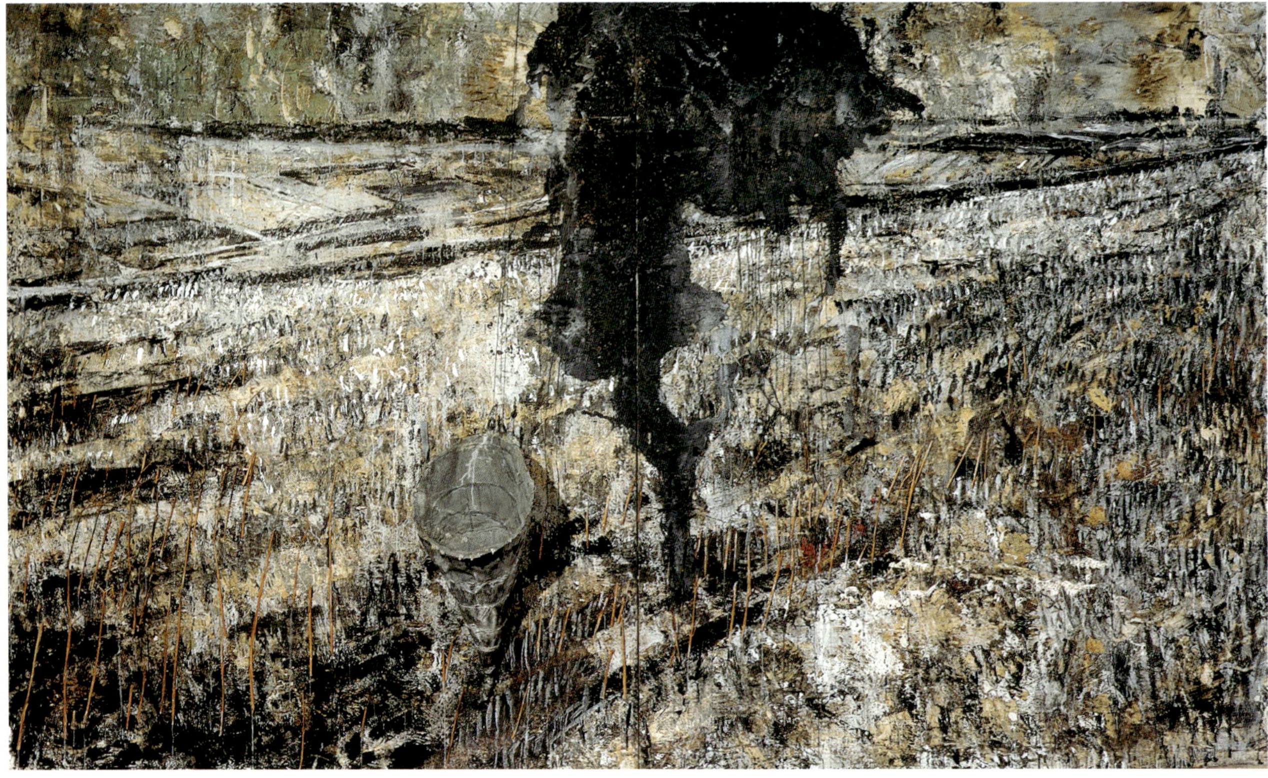

433
Outpouring, 1982-86

432
Inflammation, 1983-86

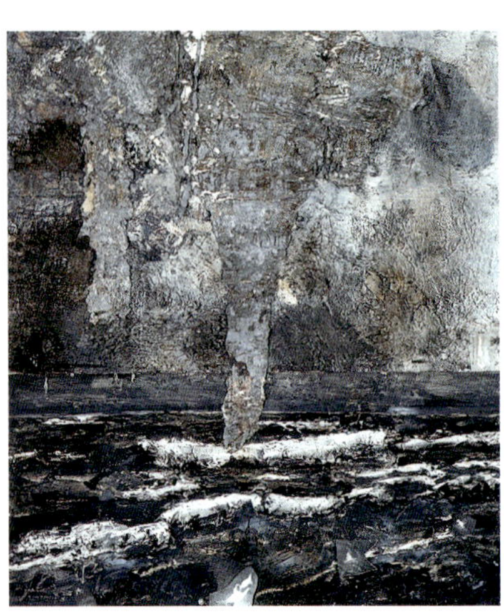

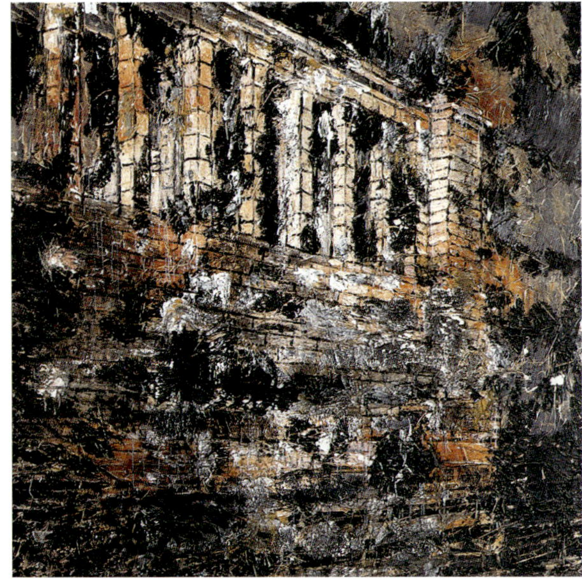

434
Columns, 1983

436
Ways of Worldly Wisdom:
The Battle of Teutoburg Forest, 1988-90

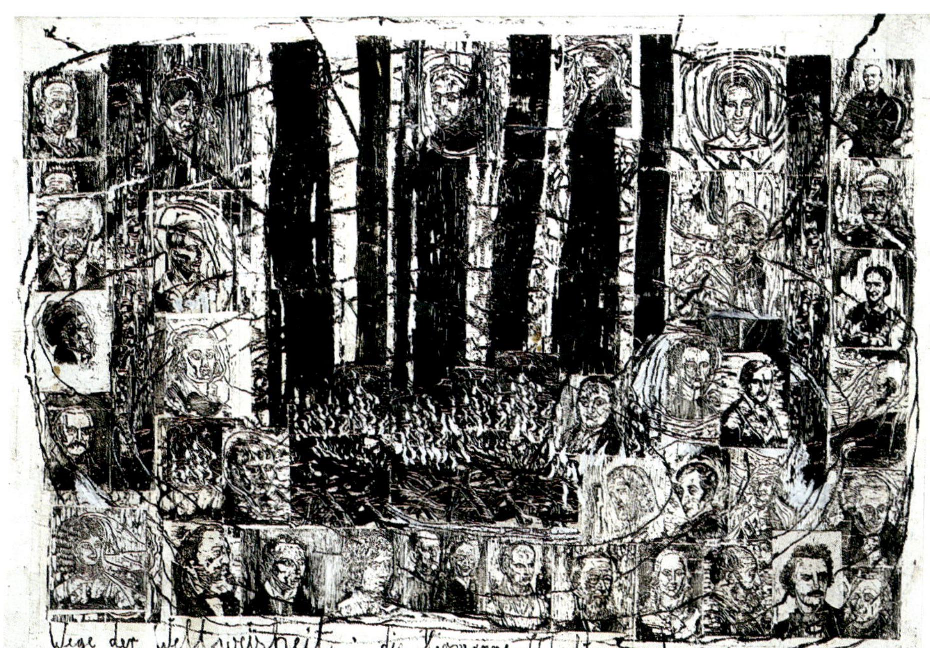

435
Jason, 1989

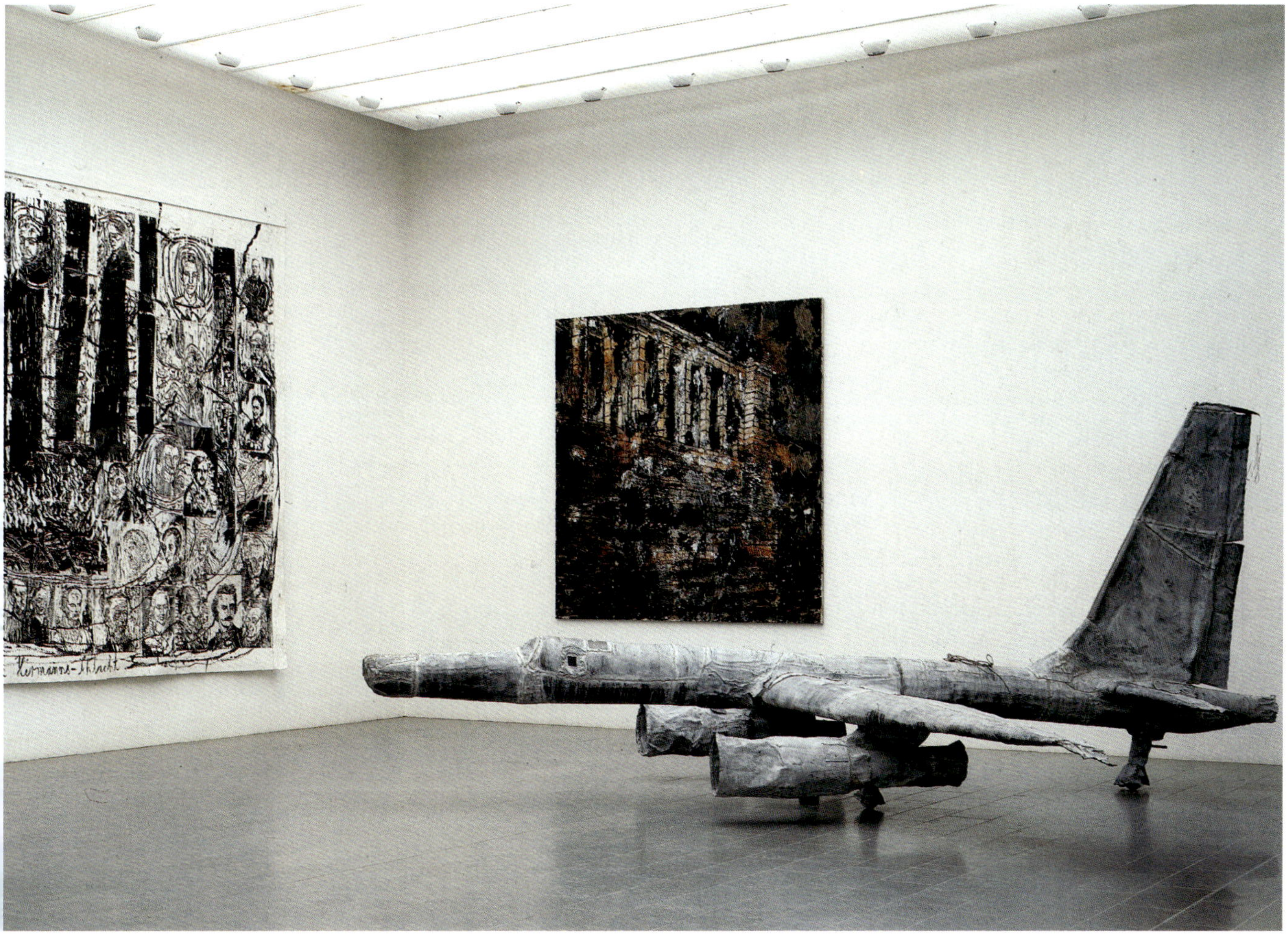

The Art of the 90s

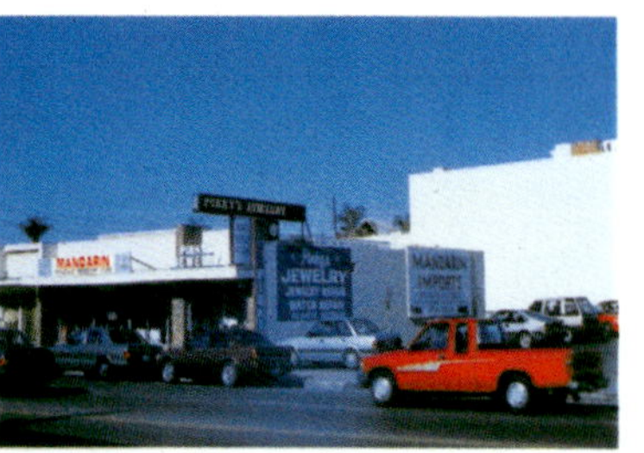

53
John Baldessari;
Pinky's Jewelry, 1996

PINKY'S JEWELRY
725 E. 8TH STREET
NATIONAL CITY, CALIF.

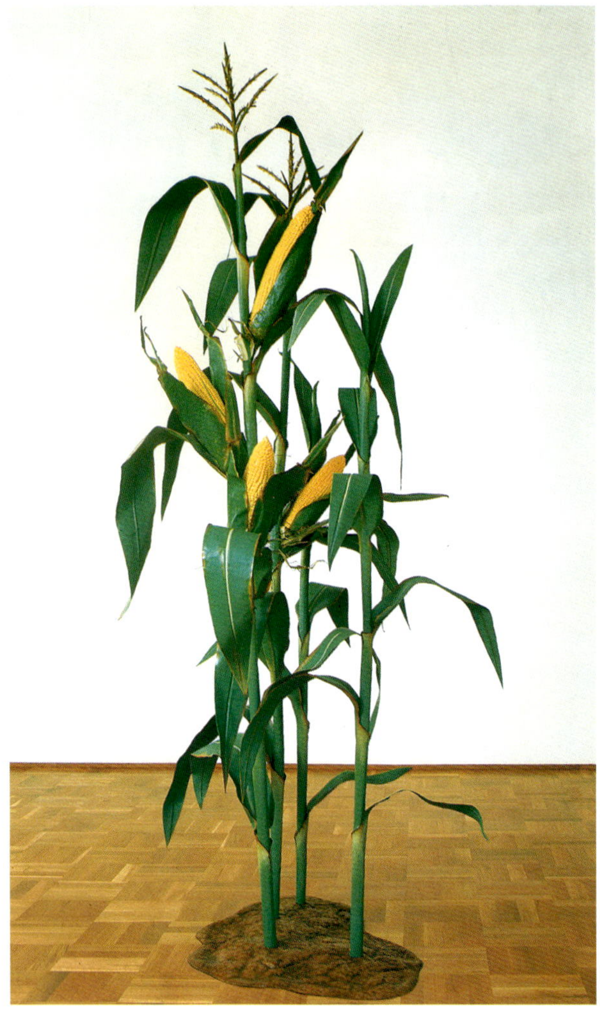

646
Jennifer Pastor: Untitled (Fall), 1994-96

918
Andrea Zittel:
A to Z Travel Trailer Unit, 1995

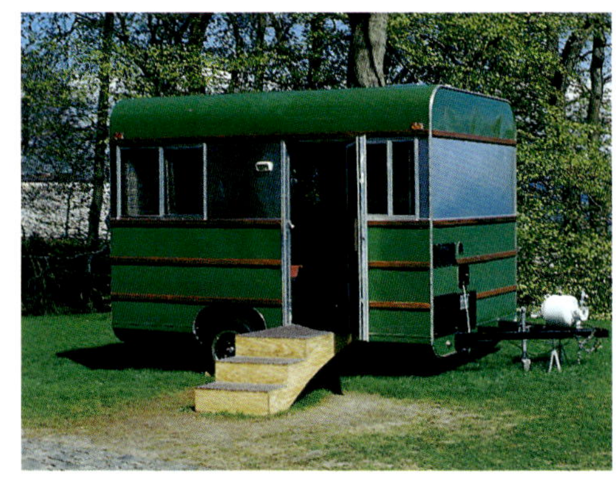

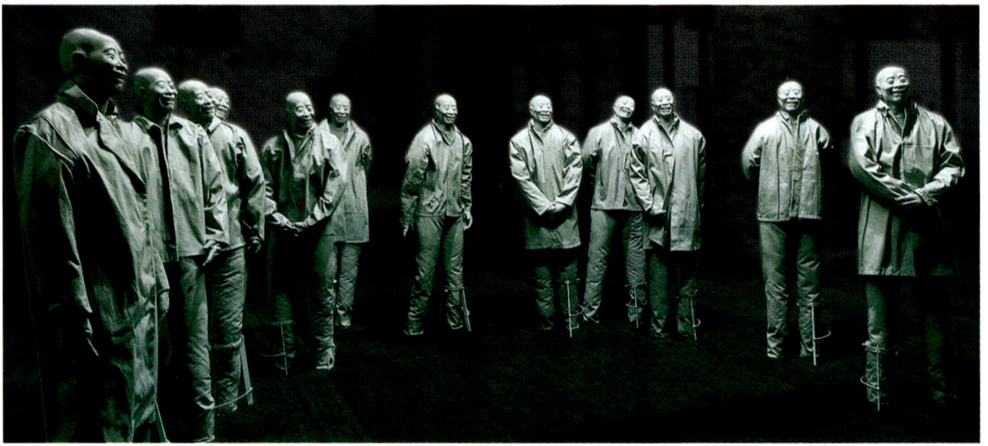

612
Juan Muñoz: Half Circle, 1997

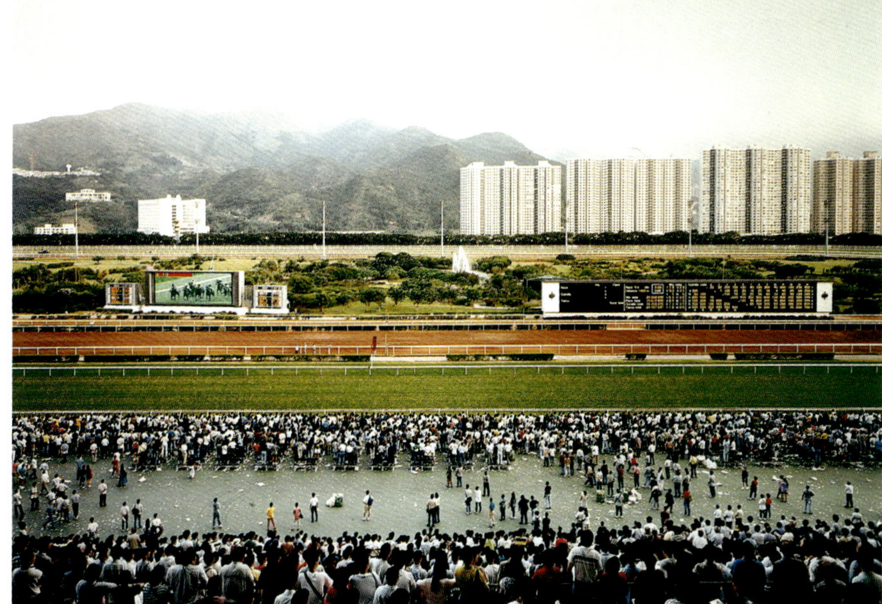

268
Andreas Gursky:
Shan Ti, 1994

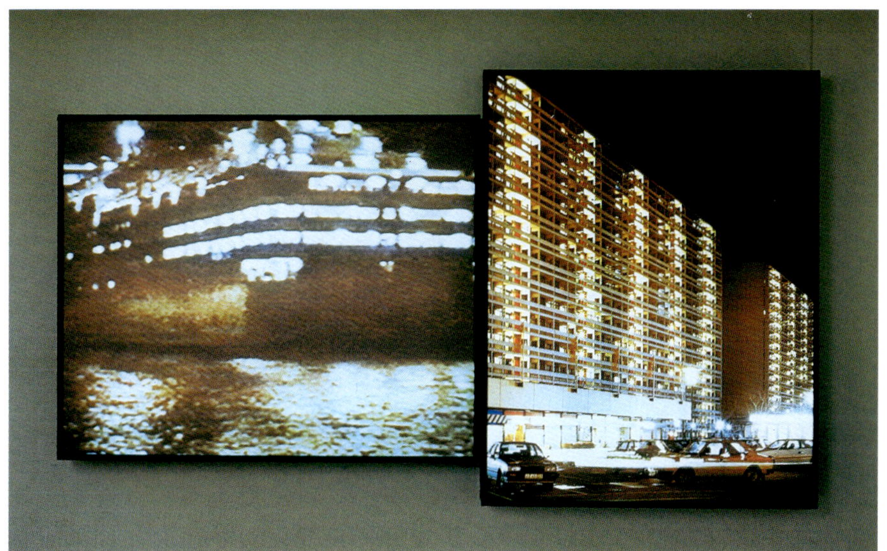

54
Lewis Baltz:
Gladsaxe, 1995

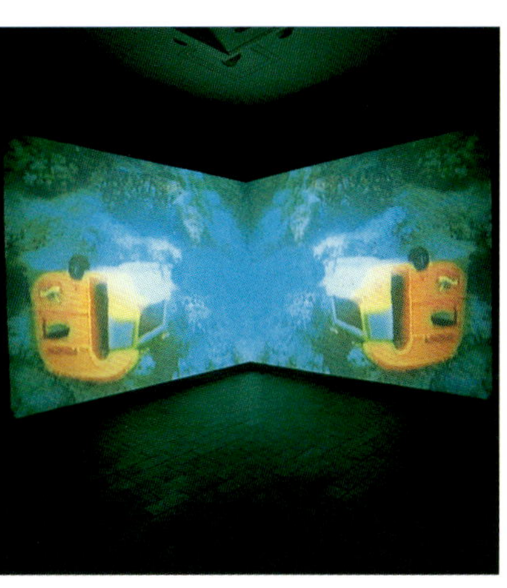

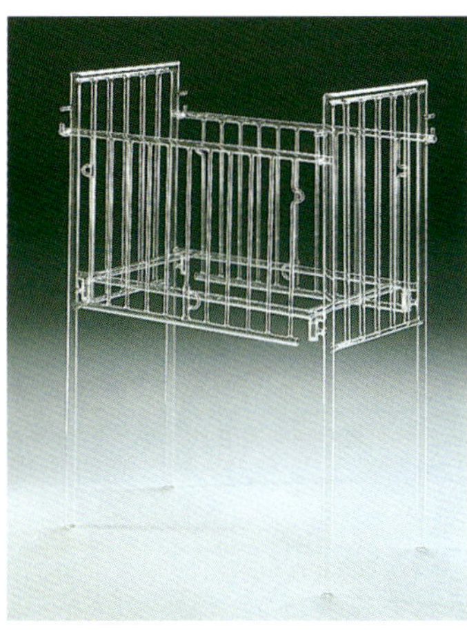

789, 286
Pipilotti Rist:
Sip My Ocean, 1996 (left)
Mona Hatoum:
Silence, 1992 (right)

Drawings and Prints

Steingrim Laursen

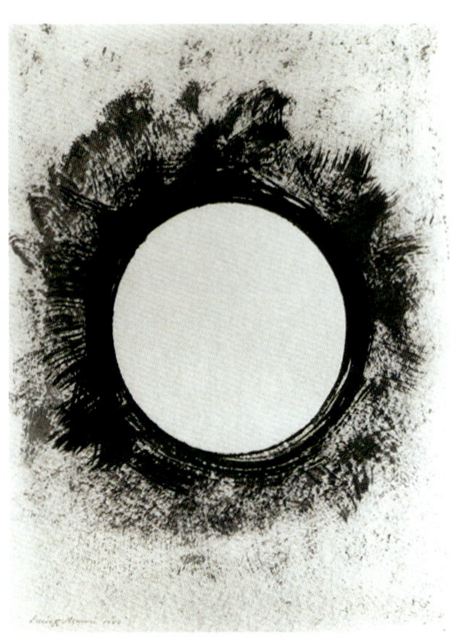

616
Barnett Newman:
Untitled, 1946

A museum is always delighted to be able to offer its public an exhibition of drawings, whether it be a temporary exhibition or an exhibition of works from its permanent collection.

It is not possible to arrange exhibitions of drawings as often as one might like, because the fragility of the paper restricts their being on display to short periods with long intervals in between.

The museum whose tight budget only rarely permits the acquisition of works that for reasons of conservation can only be shown sporadically must necessarily prefer oil on canvas to which the same restrictions do not apply, and consequently exhibitions of drawings are few and far between.

In this country there are very few graphic collections, a common denominator for drawings and prints. One exceptionally fine collection was started under the reign of Christian II in 1521, and in 1896 it was incorporated in the Department of Prints and Drawings, Royal Museum of Fine Arts in Copenhagen. Apart from this, only Vejle Art Museum and Louisiana possess collections of any consequence.

The foundation for Louisiana's collection of drawings began early with Knud W. Jensen's acquisition of a number of sketches by Niels Larsen Stevns. Hereafter the museum only acquired drawings sporadically until, in 1991, the underground exhibition rooms of the Graphics Wing were built with the optimum light and climatic conditions required by drawings and prints.

At the inauguration of the Graphics Wing, Louisiana received as a gift from the New Carlsberg Foundation a magnificent collection of drawings and prints, an important supplement to the museum's permanent collection.

Throughout the years one of the museum's benefactors, Celia Ascher, has donated primarily Suprematistic and Concrete drawings to the museum in her husband's and her own names. Additionally, in 1992 Louisiana received a bequest of exquisite works after Elena and Nicolas Calas, which together with the works already mentioned makes Louisiana's collection an important one.

Furthermore, two long-term loans add important works which the museum, with its present funds, would otherwise be unable to purchase.

Louisiana's collection is almost equally divided between American and European drawings and prints, with exceptional examples in both categories. One of the most interesting American drawings is Barnett Newman's *Untitled* from 1946. Barnett Newman was one of the leading exponents of Abstract Expressionism. He worked up to the end of the 1940s with a biomorphic form of expression, which changed around 1948 into one that rejected the European influence and conventional way of painting. Through his works and his art philosophical writings he became one of the important pioneers of an independent American art.

Louisiana's drawing by Barnett Newman is interesting because it so clearly illustrates this phase. In the centre of *Untitled* is a clearly defined circle inside which the bare paper stands out in dazzling white, whereas surrounding it an intense black circular 'aura' has been drawn on top of a light black grounding. Hereby the circle (which Newman calls "the Void") acquires even more intensity.

Newman, who was well-versed in other (so-called primitive) cultures and deeply anchored in the Jewish Cabbala, tried in his art to penetrate 'the mystical' and 'the tragic', which he saw as a precondition for life itself.

Newman regarded the problems of "the Void", with which he had worked both in painting and drawing, as an analysis of precisely these problems. "The Void" can possibly be interpreted as the sublime moment, the moment of creation, surrounded by a physical shine or aura, a conception supported by Newman's use of this form in a number of works from 1946 and 1947.

A typical European work is Alberto Giacometti's portrait of his mother from 1963, apparently a casual sketch in which the lead barely seems to touch the paper, where he probes the space with a light hand and a seeming confusion of strokes. But by concentrating these lines he draws an empathetic and inspired portrait of the mother reading a book. Giacometti reproduces the mother's appearance with great devotion and warmth, and through her expression of concentration and inner peace he also succeeds in describing the room beyond the figure. With the figure's presence and some few suggestions of the room on the sheet itself the entire drawing is filled with atmosphere and spaciousness.

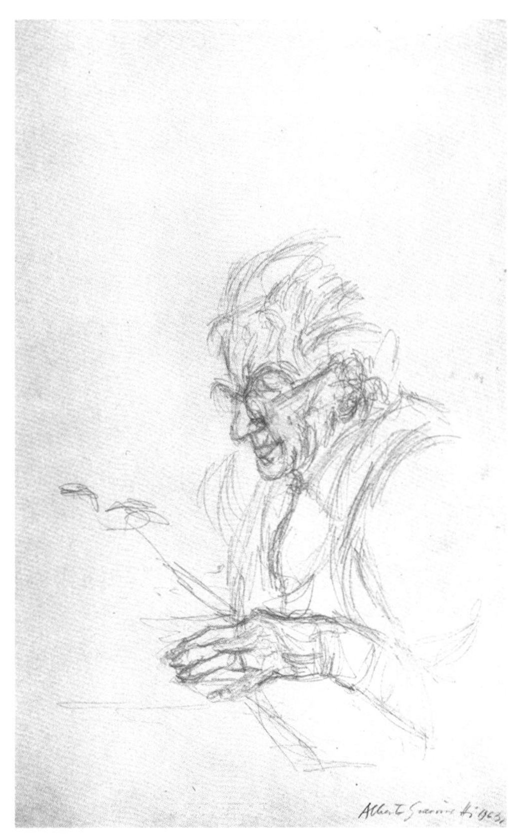

238
Alberto Giacometti:
The Mother Reading, 1963

In the series of Carl-Henning Pedersen's drawings from 1948-54, *Fantasiens fugle* ("Birds of Fantasy"), there is a different form of expression. The drawings are executed in Indian ink and, in Scandinavian Cobra style, the paper is entirely filled with markings, relating of birds of fantasy in the world of fantasy. Carl-Henning Pedersen does not draw by way of lines, but sets out to mediate his dreams using a kind of expressionist-pointillistic method that creates a greater whole by way of many small touches.

Apart from the works mentioned above, Louisiana's collection of drawings contains a great many works of distinction that deserve mention, though they cannot for lack of space be depicted or mentioned here. However, the museum's guests may look forward to becoming acquainted with these works in the museum's temporary exhibitions. Here, by a closer study of each separate drawing, one can come quite close to the artist and the moment of creation itself, which is the key to the understanding of the work's innermost being. ┤

English translation by Paula Hostrup-Jessen

665
Carl-Henning Pedersen:
Birds of Fantasy, 1948-54

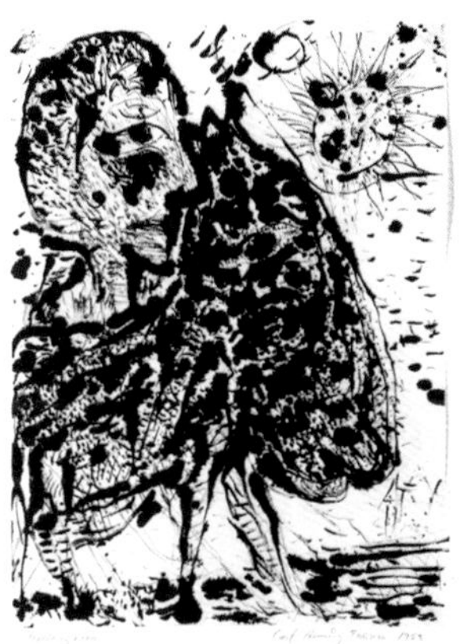

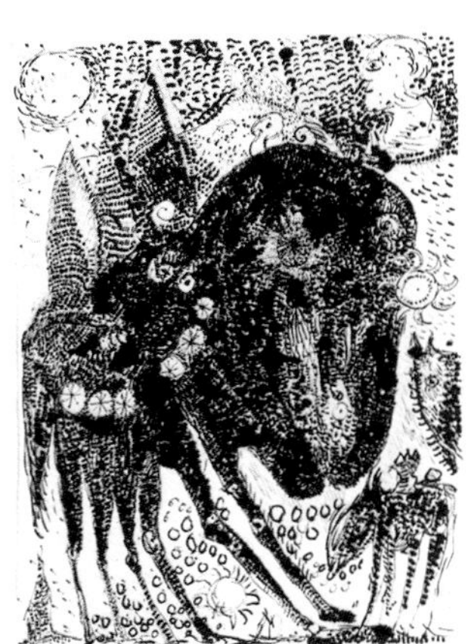

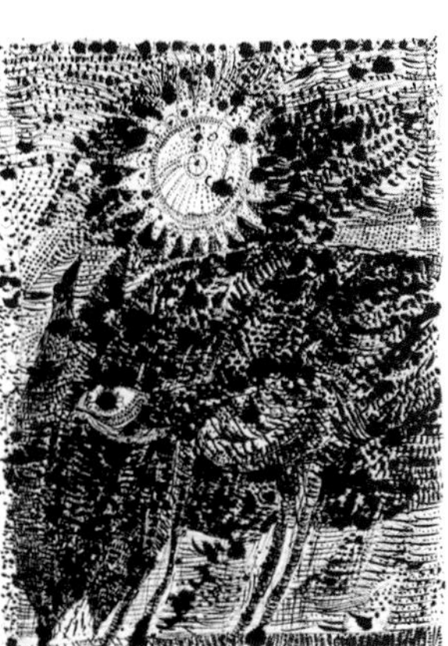

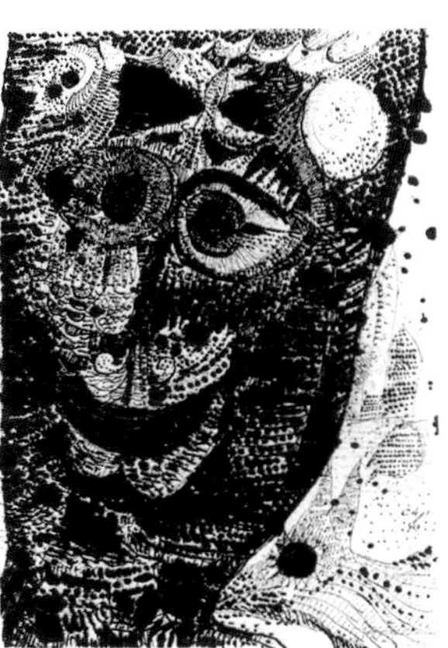

870, 869
Yves Tanguy:
Untitled, 1943-44 (left)
Untitled, 1940 (right)

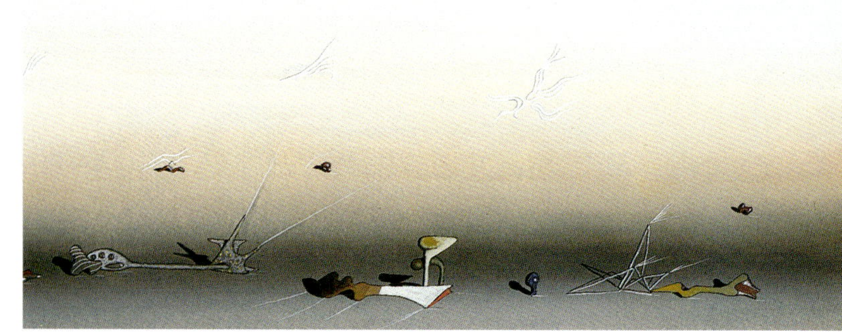

928, 807
Mark Rothko:
Prehistoric Memory, 1946 (left)
Untitled, 1944-46 (right)

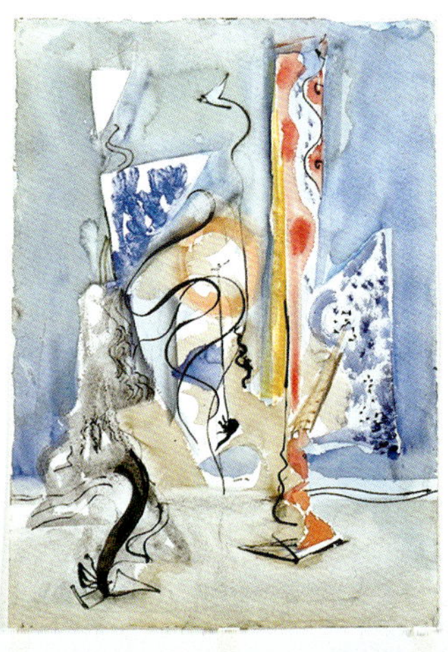

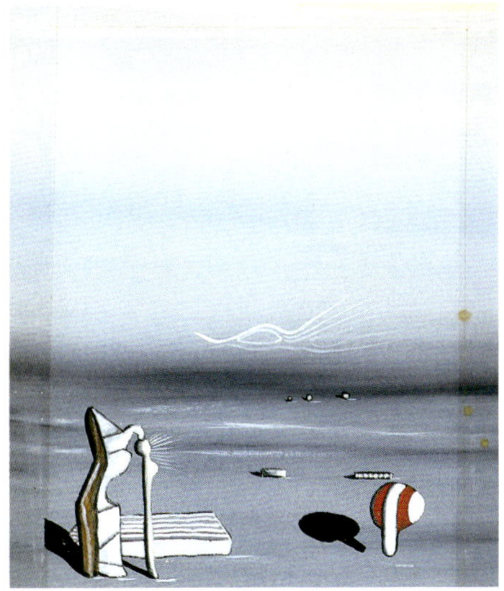

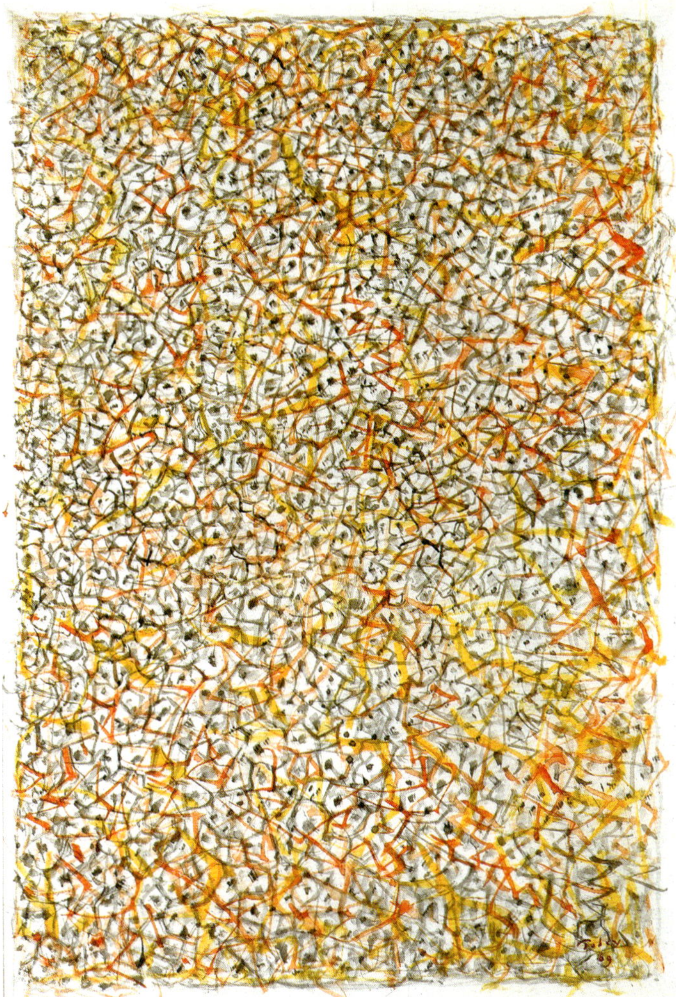

248
Arshile Gorky: Biomorphic Forms, 1946

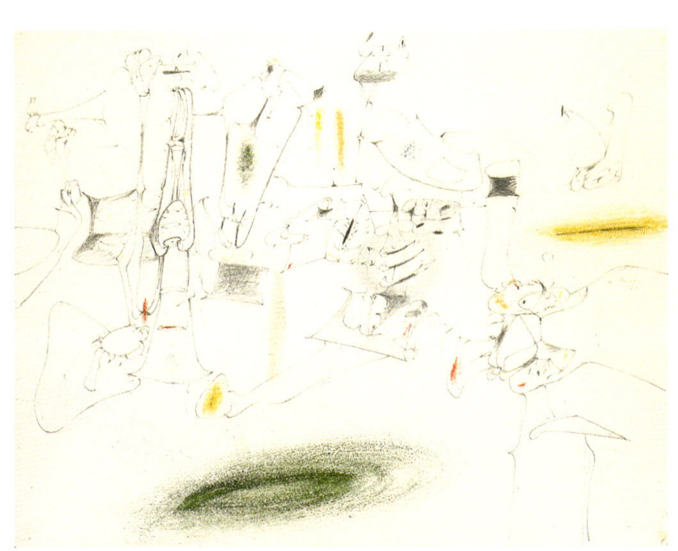

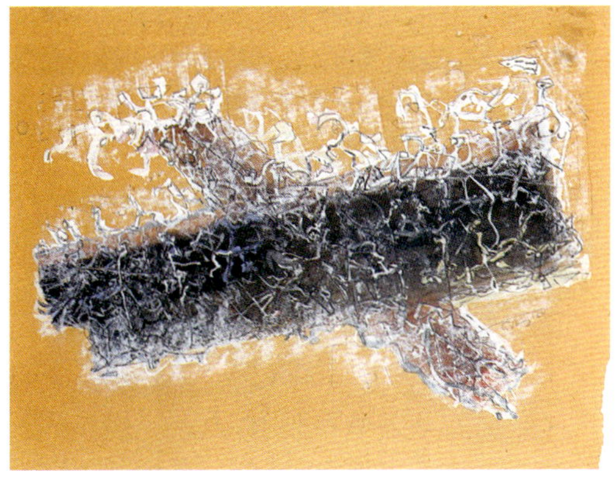

891, 890
Mark Tobey:
Untitled Composition, 1969
Intersection, 1954

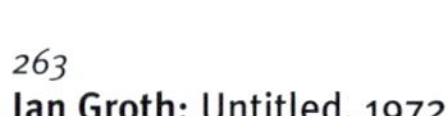

263
Jan Groth: Untitled, 1972

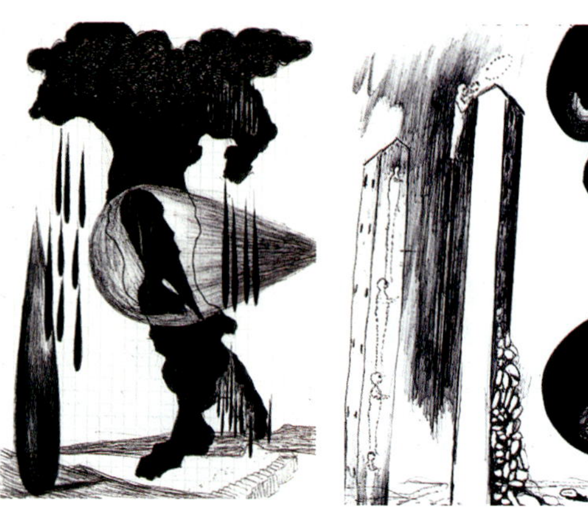

120, 121
Enzo Cucchi: Untitled, 1988

463-465
Per Kirkeby: Untitled, 1990

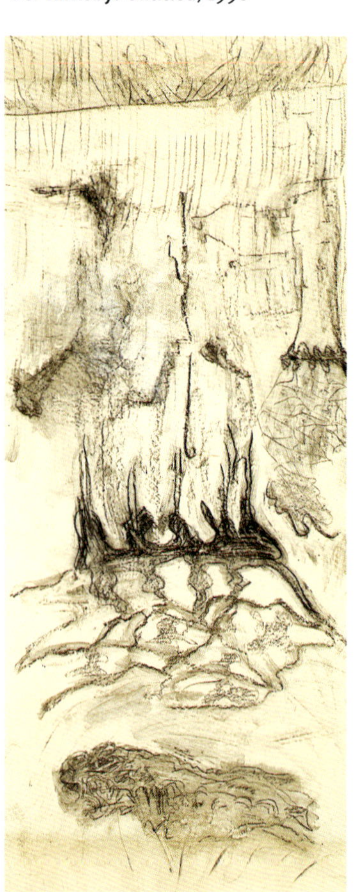

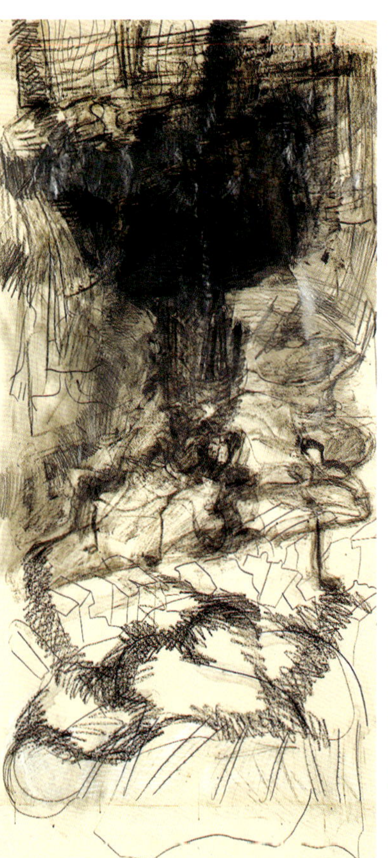

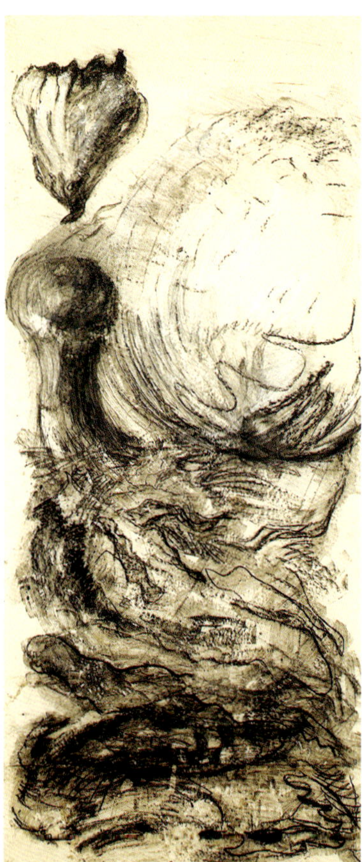

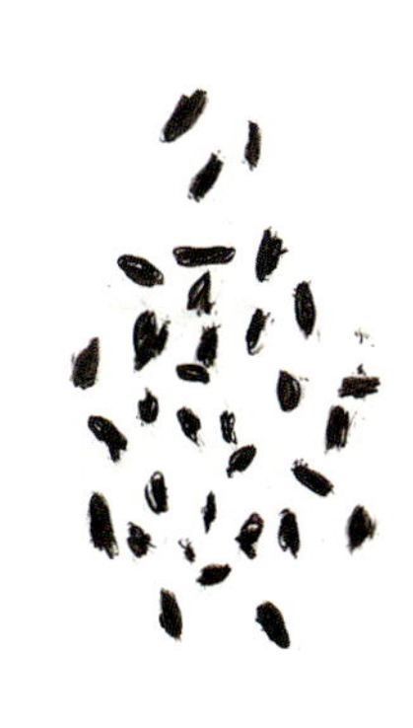

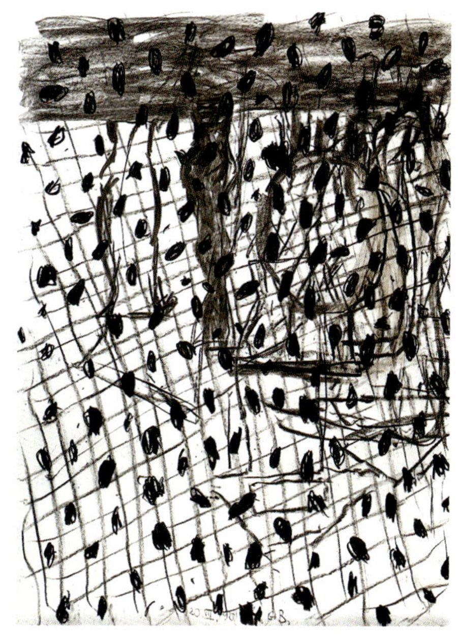

60, 62, 61
Georg Baselitz: Untitled, 1990

909
Bram van Velde:
Untitled, 1973

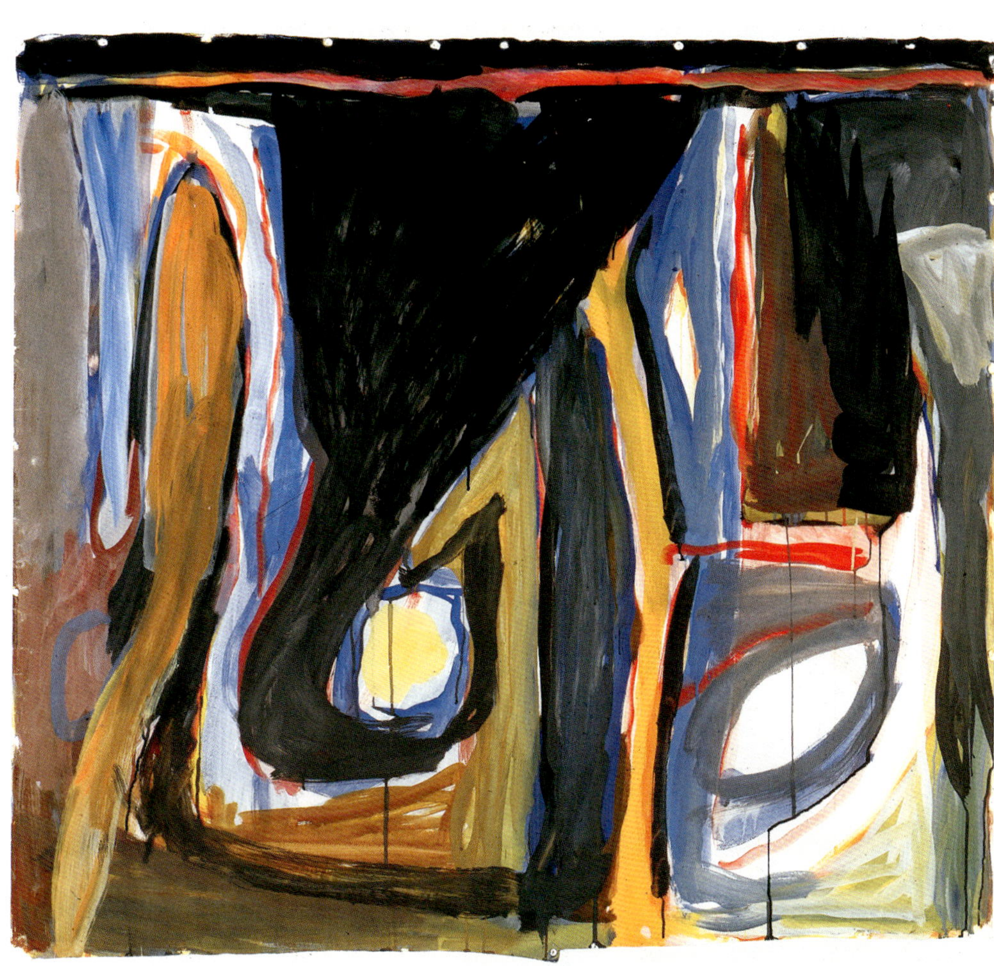

768
Robert Rauschenberg:
Die Hard, 1968

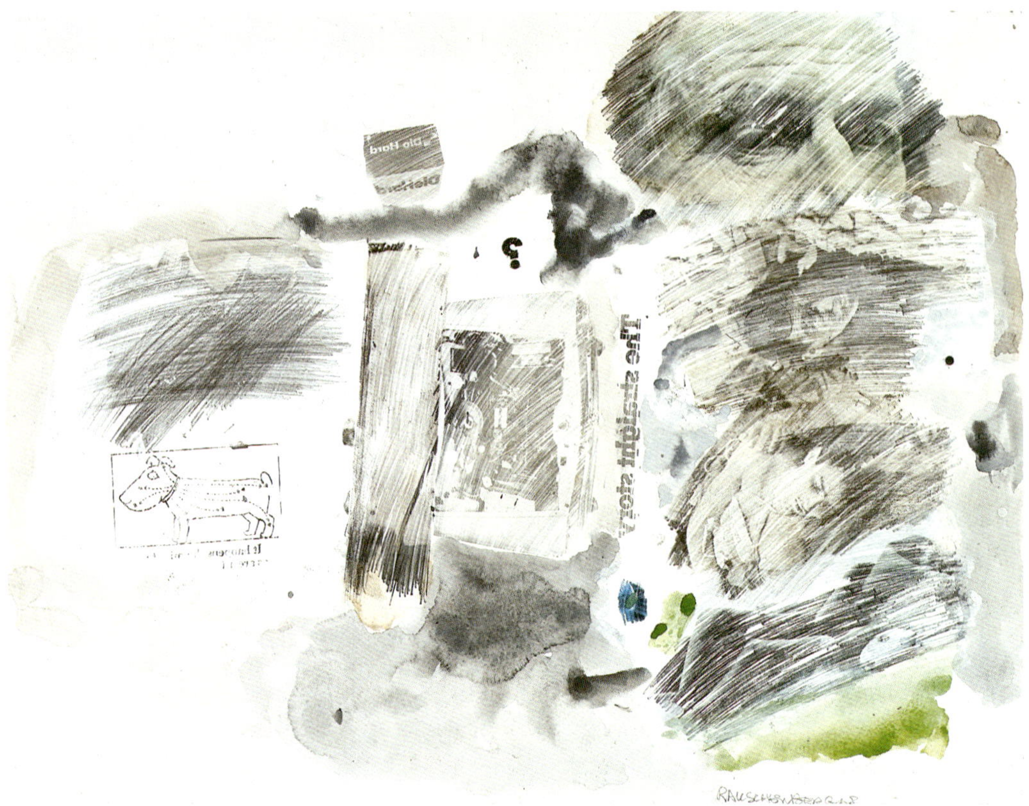

767
Robert Rauschenberg:
Booster, 1967

405, 406
Jasper Johns:
Savarin (Red), 1978 (left)
Land's End, 1979 (right)

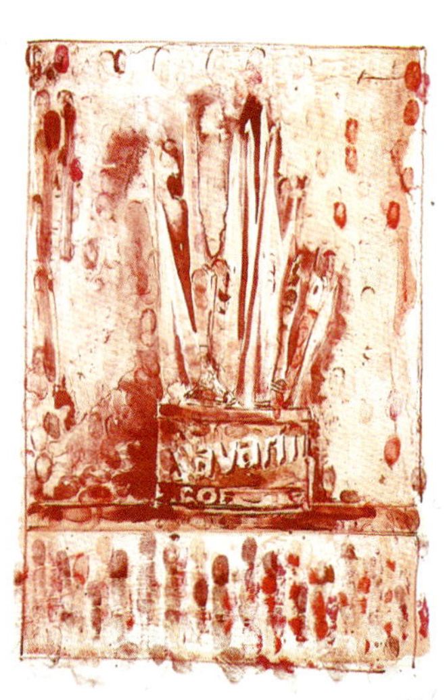

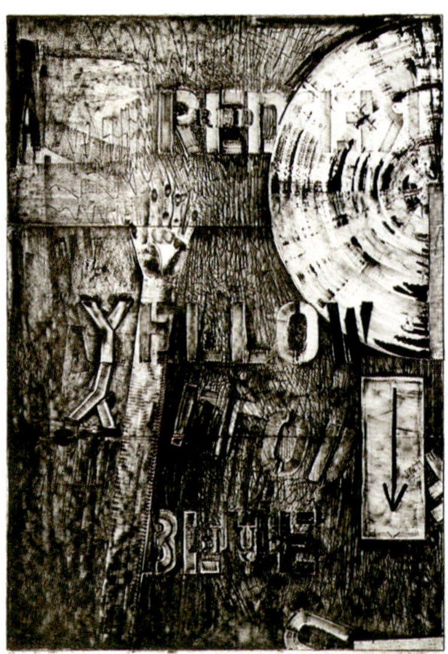

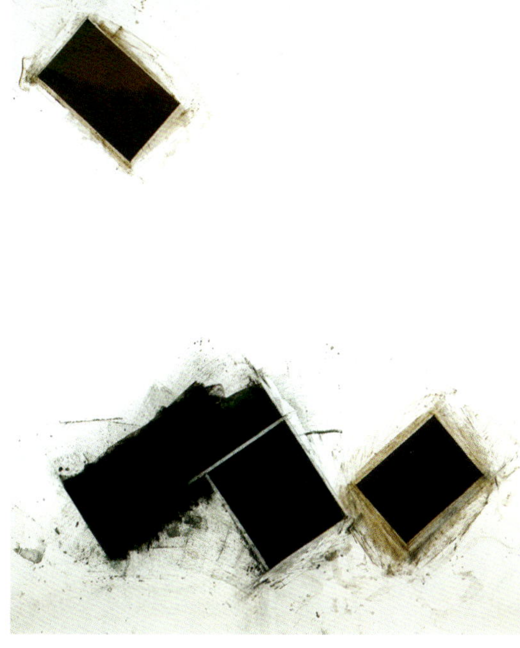

824, 825
Joel Shapiro:
Untitled (JS 929), 1990 (left)
Untitled (JS 931), 1990 (right)

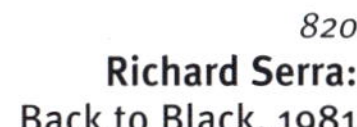

820
Richard Serra:
Back to Black, 1981

The Joseph and Celia Ascher Collection

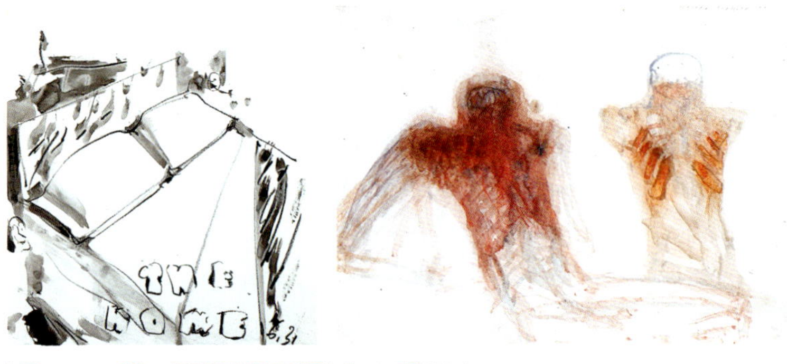

625, 748
Claes Oldenburg:
Study for Home, 1963 (left)
Walter Pichler:
Two Torsoes, 1977 (right)

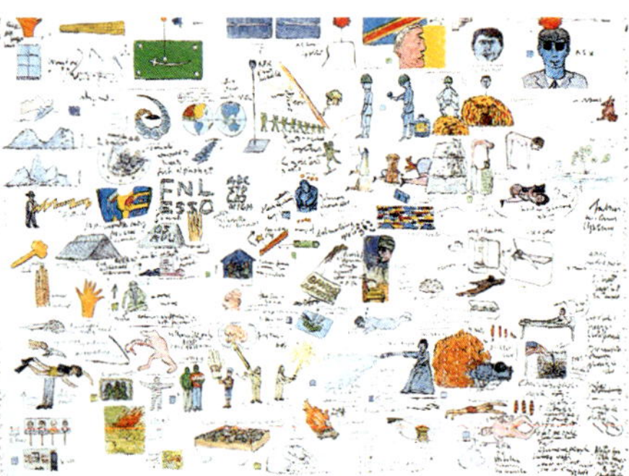

353
David Hockney:
Peter Reading, 1968

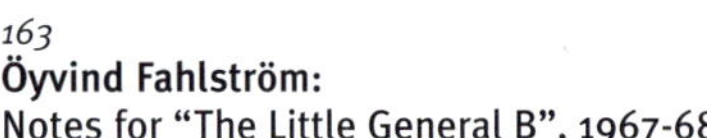

163
Öyvind Fahlström:
Notes for "The Little General B", 1967-68

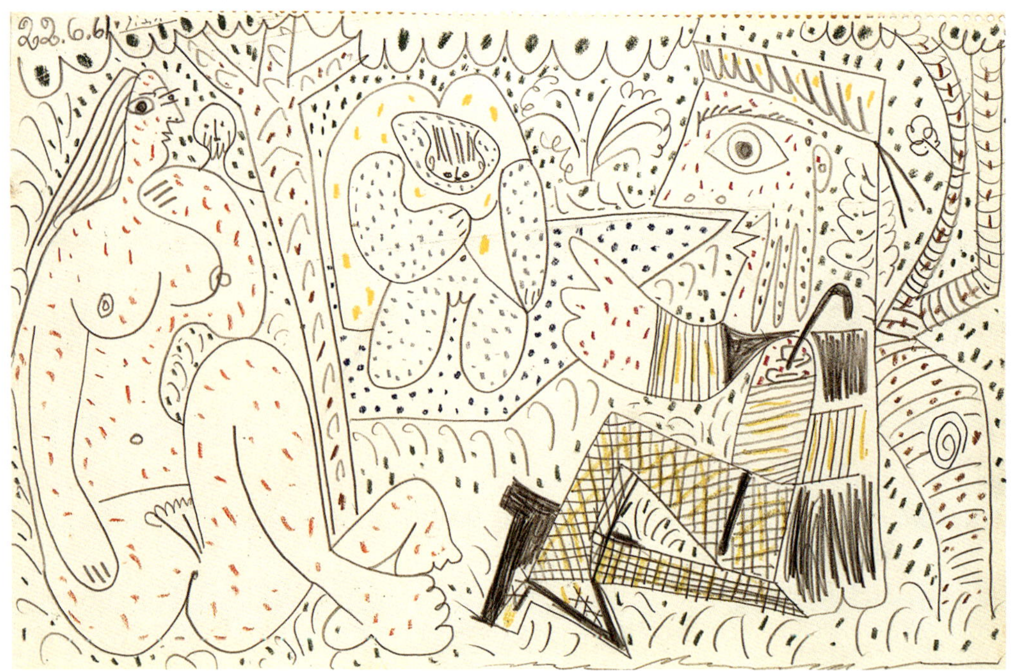

737
Pablo Picasso:
Le Déjeuner sur l'herbe, 1961

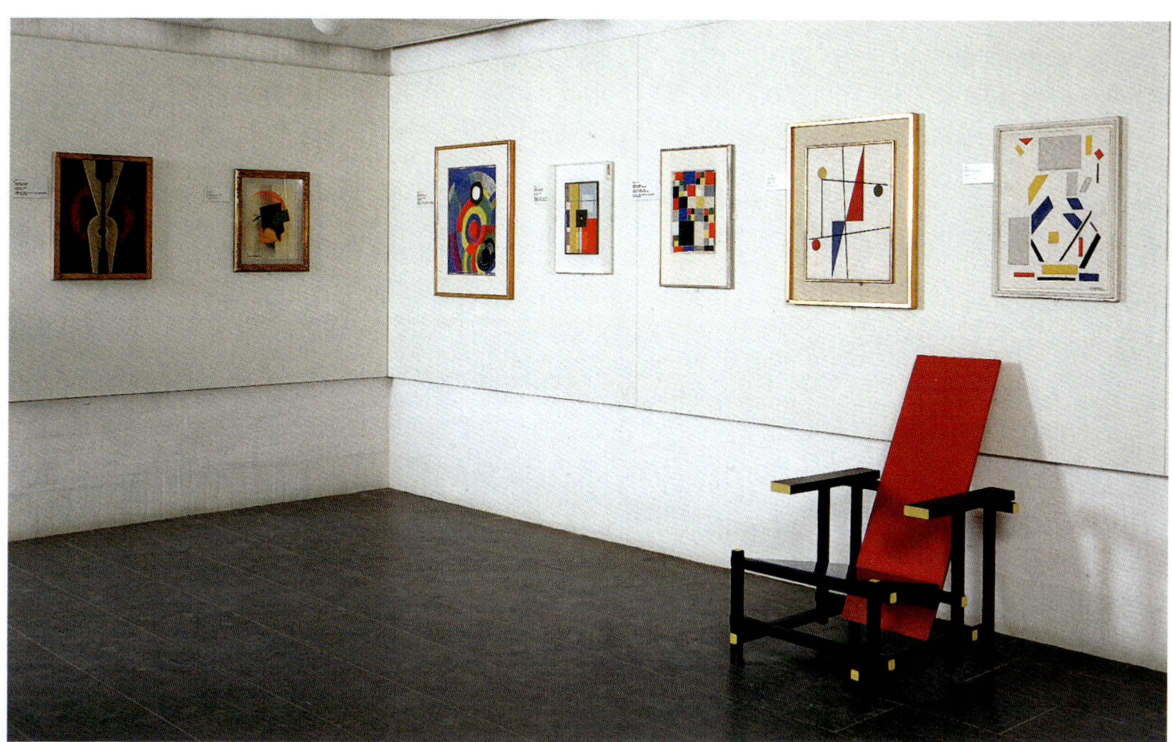

The Joseph and Celia Ascher Collection in the South Wing

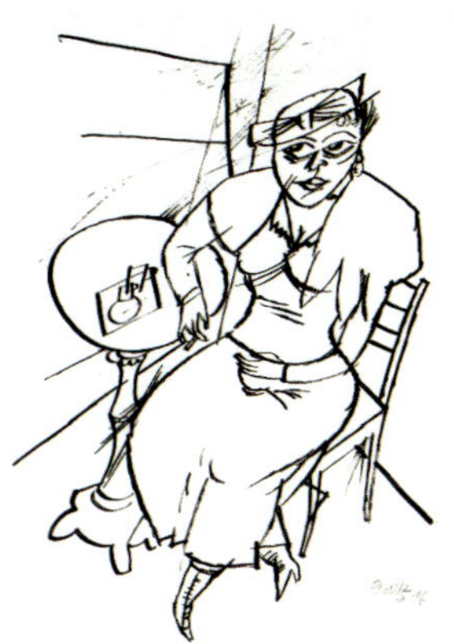

258
George Grosz:
Lady in a Café, 1916

755
Ljubov Popova:
Untitled, c. 1918

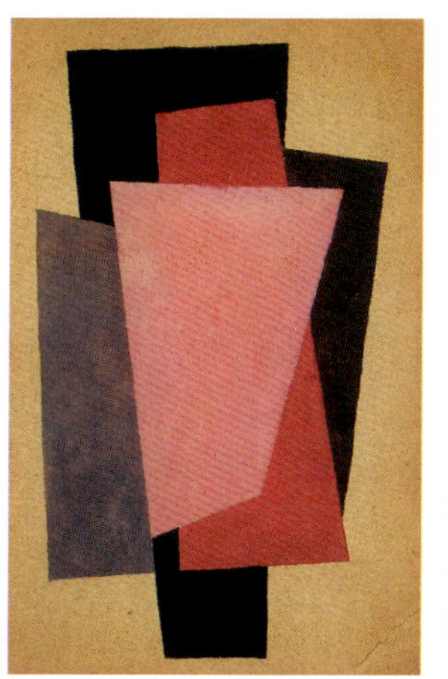

546
Kasimir Malevich:
Suprematism, c. 1920

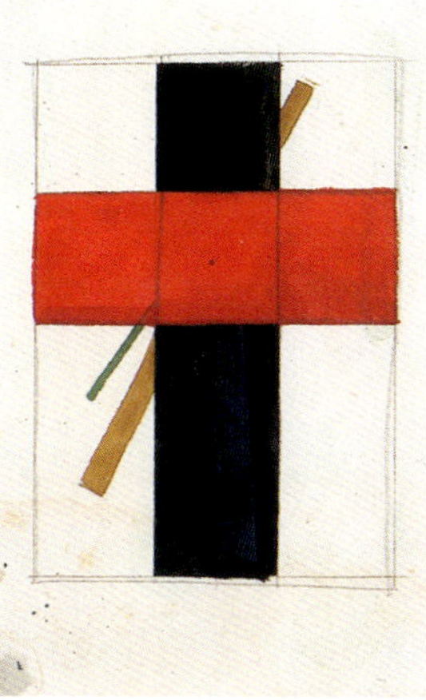

422
Lajos Kassak:
Hard Boiled Egg, 1923

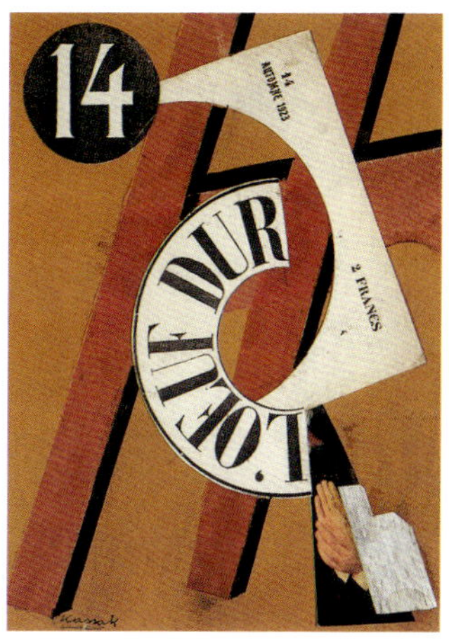

591
Lászlo Moholy-Nagy:
Pneumatic, 1926

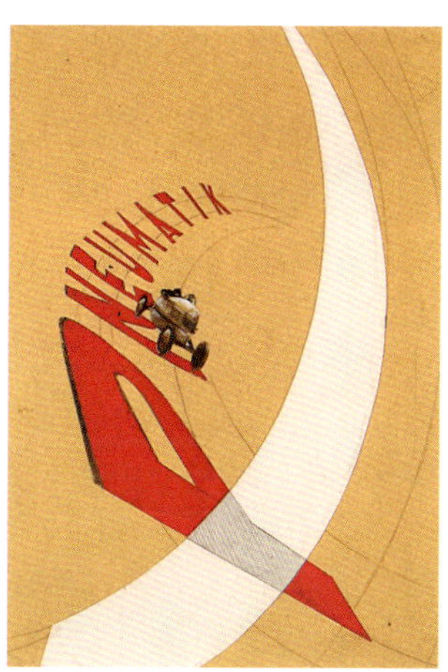

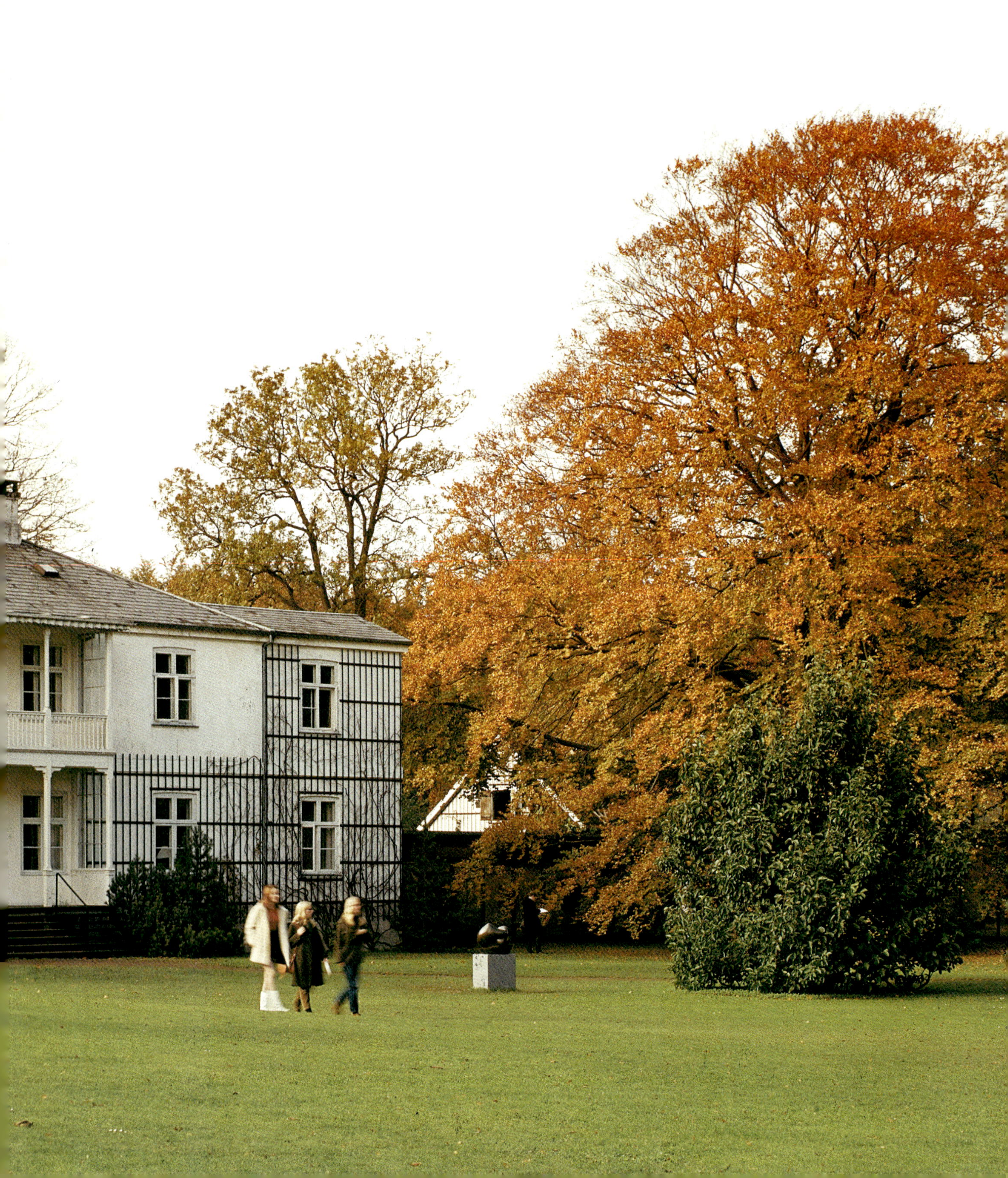

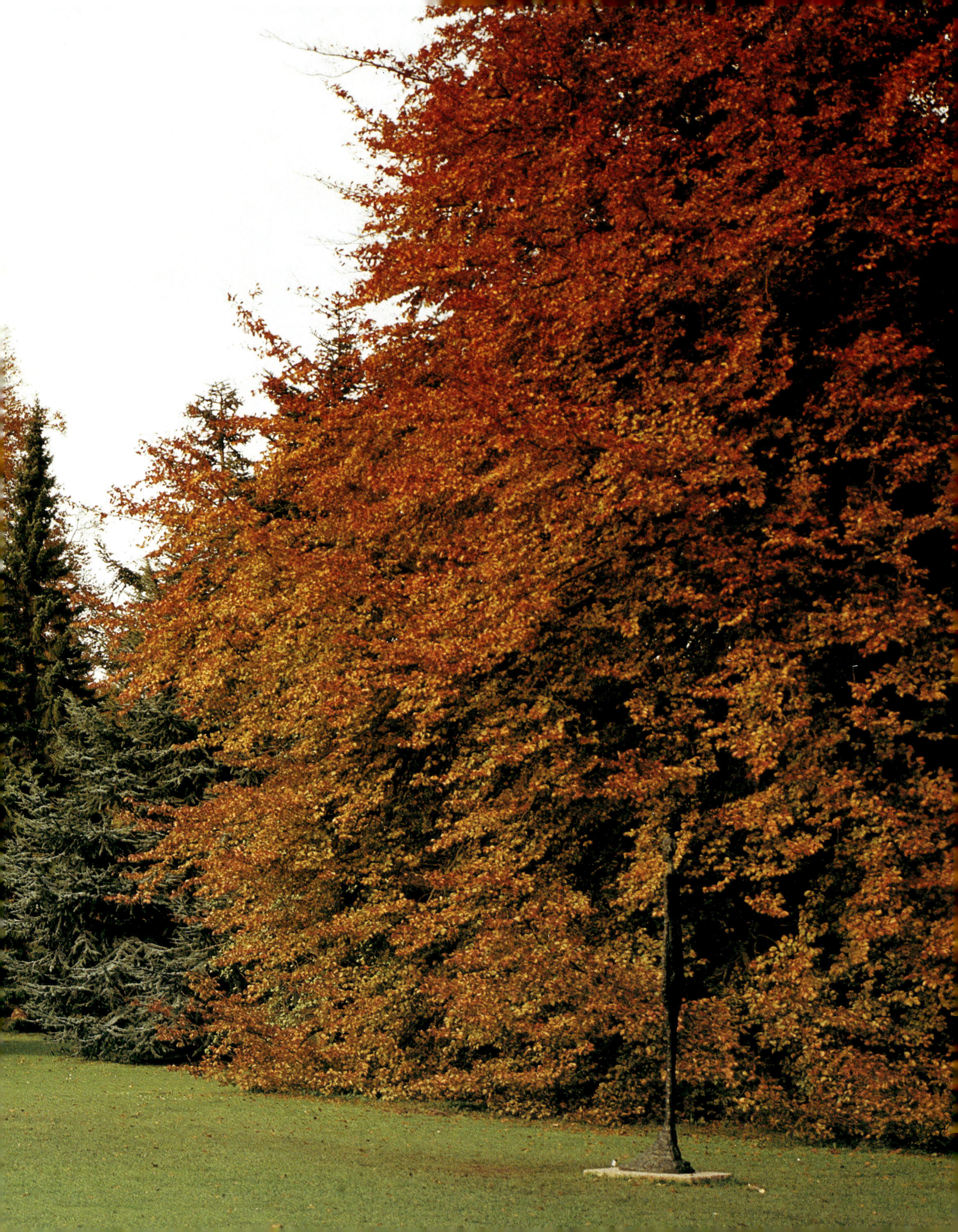

List of Works

SELECTION OF WORKS
The catalogue covers a selection of paintings, sculptures, collages, and drawings from the Louisiana Collection. The works are listed in the following order: painting, sculpture and works on paper.

TITLES AND DIMENSIONS
Original titles are emphasized. Dimensions are in cms: height x width x depth.

PURCHASES AND DONATIONS
Works purchased by the Louisiana Museum or the Louisiana Foundation are not marked. Works marked with * have been donated through The American Federation of Arts, while ** indicate that the work has been donated with The Cosmopolitan Arts Foundation as intermediary.

ABSALON
FRANCE 1964-1993
1
Bataille, 1993
Struggle
Video, 50 sec.

2
Bruits, 1993
Noises
Video, 3 min.

YAACOV AGAM
ISRAEL/FRANCE 1928
3
Structural Painting, 1964
Relief, oil/wood, 40.5 x 36.5 x 5
Donation: The Riklis Collection of McCrory Corporation**

JOSEF ALBERS
GERMANY/USA 1888-1976
4
Homage to the Square (611), 1958
Oil/masonite, 61 x 61
Donation: The Josef and Anni Albers Foundation*

5
Homage to the Square: Yellow Climate, 1961
Oil/masonite, 122 x 122
Donation: The Friends of the Louisiana Collection

6
Structural Constellation, 1961
Mechanical engraving/formica, 50 x 67

7
Homage to the Square (633), 1962
Oil/masonite, 61 x 61
Donation: The Josef and Anni Albers Foundation*

8
Homage to the Square: Broadening (1840), 1962
Oil/masonite, 61 x 61
Donation: The Josef and Anni Albers Foundation*

PIERRE ALECHINSKY
BELGIUM 1927
9
Autoportrait sans traits, 1965
Self-Portrait without Features
Oil/canvas, 75 x 90
Donation: The New Carlsberg Foundation

10
Le Doute, 1968
Doubt
Acrylic and Indian ink on paper/canvas, 201 x 251
Donation: Pierre Alechinsky

11
A l'Aveuglette, 1974
Blindly
Aquatint on paper/canvas, 186 x 286
Donation: Pierre Alechinsky

12
Le Bruit de la chute, 1975
The Noise from the Cataract
Acrylic and Indian ink on paper/canvas, 151 x 335
Donation: The Friends of the Louisiana Collection

13
Le Mystère du parfum de la dame en jaune, 1975
The Mysterious Perfume of the Lady in Yellow
Acrylic on paper/canvas, 127 x 154
Donation: Stephane Janssen**

14-16
Suite des Bouches du Rhône no. 11, 12, 13, 1976
Suite: The Estuaries of the Rhône-River No. 11, 12, 13
Indian ink/Japanese paper, three parts, 273 x 91 each

ELSE ALFELT
DENMARK 1910-1974
17
Rumligt, lyst, blåt bjergbillede, 1952
Spatial Light Blue Mountain Picture
Oil/plywood, 126 x 105

18
Monte Rosa, 1956
Oil/plywood, 207 x 102

NATHAN ALTMAN
RUSSIA 1889-1970
19
Untitled, 1916
Wood, painted, 47 x 30 x 4
Donation: Joseph and Celia Ascher, New York**

FRANCIS ALŸS
BELGIUM 1959
20-37
Déjà vu, 1993-1996
Oil/canvas, 18 works, varying dimensions

MOGENS ANDERSEN
DENMARK 1916
38
Uden titel, 1975
Untitled
Oil/canvas, 195 x 320

KAREL APPEL
THE NETHERLANDS 1921
39
Vie de la rue, 1953
Street Life
Oil/canvas, 116 x 89
Donation: Stephane Janssen**

40
Animal de la terre, 1955
Earth Animal
Oil/hessian, 89 x 146
Donation: The New Carlsberg Foundation

SHUSAKU ARAKAWA
JAPAN/USA 1938
41
Untitled, 1972
Acrylic/canvas, collage, 183 x 264
Donation: The Riklis Collection of McCrory Corporation**

42
Detail of ..., 1968
Acrylic/canvas, 85.8 x 160.5
Donation:
Elena and Nicolas Calas

43
Who Is It?, 1972
Watercolour and pencil, 88.9 x 116.8
Donation: Joseph and Celia Ascher, New York**

ARMAN
FRANCE/USA 1928
44
Concert de Munich No. 1, "Colère de violoncelle", 1963
Munich Concert No. 1, "Violoncello Anger"
Object/board, 165 x 122

JEAN ARP
FRANCE 1886-1966
45
Coupes superposées, 1947
Stacked Bowls
Bronze, 96 x 50 x 43
Donation: Marguerite Arp

46
Concrétion humaine sur coupe ovale, 1948
Human Concretion on an Oval Bowl
Bronze, 57 x 55 x 73
Donation: The New Carlsberg Foundation

47
Vénus de Meudon, 1956
Venus from Meudon
Bronze, 193 x 55 x 45
Donation: The New Carlsberg Foundation

48
Seuil aux crénaux végétaux, 1959/82
Threshold Sculpture with Plantlike Crenelations
Bronze, 230 x 137 x 25

49
Seuil-réflection, 1960/82
Threshold Sculpture: Reflection
Bronze, 246 x 260 x 30

FRANCIS BACON
IRELAND/GREAT BRITAIN
1909-1992
50
Man and Child, 1963
Oil/canvas, 198 x 147
Donation: The New Carlsberg Foundation

51
Three Studies of George Dyer, 1969
Oil/canvas, three paintings, 36 x 30 each
Donation: The New Carlsberg Foundation

OLLE BAERTLING
SWEDEN 1911-1981
52
Ogri, 1959
Oil/canvas, 180 x 91
Donation: The Riklis Collection of McCrory Corporation**

JOHN BALDESSARI
USA 1931
53
Pinky's Jewelry, 725. E. 8th Street, National City, Calif., 1996
Acrylic and jet-ink/canvas, 150 x 114

LEWIS BALTZ
USA 1945
54
Gladsaxe, 1995
Two cibachromes,
a: 123 x 155.5, b: 155.5 x 123

GEORG BASELITZ
GERMANY 1938
55
Der neue Typ, 1966
The New Type
Oil/canvas, 162 x 130
Donation: Franz Dahlem

56
Der Abgarkopf, 1984
The Abgar Head
Oil and acrylic/canvas, 250 x 200

57
Das Liebespaar, 1984
The Loving Couple
Oil/canvas, 250 x 330

58
Steinkopf, 1991
Stone Head
Oil/canvas, 300 x 250
Donation: Michael Werner

59
Dresdner Frauen: Die Heide, 1990
The Women from Dresden: Heath
Limewood, painted, 150 x 44 x 39
Donation: The New Carlsberg Foundation

60
Ohne Titel, 29. VI. 1990
Untitled
Charcoal on paper/canvas, 204.8 x 151
Donation: The New Carlsberg Foundation

61
Ohne Titel, 20. VII. 1990
Untitled
Charcoal on paper/canvas, 202.2 x 148.4
Donation: The New Carlsberg Foundation

62
Ohne Titel, 23. VII. 1990
Untitled
Charcoal on paper/canvas, 201.6 x 148.4
Donation: The New Carlsberg Foundation

BERNHARD AND HILLA BECHER
GERMANY 1931 and 1934
63
Scheibengasbehälter, 1973
Gas Tanks
Photography, black/white, 80 x 64

64
Hochöfenköpfe, 1997
Blast Furnaces
Photographs, black/white, nine works, total 173 x 143
Donation: Bernd & Hilla Becher and Sonnabend Gallery

65
Scheibengasbehälter, 1997
Gas Tanks
Photography, black/white, nine works, total 173 x 143

JOSEPH BEUYS
GERMANY 1921-1986
66
Honigpumpe am Arbeitsplatz, 1974-77
Honey Pump in the Workplace
Electromotor, steel and copper parts, plastic tubes, honey, varying dimensions

MAX BILL
SWITZERLAND 1908-1994
67
Construction, 1937
Granite, 125 x 124 x 124
Donation: The New Carlsberg Foundation

EJLER BILLE
DENMARK 1910
68
Komposition, 1938
Composition
Oil/canvas, 81 x 60

69
Komposition, 1939
Composition
Oil/canvas, 50 x 65

70
Figurer med blå dominant, 1956
Figures with Blue Dominant
Oil/canvas, 68 x 63

71
Vejby Strand, 1959
Vejby Beach
Oil/canvas, 80 x 75

72
Hvidt, blåt, grønt med rød dominant, 1960
White, Blue, Green with Red Dominant
Oil/canvas, 82 x 75

73
Blåt, gult, orange, Marrakech, 1962
Blue, Yellow, Orange, Marrakech
Oil/canvas, 65 x 55

74
Marrakech med rød dominant, 1962
Marrakech with Red Dominant
Oil/canvas, 65 x 54

75
Fugl, 1962
Bird
Oil/canvas, 45 x 39

76
Lurende fugl, 1933
Tricky Bird
Bronze, h. 16

77
Spadserende form, 1933-36
Walking Form
Bronze, h. 29

78
Fugleagtigt væsen, c. 1935
Birdlike Creature
Bronze, h. 18

79
Maske, 1936
Mask
Bronze, h. 30

80
Næbdyret, 1936
Beaked Animal
Bronze, h. 36

81
Øgle, 1936
Saurian
Bronze, l. 37

82
Øgle, c. 1936
Saurian
Concrete, 138 x 180 x 88
Donation: Ebbe Neergaard

83
Figur med fangarme, 1948-80
Figure with Tentacles
Bronze, h. 29

OLA BILLGREN
SWEDEN 1940
84
Pompejansk interiör I, 1996
Pompeian Interior I
Oil/canvas, 200 x 210

85
Pompejansk interiör III, 1996
Pompeian Interior III
Oil/canvas, 200 x 210

ROSS BLECKNER
USA 1949
86
Two Knights not Nights, 1988
Oil/canvas, 274.3 x 182.9
Donation:
The New Carlsberg Foundation, The Augustinus Foundation and The Louisiana Foundation

87
From the Three Beating as One, 1988
Oil/canvas, 152.4 x 213.4
Donation:
The New Carlsberg Foundation, The Augustinus Foundation and The Louisiana Foundation

ILYA BOLOTOWSKY
RUSSIA/USA 1907-1981
88
Tondo with Reds, 1972
Acrylic/canvas, diam. 119
Donation: The Riklis Collection of McCrory Corporation**

PETER BONDE
DENMARK 1958
89
Makulatur, 1987
Spoilage
Mixed media/masonite, 122 x 122
Donation: Kirsten and Palle Dige

ALEXANDER BORTNYIK
HUNGARY 1893-1976
90
Bildarchitektur abc, 1922
Picture Architecture ABC
Oil/canvas, 49 x 30
Donation: Joseph and Celia Ascher, New York**

HUGO ARNE BUCH
DENMARK 1927
91
Billede, 1961
Picture
Oil/canvas, 73 x 60
Donation:
Generalinde Koefoed Legat

92
Billede, 1989
Picture
Oil/canvas, 80 x 67

SCOTT BURTON
USA 1939-1990
93
Lava Rock Chair, 1981-82
Lava, 102 x 91 x 81

POL BURY
BELGIUM 1922
94
Sphère sur un cylindre, 1969
Sphere on a Cylinder
Chromium-plated brass with motor, 50 x 19 x 19
Donation: The Riklis Collection of McCrory Corporation**

ALEXANDER CALDER
USA 1898-1976
95
Quatre systèmes rouges, 1960
Four Red Systems
Iron, 195 x 180 x 180
Donation: The New Carlsberg Foundation

96
Nervures minces, 1963
Slender Ribs
Iron, 358 x 305 x 346
Donation: The New Carlsberg Foundation

97
Little Janey-Waney, 1964/76
Iron, 474 x 240 x 205

98
Almost Snow Plough, 1964/76
Iron, 432 x 325 x 287

JANET CARDIFF
CANADA 1957
99
Louisiana Walk # 14, 1996
Site specific work, audio with mixed media

CLAUS CARSTENSEN
DENMARK 1957
100
Contamineret, 010487, 1987
Contaminated, 010487
Foam rubber with china plate, 300 x 200
Donation: Kirsten and Palle Dige

101
Untitled (membrane 15), 1991
Indian ink and acrylic/plastic, 226 x 176
Donation: Kirsten and Palle Dige

CÉSAR
FRANCE 1921
102
La Victoire de Villetaneuse, 1965
The Victory at Villetaneuse
Bronze, 230 x 109 x 92
Donation: The New Carlsberg Foundation

103
Le Grand pouce, 1968
The Big Thumb
Bronze, 185 x 100 x 103

EDUARDO CHILLIDA
SPAIN 1924
104
Erabaki, 1968
Iron, 46 x 53 x 25
Donation: The Riklis Collection of McCrory Corporation**

105
Collage, 1963
Black and white paper, 24.8 x 18.4
Donation: The Riklis Collection of McCrory Corporation**

106
Esquisse de main, c. 1966
Sketch
Ink and collage/paper, 20.3 x 25.4
Donation: The Riklis Collection of McCrory Corporation**

CHRISTO
BULGARIA/USA 1933
107
Running Fence, 1976
Pencil, crayon and fabric/paper, 70 x 55

108
Running Fence, 1976
Pencil, crayon and photograph/paper, 70 x 55
Donation: Christo

109
Abu Dhabi Mastaba Stacked Oil Barrels, 1977
Abu Dhabi Mastaba
Crayon and lacquer/paper, 70 x 55

FRANCISKA CLAUSEN
DENMARK 1899-1986
110
Uden titel, 1930
Untitled
Gouache/paper, 29 x 20
Donation: The Riklis Collection of McCrory Corporation**

CHUCK CLOSE
USA 1940
111
Phil (II) Grey, 1982
Paper pulp, relief print, 175.3 x 137.2
Donation: Pace Gallery, New York

GUILLAUME CORNEILLE
BELGIUM/THE NETHERLANDS 1922
112
Le Ciel entrebâillé sur une prairie verte, 1963
Small Opening in the Sky over a Green Meadow
Oil/canvas, 55 x 38
Donation: The New Carlsberg Foundation

113
Terre radieuse, 1965
Radiant Earth
Oil/canvas, 73 x 100
Donation: The Friends of the Louisiana Collection

JOSEPH CORNELL
USA 1903-1972
114
Untitled (Canova), c. 1961
Photo-collage, 30.5 x 23

TONY CRAGG
GREAT BRITAIN 1949
115
Bottle, 1982
Mixed media, 270 x 92
Donation: Verena and Bernd Klüser

116
Big Window, 1982
Mixed media, 240 x 180

117
Spiral, 1983
Mixed media, h. 155.5, diam. 280

ENZO CUCCHI
ITALY 1950
118
Senza titolo, 1985
Untitled
Oil/canvas with objects, 270 x 400

119
Scultura Africa, 1985
Africa Sculpture
Site specific sculpture, bronze, 120 x 1000 x 200

120-122
Senza titolo, 1988
Untitled
Pen/paper, three drawings, 15.2 x 10.4 (2 works)/16.9 x 22.5
Donation: The New Carlsberg Foundation

123
Senza titolo, 1989
Untitled
Pen and Indian ink/cardboard, 16.9 x 12
Donation: Verena and Bernd Klüser

RICHARD DEACON
GREAT BRITAIN 1949
124
In Two Minds No. 1, 1985
Galvanized steel, 170 x 100 x 400

AD DEKKERS
THE NETHERLANDS 1938-1974
125
Houtgrafiek No. IV, 1970
High relief No. IV
Synthetic material, painted, 128 x 128
Donation: The Riklis Collection of McCrory Corporation**

126
Eerste fase van cirkel naar vierkant als zaagsnede, 1971
First Phase from Circle to Square as Cross Section
Wood, painted, diam. 35
Donation: The Riklis Collection of McCrory Corporation**

SONIA DELAUNAY
RUSSIA/FRANCE 1885-1979
127
Rythme-couleur no. 1916, 1973
Rythm-Colour No. 1916
Gouache/paper, 49.5 x 38
Donation: The Riklis Collection of McCrory Corporation**

128
Rythme-couleur no. 1919, 1973
Rythm-Colour No. 1919
Gouache/paper, 55.9 x 37.5
Donation: Joseph and Celia Ascher, New York

129
Projet de tissue, 1924
Study for fabric design
Gouache/paper, 57 x 24
Donation: Joseph and Celia Ascher, New York

JEAN DEWASNE
FRANCE 1921
130
Gamma sud, 1973
Gamma South
Enamel/board, 96 x 130

131
Midi soleil, 1973
Midday Sun
Enamel/board, 96 x 130
Donation: The Friends of the Louisiana Collection

JAN DIBBETS
THE NETHERLANDS 1941
132
Structure Panorama 360°, 1977
Panorama Structure 360°
Pencil/colour photographs, 80 x 140

ERIK DIETMAN
SWEDEN/FRANCE 1937
133
Livre Sterling, 1968-77
Pound Sterling
Objects/board, 210 x 732

BURGOYNE DILLER
USA 1906-1965
134
Untitled, 1940-45
Oil/canvas, 106 x 66
Donation: Joseph and Celia Ascher, New York**

JIM DINE
USA 1935
135
Wiring the Unfinished Bathroom, 1962
Oil and objects/canvas, 178 x 244

136
White Bathroom, 1962
Oil and objects/canvas,
183 x 183

137
Words for Paul's Daughters and a Little Wrench, 1971
Oil and objects/canvas, 244 x 193
Donation: The Friends of the Louisiana Collection

138
The Desire (Lessons in Nuclear Peace) for Sussi and Herbert Pundik, 1982
Acrylic and sand/masonite,
18 works, 110 x 100 each
Donation: Jim Dine

139
C-Clamp, 1962
Charcoal/paper, 64.5 x 50.5
Donation: Elena and Nicolas Calas

140
C-Clamp (in Green), 1962
Mixed media/paper, 71 x 51
Donation: Elena and Nicolas Calas

JEAN DUBUFFET
FRANCE 1901-1985
141
L'Incertaine (Corps de dame), 1950
The Uncertain (Female Figure)
Oil/canvas, 117 x 90

142
Elément de sol gris-beige (Texturologie XVI), 1958
Greyish Beige Earth Element (Texturology XVI)
Oil/canvas, 97 x 130

143
Orient de barbe, 1959
Beard Orient
Oil/canvas, 117 x 89

144
Les Implications journalières, 1977
The Daily Implications
Acrylic on paper/canvas,
222 x 290
Donation: The New Carlsberg Foundation

145-153
Sites avec personnages (E 166, E 277, E 310, E 356, E 359, E 377, E 381, E 385, E 407), 1981
Sites with figures
Acrylic/canvas, nine works,
67 x 50 each
Donation: The New Carlsberg Foundation

154
Mire G 41 (Kowloon), 1983
Acrylic on paper/canvas,
134 x 100
Donation: The Friends of the Louisiana Collection

155
Manoir d'essor, 1969/82
Dynamic Manor
Ferrocement, 400 x 540 x 520

JIMMIE DURHAM
USA 1940
156
Hermaphroditic Device, 1996
Mixed media, 131 x 192 x 14.5

157
Cotton Canvas on Polyvinyl Chloride, 1996
Mixed media, 84 x 124 x 72

MAX ERNST
GERMANY/FRANCE 1891-1976
158
Le Grand assistant, 1967/74
Great Assistant
Bronze, 156 x 223 x 70
Donation: Max Ernst

159
La Grenouille, 1967/74
Frog
Bronze, 128 x 79 x 79
Donation: Max Ernst

160
La Tortue, 1967/74
Tortoise
Bronze, 97 x 115 x 80
Donation: Max Ernst

ALEXANDRA EXTER
RUSSIA/FRANCE 1882-1949
161
Design for the decor of Faust, c. 1920
Gouache/paper, 33 x 50.2
Donation: The Riklis Collection of McCrory Corporation**

ÖYVIND FAHLSTRÖM
SWEDEN/USA 1928-1976
162
Phase Four of Sitting ... Five Panels, 1968
Tempera/paper, 60.3 x 85.5
Donation: The Riklis Collection of McCrory Corporation**

163
Notes for "The Little General B", 1967-68
Tempera and ink/paper,
44.5 x 61
Donation: Joseph and Celia Ascher, New York**

164
Notes for "The Little General A", 1968
Tempera and ink/paper,
44.5 x 60.5
Donation: Joseph and Celia Ascher, New York**

JACKIE FERRARA
USA 1929
165
A 208 Juxtu, 1980
Wood, 84 x 235 x 59

ADAM FISCHER
DENMARK 1888-1968
166
Portrætbuste, fru Ellen Fischer, 1917
Portrait Bust of Mrs. Ellen Fischer
Walnut, 42 x 12 x 23

167
Fransk soldat, 1918
French Soldier
Limestone, 51 x 19 x 22

168
Hoved, 1922
Head
Limestone, 64 x 25 x 30

169
Spiralpigen, 1928
The Spiral Girl
Cement, 74 x 18 x 16

ERIC FISCHL
USA 1948
170
Birth of Love (Second Version), 1987
Oil/canvas, 302 x 362

DAN FLAVIN
USA 1933-1996
171
Monument for V. Tatlin No. 11, 1964
Neon tube/metal plate,
243.5 x 72 x 12
Donation: Leo Castelli*

172
Untitled, 1967
Neon tube/metal box, h. 180

173
Untitled (to Barbara Lipper), 1973
Neon tube/metal frame,
243.5 x 243.5 x 24
Donation: Leo Castelli*

LUCIO FONTANA
ARGENTINA/ITALY 1899-1968
174
Concetto spaziale, 1950
Spatial Concept
Oil and glass/canvas, 50 x 100

175
Concetto spaziale, 1958
Spatial Concept
Aniline and collage/canvas,
150 x 150
Donation: The New Carlsberg Foundation

176
New York, 1962
Aluminium, 195 x 97

177
Concetto spaziale, Attese, 1966
Spatial Concept, Waiting
Water soluble colour/canvas,
103 x 84

178
Concetto spaziale, Attese, 1967
Spatial Concept, Waiting
Aniline/canvas, 74 x 60

LINDA FRANCIS
USA 1943
179
Untitled, 1981
Chalk/black paper, 141 x 107

SAM FRANCIS
USA 1923-1994
180
Untitled, 1956
Oil/canvas, 370 x 240
Donation: The New Carlsberg Foundation

181-182
Untitled, 1957-58
Watercolour and gouache/paper,
two works, 56 x 76/46 x 107
Donation: Sam Francis

183
Japan Line No. 2, 1957
Gouache/paper, 48 x 107
Donation: Sam Francis

184-188
Untitled, 1957-82
Gouache/papir, five works,
varying dimensions
Donation: Sam Francis

189
Untitled, 1958
Watercolour and gouache/paper,
105 x 75
Donation: The Augustinus Foundation

190
Untitled, 1962
Gouache/paper, 56 x 38
Donation: Paula and Philip Kirkeby, Smith Anderson Gallery

191-197
Untitled (Edge Paintings), 1966-68
Acrylic/canvas, seven works,
varying dimensions
Donation: Sam Francis

198
Untitled (Edge Painting), 1968
Acrylic and oil/canvas, 300 x 200
Donation: The Augustinus Foundation

199
Big Red II, 1979
Acrylic/canvas, 549 x 381
Donation: The Augustinus Foundation

200
Sketch for the Concert Hall, 1980
Acrylic/canvas, 85 x 282
Donation: Sam Francis

201
Sketch for the Concert Hall II, 1980
Acrylic/canvas, 89 x 353
Donation: Sam Francis

202
Untitled, 1980
Acrylic/canvas, 95 x 360
Donation: Sam Francis

203
Untitled, 1981-83
Acrylic/canvas, 271 x 896
Donation: Sam Francis

ERIK AUGUST FRANDSEN
DENMARK 1957
204
Uden titel/Singularitet, 1987
Untitled/Singularity
Oil and car tyre/canvas, 200 x 162
Donation: Kirsten and Palle Dige

ROBERT FRANK
SWITZERLAND/USA 1924
205
New York, 1979
Photograph, black/white, 41 x 50.5
Donation: Robert Frank

206
Bleecker Street N.Y.C., 1993
Photograph, black/white, 28 x 35.5
Donation: Robert Frank

207
Mabou, 1996
Photograph, black/white, 28 x 35.3
Donation: Robert Frank

WILHELM FREDDIE
DENMARK 1909-1995
208
Zolas skrivebord, 1936
Zola's Writing Desk
Assemblage, 100 x 40 x 85

209
Ildens verden, sansernes verden, de enkelte fænomeners verden, druemola, Eva, 1947
The World of Fire, The World of the Senses, the World of Separate Phenomena, Mole, Eve
Assemblage, 142 x 226 x 81

GÜNTHER FÖRG
GERMANY 1952
210
Sieben Bronzestelen, 1988
Seven Bronze Steles
Bronze, 230 x 120 (80) x 10
Donation: Günther Förg

211-212
Günther Förg Architecture Moscow 1923-1941, 1995
Photographs, black/white, two works, 280 x 170 each

NAUM GABO
RUSSIA/USA 1890-1977
213
Column, 1923/75
Glass, stainless steel, perspex, h. 193, diam. 156

ALBERTO GIACOMETTI
SWITZERLAND 1901-1966
214
Femme-cuillère, 1926
Spoon-Woman
Bronze, 144 x 51 x 23

215
Femme qui marche, 1932-34
Walking Woman
Bronze, 150 x 24 x 38

216
Petit buste sur socle, 1940-41
Small Bust on a Socle
Bronze, h. 11.8

217
Petit buste sur double socle, 1940-41
Small Bust on Double Socle
Bronze, h. 11.5

218
Petit homme sur socle, 1940-41
Small Man on a Socle
Bronze, h. 8.4

219
Petit buste de femme, 1945-46
Small Bust of a Woman
Bronze, h. 12.4

220
Petit buste d'Annette, 1946
Small Bust of Annette
Bronze, h. 16.5

221
Petit buste sur socle, 1948
Small Bust on a Socle
Bronze, h. 36.5

222
La Forêt, 1950
Forest
Bronze, 61 x 65 x 49
Donation:
The New Carlsberg Foundation and The Louisiana Foundation

223
Diego au chandail, 1953
Diego in Pullover
Bronze, h. 50.5
Donation: Lillian and P.T. Nielsens Fond

224
Buste de Diego, 1954
Bust of Diego
Bronze, h. 27
Donation:
The New Carlsberg Foundation, The Augustinus Foundation and The Louisiana Foundation

225-229
Femmes de Venise II, III, V, VII, VIII, 1956
Venice Women II, III, V, VII, VIII
Bronze, five works, h. 118 – 122.5

230
Grande tête, 1959-60
Big Head
Bronze, 96 x 27 x 28
Donation: The New Carlsberg Foundation

231
Homme qui marche, 1960
Walking Man
Bronze, 192 x 26.5 x 96.5
Donation: The New Carlsberg Foundation

232
Femme debout IV, 1960
Standing Woman IV
Bronze, 268 x 33 x 57
Donation: The New Carlsberg Foundation

233
Figurine sans bras, 1961-62
Small Figure without Arms
Bronze, h. 14.4

234
Buste de Diego, 1962
Bust of Diego
Bronze, h. 44.5
Donation:
The New Carlsberg Foundation, The Augustinus Foundation and The Louisiana Foundation

235
Buste d'Annette IV, 1962
Bust of Annette IV
Bronze, h. 59

236
Diego assis, 1964-65
Diego Seated
Bronze, h. 59.1
Donation:
The New Carlsberg Foundation, The Augustinus Foundation and The Louisiana Foundation

237
Buste d'Elie Lotar, 1965
Bust of Elie Lotar
Bronze, h. 58
Donation: The New Carlsberg Foundation

238
La Mère lisante, 1963
The Mother Reading
Pencil/paper, 50 x 32
Donation: Bruno and Odette Giacometti

HARALD GIERSING
DENMARK 1881-1927
239
Opstilling, 1923
Still Life
Oil/canvas, 54 x 74

240
Kirkegården i Svanninge, 1925
The Churchyard in Svanninge
Oil/canvas, 74 x 85

RAIMUND GIRKE
GERMANY 1930
241
Ohne Titel, 1973
Untitled
Oil and tempera/canvas 200 x 160
Donation: The Friends of the Louisiana Collection

242
Graues Bild I, 1973
Grey Picture I
Mixed techniques/canvas, 200 x 160
Donation: Peter Augustinus

ROBERT GOBER
USA 1954
243
Double Sink, 1985
Plaster, wood, metal thread, steel, latex, enamel paint, 76.2 x 213.4 x 63.5
Donation:
The New Carlsberg Foundation, The Augustinus Foundation and The Louisiana Foundation

JEAN GORIN
FRANCE 1899-1981
244
Composition le Vésinet, 1944
Composition, Vésinet
Oil/board, 53 x 44
Donation: Joseph and Celia Ascher, New York**

245
Composition no. 18, 1961
Composition No. 18
Oil/plywood, 67 x 57
Donation: The Riklis Collection of McCrory Corporation**

246
Composition spatio-temporelle no. 105, 1973
Space-Time Composition No. 105
Oil/board, 100 x 100 x 9
Donation: Suzanne Gorin

ARSHILE GORKY
USA 1904-1948
247
Untitled, undated
Oil on canvas/wood, 43.6 x 24.2
Donation: Elena and Nicolas Calas

248
Biomorphic Forms, 1946
Pencil and coloured pencil/paper, 48.5 x 63.5
Donation: Elena and Nicolas Calas

ANTONY GORMLEY
GREAT BRITAIN 1950
249
Vent, 1983
Lead, plaster, fibre-glass, 178 x 48 x 50

250
As Above so Below, 1988
Lead, plaster, fibre-glass,
188 x 181 x 35

GOTTHARD GRAUBNER
GERMANY 1930
251
Ohne Titel, 1973
Untitled
Mixed techniques, 130 x 177
Donation: Joseph and Celia Ascher, New York**

252
Rosa Kissen, 1963
Pink Cushion
Foam rubber, painted, 67 x 56
Donation: The Riklis Collection of McCrory Corporation**

ALLAN GREEN
GREAT BRITAIN 1932
253
Centered, 1974
Acrylic/canvas, 175 x 244
Donation: The Riklis Collection of McCrory Corporation**

254
Zonal, 1975
Acrylic/canvas, 137 x 183

255
Infill, 1975
Acrylic/canvas,
Two parts, total 162 x 298
Donation: Peter Augustinus

JOSEPH GRIGELY
USA 1956
256
I don't really know why, but maybe it's more abstract this way (with four untitled paintings by Per Kirkeby, 1983-84), 1996
Installation with four Per Kirkeby-paintings, oil/canvas, each 120 x 100, conversations with hearing persons, inscribed on paper and mixed media, varying dimensions

GEORG GROSZ
GERMANY 1893-1959
257
Ohne Titel, c. 1916
Untitled
Indian ink/paper, 50 x 36.5
Donation: Joseph and Celia Ascher, New York**

258
Dame im Café, 1916
Lady in a Café
Charcoal/paper, 25.4 x 21.6
Donation: Joseph and Celia Ascher, New York**

259
Ausbeuter, 1919
Exploiter
Indian ink/paper, 50 x 37.5
Donation: Joseph and Celia Ascher, New York**

JAN GROTH
NORWAY/USA 1938
260
Sign IV, 1990
Tapestry, wool, 250 x 320

261
Skulptur IV, 1990
Sculpture IV
Bronze, h. 340

262
Uden titel, 1966
Untitled
Black lithographic crayon/paper, 43 x 58

263
Uden titel, 1972
Untitled
Black lithographic crayon/paper, 62 x 88
Donation: Jan Groth

264
Uden titel, 1972
Untitled
Black lithographic crayon/paper, 62 x 88
Donation: Jan Groth

265
Uden titel, 1973
Untitled
Black lithographic crayon/paper, 62 x 88
Donation: Gertrude Mellon, New York

SVAVAR GUDNÁSON
ICELAND 1909-1988
266
Eventyrfjeldene, 1941
Fairy Tale Mountains
Oil/masonite, 74 x 84

267
Komposition, 1944
Composition
Oil/canvas, 136 x 159

ANDREAS GURSKY
GERMANY 1955
268
Shan Ti, 1994
Colour photograph, 180 x 235

269
Atlanta, 1996
Colour photograph, 180 x 220

NIGEL HALL
GREAT BRITAIN 1943
270
Wilful Reprise, 1978
Painted aluminium (seven parts), 196 x 63 x 35

271
No. 41, 1977
Charcoal drawing, 63.5 x 88.9
Donation: The Riklis Collection of McCrory Corporation**

RICHARD HAMILTON
GREAT BRITAIN 1922
272
The Solomon R. Guggenheim (Gold), 1965-66
Gold foil, fibre-glass, cellulose, 122 x 122 x 18

SVEND WIIG HANSEN
DENMARK 1922-1997
273
Mennesker i forvandling III: Det himmelske barn, 1963
People in Metamorphosis III: The Celestial Child
Oil/canvas, 205 x 325

274
Mennesker i forvandling: Tvivl, 1963
People in Metamorphosis: Doubt
Oil/canvas, 205 x 325

275
Den næseløse, 1958
Noseless
Bronze, 34 x 40 x 25

276
Delos, 1962
Bronze, 55 x 50 x 25

277
Portræt, byen, 1962
Portrait, the City
Bronze, 41 x 34 x 28

278
Siddende kvinde, 1964
Seated Woman
Bronze, 127 x 72 x 78

279
Stående kvinde, 1964
Standing Woman
Bronze, 179 x 97 x 11

280
Portræt, 1982
Portrait
Bronze, h. 38

281-283
Uden titel, c. 1980
Untitled
Indian ink and pencil/paper, three drawings, 50 x 35 each
Donation: Svend Wiig Hansen

284
Uden titel, c. 1983
Untitled
Pencil/paper, four drawings, 49.5 x 37 each
Donation: Svend Wiig Hansen

285
De kvæstede proportioner, 1984
Twisted Proportions
Indian ink and pencil/paper, 22 drawings,
31.5 x 37.2 each
Donation: Svend Wiig Hansen

MONA HATOUM
LEBANON/GREAT BRITAIN 1952
286
Silence, 1994
Glass, 127 x 92.7 x 59.1
Donation: The Friends of the Louisiana Museum of Modern Art in Denmark, Inc., USA

HENRY HEERUP
DENMARK 1907-1993
287
Solformørkelse, 1954
Solar Eclipse
Oil/hessian, 91 x 116

288
Rembrandt-fantasi, 1956
Rembrandt Fantasy
Oil/hessian, 200 x 300

289
Færdselsblomst, 1962
Traffic Signal Flower
Oil/masonite, 56 x 88

290
Bryllupskaret, 1963
Wedding Coach
Oil/plywood, 151 x 151

291
Muslingemand, 1928-30
Mussel Man
Plastelina and objects,
25 x 33 x 20

292
Flagermus, 1930
Bat
Assemblage, h. 20
Donation: Ingrid and Poul Hansen, Veksølund

293
Familien, 1930
The Family
Marble, 40 x 50

294-310
Skulpturer, c. 1930
Sculptures
Plastelina and objects,
17 works, h. 9-23

311
Frugtbarhedshornet, 1935
The Horn of Fertility
Granite, 100 x 40 x 98

312
Frueform, 1936
Female Form
Granite, 93 x 20 x 30
Donation: Elise Johansen

313
Nanna i stol, 1936
Nanna in a Chair
Granite, 94 x 41 x 35

314
Nanna figur, 1936
Nanna Figure
Marble, 77 x 30 x 18

315
Mor and barn, 1937
Mother and Child
Granite, 100 x 95 x 105

316
Strygebrætsmadonna, 1937
Ironing Board Madonna
Assemblage, 163 x 32 x 12

317
Kaffegud, c. 1940
Coffee Deity
Assemblage, 52 x 18 x 23

318
Muselmand, 1940-41
Mussulman
Assemblage, 122 x 47 x 17
Donation:
Alma and Vagn Nielsen

319
Lille billeddrejer, 1941
Small Picture Turner
Assemblage, 57 x 20 x 7
Donation: Henry Heerup

320
Dyremaske, 1943
Animal Mask
Assemblage, 56 x 64 x 18

321
Døden høster, 1943
Death Reaping
Assemblage, 81 x 70 x 53

322
Elskovshjul, 1944
Wheel of Love
Assemblage, diam. 64

323
Mand and kvinde, 1944
Man and Woman
Granite, 73 x 117 x 58

324
Fugl, 1950
Bird
Granite, 70 x 73 x 56

325
Maske, 1950
Mask
Sandstone, 37 x 52 x 16

326
Nisse, 1950
Goblin
Granite, 65 x 38 x 20

327
Nisse, c. 1950
Goblin
Wood, painted, h. 30

328
Kumme, 1950
Basin
Granite, 36 x 31 x 42

329
Pjerrotpige, 1950
Pierette
Limestone, 52 x 42 x 14

330
Venedig, c. 1950
Venice
Assemblage, h. 56

331
Uden titel, c. 1950
Untitled
Granite, 45 x 40 x 40

332
Hoved, 1951
Head
Granite, 57 x 18 x 37

333
Rødovremanden, 1953
The Rødovre Man
Granite, 70 x 65 x 44

334
Maske, 1955
Mask
Assemblage, 80 x 68 x 15

335
Mågepigen, 1955
The Gull Girl
Assemblage, 22.5 x 51 x 9

336
Påfugl, c. 1955
Peacock
Assemblage, 34 x 31 x 19

337
Portrætbuste, 1957
Portrait Bust
Granite, 46 x 33 x 32

338
Livsmøllen, 1963
The Wheel of Life
Mixed media, relief, 155 x 70 x 8

339
Tumling, 1963
Toddler
Sandstone, 70 x 22 x 22

340
Thors kat, 1964
Thor's Cat
Granite, 90 x 63 x 43

341
Vædderstele, 1965
Ram Stele
Granite, 110 x 25 x 50
Donation: Henry Heerup

342
Solbarn, 1965
Sun Child
Granite, 57 x 50 x 68

343
Troldkællinger, 1965
Witches
Granite, three parts,
75 x 140 x 40 each

344
Maske, 1965
Mask
Granite, 42 x 70 x 23

345
"Sjov i Danmark", 1945
"Fun in Denmark"
18 book illustrations
Crayon/paper, 22 x 16 each

HEIN HEINSEN
DENMARK 1935

346
OR 37, 1983
Bronze, 33 x 33 x 50

347
Uden titel, 1989
Untitled
Bronze, 90 x 67 x 65
Donation: The New Carlsberg
Foundation

BARBARA HEPWORTH
GREAT BRITAIN 1903-1975

348
Stringed Figure (Curlew), 1956
Bronze, 57 x 84 x 48
Donation: The New Carlsberg
Foundation

AUGUSTE HERBIN
FRANCE 1882-1960

349
Jaune, 1946
Yellow
Oil/canvas, 92 x 73
Donation: The New Carlsberg
Foundation

350
Vitalité, 1959
Vitality
Gouache/paper, 57.2 x 43.8
Donation: Joseph and Celia
Ascher, New York**

EWERDT HILGEMANN
GERMANY 1938

351
Cube No. 123 K, 1971
Painted iron, 60 x 60 x 60
Donation: The Riklis Collection
of McCrory Corporation**

DAVID HOCKNEY
GREAT BRITAIN 1937

352
Ubu Roi – Crossing the Ukraine,
1966
Pastel/paper, 16 x 20
Donation: Joseph and Celia
Ascher, New York**

353
Peter Reading, 1968
Ink/paper, 35.5 x 43.2
Donation: Joseph and Celia
Ascher, New York**

354
Pacific Hotel, 1968
Pencil and ink/paper,
31.8 x 25.4
Long-term loan: The Riklis Collection of McCrory Corporation

GOTTFRIED HONEGGER
SWITZERLAND 1917

355
Tableau-Relief NY 667, 1972
Oil on cardboard/canvas, 152 x 76
Donation: The Riklis Collection
of McCrory Corporation**

356
Tableau-Relief P 685, 1973
Oil on cardboard/canvas, 100 x 39
Donation: The Riklis Collection
of McCrory Corporation**

357
Tableau-Relief P 689, 1973
Oil on cardboard/canvas, 80 x 120
Donation: The Riklis Collection
of McCrory Corporation**

358
Tableau-Relief P 755, blau, 1975-76
Oil on cardboard/canvas,
240 x 240

359
Volume V, 1968
Aluminium, h. 44
Donation: The Riklis Collection
of McCrory Corporation**

ERIK HOPPE
DENMARK 1897-1968

360
Allé i Søndermarken,
to piger, 1929
Avenue in Søndermarken,
Two Girls
Oil/canvas, 106 x 103

361
Kvinde i allé, 1932
Woman in an Avenue
Oil/canvas, 107 x 135

362
Wilders Plads, 1934
Wilder's Square
Oil/canvas, 91 x 101

363
Gadebillede, 1935
Street Scene
Oil/canvas, 85 x 90

364
Blomstrende have, rød dame,
1936
Garden in Bloom, Red Lady
Oil/canvas, 90 x 100

365
Sommerdag i Søndermarken,
1944
Summer Day, Søndermarken
Oil/canvas, 75 x 86

366
Udsigt med solfyldt plæne, 1944
View with Sunny Lawn
Oil/canvas, 68 x 79

367
Efterårsskygger, 1945
Autumn Shadows
Oil/canvas, 85 x 99

368
Figur i Søndermarken, 1945
Figure in Søndermarken
Oil/canvas, 73 x 86

BRYAN HUNT
USA 1947

369
Daphne II, 1979
Bronze, 297 x 46 x 25

VILMOS HUSZAR
HUNGARY/THE NETHERLANDS
1884-1960
370
Composition, 1918-20
Oil/plywood, 48 x 37
Donation: Joseph and Celia Ascher, New York*

JÖRG IMMENDORF
GERMANY 1945
371
Malermut rundum II, 1980
Painter's Courage, Through and Through II
Synthetic resin/canvas, 250 x 200

WILL INSLEY
USA 1929
372
Interior Building Gate, Plan Section, 1970
Pencil/paper, 77.5 x 77.5
Donation: Joseph and Celia Ascher, New York*

373
Mountain Cross-Section, 1972
Pencil, coloured ink/cardboard, 76.2 x 76.2
Donation: The Riklis Collection of McCrory Corporation*

JEAN IPOUSTEGUY
FRANCE 1920
374
Remoulus, 1962
Remoulded
Bronze, seven parts, 87 x 94 x 66
Donation: The New Carlsberg Foundation

KARL ISAKSON
DENMARK 1878-1922
375
Stående model set fra ryggen, 1918-20
Standing Nude from the Back
Oil/canvas, 120 x 80

376
Portræt af fru Bertha Brandstrup, 1918-20
Portrait of Mrs. Bertha Brandstrup
Oil/canvas, 104 x 77

377
Opstilling med tulipaner, 1920
Still Life with Tulips
Oil/canvas, 59 x 74

EGILL JACOBSEN
DENMARK 1910 – 1998
378
Masker i landskab, 1942
Masks in Landscape
Oil/canvas, 70 x 85

379
Gul maske, 1943
Yellow Mask
Oil/canvas, 105 x 70

380
Masker i blåt, 1943
Masks in Blue
Oil/canvas, 98 x 71

381
Efterår, 1944
Autumn
Oil/canvas, 53 x 63

382
I bevægelse, 1944
In Motion
Oil/canvas, 99 x 72

383
Maske, 1945
Mask
Oil/hessian, 90 x 65

384
Kosmisk hav, 1945
Cosmic Ocean
Oil/canvas, 72 x 91

385
Masker i brunt, 1946
Masks in Brown
Oil/canvas, 135 x 94

GEORG JACOBSEN
DENMARK 1887-1976
386
Grøn krukke på bord, 1929
Green Jar on a Table
Oil/plywood, 100 x 77

ROBERT JACOBSEN
DENMARK 1912-1993
387
Skulptur, 1940
Sculpture
Granite, 53 x 40 x 48

388
Bevægelsesproblem, 1955
Problem of Motion
Iron, 38 x 53 x 23

389
Tobacco, 1957
Iron, 76 x 30 x 18

390
Skulptur, c. 1958
Sculpture
Iron, 58 x 60 x 27

391
Den højre røver, c. 1958
The Thief to the Right
Iron, 110 x 45 x 33

392
40-44, c. 1958
Iron, 95 x 45 x 55

393
M. Comte de la lune, 1958
The Lord of the Moon
Iron, 106 x 54 x 33

394
Multimouvement, 1959
Multimovement
Iron, 86 x 55 x 68

395
Sculpture en fer forgé, 1959
Sculpture in Wrought Iron
Iron, 48 x 43 x 33

396
Structure en mouvement, 1960
Structure in Motion
Iron, 118 x 76 x 40

NEIL JENNEY
USA 1945
397
Swimmer-Reflection, 1970
Acrylic/canvas and wooden frame, 155 x 113

ALFRED JENSEN
USA 1903-1981
398
Squaring of the Numbers, 1965-66
Oil/canvas, 193 x 193
Donation: The Friends of the Louisiana Collection

399
Earth, 1971
Oil/canvas, 188 x 188

SØREN GEORG JENSEN
DENMARK 1917-1982
400
Skulptur, 1977
Sculpture
Marble, 191 x 88 x 93

JENS ADOLF JERICHAU
DENMARK 1890-1916
401
Mennesker søger varsler III, 1915
People in Search of Omens III
Oil/canvas, 143 x 170

JASPER JOHNS
USA 1930
402
Green Target, 1957
Oil, encaustic and collage/canvas, 25.4 x 25.4
Donation: Elena and Nicolas Calas

403
Flag, 1960-69
Lead relief, multiple, 43 x 58

404
o Through 9, 1970
Lead relief, multiple, 76 x 60

405
Savarin (Red)
Lithograph, 65.8 x 50.6
Donation: The New Carlsberg Foundation

406
Land's End, 1979
Lithograph, 133 x 92
Donation: The New Carlsberg Foundation

ASGER JORN
DENMARK 1914-1973
407
Titania II, 1940-41
Oil/canvas, 120 x 115

408
Uden titel, 1943-44
Untitled
Oil/canvas, 125.5 x 100.5
Donation: The New Carlsberg Foundation

409
Den tavse myte, opus 5, 1952-53
On the Silent Myth, Opus 5
Oil/masonite, 66 x 160
Donation: Stephane Janssen**

410
Vision nocturne, 1959
Nocturnal Vision
Oil/canvas, 100 x 81

411
Uden titel, 1959
Untitled
Oil/canvas, 100 x 81

412
Dead Drunk Danes, 1960
Oil/canvas, 130 x 200

413
La Double face, 1960
Double Face
Oil/canvas, 116 x 89

414
Personnage, 1960
Figure
Oil/canvas, 114 x 144
Donation: The Danish Arts Foundation

415
Røde enge, grønne drenge, 1966-68
Red Meadows, Green Boys
Oil/canvas, 156 x 101

DONALD JUDD
USA 1928-1994
416
Untitled, 1962/87
Douglas Fir plywood, painted, 49.5 x 114 x 77.5

417
Untitled 1968/91
Douglas Fir plywood, painted, aluminium tube, 49.5 x 114 x 77.5

418
Untitled, 1969
Lacquer/anodized aluminium, 15 x 281 x 15

MENASHE KADISHMAN
ISRAEL 1932
419
Sheep, 1981
Acrylic/canvas, 138 x 111
Donation: Dov and Rachel Gottesman

DANI KARAVAN
ISRAEL 1930
420
Square, 1982
Site specific sculpture, concrete, 46 x 480 x 480

LAJOS KASSAK
HUNGARY 1887-1967
421
Architecture en image, 1923
Pictorial Architecture
Pencil/paper, 25 x 18
Donation: Joseph and Celia Ascher, New York**

422
L'Oeuf dur, 1923
Hard-boiled Egg
Collage, 24.7 x 19
Donation: Joseph and Celia Ascher, New York**

CRAIG KAUFFMAN
USA 1932
423
Untitled #1-7, 1968-69
Acrylic lacquer/plexiglass, 109 x 226 x 38

424
Untitled #2-4, 1995
Acrylic lacquer/formed acrylic plastic, 131 x 90 x 18

MIKE KELLEY
USA 1954
425-429
Apology (from "Australiana") # 1-5, 1984
Acrylic/paper, 162.5 x 122 each

ELLSWORTH KELLY
USA 1923
430
Yellow Black, 1968
Oil/canvas, 235 x 237

CLAY KETTER
USA/SWEDEN 1961
431
Surface Composite #1, 1995
Mixed media, 233 x 360 x 60

ANSELM KIEFER
GERMANY 1945
432
Inflammation, 1983-86
Oil, lead and photographs/ canvas, 320 x 280

433
Ausgiessung, 1982-86
Outpouring
Oil and mixed media/canvas, 330 x 555
Donation:
The New Carlsberg Foundation and The Louisiana Foundation

434
Säulen, 1983
Columns
Mixed media/canvas, 280 x 280
Donation:
The New Carlsberg Foundation, The Augustinus Foundation and The Louisiana Foundation

435
Jason, 1989
Lead, glass, teeth, snakeskin, 265 x 630 x 650
Donation:
The New Carlsberg Foundation, The Augustinus Foundation and The Louisiana Foundation

436
Wege der Weltweisheit: Die Hermannsschlacht, 1988-90
Ways of Worldly Wisdom: The Battle of Teutoburg Forest
Woodcut and acrylic/paper, 400 x 580
Donation: The New Carlsberg Foundation

EDWARD KIENHOLZ
USA 1927-1994
437
God Really Loves America Best, 1964
Assemblage, 55 x 38 x 45

438
The Middle Islands, 1972
Mixed media, varying dimensions

439
The Queen of the Maybe Day Parade, 1978
Mixed media (tableau), 205 x 250 x 160

PER KIRKEBY
DENMARK 1938
440
Soltemplet, 1969
The Temple of the Sun
Oil and enamel/masonite, 122 x 122

441
Fugle begravet i sne, 1970
Birds Buried in the Snow
Oil and enamel/masonite, 122 x 122

442
Uden titel, 1979
Untitled
Oil/canvas, 208 x 277
Donation: The Danish Arts Foundation

443
Uden titel, 1981
Untitled
Oil/canvas, 250 x 400

444
Uden titel, 1981
Untitled
Oil/canvas, three parts, 200 x 130

445
Uden titel, 1983
Untitled
Oil/canvas, 200 x 200

446
Landskab, 1983
Landscape
Oil/canvas, 200 x 200

447
Mor og barn, 1983
Mother and Child
Oil/canvas, 200 x 200

448
Fram, 1983
Oil/canvas, 118 x 200

449
Uden titel, 1983-84
Untitled
Six paintings, oil/canvas, 120 x 100

450
Grün Frühling, 1988
Green Spring
Oil/canvas, 200 x 170
Donation: The Friends of the Louisiana Collection

451
Beatus-Apokalypse, 1989
Oil/canvas, 290 x 350

452
Viel Später, 1992
Much Later
Oil/canvas, 300 x 500

453
Lille hoved med arm, 1981
Small Head with Arm
Bronze, 35 x 14 x 22

454
Model: To arme I, 1981
Model: Two Arms I
Bronze, 28 x 37 x 19

455
Port, 1981
Gate
Bronze, 35,5 x 23 x 15

456
Det store hoved med arm, 1983
The Big Head with Arm
Bronze, 200 x 78 x 40

457
Læsø hoved nr. IV, 1983
Læsø Head No. IV
Bronze, 66 x 32 x 25

458
Hoved og arm. Port, 1984
Head and Arm. Gate
Bronze, 85 x 67 x 76

459
Arm og hoved nr. XIII, 1984
Arm and Head No. XIII
Bronze, 55 x 26 x 16

460
Tor II, 1987
Gate II
Bronze, 240 x 170 x 60
Donation: The New Carlsberg Foundation

461
Uden titel. Murstensskulptur, 1994
Untitled. Brick Sculpture
Bricks with copper covering, 1340 x 480 x 500
Donation: The Olga and Esper Boel Foundation, The Danish Railways and The Alice Schiøtz Trust

462
Uden titel, 1988/89
Untitled
Charcoal, pencil and crayon/paper, 236 x 150
Donation: Per Kirkeby

463-465
Uden titel, 1990
Untitled
Charcoal/paper, three drawings 230 x 99 (two works) and 230 x 109
Donation: The New Carlsberg Foundation

RON B. KITAJ
USA/GREAT BRITAIN 1932
466
On a Regicide Peace, 1970
Oil/canvas, 96 x 54
Donation: Joseph and Celia Ascher, New York**

HARRY KIVIJÄRVI
FINLAND 1931
467
Viisasten kivi, 1963
The Philosophers' Stone
Diorite, 60 x 58 x 38
Donation: The Finnish Ministry of Education

468
Pieni monumentii, 1967
The Small Monument
Diorite, 154 x 60 x 32
Donation: The Finnish Ministry of Education

KONRAD KLAPHECK
GERMANY 1935
469
Logik der Frauen, 1965
Female Logic
Oil/canvas, 108 x 88
Donation: Joseph and Celia Ascher, New York**

YVES KLEIN
FRANCE 1928-1962
470
Antropométrie (ANT 52), 1960
Oil on canvas/paper, 159 x 78

471
Monoblue (IKB 75), 1960
Pigments on canvas/board, 199 x 153

472
Monogold (MG 17), 1960
Gold foil/board, 199 x 153

473
Monopink (MP 16), 1960
Pigments on canvas/board, 199 x 153

474
Eponge (SE 100), 1960
Sponge (SE 100)
Natural sponge with colour (IKB), 20 x 24 x 24
Donation: Rotraut Klein

475
Feu-couleur (FC 17), 1962
Fire-Colour (FC 17)
Tempera on cardboard/board, 106 x 94

FRANZ KLINE
USA 1910-1962
476
Untitled, 1953
Oil/paper, 22.2 x 28
Donation: Celia Ascher

IVAN KLIUN
RUSSIA 1873-1942
477
Suprematist Construction, 1920
Gouache and watercolour/board, 34 x 26
Donation: The Riklis Collection of McCrory Corporation**

478
Untitled, 1920
Pencil/paper, 17 x 10
Donation: Joseph and Celia Ascher, New York**

JIRI KOLAR
THE CZECH REPUBLIC 1914
479
Untitled, 1970
Mixed media, collage, 36.8 x 30.5
Donation: Joseph and Celia Ascher, New York**

480
Circle and Bar, 1970-71
Collage/wood, 40 x 30
Donation: The Riklis Collection of McCrory Corporation**

481
Untitled (Chiasmage), 1971
Collage, 40 x 30
Donation: The Riklis Collection of McCrory Corporation**

JOSEPH KOSUTH
USA 1945
482-483
Art as Idea as Idea (Rad-i-cal) Part I & II, 1968
I: Documentation of the printed definition, 16.3 x 13.7
II: Photostat of documentation, mounted on cardboard, 122 x 122
Donation: Leo Castelli*

JANNIS KOUNELLIS
GREECE/ITALY 1936
484
Senza titolo, 1988
Untitled
Steel plate, rails, coal sacks, 200 x 150

485
Senza titolo, 1961
Untitled
Lithographic crayon/paper, 70 x 100

BARBARA KRUGER
USA 1945
486
Untitled (You make history when you do business), 1981
Photograph, 226 x 107
Donation:
The New Carlsberg Foundation, The Augustinus Foundation and The Louisiana Foundation

MOSHE KUPFERMAN
POLAND/ISRAEL 1926
487
Untitled, 1974
Oil/canvas, 96 x 130
Donation: Joseph and Celia Ascher, New York**

488
Untitled, 1987
Oil, pastel and graphite/paper, 99.5 x 137.5
Donation: Dansk-Israelsk Kulturfond

489
Untitled, 1990
Oil, pastel and graphite/paper, 75 x 108
Donation: Dansk-Israelsk Kulturfond

ARTHUR KÖPCKE
GERMANY/DENMARK 1928-1977
490
Pudderbillede, 1962
Powder Picture
Mixed media/cardboard, 110 x 80

491
Rebus-Brevier, 1963
Picture Puzzle-Breviary
Mixed media/masonite, 70 x 101

492
Rebusbillede: Æblet falder ikke langt fra stammen, 1964
Picture Puzzle: Like Father, Like Son
Mixed media/masonite, 121 x 61

493
"Landlyst", 1965
Mixed media/wooden frame, 150 x 140

494
Actions – Pieces, 1966
Oil and collage/canvas, 200 x 140

WIFREDO LAM
CUBA 1902-1982
495
Nouvea, undated
Oil/canvas, 46 x 54.5
Donation: Elena and Nicolas Calas

496
La Femme, 1947
Woman
Ink and washing/cardboard, 91 x 73.2
Donation: Elena and Nicolas Calas

PETER LAND
DENMARK 1966
497
Peter Land d. 5. maj 1994, 1994
Peter Land, 5 May 1994
Video, 23 min.

HENRI LAURENS
FRANCE 1885-1954
498
Grande femme debout à la draperie, 1928
Tall Standing Woman, Draped
Bronze, 225 x 88 x 77.5
Donation: The New Carlsberg Foundation

JULIO LE PARC
ARGENTINA/FRANCE 1928
499
Mobile continuel blanc sur blanc, 1968-69
Continuous Mobile White on White
Mixed media, 100 x 100 x 5
Donation: The Riklis Collection of McCrory Corporation**

500
Forme en contorsion, objet cinétique, 1967
Twisted Form, Kinetic Object
Wood, steel, electromotor, 203 x 53 x 20
Donation: The Friends of the Louisiana Collection

BART VAN DER LECK
THE NETHERLANDS 1876-1958
501
Fruit Still Life, 1916
Mixed media, 28 x 38
Donation: Joseph and Celia Ascher, New York**

NIELS LERGAARD
DENMARK 1893-1982
502
Landskab, Gudhjem, 1932
Landscape, Gudhjem
Oil/canvas, 99 x 105

503
Landskab, Gudhjem, 1939
Landscape, Gudhjem
Oil/canvas, 120 x 131

504
Landskab, Gudhjem, 1940
Landscape, Gudhjem
Oil/canvas, 88 x 112

ERIK LEVINE
USA 1960
505
Rotor, 1987
Laminate, painted, 61 x 277 x 277

SHERRIE LEVINE
USA 1947
506
Bachelors (After Marcel Duchamp), 1991
Installation, six bronze castings in show cases, varying dimensions

507
Cathedral 1-9, 1995
Photographs, black/white, nine works, 25.2 x 20.5 each

SOL LEWITT
USA 1928
508
Three Cubes (Angle), 1969
Steel, painted, 160 x 305 x 305

509
Untitled (3, 2, 1, 2, 3), 1971
Wood, painted, 62 x 38 x 38

ROY LICHTENSTEIN
USA 1923-1997
510
Modern Painting, Diptych, 1967
Oil and magna/canvas, 122 x 244
Long-term loan: Roy Lichtenstein

511
Figures in Landscape, 1977
Oil and magna/canvas, 272 x 417

RICHARD PAUL LOHSE
SWITZERLAND 1902-1988
512
Reihenelemente zu rhytmischen Gruppen konzentriert, 1949/56/63
Rows of Elements in Rythmic Groups
Oil/canvas, 90 x 90
Donation: The Riklis Collection of McCrory Corporation**

513
Neun horizontale und neun vertikale Farbreihen, 1950-83
Nine Horizontal and Nine Vertical Colour Rows
Acrylic/canvas, 120 x 120

514
Grün-blau-violette Vertikale zwischen gelb-orange-rot, 1954-77
Green-Blue-Purple Verticals Between Yellow-Orange-Red
Acrylic/canvas, 120 x 120

CHARLES LONG
USA 1958
515
3 to 1 in Groovy Green, 1995
Installation, lacquer on plastic, table, sound equipment, sofa, 71 x 137 x 56

RICHARD LONG
GREAT BRITAIN 1945
516
Circle, 1972
Stone, diam. 850

517
Stone Circle, 1980
Swedish granite, diam. 400

ROBERT LONGO
USA 1953
518
Untitled (Men in the Cities), 1981
Pencil/paper, 271 x 157
Donation: The New Carlsberg Foundation, The Augustinus Foundation and The Louisiana Foundation

MORRIS LOUIS
USA 1912-1962
519-520
Charred Journal Firewritten (Untitled A, Untitled B), 1951
Acrylic/canvas, two works, 92 x 76
Donation: Marcella Louis Brenner*

521-522
Charred Journal Firewritten (II, IV), 1951
Acrylic/canvas, two works, 89 x 75
Donation: Marcella Louis Brenner*

523
Dalet Nun, 1958
Acrylic/canvas, 232 x 374
Donation: Marcella Louis Brenner*

524
Dalet Ayin, 1958
Acrylic/canvas, 230 x 375

525
Taper and Spread, 1959
Acrylic/canvas, 207 x 193
Donation: Marcella Louis Brenner*

526
Para No. 1, 1959
Acrylic/canvas, 265 x 353
Donation: Marcella Louis Brenner*

527
Addition III, 1959
Acrylic/canvas, 274 x 457
Donation: Marcella Louis Brenner*

528
Omega IV, 1959-60
Acrylic/canvas, 366 x 265
Donation: Marcella Louis Brenner*

529
Beta Epsilon, 1960
Acrylic/canvas, 261 x 394

530
Alpha Zeta, 1961
Acrylic/canvas, 266 x 610
Donation: Marcella Louis Brenner*

531
Happy Friday, 1962
Acrylic/canvas, 217 x 102
Donation: Marcella Louis Brenner*

LUCEBERT
THE NETHERLANDS 1924-1994
532
Untitled Drawing, 1955
Ink/paper, 50 x 33
Donation: Ad Petersen

VILHELM LUNDSTRØM
DENMARK 1893-1950
533
Pakkassebillede (Dagen derpå), c. 1917
Packing Box Picture (The Morning After)
Mixed media/board, 132 x 65 x 14

534
Frokost i det grønne, 1920
Le Déjeuner sur l'herbe
Oil/canvas, 200 x 264

535
Opstilling med kande, 1925
Still Life with Pitcher
Oil/canvas, 122 x 88

536
Stående model, 1926/27
Standing Nude
Oil/canvas, 196 x 131

537
Model, 1927
Nude
Oil/canvas, 146 x 97

538
Opstilling, 1928/29
Still Life
Oil/canvas, 90 x 117

539
Model, 1930
Nude
Oil/canvas, 130 x 97
Donation: The New Carlsberg Foundation

540
Opstilling, 1931
Still Life
Oil/canvas, 50.5 x 61.5

541
Opstilling, 1936
Still Life
Oil/canvas, 139 x 106

MARKUS LÜPERTZ
GERMANY 1941
542
"Der Mohr" (Linke Wange rosa, rechte Wange schwarz), 1983
"The Moor" (Left Cheek Pink, Right Cheek Black)
Bronze, painted, 45 x 20 x 32

543
Ohne Titel, 1975
Untitled
Gouache, 247 x 181.5
Donation: Michael Werner

KAZIMIR MALEVICH
RUSSIA 1878-1935
544
Suprematist Drawing, 1915-17
Pencil/paper, 19.7 x 14
Donation: The Riklis Collection of McCrory Corporation**

545
Suprematist Composition, 1915-16
Pencil/paper, 21 x 13
Donation: Joseph and Celia Ascher, New York**

546
Suprematism, c. 1920
Gouache/paper, 23 x 15
Donation: Joseph and Celia Ascher, New York**

SONJA FERLOV MANCOBA
DENMARK 1911-1984
547
To levende væsener, 1935
Two Living Creatures
Bronze, h. 53

548
Fugl med unge, c. 1940
Bird with Its Young
Bronze, h. 40

549
Skulptur, 1940-46
Sculpture
Bronze, 51 x 109 x 34

550
Skulptur, 1949
Sculpture
Bronze, 28 x 38 x 19

551
Koncentration, 1962-63
Concentration
Bronze, 58 x 56 x 48

552
Effort commun, 1963-64
Common Effort
Bronze, 107 x 107 x 50

ROBERT MANGOLD
USA 1937
553
Three Squares within a Triangle, 1975-76
Oil/canvas, 93 x 106

ROBERTO MATTA
CHILE/FRANCE 1911
554
Untitled, 1963
Oil/canvas, 113 x 146
Donation: The Friends of the Louisiana Collection

555
For the Carne con Chills. Until We Cease to Murder..., undated
Pencil and coloured pencil/paper, 36.8 x 49.5
Donation: Elena and Nicolas Calas

PAUL MCCARTHY
USA 1945
556-565
Family Tyranny/Cultural Soup, 1987
11 drawings, charcoal/paper 70 x 56/56 x 70 respectively

566
Family Tyranny/Cultural Soup, 1987
Video, 8 min./7 min.

567
Painter, 1995
Video, 50 min.

ALLAN MCCOLLUM
USA 1945
568
Over 10.000 Individual Works, 1987-89
Enamel/hydrocal, 100 x 824 x 492.5
Donation: The New Carlsberg Foundation, The Augustinus Foundation and The Louisiana Foundation

569
Ten Plaster Surrogates, 1988
Enamel/hydrostone, varying dimensions
Donation:
The New Carlsberg Foundation, The Augustinus Foundation and The Louisiana Foundation

JOHN MCLAUGHLIN
USA 1898-1976
570
Untitled, 1954
Oil/masonite, 81 x 98
Donation: Joseph and Celia Ascher, New York*

ALBERT MERTZ
DENMARK 1920-1991
571
Julestjernen, 1957
The Star of Bethlehem
Mixed media, 32 x 40

572
Bærepindeballet, 1957
Parcel Peg Ballet
Mixed media, 29 x 38 x 13

573
Et væsen med fangarme, 1957
A Creature with Tentacles
Oil/cardboard, 30 x 26

574
Klemmelus, 1957
Blister
Oil/masonite, 24 x 21

575
Løjser, 1957
Good-For-Nothing
Oil/masonite, 24 x 21

576
Samovar, 1957
Oil/masonite, 30 x 23

577
Slagterbillede, 1957
Butcher Picture
Oil/hessian, 63 x 78

578
Når grønt lyser rødt, har de vundet, 1960
When Green Shines Red, They Have Won
Oil/canvas, 73 x 91

579
Spejlmobile, 1961
Mirror Mobile
Mixed media, 42 x 48

580
Hjem, hjem, mit kære hjem, 1963
Home, Home, Sweet Home
Oil/canvas, 81 x 100

GERHARD MERZ
GERRMANY 1947
581
Iron and Canvas, 1996
Site specific work, iron rails, canvas, 305 x 1887 x 20

MARIO MERZ
ITALY 1925
582
My Home's Wind and Fibonacci Tables, 1969/82
Installation, mixed media

583
Gemma Conifera, 1981-82
Spiral Shell
Oil, lacquer spray and chalk/hessian, 200 x 432
Donation: The Friends of the Louisiana Collection

DUANE MICHALS
USA 1932
584
Playing with Matches, undated
Photograph, black/white, 50.4 x 40.5
Donation: Stephane Janssen via The Friends of the Louisiana Museum of Modern Art in Denmark, Inc., USA

HENRI MICHAUX
BELGIUM/FRANCE 1899-1984
585
Untitled, 1961
Indian ink/paper, 74 x 108

586
Untitled, 1961-62
Indian ink/paper, 74 x 108

TOMIO MIKI
JAPAN 1937
587
Ear, 1964
Aluminium, 100 x 68 x 15

588
Ear, Mirror I, 1967
Chromium plated steel, 238 x 145 x 70
Donation: Tomio Miki

JOAN MIRO
SPAIN 1893-1983
589
Personnage, 1970
Figure
Bronze, 200 x 120 x 100

JOAN MITCHELL
USA 1926-1992
590
Untitled, undated
Oil/canvas, 40.2 x 48.3
Donation: Elena and Nicolas Calas

LASZLO MOHOLY-NAGY
HUNGARY/USA 1895-1946
591
Pneumatic, 1926
Drawing and collage, 32 x 23
Donation: Joseph and Celia Ascher, New York**

HENRY MOORE
GREAT BRITAIN 1898-1986
592
Relief No. 1, 1959
Bronze, 222 x 116 x 45
Long-term loan: Henry Moore Foundation

593
Reclining Figure No. 5 (Seagram), 1963-64
Bronze, 240 x 360 x 180
Donation: The New Carlsberg Foundation

594
Reclining Figure, 1969-70
Bronze, 122 x 337 x 202
Donation: The New Carlsberg Foundation

595
Three Piece Reclining Figure: Draped, 1974-75
Bronze, 253 x 472 x 442

FRANÇOIS MORELLET
FRANCE 1926
596
Sphère, 1962
Sphere
Stainless steel, diam. 58
Donation: The Riklis Collection of McCrory Corporation**

597
A Real Artificial Flower for Celia, 1978
Pencil and collage/paper, 34.9 x 15.9
Donation: Joseph and Celia Ascher, New York**

MALCOLM MORLEY
GREAT BRITAIN 1931
598
Pacific Telephone – Los Angeles Yellow Pages, 1971
Acrylic and wax/canvas, 233 x 203

599
Sergeant I. A. Lorabel, undated
Gouache/paper, 79.4 x 106.4
Donation: The New Carlsberg Foundation

ROBERT MORRIS
USA 1931
600
Felt Piece, 1976
Felt, 160 x 270
Donation: Leo Castelli*

601
Labyrinth, 1973
Indian ink/paper, 106 x 151.2
Donation: Betty Parsons*

RICHARD MORTENSEN
DENMARK 1910-1993
602
Komposition. Objekt mellem dag and nat III, Gudhjem, 1935
Composition. Object between Day and Night III, Gudhjem
Oil/canvas, 100 x 75

603
Uden titel, c. 1939
Untitled
Oil/canvas, 135 x 110

604
Troldebillede, 1942
Troll Picture
Oil/canvas, 135 x 110

605
Udkast til "Offerscene", c. 1945
Study for "Scene of Sacrifice"
Oil/canvas, 150 x 110

606
Est-ouest, 1956
East-West
Oil/canvas, 130 x 162

607
Sud-est, 1956
South-East
Oil/canvas, 162 x 130

608
Sud, 1956
South
Oil/canvas, 130 x 162

609
Opus Normandie, 1956
Oil/canvas, 130 x 910

610
Evisa, 1960
Oil/canvas, 195 x 114

611
Un Ordre visuel arraché au chaos, 1982
A Visual Order Wrenched Out of Chaos
Oil/canvas, 180 x 180
Donation: Inger Charlotte and Richard Mortensen

JUAN MUÑOZ
SPAIN 1953
612
Half Circle, 1997
12 figures, resin polyester material, varying dimensions

613
Neal's Last Words, 1997
Resin polyester material, silicone,motor, mirror, varying dimensions

DAVID NASH
GREAT BRITAIN 1945
614
Elm Bowl, 1988
Elm, h. 139, diam. 110

LOUISE NEVELSON
RUSSIA/USA 1899-1988
615
Royal Tide III, 1960
Wood, painted, 198 x 152

BARNETT NEWMAN
USA 1905-1970
616
Untitled, 1946
Ink/paper, 61 x 45.7
Donation: Annalee Newman

617
Untitled, 1960
Ink/paper, 30.2 x 22.6
Donation: Annalee Newman

BEN NICHOLSON
GREAT BRITAIN 1894-1982
618
Silver Dust, 1961
Oil/board, 62 x 70
Donation: The Riklis Collection of McCrory Corporation**

619
Wall Landscape, 1968
Oil on canvas/board, 49 x 42
Donation: The Riklis Collection of McCrory Corporation**

ISAMU NOGUCHI
USA 1904-1988
620
Queen of Spades, 1986
Basalt, 113 x 98 x 72
Donation: The Estate of Isamu Noguchi

KENNETH NOLAND
USA 1924
621
Up Cadmium, 1966
Acrylic/canvas, 184 x 540

BJØRN NØRGAARD
DENMARK 1947
622
Spiralen, 1980
The Spiral
Mixed media, 203 x 167 x 115

JOHAN OJA
FINLAND 1956
623
Playing Dandelion, 1990
Video, 6 min.

CLAES OLDENBURG
SWEDEN/USA 1929
624
Lunch-Box, 1961
Fabric, painted, 70 x 45

625
Study for Home, 1963
Pencil/paper, 47.5 x 44.5
Donation: Joseph and Celia Ascher, New York*

626
The Chair, 1963
Watercolour and chalk/paper, 35 x 27.3
Donation: Joseph and Celia Ascher, New York*

627
Study for a Heroic Monument in the Form of a Bent Typewriter Eraser, 1970
Pencil/paper, 36.8 x 36.8
Donation: Joseph and Celia Ascher, New York*

DENNIS OPPENHEIM
USA 1938
628
Attempt to Raise Hell, 1974
Mixed media, 80 x 65 x 65

629
Removal Transplant New York Stock Exchange, 1969
Speed marker, photograph and paper/cardboard, 70.5 x 55.3

630
Concentration Pit, 1970
Map, photograph, chalk sketch on paper/cardboard, 70.5 x 55.5

631
Two Stage Transfer Drawing, 1971
Speed Marker, photograph and paper/cardboard, two parts, 71 x 56 each

632
Study for The Bad Cells are Comin', 1988
Chalk and gouache/paper, 127 x 195.5
Donation: Dennis Oppenheim

KIRSTEN ORTWED
DENMARK 1948
633-635
B2, B3, B4, 1997
Cast aluminium/bronze and stainless steel, three works, 85 x 207 x 59 each
Donation: The New Carlsberg Foundation

NAM JUNE PAIK
KOREA/USA 1932
636
TV Monitor, 1974
Radio cabinet and TV-monitor, 42 x 34 x 33

MIMMO PALADINO
ITALY 1948
637
Study for Painting, 1982
Oil/canvas, 32 x 42

638
Chimera, 1983
Mixed media on canvas/board, 165 x 264

639-642
Angoli del nord, 1981
Northern Corners
Acrylic, Indian ink, chalk, watercolour and pastel/paper, four sheets, 74.5 x 100 each
Donation: The Friends of the Louisiana Collection

642-644
Angoli del nord, 1982
Northern Corners
Acrylic, Indian ink, chalk, watercolour and pastel/paper, three sheets, 70.5 x 100.5 each
Donation: Mimmo Paladino

ED PASCHKE
USA 1939
645
Romanzi, 1985
Oil/canvas, 173 x 232

JENNIFER PASTOR
USA 1966
646
Untitled (Fall), 1994-96
Painted copper and plastic, 305 x 198 x 145

CARL-HENNING PEDERSEN
DENMARK 1913
647
Fugleleg, 1938
Birds' Play
Oil/canvas, 50 x 40

648
Rødt, blåt billede, 1942
Red, Blue Picture
Oil/hessian, 99 x 89

649
Spillekonge, 1949
King of the Game
Oil/hessian, 122 x 101

650
Mennesker og havet I, 1949
People and the Sea I
Oil/canvas, 160 x 207

651
Himlens guder og gul fugl, 1949
Gods of Heaven and a Yellow Bird
Oil/canvas, 121 x 102

652
Stjernehoveder, 1949
Star Heads
Oil/hessian, 102 x 121

653
Romersk landskab, 1950
Roman Landscape
Olie/hessian, 160 x 207

654
Stjerne and røde tårne, 1950
Star and Red Towers
Oil/hessian, 100 x 118

655
Gråt rytterbillede med vingeheste, 1957
Grey Rider and Winged Horses
Oil/canvas, 124 x 180

656
Legende: Menneskene og havet, 1957
Legend: Man and the Sea
Oil on canvas/masonite, 243 x 400

657
Sort stjerne, 1958
Black Star
Oil/canvas, 177 x 295

658
Blomstrende figurbillede, 1972
Figure in Bloom
Oil/canvas, 125 x 105
Donation: Carl-Henning Pedersen

659
Stjernefigurer, 1972
Star Figures
Oil/canvas, 125 x 105
Donation: Carl-Henning Pedersen

660
"Time" med gul "gåde", 1973
"Hour" with Yellow "Riddle"
Oil/canvas, 117 x 97
Donation: Carl-Henning Pedersen

661
Havets guder, 1973
Gods of the Sea
Oil/canvas, 206 x 160

662
Bourgogne, 1981
Oil/canvas, 127 x 104
Donation: Carl-Henning Pedersen

663
Ventende forår, 1981
Coming Spring
Oil/canvas, 124 x 104
Donation: Carl-Henning Pedersen

664
Vinterbillede, 1982
Winter Picture
Oil/canvas, 124 x 104
Donation: Carl-Henning Pedersen

665
Fantasiens fugle, 1948-54
Birds of Fantasy
Indian ink/Japanese paper, 50 drawings, 31 x 41 each
Donation: Carl-Henning Pedersen

666-728
Nepal-suite, 1960
Watercolour and pen-and-ink drawing/paper, 63 watercolours, varying dimensions
Donation: Carl-Henning Pedersen and Sidsel Ramson

A.R. PENCK
GERMANY 1939
729
Requiem für Waltraud (N-Komplex), 1976
Requiem for Waltraud (N-Complex)
Oil/canvas, 285 x 285

730
Schierz DDR, 1984
Dispersion/canvas, 130 x 160

731
Ohne Titel, 1987
Untitled
Indian ink and crayon/paper, 60.2 x 88.5
Donation: Galerie Michael Werner

732
Gorbatjov I, 1987
Pencil, Indian ink, crayon/paper, 60.2 x 88.5
Donation: Galerie Michael Werner

733
M.P.B. (Marie Puck Broodthaers), 1987
Indian ink, crayon/paper, 60.2 x 88.5
Donation: Galerie Michael Werner

734
Ohne Titel, undated
Untitled
Watercolour/paper, 74.3 x 48.9
Donation: Joseph and Celia Ascher, New York**

735
Ich und Dani, undated
I and Dani
Indian ink/paper, 50.8 x 83.2
Donation: The Riklis Collection of McCrory Corporation**

PABLO PICASSO
SPAIN/FRANCE 1881-1973
736
Femme et joueur de diaule III, 1956
Woman and Flute Player III
Oil/canvas, 89 x 116
Donation: The New Carlsberg Foundation and The Louisiana Foundation

737
Le Déjeuner sur l'herbe, 1961
Oil/canvas, 130 x 97
Donation: The Picasso Foundation and The Louisiana Foundation

738
Le Joueur de cartes II, 1971
The Card Player II
Oil/canvas, 114 x 146
Donation: The New Carlsberg Foundation

739
Le Déjeuner sur l'herbe, 1961
Pastel/paper, 26.6 x 40.6
Long-term loan: Celia Ascher

WALTER PICHLER
AUSTRIA 1936

740
Projekt "Guter Freund", 1968
Project "Good Friend"
Ink/paper, 25.4 x 29.2
Long-term loan: The Riklis Collection of McCrory Corporation

741
Fragendes Objekt, 1968
Inquiring Object
Pencil/paper, 26 x 32.4
Donation: Joseph and Celia Ascher, New York**

742
Hügelketten, 1972
Ridge
Pencil/paper, 21 x 26.7
Donation: Joseph and Celia Ascher, New York**

743
Figur mit Speer, 1972
Figure with Spear
Ink/paper, 27.5 x 20.8
Donation: Joseph and Celia Ascher, New York**

744
Figur mit Pfeil in der Türöffnung, 1972
Figure with Arrow in the Doorway
Ink and pencil/paper, 29.7 x 40
Donation: Joseph and Celia Ascher, New York**

745
Verschiedene Zeichen und badendes Mädchen, 1973
Various Signs and Bathing Girl
Pencil and coloured pencil/paper, 34.9 x 27.9
Donation: Joseph and Celia Ascher, New York**

746
Tag der Entscheidung, 1973
The Day of Judgement
Pencil, ink, chalk/paper, 24.8 x 57.8
Donation: Joseph and Celia Ascher, New York**

747
Der Zeichner, 1977
The Draughtsman
Tempera and pencil/paper, 21 x 29.2
Donation: Joseph and Celia Ascher, New York**

748
Zwei Torsos, 1977
Two Torsoes
Tempera/paper, 21 x 29.2
Donation: Joseph and Celia Ascher, New York**

749
Abgestürzter II, 1978
The Fallen II
Ink and tempera/paper, 34.5 x 49.5
Donation: Joseph and Celia Ascher, New York**

750
Gespräch mit einem Radfahrer, 1982
Conversation with Bicyclist
Pencil and watercolour/paper, 20.3 x 29.5
Donation: Joseph and Celia Ascher, New York**

751
Ohne Titel, 1983
Untitled
Pencil and watercolour/paper, 20.3 x 29.2
Donation: Joseph and Celia Ascher, New York**

SIGMAR POLKE
GERMANY 1941

752
Sieht man ja was es ist, 1984
One Surely Sees What It Is
Acrylic/canvas, 223 x 300
Donation:
The New Carlsberg Foundation, The Augustinus Foundation and The Louisiana Foundation

753
Ohne Titel, 1983
Untitled
Gouache, watercolour, spray colour/paper, 99.5 x 69.8

754
Ketten von Perlen, 1988
Strings of Pearls
Synthetic resin, synthetic sealing wax/polyester, 300 x 225

LJUBOV POPOVA
RUSSIA 1889-1924

755
Untitled, c. 1918
Gouache/paper, 33 x 22
Donation: Joseph and Celia Ascher, New York**

ARNULF RAINER
AUSTRIA 1929

756
Blind und stumm, 1969
Blind and Numb
Oil on photograph/wood, 95 x 71

757
Mit Perücke, 1969/71
With Wig
Oil on photograph/wood, 91 x 72
Long-term loan: Arnulf Rainer

758
Gesichtskolorierung, 1970/75
Face Painting
Oil on photograph/wood, 95 x 73
Long-term loan: Arnulf Rainer

759-764
Totenmasken, 1978/79
Death Masks
Oil/photograph, six pictures, 61 x 50 each

ROBERT RAUSCHENBERG
USA 1925

765
Tideline, 1963
Oil and silkscreen/canvas, 213 x 152

766
Untitled (First Apollo Landing), 1965
Oil and silkscreen/canvas, 101 x 76

767
Booster, 1967
Colour lithography and silkscreen/paper, 220 x 105

768
Die Hard, 1968
Pencil and lithography and silkscreen paper, 57 x 75.5
Donation: Joseph and Celia Ascher, New York*

MAN RAY
USA 1890-1976

769
Portrait of Meret Oppenheim, 1934
Solarised photograph, 29 x 22
Donation: Elena and Nicolas Calas

MARTIAL RAYSSE
FRANCE 1936

770
Souviens-toi de Tahiti en septembre 61, 1963
Do You Remember Tahiti in September 61
Acrylic, silkscreen and objects/canvas, 180 x 170

771
Jeune fille vénétienne, 1963
Young Venetian Girl
Acrylic, silkscreen and objects/canvas, 36 x 48
Donation: Puk and Hans Vieth

JAMES REINEKING
USA 1937

772
Untitled, 1985
Steel, 75 x 350 x 62.5

AD REINHARDT
USA 1913-1967

773
Abstract Painting, 1959
Oil/canvas, 203 x 102
Donation: The Riklis Collection of McCrory Corporation*

REINHOUD
BELGIUM 1928-1982

774
Je n'ai rien vu, 1963
I Haven't Seen Anything
Bronze, 63 x 38 x 34
Donation: The New Carlsberg Foundation

775
La Cage, 1978
The Cage
Copper, 58 x 21 x 21
Donation: Stephane Janssen**

CARL FREDRIK REUTERSWÄRD
SWEDEN 1934

776
Game With Round Dice, 1962
Tempera and lacquer/canvas, 125 x 125

777
Birth of a Planet, 1963
Oil/masonite, 89 x 118

778
Non-Violence, 1989
Bronze, marble, multiple, 22.5 x 30 x 12
Donation: Carl Fredrik Reuterswärd

GERMAINE RICHIER
FRANCE 1904-1959

779
L'Orage, 1947-48
Storm
Bronze, 189 x 72 x 58
Donation: The Richier Family

780
L'Ouragane, 1948-49
Hurricane
Bronze, 179 x 71 x 47
Donation: The Richier Family

781
Le Berger des Landes, 1952
Shepherd from Les Landes
Bronze, 149 x 89 x 60
Donation: The New Carlsberg Foundation

782
La Tauromachie, 1953
Bull Fight
Bronze, 116 x 54 x 101
Donation: The Richier Family

783
La Sauterelle, 1956
Grasshopper
Bronze, 137 x 99 x 176
Donation: The Richier Family

GERHARD RICHTER
GERMANY 1932

784
1025 Farben, 1974
1025 Colours
Enamel/canvas, 254 x 254

GEORGE RICKEY
USA 1907

785
One Up One Down, Oblique Variant IV, 1974
Steel, 450 x 400 x 37

BRIDGET RILEY
GREAT BRITAIN 1931

786
Cataract, 1965
Gouache/paper, 28 x 32
Donation: The Riklis Collection of McCrory Corporation**

787
Study for Cataract, 1967
Gouache/paper, 69 x 67.5
Donation: The Riklis Collection of McCrory Corporation**

788
Red Crossing Turquoise Elongated Triangles, 1968
Gouache/paper, 101.6 x 26.7
Donation: The Riklis Collection of McCrory Corporation**

PIPILOTTI RIST
SWITZERLAND 1962
789
Sip my Ocean, 1996
Video installation

LARRY RIVERS
USA 1923
790
The Queen, undated
Oil/masonite, 50.5 x 40.5
Donation: Elena and Nicolas Calas

DOROTHEA ROCKBURNE
CANADA
791
Untitled, 1974
Drawing/paper, 76.2 x 101.6
Donation: Ileana Sonnabend**

DIETER ROTH
GERMANY 1930
792
Fremdbildnis als Selbstbildnis, 1974
Portrait of a Stranger as Self-Portrait
Acrylic, glue, serigraphy and off-set print/cardboard, 50 x 70
Donation: Martin S. Ackerman Foundation**

793
Selbstbildnis als Maserati, 1974
Self-Portrait as a Maserati
Acrylic, glue, serigraphy and off-set print/cardboard, 50 x 70
Donation: Martin S. Ackerman Foundation**

794
Vier Rübensaftpumper an der Quelle, 1974
Four Sugar Beet Pumps at the Well
Acrylic, glue, serigraphy and off-set print/cardboard, 50 x 70
Donation: Martin S. Ackerman Foundation**

795
Selbstbildnis als Hosenmatz, 1974
Self-Portrait as A Toddler
Acrylic, glue, serigraphy and off-set print/cardboard, 50 x 70
Donation: Martin S. Ackerman Foundation**

796
Deutscher Teufel, als gekreuzigte Schokoladenbombe versagend, 1974
German Devil as A Crucified, Unexploded Chocolate Bomb
Acrylic, glue, serigraphy and off-set print/cardboard, 50 x 70
Donation: Martin S. Ackerman Foundation**

797
Fremdbildnis unter Bekannten, 1974
Portrait of a Stranger Among Friends
Acrylic, glue, serigraphy and off-set print/cardboard, 50 x 70
Donation: Martin S. Ackerman Foundation**

798
Selbstbildnis als Hasenschaukel, 1974
Self-Portrait as A Hare Swing
Acrylic, glue, serigraphy and off-set print/cardboard, 50 x 70
Donation: Martin S. Ackerman Foundation**

799
Käse, 1969
Cheese
Collage with objects, 96 x 65

800
Cacao, Cocoa, 1969
Serigraphy with cocoa powder, 72 x 102

801
Schimmel, 1969
Mould
Paper prepared with mould fungus, 99 x 80

802
Salami, 1969
Sausage in a closed plastic folder, 96 x 65

803
Postcard, 1969
Two boards, 65 x 95 each
Donation: Dieter Roth

804
Containers, 1972
Mixed media, varying dimensions

MARK ROTHKO
LITHUANIA/USA 1903-1970
805
Untitled, 1964
Oil and acrylic/canvas, 176 x 168
Donation: The Mark Rothko Foundation*

806
Untitled, 1968
Acrylic and paper/board, 61 x 46
Donation: The Mark Rothko Foundation*

807
Untitled, 1944-46
Watercolour, tempera and ink/paper, 53.5 x 38.2
Donation: The Mark Rothko Foundation*

928
Prehistoric Memory, 1946
Watercolour, gouache/paper, 65.5 x 49
Long-term loan

ROBERT RYMAN
USA 1930
808
Untitled, 1961
Oil/canvas, 190 x 190

809
Canon, 1978
Oil/canvas with metal, 81 x 76
Donation: The Riklis Collection of McCrory Corporation*

NIKI DE SAINT-PHALLE
FRANCE 1930
810
Drame de coup de feu, 1961
Gun Tragedy
Mixed media, two parts, 22 x 155 and 15 x 30

DAVID SALLE
USA 1952
811
Wearing Down, 1989
Oil and acrylic/canvas, two parts, 189 x 243
Donation: The New Carlsberg Foundation

ANTONIO SAURA
SPAIN 1930
812
Giselle dans un fauteuil, 1967
Giselle in an Armchair
Oil/canvas, 162 x 130
Donation: The Helia and Edward Goldschmidt Fondation

JAN SCHOONHOVEN
THE NETHERLANDS 1914-1994
813
R-69.3, 1969
Papier mâché/plywood, 104 x 104 x 5
Donation: The Riklis Collection of McCrory Corporation**

814
MV3, 1968
Ink/paper, 40 x 20.3
Donation: Joseph and Celia Ascher, New York**

815
T-71.43, 1971
Indian ink/paper, 42 x 26
Donation: The Riklis Collection of McCrory Corporation**

SEAN SCULLY
IRELAND/USA 1945
816
Field, 1985
Oil/canvas, three parts, 244 x 305
Donation: The Friends of the Louisiana Collection

817
Italian Painting No. 1, 1979
Oil/canvas, 213 x 71
Donation: The Riklis Collection of McCrory Corporation**

NOBUO SEKINE
JAPAN 1942
818
Phases of Nothingness, 1970
Granite and steel, 625 x 435 x 216
Donation: The Japan Foundation

819
Phases of Nothingness – Nine Pieces, 1978
Stone and stainless steel, varying dimensions

RICHARD SERRA
USA 1939
820
Back to Black, 1981
Lithography, 131.5 x 155
Donation: The New Carlsberg Foundation

821
The Gate in the Gorge, 1986
Corteen-steel, two parts, 350 x 1200 and 350 x 1045

JOEL SHAPIRO
USA 1941
822
Untitled, 1983
Wood, 77.5 x 22 x 29.5
Donation: Joel Shapiro

823
Untitled, 1985-86
Bronze, 426 x 368 x 330
Donation: The New Carlsberg Foundation

824
Untitled (JS 929), 1990
Charcoal/paper, 152.5 x 137

825
Untitled (JS 931), 1990
Carcoal/paper, 183 x 147

CINDY SHERMAN
USA 1954
826
Untitled #80, 1980
Colour photograph, 51.8 x 62.2
Donation: The New Carlsberg Foundation

827
Untitled #109, 1982
Colour photograph, 92.5 x 92.5

828
Untitled #128A, 1983
Colour photograph, 93.9 x 60.2
Donation: The New Carlsberg Foundation

829
Untitled #129, 1983
Colour photograph, 90 x 60
Donation: The New Carlsberg Foundation

830
Untitled #149, 1985
Colour photograph, 184.5 x 126.8

MICHAEL SINGER
USA 1945
831
Cloud Hands Ritual Series 80/81, 1980-81
Wood and stone, 143 x 511 x 510

832
Cloud Hands Ritual Series, 1982
Charcoal, chalk and ink/paper, 125 x 95

KIKI SMITH
GERMANY/USA 1954
833
Untitled, 1990
Ink/paper, 50.8 x 76.2

LEON POLK SMITH
USA 1906-1996
834
Correspondance Red/White/Black, 1968
Acrylic/canvas, 107 x 84
Donation: The Riklis Collection of McCrory Corporation*

835
Circle and Square, 1973
Collage and pencil/paper, 71.7 x 58.4
Donation: Elena and Nicolas Calas

TONY SMITH
USA 1912-1980
836
The Elevens Are Up, 1963
Steel plates, painted, two parts, 249 x 249 x 61 each
Donation: Tony Smith Estate

837
Moondog, 1964
Bronze, 84 x 70 x 64

K.R.H. SONDERBORG
DENMARK/GERMANY 1923
838
Ohne Titel, 1965
Untitled
Indian ink/paper, 105 x 75
Donation: The New Carlsberg Foundation

KEITH SONNIER
USA 1941
839
Expanded Sel Diptych I, 1979
Neon tube, 309 x 304
Donation: Leo Castelli*

JESUS RAFAEL SOTO
VENEZUELA 1923
840
Le Grand bleu, 1964
The Big Blue
Oil/wood, masonite, 180 x 100 x 15
Donation: The Helia and Edward Goldschmidt Foundation

841
Vibration grise et blanche, 1966
Grey and White Vibration
Painted wood and nylon string, 156 x 106 x 35
Donation: The Riklis Collection of McCrory Corporation**

842
Carré virtuel violet, 1979
Virtual Purple Square
Oil, wood, aluminium and nylon, 122 x 122 x 55
Donation: The Friends of the Louisiana Collection

HENRYK STAZEWSKI
POLAND 1894-1988
843
Relief Malowany, 1961
Collage, 36 x 38
Donation: Joseph and Celia Ascher, New York**

844
Composition with Blue and Yellow, 1960
Oil, acrylic and wood/board, 41 x 51
Donation: Joseph and Celia Ascher, New York**

845
White Relief No. 17, 1963
Acrylic/plywood, 58 x 112
Donation: The Riklis Collection of McCrory Corporation**

FRANK STELLA
USA 1936
846
Bam, 1966
Fluorescent alkyd/canvas, 244 x 275

847
Ctesiphon II, 1967
Polymer and fluorescent polymer/canvas, 310 x 610

VARVARA STEPANOVA
RUSSIA 1894-1958
848
Untitled, undated
Watercolour and pencil/paper, 35.5 x 22
Donation: Joseph and Celia Ascher, New York**

NIELS LARSEN STEVNS
DENMARK 1864-1941
849
Selvportræt, 1920
Self-Portrait
Oil/canvas, 48 x 32

850
Selvportræt, 1927
Self-Portrait
Watercolour/paper, 34 x 26

851
Agri Baunehøj, Købmanden mejer korn, 1928
Agri Baunehøj, The Grocer Reaps Grain
Oil/canvas, 64 x 97

852
Udsigt mod Bokul, Gudhjem, 1929
View to Bokul, Gudhjem
Oil/canvas, 80 x 112

853
H. C. Andersen læser op i Collins have, 1931
Hans Christian Andersen Reads Aloud in Collin's Garden
Watercolour/paper, 142 x 162

HIROSHI SUGIMOTO
JAPAN/USA 1948
854
Marmar Sea, Silivli, 1991
Photograph black/white, 51 x 61

855
Orange Drive-in, Orange, 1993
Photograph black/white, 51 x 61

856
Tri City Drive-in, San Bernadino, 1993
Photograph, black/white, 51 x 61

857
Union City Drive-in, Union City, 1993
Photograph, black/white, 51 x 61

858
English Channel, Weston Cliff, 1994
Photograph, black/white, 51 x 61

859
Tyrrhenian Sea, Conda, 1994
Photograph, black/white, 51 x 61

JØRGEN HAUGEN SØRENSEN
DENMARK 1934
860
Dunkedyret, 1961
Tapping Animal
Bronze, 60 x 42 x 93
Donation: The New Carlsberg Foundation

861
De der suger og de der bider, 1978-79
Those that Suck and Those that Bite
Travertine, 81 x 73 x 148

862
Landskab med bro, 1979
Landscape with Bridge
Travertine, eight parts, 66 x 131 x 212

SOPHIE TAEUBER-ARP
SWITZERLAND/FRANCE 1889-1943
863
Equilibre, 1932
Equilibrium
Oil/canvas, 46 x 37
Donation: Joseph and Celia Ascher, New York**

TAKIS
GREECE/FRANCE 1925
864
Signal, 1955-58
Iron and bronze/stone, h. 295

865
Rotating Construction, 1969
Mixed media and plexiglass box, 28.2 x 28 x 9.7
Donation: Elena and Nicolas Calas

866
Three Stalks Willow Wasp, undated
Metal, h. 92
Donation: Elena and Nicolas Calas

867
Magnetized Wires, undated
Magneto, metal and wooden board, 12 x 28.5 x 17.4
Donation: Elena and Nicolas Calas

YVES TANGUY
FRANCE 1900-1955
868
Sans titre, 1938
Untitled
Gouache/paper, 19 x 17.7
Donation: Elena and Nicolas Calas

869
Sans titre, 1940
Untitled
Gouache/paper, 10.1 x 7.6
Donation: Elena and Nicolas Calas

870
Sans titre, 1943-44
Untitled
Gouache/paper, 12.7 x 30.4
Donation: Elena and Nicolas Calas

871
Personnage, 1944
Figure
Gouache/paper, 30.4 x 25.4
Donation: Elena and Nicolas Calas

MARK TANSEY
USA 1949
872
Leonardo's Wheel, 1992
Oil/canvas, 235 x 235
Donation:
The New Carlsberg Foundation, The Augustinus Foundation and The Louisiana Foundation

ANTONIO TAPIES
SPAIN 1923
873
Ocre, 1963
Colour, sand, asphalt/canvas, 275 x 400
Donation: The Friends of the Louisiana Collection

SAM TAYLOR-WOOD
GREAT BRITAIN 1967
874
Killing Time, 1994
Video installation, 48 min.

PAUL THEK
USA 1933-1988
875
Calligraphic Runner, 1975
Gouache/paper, 58 x 85

876
Diving Swan, 1975
Gouache/newspaper,
57.8 x 85

ERIK THOMMESEN
DENMARK 1916
877
Hoved, 1951
Head
Granite, 77 x 61 x 46

878
Mor og barn, 1955
Mother and Child
Teak, 48 x 33 x 36

879
Mand og kvinde, 1956
Man and Woman
Teak, 115 x 68 x 65

880
Kvinde, 1960
Woman
Bog oak, 150 x 69 x 46

JEAN TINGUELY
SWITZERLAND 1925-1991
881
Relief métamécanique, 1956
Metamechanical Relief
Metal, wood and electromotor,
47 x 123 x 17
Donation: The Friends of the
Louisiana Collection

882
Relief métamécanique, 1957
Metamechanical Relief
Metal, wood and electromotor,
99 x 60 x 23

883
Baluba vert, 1962
Green Baluba
Iron, wood, electromotor and
feather tassel, 135 x 52 x 42

884
Bascule, 1965
Seesaw
Iron and electromotor,
136 x 192 x 125

885
Drawing for "Bascule", 1968
Indian ink/paper, 38 x 50
Donation: Ad Petersen

886
Rotozaza no. 1, 1968
Pencil, ink and Indian ink/paper,
58 x 63
Donation: The Riklis Collection
of McCrory Corporation**

RIRKRIT TIRAVANIJA
THAILAND/USA 1961
887
Untitled, 1995
Mixed media, 390 x 295 x 300

GERARD TITUS-CARMEL
FRANCE 1941
888
L'Usage du nécessaire, 1972
The Use of The Necessary
Pencil/paper, 151 x 250

889
Summer Sticks au centre croisé,
1974
Summer Sticks Crossed in the
Centre
Collage and pencil/paper, 75 x 105
Donation: Puk and Hans Vieth

MARK TOBEY
USA 1890-1976
890
Intersection, 1954
Tempera/paper, 22 x 30
Donation: Joseph and Celia
Ascher, New York*

891
Untitled Composition, 1969
Watercolour and gouache/
Japanese paper, 55 x 39
Donation: The Friends of the
Louisiana Collection

GEORGE TRAKAS
CANADA/USA 1944
892
Self Passage, 1986-88
Site specific sculpture,
wood and steel

893-895
Routes from the Heart, 1992
Charcoal and pencil/grey paper,
three sheets, I: 56 x 76,
II: 97 x 127, III: 97 x 127
Donation: George Trakas

RICHARD TUTTLE
USA 1941
896
Talk, 1965
Acrylic/plywood, 99 x 61 x 3

897
Hill, 1965
Acrylic/plywood, 94 x 110 x 3

898
The Garden, 1966
Pinewood, diam. 100
Donation: Betty Parsons*

899
Garden Sculpture, 1973/1995
Bronze, seven elements, h. 275

CY TWOMBLY
USA 1929
900
Untitled, 1960
Chalk/paper, 69 x 99
Donation: Duncan McGuigan*

GÜNTHER UECKER
GERMANY 1930
901
Kreis-Kreise, 1967
Circle
Oil and nails/board, 87 x 87

902
Weisses Feld, 1983
White Field
Nails/board, 150 x 150

PER OLOF ULTVEDT
FINLAND/SWEDEN 1927
903
Untitled, c. 1965
Assemblage, 42 x 47

AVIVA URI
ISRAEL 1927
904
Untitled, 1975
Coloured chalk and charcoal
/paper, 70 x 78.5
Donation: Yona Fischer and
Dansk-Israelsk Kulturfond

SERGE VANDERCAM
BELGIUM/DENMARK 1924
905
Le Rendez-vous, 1972
The Meeting
Oil/canvas, 130 x 99
Donation: Stephane Janssen**

VICTOR VASARELY
HUNGARY/FRANCE 1908-1997
906
Citra, 1955-59
Oil/canvas, 110 x 100
Donation: The Riklis Collection
of McCrory Corporation**

907
Zilah, 1957
Oil/canvas, 162 x 130
Donation: The New Carlsberg
Foundation

908
Tridim TT, 1969
Acrylic/board, 90 x 45
Donation: The Riklis Collection
of McCrory Corporation**

BRAM VAN VELDE
THE NETHERLANDS
1895-1981
909
Untitled, 1973
Gouache/paper, 132 x 150
Donation: Stephane Janssen**

CAREL VISSER
THE NETHERLANDS 1928
910
Piled Beams, 1964
Welded steel, 70 x 70 x 40
Donation: The Riklis Collection
of McCrory Corporation**

ANDY WARHOL
USA 1928-1987
911
Close Cover before Striking,
1962
Acrylic/canvas, 183 x 137

912
Jackie, 1964
Silkscreen/canvas, 51 x 42

913
Four Marlons, 1966
Silkscreen/canvas, 204 x 348

914
Mao, 1972
Silkscreen and acrylic/canvas,
208 x 148

915
Shadow, 1978
Silkscreen and oil/canvas,
193 x 132

916
Portrait of Joseph Beuys, 1979
Silkscreen and diamond
dust/canvas, 101 x 101

RYSZARD WINIARSKY
POLAND 1937
917
Surface No. 94, 1971
Acrylic/wood, 100 x 100
Donation: The Riklis Collection
of McCrory Corporation**

ANDREA ZITTEL
USA 1965
918
**A to Z Travel Trailer Unit
Customized by Kristin and Todd
Kimmell,** 1995
Mixed media, 292 x 238 x 518

WILLY ØRSKOV
DENMARK 1920-1990
919-921
Uden titel (pneumatiske skulp-
turer), 1967-68
Untitled (pneumatic sculptures)
Rubber, nylon, three sculptures,
320/275/150 x 11

922
Uden titel, 1972
Untitled
Bronze, 95 x 155 x 206
Donation: The New Carlsberg
Foundation

923
Uden titel, 1973
Untitled
Bronze, 126 x 133 x 63

924
Uden titel, 1979-80
Untitled
Bronze, 211 x 192 x 149

925
Uden titel (pneumatisk skulp-
tur), undated
Untitled (pneumatic sculpture)
Rubber and nylon, 28 x 508

926
Uden titel, 1982
Untitled
Lithographic crayon/paper,
109 x 109
Donation: Willy Ørskov

927
Uden titel, 1984
Untitled
Lithographic crayon/paper,
110 x 110
Donation: Willy Ørskov

Photographers

Kim Agersten /Polfoto 58, 67
Ebbe Andersen /Politikens Pressefoto 49, 51
Svend Erik Andersen 47
Anders Askegård /Billedhuset 61
Anders Bentzon 45, 47-50, 52, 55-58
Suste Bonnén 61
Bo Boustedt 42, 43
Poul Buchard /Strüwing Reklamefoto 14, 16-18, 20, 22, 23, 29-32, 34, 35, 36-37, 38-42, 44, 48, 50, 51, 53, 54, 56-58, 60, 61, 63, 64, 67, 68-69, 74, 76-115, 117-125, 126-127
Nanna Büchert 46
Delta /Jørgen Schytte /Polfoto 43
Det Kongelige Bibliotek 38
Jørn Freddie 39-43, 55, 57
Jens Frederiksen 8, 9, 12-23, 25, 31, 33, 43, 45, 58, 61, 63, 66, 70-73, 75, 115
Mads Gamdrup 108
Marianne Grøndahl 51-54, 64
Jean-Claude Guiter 55
Gunilla 39
Lars Hansen /Politikens Pressefoto 49
Keld Helmer-Petersen 17, 20, 26, 64
C. Henriksen /Dagens Nyheder 38
Jesper Høm 39
Steen Jakobsen /Nordfoto 60
Kirsten Jappe 63
Birgitta Jönsson 41
Esben Kaalund 54
Tove Kurtzweil 67-68
Lennart Larsen 34
Stefan Lindblom 55
Jens Lindhe 11, 16, 24, 27, 29, 32, 33
Susanne Mertz 46, 47
Jan-Olof Mångård /Smålands Posten 47
Peter Nagel 6-7
Ernst Nielsen 61
Gregers Nielsen 60, 62, 63, 65
Harry Nielsen /Aktuelt's Pressefoto 56
Knud Rauff Nielsen /Fredensborg Fotografi 58-61, 63, 64, 67
Stefan Kai Nielsen 44, 48
Ole Nørgård 26
Ad Petersen 52
Hans Petersen 41, 43
Steen Møller Rasmussen 45, 67
Bent Ryberg /Planet Foto 26, 57, 77, 87, 93, 95, 105, 106
Peter Schandorf 49
Ole Schelde 42
Louis Schnakenburg 15, 40, 42, 46, 47, 58, 65
Antonio Sperlazzo 46
Else Tholstrup 43
Lisbeth Thorlacius 64
Maya Ussing 62
Kirsten Vaamonde /Medieskolen 61
Børge Venge 40
Mogens von Haven 39
Hans Erik Wallin 58, 89

Cover: **Jens Lindhe**

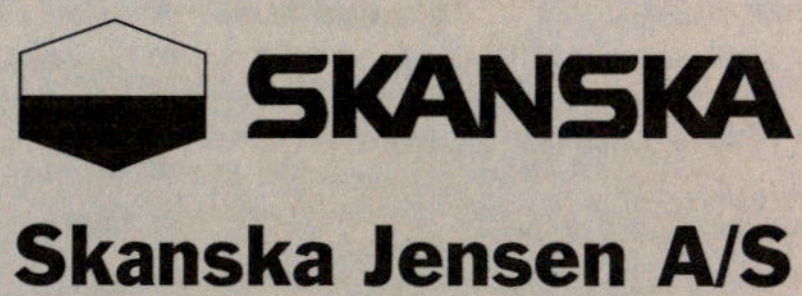

Skanska Jensen A/S

Building contractor sponsoring Louisiana in connection with improvement of the facilities for visitors and staff at Louisiana in 1997/1998